IN THE DRAGON'S SHADOW

SEBASTIAN STRANGIO

IN THE

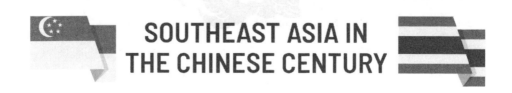

DRAGON'S

SHADOW

SOUTHEAST ASIA IN
THE CHINESE CENTURY

YALE UNIVERSITY PRESS
NEW HAVEN AND LONDON

For information about this and other Yale University Press publications, please contact:
U.S. Office: sales.press@yale.edu   yalebooks.com
Europe Office: sales@yaleup.co.uk   yalebooks.co.uk

Set in Minion by IDSUK (DataConnection) Ltd
Printed in Great Britain by CPI Group (UK) Ltd, Croydon, CR0 4YY

Library of Congress Control Number: 2020938041

ISBN 978-0-300-23403-9

A catalogue record for this book is available from the British Library.

10 9 8 7 6 5 4 3 2 1

For Felix

CONTENTS

ILLUSTRATIONS

PLATES

1. Chinese President Xi Jinping participates in a parade celebrating the 70th anniversary of the founding of the People's Republic of China in Beijing on October 1, 2019. Photo by Kevin Frayer/Getty Images.
2. A cartoon published in *Le Petit Journal* on January 16, 1898.
3. The Mekong Exploration Commission at Angkor Wat in 1866. Unknown engraver after Émile Gsell.
4. The Mekong River at Pakbeng, Laos. Author photo.
5. Ornamental gate at the Chinese-run Golden Triangle Special Economic Zone, northwestern Laos. Author photo.
6. Chinese police escort Naw Kham to his execution in Kunming on March 1, 2013. Hap/Quirky China News/Shutterstock.
7. Zhao Wei pictured in a promotional brochure produced by his company. Author photo.
8. A Vietnamese infantryman beats back invading Chinese troops on a mural at a military cemetery outside Sapa in northern Vietnam, March 2003. Author photo.
9. An unauthorized march in Hanoi on March 14, 2016, marking the anniversary of a 1988 naval clash with China in the Spratly Islands. Hoang Dinh Nam/AFP via Getty Images.
10. Prime Minister Hun Sen of Cambodia attends a state funeral in the capital Phnom Penh in June 2015. Author photo.
11. A Chinese-run casino in Sihanoukville, on the Cambodian coast. Author photo.
12. A Chinese railway bridge under construction in the hills of China's Yunnan province. Author photo.

13. Chinese shops at the Sanjiang Market in Vientiane, Laos. Author photo.
14. Thailand's Prime Minister Prayuth Chan-ocha attends a birthday ceremony for Princess Maha Chakri Sirindhorn in Bangkok in April 2015. Dario Pignatelli/Bloomberg via Getty Images.
15. Yaowarat Road, Bangkok. Mladen Antonov/AFP via Getty Images.
16. Aung San Suu Kyi speaks at an election campaign rally in Shan State on September 6, 2015. Author photo.
17. A vista of Mong La, the capital of Special Region No. 4. Author photo.
18. A statue of Admiral Zheng He at the Tay Kak Sie Temple in Semarang, Indonesia. Arterra/Universal Images Group via Getty Images.
19. Xi Jinping and Lee Kuan Yew unveil a commemorative bust of Deng Xiaoping in Singapore on November 14, 2010. Munshi Ahmed/Bloomberg via Getty Images.
20. The showroom of Forest City in Johor Bahru, on the tip of peninsular Malaysia. Author photo.
21. A cartoon published in May 2017 by the Malaysian cartoonist Zunar. Courtesy of Zunar/www.zunar.my.
22. Riots in Jakarta on May 14, 1998. Patrick Aventurier/Gamma-Rapho via Getty Images.
23. Kopi Es Tak Kie (est. 1927), the oldest café in Glodok, Jakarta's Chinatown. Author photo.
24. Philippine President Rodrigo Duterte with outgoing national police chief Ronald "Bato" dela Rosa during a handover ceremony in Manila on April 19, 2018. Noel Celis/AFP via Getty Images.
25. An aerial view of Thitu Island, November 26, 2005. The Asahi Shimbun via Getty Images.

MAPS

ACRONYMS

1MDB	1Malaysia Development Berhad
ADB	Asian Development Bank
AIIB	Asian Infrastructure and Investment Bank
APEC	Asia-Pacific Economic Cooperation
ARIA	Asia Reassurance Initiative Act
ARSA	Arakan Rohingya Salvation Army
ASEAN	Association of Southeast Asian Nations
BBSEZ	Beautiful Boten Specific Economic Zone
BN	National Front (Barisan Nasional)
BRI	Belt and Road Initiative
CAFTA	China–ASEAN Free Trade Agreement
CCP	Chinese Communist Party
CMEC	China–Myanmar Economic Corridor
CNRP	Cambodia National Rescue Party
COC	Code of Conduct in the South China Sea
CP Group	Charoen Pokphand Group
CPB	Communist Party of Burma
CPM	Communist Party of Malaya
CPP	Cambodian People's Party
CPT	Communist Party of Thailand
CSIS	Centre for Strategic and International Studies (Indonesia)
DAP	Democratic Action Party
EAS	East Asia Summit
ECRL	East Coast Rail Link
EDCA	Enhanced Defense Cooperation Agreement
EDSA	Epifanio de los Santos Avenue
EEZ	Exclusive Economic Zone

FOIP	Free and Open Indo-Pacific
FPI	Islamic Defenders Front (Front Pembela Islam)
G30S	September 30th Movement (Gerakan 30 September)
GDP	Gross Domestic Product
GLC	government-linked company
GMS	Greater Mekong Subregion
GTSEZ	Golden Triangle Special Economic Zone
HSR	high-speed rail
ILD	International Liaison Department
IMF	International Monetary Fund
ISEAS	Institute of Southeast Asian Studies (Singapore)
KIA	Kachin Independence Army
LMC	Lancang–Mekong Cooperation
LPRP	Lao People's Revolutionary Party
MDT	Mutual Defense Treaty
MRC	Mekong River Commission
MSR	21st Century Maritime Silk Road
NCPO	National Council for Peace and Order
NDAA	National Democratic Alliance Army
NEP	New Economic Policy
NLD	National League for Democracy
NSEC	North–South Economic Corridor
NUS	National University of Singapore
OCAO	Overseas Chinese Affairs Office
PAP	People's Action Party
PAS	Malaysian Islamic Party (Parti Islam Se-Malaysia)
PDRC	People's Democratic Reform Committee
PH	Alliance of Hope (Pakatan Harapan)
PKI	Communist Party of Indonesia (Partai Komunis Indonesia)
PL	Pathet Lao
PLA	People's Liberation Army
PLAN	People's Liberation Army Navy
POGO	Philippine Online Gaming Operation
PPBM	Parti Pribumi Bersatu Malaysia
PRC	People's Republic of China
RCEP	Regional Comprehensive Economic Partnership

SEZ	Special Economic Zone
TPP	Trans-Pacific Partnership
UDG	Union Development Group
UMNO	United Malays National Organization
UN	United Nations
UNTAC	United Nations Transitional Authority in Cambodia
UWSA	United Wa State Army
UXO	unexploded ordnance
VCP	Vietnamese Communist Party
VFA	Visiting Forces Agreement
VOC	Dutch East India Company (Vereenigde Oostindische Compagnie)

A NOTE ON TERMINOLOGY

This book ranges over considerable historical and geographic terrain. As such, it takes a practical approach to names and terminology, opting for familiarity over lexicological consistency. Chinese names are presented in the mainland's *pinyin* transliteration system, except in instances where names originate from regional dialects of Chinese, like Hokkien or Cantonese, or where an alternative transliteration is more likely to be familiar. Thus, "Chiang Kai-shek" over "Jiang Jieshi," and "Teochew" rather than "Chaozhou." Several Southeast Asian languages lack agreed-upon systems of transliteration. Here, too, I have employed the versions of names most likely to be recognized by English-speaking readers.

An analogous approach is taken to the South China Sea, where competing maritime claims have given rise to a catalog of clashing nomenclature. In Chinese, the South China Sea is *Nanhai* ("South Sea"). The Vietnamese call it *Bien Dong* ("East Sea"). To Malaysians, it is *Laut China Selatan*, a direct translation of the English name. Since 2011, the Philippines has referred to the "West Philippine Sea." In 2017, Indonesia declared the creation of the "North Natuna Sea." In a similar way, islands, reefs, and low-tide features all bear multiple names. In general discussions, "South China Sea" and the other standard English-language names are employed, except in instances where the text focuses on a particular location.

Another important question involves the competing usages of "Myanmar" and "Burma." In Burmese, the two terms are basically synonymous. For centuries, the term *myanma* has been used to refer to the various kingdoms that rose and fell in the Irrawaddy River valley. The word *bama* is a colloquial variant, which the British later glossed into "Burma." The country's name became a subject of controversy only in 1989, when its military government changed the country's English name from "Burma" to "Myanmar," claiming that the latter was more inclusive of the nation's minority ethnic groups. However, many disputed this claim, and the use of "Burma" became a symbol of opposition to the junta—a dispute that has cooled somewhat since the country's political opening in 2011.

Throughout this book I have opted for "Burma." This is mostly because it is better adopted to English usage, with distinct noun and adjectival forms. Given its presence in much writing on the country, I also hope to reduce needless jumping between the two terms. "Burmese" refers to citizens of Burma, whatever their ethnolinguistic origin, and for its official language. "Burman" refers to the country's majority ethnic group. For the sake of consistency and familiarity, I have followed the remaining pre-1989 usages. Hence, "Rangoon" over "Yangon," and "Arakan" over "Rakhine."

Given the ethnic diversity of many Southeast Asian nations, it is important to maintain clear distinctions between nationalities and ethnic groups. In some cases, this is straightforward, as in the distinction between "Burmese" and "Burman." In a similar fashion, "Cambodian"/"Khmer" and "Malaysian"/ "Malay." Where the nomenclature is less accommodating, the distinction is made thus: "Lao" vs. "ethnic Lao," "Thai" vs. "ethnic Thai," etc. I have also drawn a distinction between "Thai"—the citizens and majority ethnic group of Thailand—and "Tai," which refers to members of the wider ethnolinguistic family to which the Thais belong.

How to describe Southeast Asia's large ethnic Chinese diaspora presents a thornier set of problems. There are many terms used in reference to the ethnic Chinese living outside of China, with varying (and overlapping) cultural, legal, and political meanings. In English, the phrase "Overseas Chinese" is frequently employed to refer to the tens of millions of ethnic Chinese living outside China, Hong Kong, Macao, and Taiwan, though its usage is opposed by some scholars. "Overseas Chinese" is a rough equivalent of the Chinese term *huaqiao* (华侨, "sojourner"), which suggests that those so described are temporarily resident outside China and intend to return. This carries an implication that the political loyalties of *huaqiao* lie not with their countries of residence but with China.

In contemporary English usage, "Overseas Chinese" has largely shed this connotation. It is now used as a general term for ethnic Chinese abroad, the majority of whom were born outside China, hold foreign citizenship, and have no intention of "returning" permanently to the land of their ancestors.

The Chinese meaning has remained stickier, however, as the People's Republic of China (PRC) continues to use *huaqiao* to refer to its own citizens residing abroad. Despite this divergence, I use "Overseas Chinese" to refer to Southeast Asians with Chinese ancestry, along with "ethnic Chinese" (*huaren*, 华人) and related nation-specific phrases: "Sino-Burmese," "Indonesian Chinese," etc.

For the purposes of this book, the most salient distinction to bear in mind is the one between ethnic Chinese who are citizens of Southeast Asian countries, and the large number of PRC nationals who have emigrated to Southeast Asia since 1978. The phrase "new migrants," or *xin yimin* (新移民), refers to this new and quite different cohort.

1. China and Southeast Asia

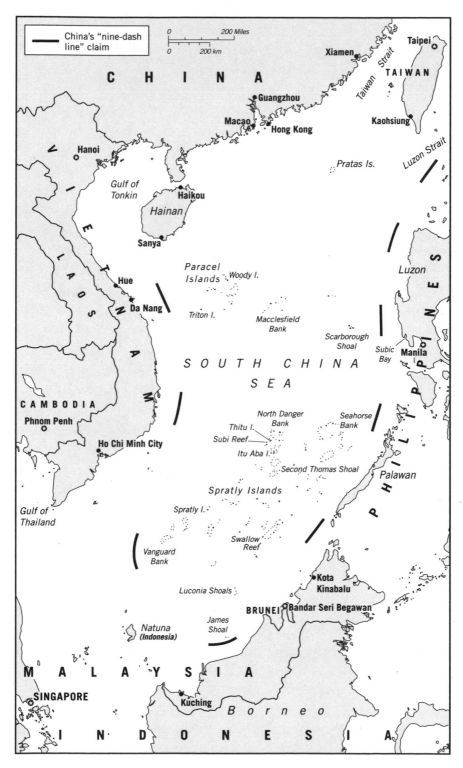

2. The South China Sea

INTRODUCTION

Rising from the water like a frosted wedding cake, the MS *World Dream* glided into the port of Subic Bay to a characteristically sunny Filipino reception. Municipal officials lined up along the wharf to welcome the cruise ship, waving small Philippine flags and draping floral leis around the necks of disembarking passengers. A band played and a line of dancers whirled along the pier in ethnic garb. Outside, special souvenir stalls had been erected and tour buses stood idling at the ready.

For the authorities at Subic Bay, which once hosted the largest American naval base outside the United States, the arrival of the *World Dream* on the morning of January 16, 2019 was ample cause for celebration. Since 1992, the year of the base's closure, the Philippines had struggled to fill the economic hole left by the departure of thousands of American sailors and their families. Now, the gleaming German-built cruise ship towered over Subic's Alava Wharf, which once berthed the nuclear-powered aircraft carriers of the US Navy. In place of American sailors looking forward to raucous spells of shore leave, it carried some 3,000 tourists from mainland China. They came with parasols, camera phones, and—most importantly—plenty of money to spend.

As the Chinese visitors stepped off the pier, they wandered into the heart of the former American base. They strolled past Building 229, the old base headquarters, and passed ex-naval warehouses and administrative buildings, their identification numbers still stenciled in black on peeling white facades. Some visited the public restrooms next to an overgrown mini-golf course once used by US personnel. Others dragged roller suitcases down leafy Dewey Avenue, named after the US commander who defeated the Spanish fleet at Manila Bay in 1898, marking the start of the bloody American conquest of the Philippine islands.

Situated on a magnificent natural harbor on the island of Luzon, the US Naval Base Subic Bay was central to the story of America's rise as a Pacific power in the twentieth century. Occupied by the US after its victory in the Spanish–American War, Subic had figured in every overseas US military engagement of the twentieth century, from the Boxer Rebellion to Desert Storm. With its wealth of sheltered deep-water anchorages and mammoth naval airfield, the base served as "the service station and supermarket" of the US Seventh Fleet, providing the training, repair, resupply, and recreation facilities that kept the Pacific armada afloat.[1] There was no more imposing symbol of Washington's global military reach.

Today, the Subic area is still dotted with the vestiges of empire. Weathered signs hang on ragged cyclone fencing. Disintegrating Quonset huts and empty concrete ammunition bunkers slumber in the jungle. In the nearby town of Olongapo, an American Legion Office still sits amid the faded go-go bars and discos spawned by the large US troop presence. In 1992, the base was forced to close due to a fateful convergence of Filipino nationalism, the end of the Cold War, and the eruption in June 1991 of Mount Pinatubo, which severely damaged its facilities and forced the abandonment of Clark, the US Air Force base 45 kilometers to the north. The area was subsequently converted into the Subic Bay Freeport Zone, a duty-free service and logistics hub, though it never fully recovered from the American withdrawal.

Now, nearly 30 years later, the local authorities were turning to China to revive the economy. In 2018, cruise ships like the *World Dream* made 19 layovers at Subic, many of them filled with newly prosperous mainland Chinese tourists. Wilma T. Eisma, chairperson of the Subic Bay Metropolitan Authority, described them as a "game changer" for the area—at least until the coronavirus pandemic of 2020, which brought the global cruise industry to a shuddering halt.[2] It wasn't just Subic Bay that was looking to China. A Chinese firm had recently announced plans to invest $2 billion[3] in an industrial park at the former Clark Air Base, while Chinese state banks had plans to fund a railway connecting the two former bases under the Belt and Road Initiative (BRI), President Xi Jinping's globe-spanning infrastructure scheme. At the same time, two more Chinese companies were angling to take over a failing South Korean shipyard at Subic Bay—a worrisome prospect for the US government, given its close proximity to the hotly disputed South China Sea.[4]

The arrival of Chinese economic power in these former nerve-centers of the American military reflected a deeper shift in the balance of power in Southeast Asia. While the closure of Subic and Clark did not result in a wholesale American withdrawal from the region—the US Navy shifted its ship maintenance yards and supply depots to other Asian countries, including Japan and Singapore—it did mark an important watershed. The base closures represented the largest reduction of American forces in the western Pacific up to that point. For the first time in four centuries, there were no foreign troops in the Philippines. A strategic vacuum yawned, and the Chinese stood ready to fill it.

In February 1992, nine months before the US flag was lowered at Alava Wharf, China's legislature passed a bill laying claim to more than 80 percent of the South China Sea, the Asian seaway that serves as a major conduit of global trade. The innocuously titled Law Concerning Territorial Waters and Adjacent Regions marked the beginning of China's increasingly muscular attempts to extend its control over the important ocean expanse. That same month, China's paramount leader Deng Xiaoping wound up what would later become known as his Southern Tour, which revived China's economic reforms following its violent crackdown on pro-democracy protests in 1989.

At the time of Deng's tour, few American observers thought China likely to emerge as a viable economic competitor in the foreseeable future: in 1992, the nation's per capita GDP sat at just $366, and its exports amounted to less than $85 billion. But 25 years later, its per capita GDP had grown more than 20-fold; the value of its exports had increased 26 times over.[5] In 2013, China surpassed the US to become the world's top trading nation, and the following year, overtook the US to become the world's largest economy, at least in terms of purchasing power parity.[6] This booming economic emergence has fueled a crash-program of defense modernization that poses the most serious challenge to US military supremacy in the Pacific since the end of World War II.

Nowhere is China's economic and military emergence more apparent than in Southeast Asia, the dynamic and diverse region straddling the critical intersection of the Indian and Pacific oceans. Since the end of the Cold War, China has risen from a mid-table power in Southeast Asia to an economic, military, and even cultural force in the 11 nations of the region: Vietnam, Cambodia, Laos, Thailand, Burma, Singapore, Malaysia, Indonesia, Brunei, East Timor, and the Philippines. Today, China is Southeast Asia's top trade partner and source of tourism, and contributes a rapidly growing proportion of its foreign direct investment. From the Mekong River to the South China Sea, China's power is rapidly reshaping the region.

I first started following this story from Cambodia, where I lived and worked from 2008 to 2016, covering Southeast Asia from the country's dilapidated capital, Phnom Penh. This small, conflict-torn country offered a unique angle on the changes that had taken place since the end of the Cold War. In March 1992, as the US Navy was leaving Subic Bay, the United Nations (UN) was arriving in Cambodia, part of a $2 billion multinational peacekeeping mission intended to end a long civil war and rebuild the country as a liberal democracy. If Subic Bay symbolized the passing era of the Cold War, Cambodia symbolized the promise of what was to come: a world finally made safe for democracy.

With the arrival of the UN's democracy-building mission, Cambodia became a tattered vessel for the optimistic spirit of the age: a global project of betterment. But it soon became clear that Cambodia, and the world, were moving in a different direction. Hun Sen, a former Khmer Rouge commander who had been in power since 1985, quickly wrested control of the new democratic institutions implanted by the UN. At first, to keep Western aid flowing, he retained the trappings of democracy, granting political parties and human rights groups considerable freedom. But when opposition to his rule mounted, these spaces were hastily closed over. After a jolting loss of support at national elections in 2013, the Cambodian government dissolved the main opposition party, arrested its leader for treason, and assaulted civil society and the press. At the next election in 2018, Hun Sen's party won every seat in parliament.

Standing behind Cambodia's strongman was a new foreign ally: one with capacious pockets and little commitment to the liberal democratic norms that supposedly emerged triumphant from the Cold War with the Soviets. During the eight years I spent in Cambodia, China ticked off milestone after milestone: it became the country's top trade partner, then its leading foreign investor and aid-giver. Defense ties deepened. In 2017, China became the number one source of tourists to Cambodia, and a magnet for Chinese expatriates and businesspeople. China's backing changed the game in Cambodia. By reducing Hun Sen's need for Western support, it also lessened his need to sustain the pretense of democracy. Under his rule, Cambodia largely reverted to what it had been before 1992: an authoritarian, single-party state.[7]

Like the *World Dream* at Subic Bay, Cambodia's parabolic trajectory—from open authoritarianism to quasi-democracy and back again—epitomized a wider shift. Everywhere that I traveled and reported in the region, China's rising influence was evident. From Vientiane to Johor Bahru, China's banks, energy companies, tech firms, and real-estate conglomerates were an increasingly visible presence; so too were its students, tourists, and businesspeople. In the borderlands separating China from mainland Southeast Asia, new infrastructure and transport networks were plowing through ancient geographic barriers, opening remote areas to a transformative southward sweep of Chinese capital and immigration. In the South China Sea, which laps the shores of eight Southeast Asian nations, Beijing was asserting its naval power and constructing artificial islands, complete with airstrips and radar installations, in defense of audacious maritime claims. Meanwhile, China's cultural power was washing over the ethnic Chinese communities of the region, altering ideas of what it meant to be Chinese in Southeast Asia.

Southeast Asia is unusually exposed to the expanding power of the new China. Three Southeast Asian nations share land borders with China, and five are directly affected by its claims in the South China Sea. All dwell in the lengthening shadow of its power: economic, political, military, and cultural. The numbers alone tell a striking story. In 2007, China surpassed the US to become the third-largest trading partner of Southeast Asia after Japan and the European Union. Two years later, it had leapt into first position. In 2012, it became the largest source of tourists to the region as well. While Chinese investment in Southeast Asia has grown more slowly, it now sits behind just Japan as the region's second biggest source of foreign investment.

The Southeast Asian attitude to China's sudden rise can best be described as fraught. As China has become the most important economic partner to nearly every nation in the region, it has also become their thorniest foreign policy challenge. A survey of Southeast Asian regional experts and policymakers conducted in late 2019 by the ISEAS–Yusof Ishak Institute in Singapore found that 38 percent of respondents thought "China will become a revisionist power with an intent to turn Southeast Asia into its sphere of influence," while less than one-tenth saw China as "a benign and benevolent power."[8] In Burma, unease about growing Chinese influence contributed to a rapid opening to the West. In Malaysia, it helped bring down a corrupt government. Beijing's aggressive actions in the South China Sea have touched off protests in Manila and riots in Ho Chi Minh City. Everywhere, peoples and governments are grappling with the question of how best to deal with the nuclear-armed superpower standing up on their doorstep.

This ambivalence grows from the region's geography. Southeast Asia begins as a southward extension of the Chinese subcontinent, before breaking apart into a scattering of islands that stretch across the mid-point of the Indian and Pacific oceans. China's size and propinquity make it both a natural source of disquiet, and a reality that no Southeast Asian nation can feasibly ignore. The starkest example is Vietnam, a nation whose history has been driven in many ways by the tension between emulating China and resisting it. But the same is true, to varying lesser degrees, of the all the Southeast Asian nations.

For Southeast Asia, China's return to wealth and power carries echoes of the distant past. For more than a millennium the two regions have been closely connected by trade, tribute, and cultural transmissions. Up to the nineteenth century, China enjoyed an unassailable primacy in the lands to its south. Southeast Asian kings, sultans, and tribal princes prostrated themselves before the Chinese emperors, and the waters of the Nanyang—the "southern ocean"—supported a thriving trade between the two regions. Commerce brought waves of settlers from southern China, who spread their culture, languages, and technology throughout Southeast Asia, while retaining strong connections to their homeland. Their descendants today form significant populations in every Southeast Asian nation; in Singapore, they are a majority. In many senses, the region boasts a "longer, more varied, and more sustained history of relations with China than any other."[9]

Where imperial China seldom intervened in the affairs of the Southeast Asian kingdoms and sultanates, content with their rulers' ritual genuflections, its modern successor has been less complacent. Since the founding of the communist People's Republic of China (PRC) in 1949, after a century of internal chaos and ascendant Western imperialism, China has blazed a turbulent path toward a new era of wealth and power. During its first three decades, the PRC sought to achieve this through the active support of communist insurgencies across the region, poisoning its relations with many Southeast Asian governments. In the late 1970s, when Deng Xiaoping threw aside Maoist ideology in favor of opening and economic reform, Beijing normalized its relations with the region, declared itself a "good neighbor," and began building its influence via trade, investment, and accommodating diplomacy. But suspicions of the PRC's intentions remain widespread. As Beijing has more aggressively moved to reclaim its former position of prominence in

Southeast Asia, especially under President Xi Jinping, who took office in 2012, fears of Chinese coercion and subversion have revived—shadowed by a deeper, more subliminal fear of vassalage to a revived Chinese empire.

How Southeast Asia views and responds to the challenge of China's rise has global implications. The region is home to a young and growing population of 650 million, with a $2.8 trillion economy that is the fifth-largest in the world after the US, China, Japan, and India. By 2030, it is projected to rise to fourth place. Through the Association of Southeast Asian Nations (ASEAN), which unites ten Southeast Asian countries, it is an increasingly important player on the diplomatic stage. It straddles vital arteries of global trade, including the Straits of Malacca, one of the world's busiest shipping routes. All this makes Southeast Asia of crucial strategic significance not just to China, but also to rival powers, including the US, which harbor concerns about China's waxing power and ambition.

The interests of major powers have always collided in Southeast Asia. Fate gifted the region the gentle currents and strong monsoon winds that made it a hinge of global trade and a rich prize of empire. Starting in the sixteenth century, Southeast Asia was conquered and carved up by the Portuguese, British, Dutch, Spanish, French, and Americans, each bent on the pursuit of riches and glory. In the twentieth century, the region became a crucial arena of the Cold War, split between hostile communist and non-communist camps, a conflict that turned hot in the jungles of Indochina. As China's emergence stirs up anxieties across the Western world, Southeast Asia has once again become the focus of a global contest for power.

The research and writing of this book coincided with a watershed in American attitudes toward China. Under President Donald Trump, the Obama administration's cautious "rebalance" to Asia has given way to a strident and increasingly confrontational China policy. This has since crystalized into a broadly bipartisan consensus: one of the few that pertains in Washington today. American officials speak of Beijing as a hostile power that is seeking to dominate Asia and overturn the US-backed global security order, already knocked off its axis by Trump's ascent to the Oval Office. Politicians and pundits sketch the lines of a grand ideological struggle, even a new Cold War, pitting authoritarian China against the democracies of the West.

In Southeast Asia, views of China are more anguished and complex. Dwelling in China's shadow, the region does not enjoy the luxury of simple binaries. While Southeast Asian governments view Chinese behavior with justified alarm, China's economic centrality to the region makes it something they cannot ignore, as much as they might wish to. Indeed, there are even important questions of principle on which they agree or sympathize with it. Beyond this, it is tricky to generalize about Southeast Asian views of China. Each of its 11 nations faces similar challenges in adapting to the changing balance of power in the Indo-Pacific, yet no two countries approach China in quite the same way. In each case, views of the Middle Kingdom have been shaped by long patterns of interaction: by the multifarious ways that China and its people have been encountered, seen, and understood through history. Like the facets of a gemstone, each splits the same light in different ways.

This consideration has dictated the book's structure, which proceeds through the region country by country, in rough order of their geographic and cultural proximity to China. Chapter 1 situates Southeast Asia in the wider context of China's geopolitical ambitions, and its long march back to national wealth and power. It sketches the long history of interactions between China and the lands to its south, and describes Southeast Asia's attempts to navigate a dawning era of superpower struggle. Chapter 2 then moves to the Southeast Asian mainland, describing the process of economic integration that is breaking down an age-old geographic barrier, opening the region to an unprecedented flow of Chinese investment and immigration. Chapter 3 turns to Vietnam, the nation with the most intimate and tortured relationship to China. Chapter 4 examines Cambodia and Laos, the two small satellites of mainland Southeast Asia, where China's economic presence is more marked than anywhere else in the region. Chapters 5 and 6 look in turn at Thailand, the anchor of the Southeast Asian mainland, and Burma, enclosed at the crossroads of Asia's two giants: China and India.

The book's attention then turns to the oceans. Chapter 7 describes the origins and nature of China's maritime ambitions, and its impact on the Southeast Asian nation perhaps most reliant on the unimpeded global flow of goods and capital: Singapore. Chapters 8 to 10 examine China's relationships with the nations of the historically more remote (from a Chinese perspective) Malay maritime world: Malaysia, Indonesia, and the Philippines. Due to restrictions of time and space, this book regretfully omits detailed discussions of Brunei and East Timor, the two smallest Southeast Asian nations by population. Both countries would have undoubtedly made worthy additions to the story told in this book, underlining further the multifariousness of the region's responses to a rising China. Finally, a short Afterword offers some thoughts on the likely trajectory of Southeast Asia through the twenty-first century, as it seeks safe and prosperous passage through the reefs of an increasingly turbulent world.

1
PIVOT OF THE INDO-PACIFIC

President Xi Jinping looked down from the rostrum as China's armed forces paraded in great waves along the Avenue of Eternal Peace. First came thousands of soldiers, marching by in great lockstep squares. Then came a display of tanks, drones, and heavy weaponry, including the world premiere of the fearsome DF-41 ballistic nuclear missile, which growled past on 16-wheeled carriers. The military spectacle was followed by floats extolling the achievements of Xi's Chinese Communist Party (CCP). Cheering youngsters shook plastic torches before a giant image of Mao Zedong. Floats marked the "Four Modernizations" of Deng Xiaoping, and the "Three Represents" of Jiang Zemin, the 2008 Beijing Olympics and China's achievements in high-speed rail.

The date was October 1, 2019, and the occasion was the 70th birthday of the communist People's Republic of China (PRC). Before the parade, President Xi had delivered a short speech, standing directly above the huge portrait of Mao that hangs from Tiananmen, the Gate of Heavenly Peace. Xi wore a black Zhongshan suit similar to the one Mao had worn 70 years before, when he had stood on the same spot to proclaim the PRC's founding. "There is no force that can shake the foundation of this great nation," Xi told the crowds assembled in Tiananmen Square. "No force can stop the Chinese people and the Chinese nation forging ahead."[1]

The tightly choreographed parade, with its war machines and marching bands, was a compelling display of the growing power and ambition of the world's most populous nation. Shortly after taking office on November 15, 2012, Xi Jinping vowed to restore China to its ancient prominence and glory. He spoke of a "China Dream" and a "great rejuvenation of the Chinese nation." As Xi consolidated power at home, reinforcing the CCP's position at the heart of the nation's political and economic life, he became more assertive abroad.

Shrugging off the caution and humility of his predecessors, he openly declared China's arrival as a great power. Addressing the CCP's 19th National Congress in October 2017, Xi proclaimed a "new era" in which China would take center stage in the world and "make a greater contribution to humankind."[2]

In its broad outlines, Xi's goal is the same as that pursued by past generations of Chinese nationalists and political leaders, from Mao to the Nationalist leader Chiang Kai-shek: the restoration of China's national "wealth and power" (*fuqiang*) after a long period of disunity and weakness.[3] This project of national renewal is driven by a profound sense of victimhood arising from what the CCP refers to as the "century of humiliation," a melancholy period of subjugation by the Western imperial powers that began with imperial China's defeat in the Opium War of 1839–42, and ended with the PRC's establishment in 1949, when Mao proclaimed, "Ours will no longer be a nation subject to insult and humiliation. We have stood up."[4]

If Xi's ends are familiar, however, his means are in many ways unprecedented. For the first time in half a millennium, China has taken to the seas, asserting sovereignty over most of the South China Sea on the basis of dubious historical claims, and rapidly building its navy into a "blue-water" armada capable of projecting power far from its shores. At the same time, China has pushed for the reform of key international institutions to better reflect the country's interests and preferred norms. It has established an array of new financial institutions to supplement American-dominated institutions like the International Monetary Fund and World Bank. In 2015, China launched the Asian Infrastructure Investment Bank (AIIB), headquartered in Beijing, to support infrastructure development across the region. The AIIB currently counts 76 members, including nearly every Asian country.

By far the most ambitious Chinese undertaking is the Belt and Road Initiative (BRI), announced in 2013. Likened by some to a new Marshall Plan, the BRI envisions the investment of tens of billions of dollars in the construction of an international network of roads, railways, pipelines, ports, fiber optic cables, and industrial zones that will run from Vladivostok to the Atlantic Ocean. Consisting of overland and maritime components—the Silk Road Economic Belt and the 21st Century Maritime Silk Road—the BRI aims to bind the Eurasian landmass into a single geoeconomic zone with China at its core. In late 2014, China announced the establishment of the Silk Road Fund, endowed with $40 billion to support BRI infrastructure projects. The BRI has since involved into the primary rubric and organizing scheme for China's multitude of global engagements.

Western observers frequently misdiagnose these efforts as an attempt to overturn and replace the existing US-backed global security order established at the end of World War II. In reality, Chinese attitudes are more ambivalent. Few nations have benefited more from US hegemony than China, and its leaders have little interest in tearing down the very structures that have aided their country's economic advancement. Like any great power, China seeks changes in the governance of international institutions, in order that they better reflect its growing prominence, while creating new institutions and mechanisms when it senses a need. Evan Feigenbaum describes China's strategy as one of "portfolio diversification," rather than the wholesale replacement of institutions and systems. "In the majority of instances and institutions," he writes, "Beijing pursues structural change by demanding changes to the existing framework."[5]

While China is not seeking to replace the US as the global hegemon, it does want to reclaim something of the centrality it enjoyed in East Asia prior to its subjugation by the Western empires and imperial Japan in the nineteenth and twentieth centuries. In May 2014, Xi announced that it was time for "Asian people to run the affairs of Asia, solve the problems of Asia, and uphold the security of Asia," a remark that seemed to imply China's desire to displace the US military from East Asia. While some have expressed doubts as to whether this comment amounted to a serious statement of policy,[6] recent Chinese actions have made it abundantly clear that Xi intends to expunge past humiliations, gain the respect of the global community, and restore China to its former and "natural" place at the center of the Asian order.

Southeast Asia occupies a pivotal role in this project of national rejuvenation. This stems from the challenging realities of China's strategic environment. Seen from Beijing, Asia is a claustrophobic place: on three sides, China is enclosed by land borders with fourteen nations, including nuclear-armed rivals India and Russia. Off its east coast, it confronts an island barrier, running from Russia's Kamchatka Peninsula in the north to the island of Borneo in the south, constraining its access to the oceanic thoroughfare. Forming part of this barrier are three US treaty allies—Japan, South Korea, and the Philippines—as well as Taiwan, which enjoys close ties to Washington. As Meng Xiangqing of China's National Defense University laments, these are airless confines for an aspiring great power: China "borders on big powers on land and is encircled by an island chain in the sea," he writes. As such, it "has never been able to enjoy any benefit from having both the land and the sea."[7]

The constraints facing the extension of Chinese power to the north, east, and west place a special emphasis on the small nations lying to the south. Sprawling across fifty sun-drenched degrees of longitude between the Pacific and Indian oceans, Southeast Asia is at once China's backyard, and its primary vulnerability. As its economy has grown, China has become heavily reliant on the busy sea-lanes that run through the region, especially through the Straits of Malacca, the congested neck of water separating the Malay Peninsula and the east coast of Sumatra in Indonesia. Each year, nearly 90,000 container vessels—more than half of the world's merchant fleet tonnage—pass through this narrow chute. These ships bear around a quarter of the world's trade and a third of its crude oil and refined fuels, making the Malacca Straits the second most important global oil transit chokepoint after the Strait of Hormuz.[8]

As China's economy has grown, Chinese strategists have become concerned about their nation's heavy reliance on the Malacca Straits, both as a conduit for China's energy supplies and as an outlet for its own exports. In November 2003, then-President Hu Jintao declared that "certain major powers" were bent on controlling the straits, and called for the adoption of new strategies to mitigate what he described as China's "Malacca dilemma."[9] Despite increased overland imports from Russia and Central Asia, China remains dependent on oil transported via the straits. In 2018, approximately 70 percent of its total oil needs came from imports, around 80 percent of which were shipped through the straits.[10] One of Beijing's core strategic priorities is therefore to protect these routes from foreign interdiction, while diversifying its sources of energy.

On both these counts, Southeast Asia is paramount. Mainland Southeast Asia, a region geographically contiguous with China, presents Beijing with alternative overland routes to the Indian Ocean, and the possibility of materializing, via the construction of roads, railways, and oil pipelines, the western "coast" that China lacks. In the maritime region of Southeast Asia, China has broken with the continental orientation of the old Chinese empire and leapt out into the oceans, erecting artificial islands on rocks and low-tide elevations in the South China Sea, while rapidly developing a powerful navy capable of securing the sea-lanes that have sustained its economic renascence. Xi's road to rejuvenation thus runs directly through the mountain passes and island straits of Southeast Asia.

China's interest in Southeast Asia is nothing new. For more than two millennia, the region was China's imperial backyard and its main arena of commercial interaction with the outside world. Dating back at least to the Song dynasty (960–1279), Chinese trading junks crisscrossed the Nanyang, or "southern ocean," as the Chinese termed it, their sails filled with monsoon winds, while Yunnanese mule trains snaked their way through the narrow mountain passes of southern China into the Buddhist kingdoms of mainland Southeast Asia. Chinese merchants exchanged silk, tea, and porcelain for a range of goods, exotic and mundane: sea cucumbers from Makassar; edible birds' nests from Sarawak; jade and gems from Burma; rice from Siam; sticklac and ivory from the Lao states.

The streams of commerce brought large numbers of people from China, including merchants and monks, coolies and literati, political rebels and refugees fleeing dynastic collapse. These arrivals helped diffuse Chinese culture and technology throughout Southeast Asia, and catalyzed the region's commercial life. Many settled and intermarried with local populations, becoming in time an integral part of the societies to which they belonged. Later, the region's ethnic Chinese would also play important roles in major events in their ancestral homeland, from the Xinhai Revolution of 1911 to the economic revolution of the post-1978 era.

For most of recorded history, the Chinese empire has had a southward drift. As China's gaze remained fixed on the fearsome steppe peoples from the wind-swept north, Chinese culture and political power expanded slowly southward from its civilizational heartland in the Yellow River basin, a movement that one historian has likened to "the westward movement of American history and the eastward movement of Russian history."[11] China's "march toward the tropics," a centuries-long process that involved the absorption of borderlands and the gradual sinicization of their indigenous inhabitants, brought it into prolonged contact with the lands and peoples of today's Southeast Asia.[12] It involved direct rule over parts of modern-day Vietnam and Burma, and the annexation of regions, like the Chinese provinces of Yunnan and Guangxi, which had more in common with mainland Southeast Asia than the northern empire that absorbed them. It also displaced peoples from southern China, who migrated down through the mountain passes into the fertile lowland river valleys of the Southeast Asian mainland. When this advancing frontier was halted by European imperial conquest in the nineteenth century, it continued in the form of large-scale emigration from the ports of southern China to the labor-hungry Western colonies of the Nanyang.[13]

Imperial officials viewed these southern lands through the lens of China's classical worldview: one that took the empire to be the center of civilization, with an emperor who ruled "all under heaven" (*tianxia*). From this perspective, the southern lands were wild tracts populated by less civilized peoples, whom one sixteenth-century Ming emperor likened to "the birds and beasts, without human morality."[14] Most of the time, there was no need to dominate these "barbarians" by force. Provided they acknowledged the superiority of the Celestial Emperor, civilization would flourish and harmony would reign. The concrete manifestation of this worldview was the imperial tribute mission, in which Southeast Asian kings and sultans dispatched periodic gift-bearing embassies to the Chinese capital. In return for performing the *kowtow*, a ritual prostration at the feet of the emperor, ambassadors received imperial seals of investiture and lavish gifts—silk, sable furs, fine porcelain—symbolizing his power and largesse.

If the Chinese viewed these tributary rituals as confirmations of their virtue and supremacy, Southeast Asia's rulers participated for a more practical reason: to gain access to trade.[15] By the time of the Ming dynasty (1368–1644), commerce with China had become so important to the region that many of its kings and sultans were willing to flatter Chinese conceits in order to gain access to China's huge market—a dynamic that has some echoes in the present. In any event, they had little alternative. As the historian Yuan-kang Wang writes, "there were no other allies of significance that could be counted upon to balance Chinese power. . . . Relative weakness, geographic proximity, and lack of a counterbalancing ally forced them to accept Chinese dominance."[16]

The arrival of the European powers in Southeast Asia in the sixteenth century—first as traders, then as conquerors—ended China's southward expansion and severed these tributary relationships, along with many of the complacent illusions that sustained them. France's conquest of Tonkin (northern Vietnam) in 1885 cut off China's last, and closest, tributary bond in the region, bringing the whole of modern Southeast Asia—bar the Kingdom of Siam, which remained independent—under some form of alien control. China itself was reduced to a semi-colonial status, forced open to trade after the first Opium War in 1839–42, its vaunting civilizational pretensions forced into the humble constraining jacket of the modern nation-state.

China's return to Southeast Asia therefore marks the closing of a brief historical parenthesis—five hundred years at the most—in which Western power was predominant in Asia. It forms one part of the broader global shift of power and wealth that Gideon Rachman of the *Financial Times* has termed "Easternization."[17] China's expanding presence in Southeast Asia—from its island-fortresses in the South China Sea to the quickening diffusion of its money, people, and ideas throughout the region—represents a resumption, through varied means, of its historical expansion to the south.

Of course, Southeast Asia is a vastly different place today compared to even a century ago. While Western imperialism temporarily halted China's march toward the tropics, a more enduring obstacle came in the form of the Southeast Asian nationalisms that it helped to provoke.[18] Fortified by a potent new sense of national pride and identity, tempered in some instances by ferocious struggles against Western colonial rule, the independent nation-states of Southeast Asia were (and remain) fiercely defensive of their sovereignty— and much less willing to assume positions of deference. Moreover, unlike in the precolonial era, when there was no other significant force to counterbalance Chinese power, today's Southeast Asia is crowded with rivals. The 11 nations of the region boast strong economic, political, and cultural ties not only to China but also to the US, Japan, the European Union, Australia, India, and many other countries, which collectively provide a strong counterweight to China's rising power and influence.

China's economic renewal has also coincided with Southeast Asia's increasing cohesiveness as a region. The idea of "Southeast Asia" is a very recent one. It originated as a term of simple geographic convenience, referring to the space between more firmly defined regions. While the phrase and its variants ("South-Eastern Asia," "Sudostasien," etc.) have been employed by Western writers since the mid-nineteenth century, its modern use dates to the formation of Louis Mountbatten's South East Asia Command by the Allies during World War II.[19] The term then entered widespread popular use during the Cold War, when it was taken up by US military planners and the thriving academic field of "Southeast Asian Studies" that emerged around the same time.[20]

The term "Southeast Asia" suggests a misleading degree of unity. On nearly every metric, the region presents a picture of bewildering diversity. It is "Muslim, Buddhist, Catholic, Confucian-Taoist," writes Benedict Anderson, "colonized by Spaniards in the sixteenth century, by the Dutch in the seventeenth, by the French and the British in the nineteenth, and by the Americans in the twentieth."[21] Today, its peoples speak a profusion of mutually incomprehensible languages. It includes gleaming Singapore and impoverished Laos, and stretches from the azure waters of the Banda Sea to the dun foothills of the Himalayas. That this collection of lands and peoples came to be grouped into a single geographic unit is an outcome of both political convenience and historical contingency. Yet as Donald Emmerson argues, assigning a name to the region, however arbitrarily, also "helped to bring about the reality to which it now refers."[22]

The main vehicle for the region's emergence was the Association of Southeast Asian Nations (ASEAN), established in 1967 with Singapore, Malaysia, Indonesia, Thailand, and the Philippines as founding members. ASEAN has since outgrown its narrow anti-communist origins to embrace ten of the eleven nations generally recognized to constitute Southeast Asia. (The remaining exclusion is East Timor, which applied for ASEAN membership in 2011.) During the 1980s and 1990s, ASEAN provided the framework for what became known as the Southeast Asian "miracle," a period of surging economic advancement that saw the region's cities swell and towers of glass and steel rise above the stone colonial edifices of Kuala Lumpur and Jakarta.

As regional economic integration has proceeded, and cheap regional airlines have bound the region and its people more tightly together, this negative space—south of China and east of India, part-Indo and part-Pacific—has started to develop a positive identity and coherence of its own. ASEAN has many shortcomings (of which more later), but under its auspices a fragmented region once termed "the Balkans of Asia" has attained a degree of peace and prosperity. As the historian Leonard Andaya writes, " 'Southeast Asia' is no longer simply a term of convenience. Southeast Asians themselves now think regionally."[23]

If Southeast Asia is central to China's regional ambitions, it also presents uniquely challenging terrain—in large part due to China's past actions in the region. From the PRC's founding in 1949 up to the late 1970s, Southeast Asia was Mao's laboratory of revolution, through which he sought to reclaim for China, through his leadership of world communism, its former wealth and prominence. By the 1960s, almost every Southeast Asian country had strong, capable communist movements, influenced and in many cases actively supported by Beijing. The parachute seeds of Maoism spread widely: from

Singapore to Phnom Penh, students, intellectuals, and trade unionists bran-dished Mao's "Little Red Book" of ideological aphorisms. Burmese, Indonesian, Malayan, and Thai revolutionaries converged on Beijing for political training. Chinese radio stations beamed out red propaganda in a dozen languages.

The result was that, by the time of Mao's death in 1976, China had alien-ated most of Southeast Asia. Fears of Chinese communist subversion spurred the founding of ASEAN: its five founding members were all staunchly anti-communist, and two of them—Indonesia and Singapore—would refuse to recognize the PRC until the final years of the Cold War. Even in Vietnam, where a communist revolution triumphed in 1975 with Chinese support, ideological solidarity soon collapsed into fierce nationalist enmity with roots in the distant past.

As in China itself, the task of cleaning up Mao's mess fell to Deng Xiaoping, the diminutive Sichuanese party veteran who emerged from the political maelstrom to become China's paramount leader in 1978. Deng shared Mao's ambitions—he, too, wanted to make China rich and strong—but he differed greatly in the means he employed. In place of revolutionary shock therapy, Deng advocated economic reform and the patient accumulation of national power under a cloak of self-effacement. In a famous 24-character slogan, he instructed his colleagues: "Hide our capacities and bide our time. Be good at maintaining a low profile. Never claim leadership." Seeking stability in China's immediate neighborhood, and recognizing Southeast Asia's importance to his program of "reform and opening," Deng also moved to mend ties with the ASEAN states. He phased out China's support to the region's communist movements, focused on trade, and adopted a humble international posture.

China's changing strategy toward Southeast Asia was spurred by US President Richard Nixon's landmark visit to Beijing in February 1972, and the broader Sino-American rapprochement that resulted. In the aftermath of the Nixon visit, China established formal diplomatic relations with Malaysia, the Philippines, and Thailand. In late 1978, when Vietnam invaded Cambodia and toppled its Chinese-supported Khmer Rouge regime, China aligned with ASEAN and the US to form a new strategic front against Soviet-backed Vietnam and its Cambodian client-state: a partnership that provided the basis for a steady improvement in relations between China and ASEAN through the 1980s. As the CCP weathered international condemnation for its brutal handling of the Tiananmen Square protests in 1989, it found supportive friends in Southeast Asia, where governments shared its sensitivities about perceived outside interference in their affairs.

By the end of the Cold War, Beijing had established diplomatic ties with all ten Southeast Asian nations—even the toxically anti-Chinese Suharto regime in Indonesia—and normalized relations with Vietnam. China also began to engage for the first time with ASEAN, a body that it had previously viewed with suspicion. In 1991, it became a "consultative partner" to the organization, and began to pursue a new policy of friendly coexistence and peaceful development with the nations lying along its periphery.

Despite stirrings of apprehension about Chinese actions in the South China Sea, security concerns were soon eclipsed by economics. In mid-1997, Southeast Asia was rocked by the Asian financial crisis, which began with the floating of the Thai baht in July of that year, and subsequently brought the region's economic "miracle" to a shuddering halt. The effects were particularly dire in Thailand and Indonesia, where the local currencies shed half their value or more, banks and companies collapsed, and millions were thrown out of work. In the aftermath of the crisis, China played a central role in easing the economic pain, offering financial aid and supportive proclamations that differed from the sluggish reaction of the US and the harsh diktats of the International Monetary Fund. Most importantly, China refrained from devaluing its own currency, a move that earned it praise from leaders across the region. As David Shambaugh writes, Beijing's assistance to the affected countries "punctured the prevailing image of China in the region as either aloof or hegemonic and began to replace it with an image of China as a responsible power."[24]

To build on the goodwill generated by its response to the 1997 crash, China mounted a concerted diplomatic "charm offensive" in Southeast Asia.[25] Leaders spoke of the nation's "peaceful rise," and Chinese President Jiang Zemin declared that his nation would "forever be a good neighbor, a good partner, and a good friend" to the region.[26] In the late 1990s and early 2000s, high-level state visits were kicked into dizzying rotation. Beijing increased its involvement with ASEAN; by 2009, it was engaging the bloc through 48 separate mechanisms.[27] For the first time, it also opened multilateral discussions concerning maritime disputes. In 2002, China and ASEAN signed a Declaration on the Conduct of Parties in the South China Sea, which succeeded in dampening maritime tensions, at least for the time being. The following year saw the signing of a China–ASEAN Free Trade Agreement (CAFTA), which came into effect in 2010, boosting trade between the two regions.

Southeast Asia's importance to China was reflected in its increasing knowledge of the region and its peoples. After the isolation of the Mao years, the 1990s and early 2000s saw a marked improvement in China's academic expertise on Southeast Asia. A survey conducted in 2001 noted the appearance of 607 publications on various aspects of Southeast Asia since 1990.[28] Much of this academic expertise was concentrated in southern China, particularly at universities in the provinces of Fujian, Guangdong, Guangxi, and Yunnan, reflecting the region's long-standing cultural and migratory linkages with Southeast Asia. In more recent years, this has expanded beyond the south to include research institutes and government think-tanks in Beijing, such as the Chinese Academy of Social Sciences and the China Institute of International Studies, and new centers of Southeast Asian studies in major inland cities like Chongqing and Xi'an.[29]

This growing body of expertise fed into the quality of China's diplomacy toward the region. In the 1990s, the wooden officials of the Deng Xiaoping era started being phased into retirement and replaced with a younger generation of diplomats, frequently fluent in Southeast Asian languages, and often in English as well. The Ministry of Foreign Affairs began encouraging its diplomats to undertake multiple rotations to the same country in order to develop the local contacts in business and politics that would later serve them well as ambassadors.[30]

A key part of China's strategy in Southeast Asia was its deployment of "soft power" throughout the region. Chinese ambassadors gave donations to Chinese-language schools in Malaysia, and speeches at the opening of new Confucius Institutes from Laos to Singapore.[31] China expanded its media operations in Southeast Asia, broadcasting in local languages, and poured money into scholarships designed to bring Southeast Asian students to Chinese universities. By 2016, an estimated 80,000 students from Southeast Asia were enrolled at universities in mainland China—many on scholarships offered under the BRI.[32]

China's "soft power" push involved a proliferation of friendship visits, training programs, and all-expenses-paid "study tours" for journalists, academics, and government officials. One Malaysian think-tank analyst recalled a trip in which members of his institution were ferried from hi-tech industrial parks to cultural sights to bullet trains. He summarized the trip's agenda as "demonstrations of Chinese competence, one after another." In a similar way, China deepened its outreach to the economically prosperous ethnic Chinese minorities of Southeast Asia. As Beijing sought to thicken business connections and curry support for Chinese initiatives, Overseas Chinese community organizations, chambers of commerce, and clan and dialect associations became the targets of special attention.

Despite these efforts, China has never quite succeeded at "soft power" in Southeast Asia. Its wooing of the region was based not on natural attraction, nor on appeals to its rich and fascinating history. These various initiatives rather involved variations on China's predominant theme: its economic strength. True to the CCP's materialist roots, many Chinese strategists have assumed that China's economic weight would exert an inevitable and irresistible pull on the small nations along its periphery. As Hou Songling of the Institute of Southeast Asian Studies at Jinan University has explained, "economics are the priority and politics will follow; economics will carry forward and spur politics."[33] Yan Xuetong, another leading Chinese scholar, has argued that China should let small nations benefit economically from their relationships, "and in return we get good political relationships. We should 'purchase' the relationships."[34] This "soft" power has also had a harder edge: if a foreign country's policy ran counter to its interests, China could cut off trade or employ other forms of economic coercion. Buried in China's talk of mutual prosperity was a stark choice: flourish within a Chinese orbit, or languish outside of it.

If Southeast Asians harbored concerns about Beijing's intentions, they could at least give the Chinese credit for showing up. China's regional charm offensive coincided with a period of ambivalent US engagement with Southeast Asia, which set in following the terrorist attacks of September 11, 2001.[35] Preoccupied with planning and launching the invasions of Afghanistan and Iraq, and then coping with the political chaos and diplomatic fallout that ensued, President George W. Bush skipped major regional summits, and most US engagement with Southeast Asia was framed in terms of the global "war on terror." The Bush administration's combination of strategic neglect and aggressive unilateralism contrasted starkly with China's persistent engagement and assertions of respect for national sovereignty. By the time Beijing hosted the 2008 Olympics, an event widely seen as a coming-out party for the new China, the nation's leaders could mount a good argument that they had fulfilled the promise of China's "peaceful rise."

In September 2008, however, just a month after the Olympic Opening Ceremony in the Chinese capital, a massive economic crisis detonated in the US financial sector, blowing a hole in the global economy. The crash of 2008–9 would become another turning point. It not only battered the US economy and triggered a worldwide recession; it also discredited the prevailing American model of financialized capitalism and burnished China's state-led approach to economic management. Far from simply weathering the crisis, China accounted at the height of the recession for an astonishing 50 percent of the world's economic growth.[36] In the halls of power in Beijing, the crisis was a watershed: in the journalist John Pomfret's words, it "strengthened the impression that the future belonged to China while America's greatest moment had passed."[37]

The year 2009 saw a sudden shift in the tone and content of Chinese declarations, which became more assertive on a range of issues, from monetary policy to the virtues (or otherwise) of Western-style democracy. China also revived a series of mostly dormant territorial disputes with its neighbors, including those in the South China Sea. In May 2009, it submitted a map to a United Nations commission that featured the so-called "nine-dash line," a looping U-shaped boundary that claimed Chinese sovereignty over the majority of the South China Sea, including swathes of ocean claimed by Vietnam, the Philippines, Malaysia, Brunei, and Taiwan.[38] China's move incited an immediate and furious response from the affected Southeast Asian states.

China's stridency, on this question and others, has only increased since Xi Jinping's accession to the leadership in 2012. In late 2013, China began dredging operations aimed at transforming contested specks of rock and coral in the middle of the South China Sea into man-made island fortresses. By 2017, it had created seven of these features in the Spratly Islands, equipping them with administrative buildings, munitions depots, runways, fighter jet hangars, radar systems, and missile shelters. At the same time, it became more willing to employ various forms of economic coercion against other states, and take assertive actions to shape other nations' public opinion and political outcomes in ways favorable to Chinese interests.

Contrary to China's oft-repeated doctrine of non-interference, many of these influence efforts blurred the line between legitimate cultural outreach and active involvement in the affairs of target nations—a form of intervention that has been dubbed "sharp power."[39] One medium of influence was the CCP's secretive International Liaison Department (ILD). Established in 1950 to coordinate Beijing's contacts with foreign communist parties, the ILD has since been retooled as a means of maintaining ties with members of opposition political parties, as well as non-state groups, like ethnic armed rebel groups in Burma, which are seen as important to Chinese interests.

The most controversial form of influence operation has involved attempts to strengthen relations with Southeast Asia's ethnic Chinese. As in the US and Australia, where the CCP's wooing of Chinese diaspora communities has been the subject of recent alarm, state efforts have extended beyond cultural outreach, seeking to convert Chinese cultural affinities into sympathy for PRC state policies and support for official schemes like the BRI. While many Southeast Asian Chinese have resisted (or simply ignored) Beijing's attempts to harness their support, these efforts have nonetheless generated unease across the region, where citizens of Chinese descent have frequently been suspected of dual loyalties.

All the while, China has continued to assert that its new strength will be a force for international harmony rather than conflict or domination. In October 2013, Xi Jinping convened a special conference on "diplomatic work with neighboring countries," in which he called for the transformation of China's immediate neighborhood, including Southeast Asia, into a "community of common destiny."[40] However much Beijing might woo its southern neighbors, this "win-win" sloganeering jars with the realities of China's present approach to the region: one that is increasingly less charm and more offensive.

For the nations and peoples of Southeast Asia, proximity to Asia's largest power has always been a mixed blessing. As Malaysia's former prime minister Tun Abdul Razak observed in 1971, the fact that the Southeast Asian countries dwell in China's neighborhood means that they are always "the first to live with the consequences of her policies."[41] Southeast Asia was the region where the fires of Maoism burned the hottest. It is also where the effects of China's rising economic and political power have been most marked, for better and for worse.

On the one hand, the region has benefited greatly from a surge of trade, private sector investment, and development aid from China. In 1990, China's trade with the region was worth just over $7.5 billion; by 2018, it had risen to some $642 billion—a more than 85-fold increase.[42] Today, China is by far the leading trading partner of eight of the ten ASEAN countries, as well as of the region as a whole. From 2013 to 2018, China's trade with the Southeast Asian bloc totaled $2.37 trillion, compared to $1.33 trillion for the US and $1.32 trillion for Japan.[43] It is also the leading source of tourists to the region. Chinese investment flows into ASEAN have increased at a slower clip, but have jumped sharply since the announcement of the BRI in 2013; in 2018, China was the second-largest investor in ASEAN from outside the region, behind Japan.[44]

In theory, Chinese state-backed financing under the BRI could help the poorer Southeast Asian countries modernize their infrastructure and raise their populations to prosperity. According to the Asian Development Bank (ADB), the developing countries of Asia alone require infrastructure investments of about $1.7 trillion per year to maintain growth, reduce poverty, and mitigate climate change—a need that China's BRI is ideally poised to fill.[45] Many Southeast Asian governments also find it appealing that Chinese support is offered without overt political conditions, unlike Western nations and international financial institutions, which often tie their aid and financing to a range of good governance and human rights benchmarks.

On the other hand, many of these economic benefits have been double-edged. Booming trade figures conceal China's large and growing trade surpluses with a number of its major trading partners in Southeast Asia, fueled by an influx of low-priced Chinese agricultural produce and manufactured goods that have undercut local industries, especially since CAFTA came into force in 2010. Moreover, Chinese investment—especially state-backed infrastructure projects—has relied heavily on the use of Chinese workers and technology, a perennially sensitive issue across much of the region.

Exported south, China's state-driven development model has had a range of deleterious effects, from environmental degradation and illegal logging to the forced displacement of local populations for infrastructure projects. While Chinese financial support is free of explicit political conditionalities, it comes with strings of a different kind: harsh financing terms that have stoked fears of over-indebtedness to Chinese state banks. All of these fears help account for the joke that I have heard across the ASEAN region, from Palawan to Sihanoukville: that the arrival of Chinese capital, goods, traders, or workers was turning the nation, or some part of it, into "a province of China." Although an exaggeration, the joke speaks to the profound unease that many Southeast Asians feel at the giant awakening to their north.

China's size and proximity confers on its leaders a special responsibility of convincing the Southeast Asian nations of its friendly intentions. Instead, many of its recent actions have sent the opposite message. For all the talent of its diplomatic corps, Chinese officialdom has shown it has a tin-ear for public opinion, and a general insensitivity to the negative responses provoked by its rising power—even to the idea that China's policies could evoke such resentment in the first place. These traits are especially notable in the region's more open societies. As befits an authoritarian party-state with little space for independent political organization, the PRC is adroit at dealing with states and governments—no nation does state pageantry better—yet is congenitally clumsy in its dealings with populations and organizations lying outside the remit of the state.

This blinkered approach encapsulates the condition that Edward Luttwak has diagnosed as "great-state autism"—the difficulty that large powers face in breaking free of entrenched ways of thinking, acting, and behaving.[46] Bilahari Kausikan, the outspoken former Permanent Secretary of Singapore's Foreign Ministry, put China's behavior down to the re-emergence of a kind of imperial hauteur: a demand that its size and prominence be acknowledged by a general subservience to Chinese interests. "Everybody has accepted China as a geopolitical fact," he told me in an interview in 2017, "but the Chinese infer from this geopolitical fact a new norm for East Asian international relations: that there is a new hierarchy with China at the apex."

This has given rise to an apparently widespread perception that opposition to Chinese initiatives can only be due to recalcitrance, ill-intention, or the malign influence of outside powers. This imperious attitude was epitomized during the 17th ASEAN Regional Forum in Hanoi in July 2010, when Yang Jiechi, then Minister of Foreign Affairs, declared that maritime disputes between China and ASEAN member states in the South China Sea would not be negotiated multilaterally. "China is a big country and other countries are small countries," he reportedly told Southeast Asian leaders, "and that's just a fact."[47] Even as Beijing claims to safeguard other nations' sovereignty, its behavior carries an unmistakable echo of colonial powers past.

China's "great-state autism" is most glaring—and potentially most dangerous—on the question of its relationship to Southeast Asia's ethnic Chinese diaspora.

An estimated 32.7 million ethnic Chinese live across the ten nations of ASEAN, most of them the descendants of poor immigrants who moved south during the high noon of European colonialism in the late nineteenth and early twentieth centuries.[48] These Chinese communities have played a central role in the making of modern Southeast Asia. Their commercial networks helped drive the Southeast Asian "miracle" in the 1980s and 1990s and they remain central to the region's economic life today, enmeshed in the commanding heights of politics and business.

At the same time, these Chinese communities have long been a source of resentment among "native" Southeast Asians. Since colonial times, they have been accused of profiting at the expense of ethnic majorities, advancing the interests of the Chinese state, or both. This has made ethnic Chinese the frequent targets of discrimination and violence, most notably during the rolling street riots that seized Indonesia in May 1998. As Michael Vatikiotis writes, it is not the threat of a Chinese naval or overland invasion that most worries the peoples and governments of the region. Rather, it is the "subliminal, unspoken fear of mass migration from China, as well as China's putative extra-territorial claim over the ethnic Chinese communities of the region."[49]

People from China began settling in Southeast Asia around the thirteenth century, in line with its growing commercial presence in the region. But the major waves of immigration date from the mid-nineteenth century, when famine, overpopulation, and political upheaval pushed millions of young men to emigrate from the coastal regions of Fujian and Guangdong provinces. While some set off for California, or the island plantations of the Caribbean, most went to Southeast Asia, where work was plentiful in the mines and plantations of colonial Java, Malaya, and French Indochina, as well as in independent Siam. So strong was the connection between Chinese immigration and Western imperialism, the historian Wang Gungwu writes, that "it could almost be said that Chinese trade followed European flags."[50] By 1900, there were 120,000 Chinese in southern Vietnam, 200,000 in Bangkok, and more than 60,000 in the Rangoon area.[51] While many of these immigrants remained poor, a significant number flourished under colonial rule, slotting into roles as tax collectors and economic middlemen between the European authorities and native populations.

Things began to change in the late nineteenth century, when nationalism arose in China and subsequently spread, via telegraph and steamship, to the

Chinese communities abroad. Prior to this, few would have considered themselves "Chinese" in the modern sense of the term. Most spoke southern regional languages like Hokkien and Teochew that were unintelligible to Mandarin-speakers, and would more likely have identified themselves by dialect, clan group, or district of origin. Suddenly, these "Nanyang Chinese" began to play active roles in the events roiling their homeland. From the early twentieth century, they offered a pool of support for those seeking the overthrow of the Qing dynasty and its replacement with a modern republic. The republican leader Sun Yat-sen would later describe the Southeast Asian Chinese as "the mother of the revolution" that toppled the Qing in 1911.[52]

Political divisions among the ethnic Chinese of Southeast Asia mirrored those in China proper. Some supported the Nationalist republic led by Chiang Kai-shek, others the Communist movement led by Mao. In the 1930s, when the Nationalists and Communists formed a United Front to fight the invading Japanese armies, Southeast Asia's Overseas Chinese similarly banded together and raised funds to support the struggle.

As Chinese identity sharpened across the Nanyang, however, colonial officials came to view Chinese populations as disloyal and potentially subversive. One British cabinet assessment from the 1950s described the ethnic Chinese of Southeast Asia as "almost automatic agencies of the Peking Government."[53] The same was true of indigenous elites, already resentful at the wealth and privilege of their nations' ethnic Chinese populations. King Vajiravudh (Rama VI) of Siam, who infamously referred to his kingdom's Chinese as "the Jews of the East," probably spoke for many early Southeast Asian nationalists when he wrote in 1914, "No matter where they live, what nationality they assume, Chinese remain essentially Chinese."[54]

The coming of independence after World War II brought further challenges for the region's ethnic Chinese. As Benedict Anderson notes, "Colonial subjecthood could be worn lightly: modern citizenship could not."[55] The PRC's export of communism led many Southeast Asian governments to accuse the Chinese of acting as a "fifth column" for Beijing—a claim that was all the more insidious for containing a grain of truth. This resulted in a range of restrictions, including bans on the Chinese language, travel to China, and ethnic Chinese participation in key professions. Their practical effect was to ghettoize the Chinese in the private commercial sector, where they flourished, boasting close connections to "native" political leaders and access to an intricate "bamboo network" of Overseas Chinese financial connections spanning the region. In 1995, an Australian government study estimated that the ethnic Chinese of Southeast Asia generated a collective GDP of $450 billion, not far short of China's then-GDP of around $500 billion.[56]

China's policy toward its Southeast Asian offspring has always been a complex and delicate issue. For much of its history, the Chinese empire disdained those who left its shores, viewing them as outcasts, even criminals. When the Dutch sent the Qianlong Emperor an apology for a vicious massacre of Chinese in Batavia (Jakarta) in 1740, he is reported to have replied that he was "little solicitous for the fate of unworthy subjects who, in the pursuit of lucre, had quitted their country and abandoned the tombs of their ancestors."[57] With the rise of Chinese nationalism things moved to the other extreme. In 1909, the Qing dynasty claimed jurisdiction over all ethnic Chinese, no matter where they resided, on the basis of blood, a position inherited by the Republic of China after 1912, a further reason why ethnic Chinese loyalties aroused such concerns in Southeast Asia.

Upon taking power in 1949, the PRC faced the challenge of what policy to take toward the Overseas Chinese of Southeast Asia. In general, its approach has shifted according to its perceived national interests. In the 1950s, hoping to cultivate good relationships in Southeast Asia, the PRC's first premier Zhou Enlai disavowed responsibility for the region's ethnic Chinese, encouraging them to be loyal to their new nations of residence. But ambiguities lingered, especially given China's steadfast support for the region's communist movements, some of which (as in Malaya) consisted disproportionately of ethnic Chinese. The issue was also complicated by the fact that the CCP and Chinese Nationalists, or Kuomintang, now ensconced on Taiwan, continued to compete for the loyalties and support of the ethnic Chinese of Southeast Asia.

As China opened its economy and sought improved ties with the ASEAN countries in the late 1970s, the policy changed again. In 1980, Beijing passed a new Nationality Law that abolished dual nationality, marking for the first time a clear distinction between *huaqiao* (Chinese citizens living overseas) and *huaren* (foreign citizens of Chinese descent). Henceforth, ethnic Chinese could choose to be citizens of China or their nations of residence—but not both. This helped mend relations with the Southeast Asian states; it also opened China's access to the financial resources of the "bamboo network." After Deng initiated his economic reforms in late 1978, ethnic Chinese businesspeople in Thailand, Indonesia, and Malaysia were among the first to sink money into the mainland. By 1989, investment in China from ethnic Chinese abroad amounted to some $30 billion. Most of this was from Hong Kong and Taiwan, but as much as 10 percent of it came from Southeast Asia.[58]

In recent years, as China's power has grown, its economic and cultural ties to Southeast Asia's Chinese communities have expanded, affecting them in subtle but potentially significant ways. As some Southeast Asian Chinese have re-established or strengthened commercial links to mainland China, others have oriented themselves toward mainland notions of Chineseness. A rough proxy for this change is the decline in their use of Chinese regional languages like Hokkien and Cantonese, and the adoption (especially by younger generations) of *putonghua*, the Mandarin Chinese favored on the mainland.

More significantly, the Chinese government has also oriented itself more closely toward the ethnic Chinese diaspora. Under Xi Jinping, China is beginning to abandon the caution that has marked its approach to Overseas Chinese affairs since the 1980s. It has recently adopted a more proactive policy that that describes ethnic Chinese abroad as part of a "Greater China," and endeavors to convert business ties and cultural affinities into sympathy for Chinese goals and support for key state initiatives like the BRI. In a 2014 speech, Xi described ethnic Chinese living overseas as "members of one big Chinese family" and referred to national rejuvenation as a "common dream" of all Chinese, whether or not they were PRC citizens.[59] In 2017, at an Overseas Chinese work conference, he similarly declared, "The realization of the great rejuvenation of the Chinese nation requires the joint efforts of Chinese sons and daughters at home and abroad."[60]

The importance Beijing places on the ethnic Chinese overseas became clear in March 2018, when it placed its Overseas Chinese Affairs Office under the control of the United Front Work Department, the CCP's traditional arm for developing alliances with non-communist groups, including the global Chinese diaspora.[61] In 2015, China introduced the *huayi ka*, a special "green card" for foreign citizens of Chinese origin, according them most of the privileges of PRC citizens. Given their relative wealth and prominence, one leading Chinese scholar proclaimed, the ethnic Chinese overseas constituted Xi Jinping's "economic weapon."[62]

Beijing's outreach to the Overseas Chinese makes sense given their past contributions to China's development. It nonetheless carries significant risks for

Southeast Asians of Chinese extraction. While levels of assimilation differ greatly across the region, the acceptance of the ethnic Chinese into Southeast Asian societies has rested on the preservation of a firm but fragile distinction between *huaren* and *huaqiao*: between Chinese cultural affinities and political loyalty to the Chinese state. As the Chinese government starts to claim ethnic Chinese abroad as members of a putative "Greater China," it is beginning to muddy the distinction, reawakening dormant suspicions of dual loyalties.[63]

The situation has been complicated by two more recent developments. The first is the mounting public pressure within China, resulting from several decades of "patriotic education" and official state nationalism, for Beijing to protect ethnic Chinese "compatriots" living in Southeast Asia, especially in the event of another outbreak of anti-Chinese violence or discrimination. The second is a new generation of Chinese emigrants and expatriates that have accompanied the flow of Chinese capital into Southeast Asia since 1978. Since the Chinese government has a legitimate interest in the welfare of its citizens abroad, this new influx of people has only underlined the importance of maintaining the crucial distinction between Chinese citizenship and Chinese ethnicity. Worryingly, Beijing has begun referring to all ethnic Chinese abroad by a new term: *haiwai qiaobao*, or "Chinese compatriots overseas."[64] This raises doubts that it has the wisdom or sensitivity to distinguish between passport-carrying PRC citizens, and the ethnic Chinese who have long called the lands of Southeast Asia home.

The same doubts also attach to some Southeast Asians. While the region's ethnic Chinese appear well assimilated, there are still small but vocal minorities in some nations that have never fully accepted them as members of the national community. This is especially the case in Muslim-majority Indonesia and Malaysia, where nationalist and religious demagogues continue to find profit in painting all Chinese—whether PRC nationals or citizens of their own country—as an undifferentiated foreign "other." Caught between a rising China abroad and a rising nativism at home, the ethnic Chinese of Southeast Asia face an ominous blurring of the lines.

As China has shrugged off its old caution and adopted a more assertive foreign policy, it has naturally provoked pushback from other major powers, especially the US. In 2011, the Obama administration announced a "pivot" in American foreign policy, redirecting its attention and resources from the

Middle East back toward Asia, in a bid to counter China's strategic ambitions. As President Obama said in an address to the Australian parliament in 2011, "After a decade in which we fought two wars that cost us dearly, in blood and treasure, the US is turning our attention to the vast potential of the Asia-Pacific region."[65] The pivot, later rebranded the "rebalance," promised a significant augmentation of Washington's diplomatic, economic, and military presence in Southeast Asia, in a bid to reassure American partners and counterbalance China's increasing heft.

While it would fall short of its ultimate goals, in large part due to the continuing turmoil in the Middle East, the "rebalance" went a considerable way to redressing the neglect of the Bush years. Hillary Clinton became the first US Secretary of State to visit all ten ASEAN nations; Washington appointed its first ambassador to ASEAN; the US elevated relations with Vietnam, Singapore, and the Philippines; and the administration played a key role in coaxing military-ruled Burma from its cocoon of isolation. Obama also painstakingly negotiated the Trans-Pacific Partnership (TPP), a free-trade pact involving twelve nations, including four from Southeast Asia. Always underwhelming in its execution, the "rebalance" did not long survive the election of President Trump, who withdrew from the TPP during his first days in office, deriding it as "a bad, bad deal" for American workers.

The Trump administration has since replaced the "rebalance" with a more openly belligerent stance toward China. Whereas the Obama administration saw Beijing as both competitor and partner, recent American policy documents have depicted China as an unqualified adversary and a fundamental threat to American interests. As the unclassified summary of the January 2018 US National Defense Strategy alleges, China has adopted "an all-of-nation long-term strategy" that "seeks Indo-Pacific regional hegemony in the near-term and displacement of the United States to achieve global preeminence in the future."[66] A similar view suffuses the administration's Free and Open Indo-Pacific (FOIP) strategy, first announced by Trump during an Asia-Pacific Economic Cooperation meeting in Vietnam in November 2017. The FOIP lays out a vision for a regional order built around a "Quad" of regional democratic powers: the US, Japan, India, and Australia. The FOIP strategy is implicitly aimed at containing Beijing's ability to dominate Asia, and ensuring, in Secretary of State Mike Pompeo's words, "that China retains only its proper place in the world."[67]

This new anti-China mood is not confined to Trump and his acolytes. From Senator Elizabeth Warren to Steve Bannon, bipartisan opinion has converged on a view of China as a predatory power that bullies its neighbors, seeks to export its authoritarian political model, and purposefully employs "debt-trap diplomacy" to ensnare developing nations.[68] This monochrome image is typically set against an idealized vision of American primacy and the US-led "liberal international order" that China is allegedly working to supplant.[69] The 2017 US National Security Strategy describes a struggle "between free and repressive visions of world order."[70] Kiron Skinner, until recently the State Department's director of policy planning (a post once held by the diplomat George Kennan), even described competition with China in civilizational and racial terms, as being "the first time that we will have a great power competitor that is not Caucasian."[71]

The view from Southeast Asia is considerably more complicated. China's centrality in the region makes it a reality no nation can ignore, much less defy openly. As one senior Singaporean Foreign Ministry official put it, "No country in Southeast Asia wants to set itself against Beijing." More than that, China's economic ties with Southeast Asia give the region a strong stake in its continued growth and stability—not least since all the alternatives would likely be worse. Southeast Asians are keenly aware that periods of Chinese instability have often coincided with destabilizing flows of people southward. The fall of the Ming dynasty in the seventeenth century led to a large stream of refugees into Southeast Asia, as did the internal upheavals of the late Qing and the fall of the Chinese mainland to the communists in 1949. A similar event today would have massively disruptive implications for the region.

The prevailing US view also overlooks important areas of common interest between China and Southeast Asia. The two regions share an history of bruising encounters with Western imperial power in the nineteenth and twentieth centuries, an experience that has inculcated a common zeal for national sovereignty and an extreme allergy to any hint of outside interference in their affairs. This has also made many Chinese and Southeast Asian leaders congenitally skeptical of the Western claim, especially ascendant since the end of the Cold War, that there is a single, universal standard of political development.

It is on this question that the US most often reveals its own liberal variant of "great-state autism": a tendency to view the region's political developments through the lens of its own sense of exceptionalism, the idea that America's national interests harmonize in some essential way with the interests of people everywhere, that the American way of life is "the ultimate destiny of humankind."[72] Based on conversations I have had in Southeast Asia's capitals, however, the idea of the US as a universal political model is generally viewed as quaint and parochial, if not an open threat. This perception has only been reinforced by the nativism and unilateralism of the Trump administration.

Moreover, the recent history of American intervention in Southeast Asia presents a grayer picture than most recent paeans to the "liberal international order" admit. While Southeast Asia, like China, has benefited greatly from the US-backed security order, the "ordering" of the region was a bloody business. It involved America's long and destructive war in Indochina, its backing for vicious anti-communist purges in Indonesia in 1965–6, and sustained US support for a procession of anti-communist autocrats, from Thailand's Marshal Sarit Thanarat to President Suharto of Indonesia to Ferdinand Marcos of the Philippines. While most ASEAN nations fear a dominant China and strongly desire a US military presence to help counterbalance it, few yearn for liberal prescriptions. The result is that in those places where the US and other Western powers have been most heavy-handed in their criticisms of Southeast Asian governments on questions of democracy or human rights, a pragmatic China has made quick inroads.

China's foreign policy pragmatism has led some American observers to assert that it is seeking actively to undermine democracy or export its authoritarian system to the world. Elizabeth C. Economy of the Council on Foreign Relations writes of "China's push to shape other countries' political systems" and its intention "to reshape the international system in its own image."[73] At first glance, this claim might seem merited in the case of Southeast Asia. The Xi Jinping years have coincided with a wave of apparent democratic reverses in the region: a return to military rule in Thailand; bloody populism in the Philippines; ethnic cleansing in Burma; autocratic ascendancy in Cambodia; and embezzlement in Malaysia on a grand scale. At the same time, Chinese leaders are speaking more confidently about what their own experience can offer developing countries. In 2016, Xi declared that the Chinese people were "fully confident in offering a solution to humanity's search for better social systems." The following year, he declared that China was "blazing a new trail for other developing countries to achieve modernization."[74]

While democracy has certainly eroded across Southeast Asia, it is easy to exaggerate China's role in this trend. The region's patterns of authoritarianism and political dysfunction long pre-date the era of Xi. The reasons for this are complex, and cannot easily be abstracted from the social, political, and historical context of the nations in question. In some, they have their roots in the colonial era, when European powers manipulated racial divisions to control subject populations and facilitate the extraction of natural resources, handing on serious nation-building challenges to the independent states that succeeded them. In others, they are underpinned by pre-modern traditions of authority that raised kings and princes high above the worldly realm, shaping political cultures opposed to the idea of popular sovereignty.[75] Others still mirror the present situation in Western democracies, including the US, where authoritarian populism has arisen in response to the failures of ruling elites to deliver broad prosperity and equitable development.

China's critics are right about one thing: it has not certainly helped the situation. Its no-questions-asked approach to human rights abuses, and its diplomatic and financial support for the governments committing them, has helped embolden authoritarian leaders in Southeast Asian countries, much as American support did during the Cold War. But for all the talk about China offering new solutions to developing countries, it has been mostly indifferent to how they govern themselves. Rather than pursuing an authoritarian equivalent to Western democracy promotion efforts, the Chinese government works with the realities that exist, exploiting them in order to advance its strategic goals, asserting all the while that "it is the right of every sovereign state to choose its own development path."[76] Even when this nod to sovereignty is undermined by China's own actions, it is a message that finds a receptive audience in Southeast Asia.

It is also a mistake to ascribe more coherence to China's plans than exists in practice. To speak of Chinese influence in Southeast Asia is to speak not of one thing, but of many. One leading Thai scholar describes China as "a dragon of many shades and colors" in order to reflect the "multiplicity and flexibility" of its activities in the region.[77] While it is never easy to determine where the Chinese state ends and private initiatives begin, China's influence spills beyond the decrees and policies of the central state to include countless individual actors, from businesspeople and students to petty traders, smugglers, and criminals, whose ends frequently run counter to official schemes like the BRI—even as they ape its rhetoric. In his book *The Souls of China*, Ian Johnson observes that content generally comes late to Chinese projects. He describes

China as "the land of soft openings. Projects are first announced to big fanfare, structures erected as declarations of intent, and only then filled with content."[78] This offers a useful reminder that Chinese initiatives like the BRI, often depicted as a masterplan for global economic domination, remain very much works in progress. Beneath the radiant banners and headline announcements, China's strategy in Southeast Asia is more improvised, contradictory, and chaotic than at first it might appear.

As Sino-American competition becomes more intense, Southeast Asian nations have sought to avoid any scenario in which they might be forced to choose sides. So, too, has ASEAN. While it was established in 1967 as a response to Chinese communist subversion, ASEAN's fundamental purpose was to create a mechanism by which the small nations of the region could attain some measure of autonomy in the midst of great power competition. As Singapore's first Foreign Minister S. Rajaratnam then argued, ASEAN had to fill the region's vacuum on its own, "or resign itself to the dismal prospect of the vacuum being filled from outside."[79] ASEAN has since succeeded in establishing itself as a key part of the regional diplomatic architecture, and an increasingly cohesive presence at the fulcrum of the Indian and Pacific oceans.

So far, ASEAN's preferred approach has been to bind the Chinese Gulliver with a thousand multilateral threads, to socialize it into the "ASEAN way": the bloc's signature mode of sometimes glacial consensus-based diplomacy. It is an approach that amounts to a sort of narcotization by summitry. At the same time, China's rising power has brought ASEAN's various shortcomings into relief. The very things that have allowed ASEAN to bridge the wide differences in its member states' interests—its operating principles of non-interference and consensus—have limited how far it can go in forging unified political positions.

Currently, the ten ASEAN nations differ considerably on the question of China in general, and on the South China Sea disputes in particular, opening up gaps into which Beijing has thrust wedges of economic inducement. In recent years, China has convinced or pressured its closest Southeast Asian partners—particularly Cambodia and Laos—to veto or dilute criticisms of its aggressive maritime activities and prevent the bloc from taking a unified position on the disputes. As China's power increases, it thus poses fundamental challenges to ASEAN's cohesion, and perhaps, in time, to the very idea of "Southeast Asia" itself.

China and the US are not the only outside powers actively engaged in Southeast Asia. Another important player in this story is Japan: the region's quiet achiever. Tokyo has its own baggage in Southeast Asia, where its occupying armies committed savage atrocities before and during World War II. Since the 1970s, however, accommodating diplomacy and injections of capital investment have helped transform Japan's image "from a fearsome samurai state or a rapacious merchant state to a peace-fostering, alms-giving, and community-building state."[80] Today, Japan is the world's third-largest economy after China and the US, its fourth-largest trading nation, and a global leader in precision manufactures and other advanced technologies. Japanese investment and aid were key ingredients in the Southeast Asian "miracle," and the country remains the largest outside investor in ASEAN. Between 2013 and 2018, Japan's investment in the region came to $102.3 billion, nearly twice as much as the $52.8 billion it received from China.[81]

Under Prime Minister Shinzo Abe, who took office for the second time in 2012, Japan has gone a considerable way to developing its own ability to counter China and reassert a leadership role in Southeast Asia. Abe's government has quietly expanded military consultations and cooperation with nearly every Southeast Asian nation. After China, it possesses the second-largest navy in Asia. Under its own multibillion-dollar connectivity initiative, Japan has funded critical infrastructure projects from Luzon to Tenasserim. Richard Javad Heydarian, one of the Philippines' leading foreign policy commentators, describes Japan as the region's "stealth superpower"[82]: large enough to be helpful, yet not so large as to incite fear and anxiety.

The other potential regional counterweight, India, presents a more cryptic picture. In 2014, amid widespread apprehension over China's ambitions, Prime Minister Narendra Modi announced the "Act East" policy: an attempt to enhance India's political and economic ties to Southeast Asia. An update on the "Look East" policy promulgated in 1991, Modi's initiative has yielded some significant results: in January 2018, he hosted all ten ASEAN leaders in New Delhi for the first time. For the most part, however, the vast, kaleidoscopic republic remains overwhelmingly inward-looking, its strategic attention consumed by its jittery nuclear rivalry with Pakistan. Despite the strong imprint that its classical civilization left on pre-modern Southeast Asia, visible today in its sinuous Indic scripts and enigmatic religious monuments, New Delhi remains a relatively weak player in the region. Even so, India remains

Asia's sleeping giant, its very latency serving as a bulwark against the westward spread of Chinese power and influence. In addition to Japan and India, the European Union, South Korea, Russia, Taiwan, and Australia all have a strong economic and diplomatic presence in the region, giving the Southeast Asian states added room for maneuver.

In general, China has presented each of the Southeast Asian states with a similar challenge: how to benefit from its booming economy while safeguarding its sovereignty from the perils of overdependence. As the following chapters show, each nation has met this challenge in its own way. Some have harnessed Chinese power as a shield against Western pressures to enact democratic reforms, or as a means of developing their infrastructure and lifting their populations out of poverty. Others have sought to offset China's clout by building up economic and security ties to the US, Japan, India, and other powers. All have been promiscuous in tilting, balancing, and hedging their bets. In their own way, within the limits available to them, the nations and peoples of Southeast Asia are all learning to adjust themselves to life in China's shadow.

2
MARCHING TOWARD THE TROPICS

On a hot, humid morning in June 1866, six Frenchmen cast off from the waterfront in Saigon and ventured into the hazy green unknown. Led by Ernest Doudart de Lagrée, a 43-year-old Crimean War veteran with an history of chronic laryngitis, the group traveled in "two minuscule steam-driven gunboats," according to the historian John Keay, accompanied by a support crew of 20 and an "inordinate quantity of liquor, flour, guns, and trade goods."[1] All this was laid aside in support of their mission: to chart the mighty Mekong River upstream from its delta in southern Vietnam into wild regions then untrodden by European explorers.

As Western imperialism reached its zenith in the mid-nineteenth century, the Mekong region became the subject of fevered competition between rival European powers. In London and Paris, colonial functionaries swooned at explorers' embellished accounts of the trade that flourished in the mist-shrouded borderlands lying between imperial China and the kingdoms to its south. "If one believes the travelers' tales, these valleys contain active and industrious peoples who trade with the Celestial Empire," wrote de Lagrée's tempestuous deputy Francis Garnier, who dreamt of gaining access to "the mines of amber, serpentine, zinc, gold, and silver that lie along the upper course of the Mekong."[2]

By the time the Mekong Exploration Commission set off from Saigon, these treasures seemed ready for the taking. The Qing dynasty that had ruled China since the mid-seventeenth century was reeling from the twin blows of Western imperial assault and internal rebellion. Following its victory in the first Opium War in 1842, Great Britain had forced the empire open to trade and Western powers had carved up the Chinese coast into a patchwork of enclaves, treaty ports, and foreign concessions. The war's 1860 sequel saw European armies burn and loot the emperor's summer palace on the outskirts of Beijing. These humiliating capitulations fed into an outbreak of paralyzing internal revolts, including the Taiping Rebellion of 1850–64, which brought Qing rule to the verge of collapse. As Chinese power weakened, Beijing's hold over its protective ring of Southeast Asian vassal states began to loosen, opening up fresh opportunities for imperial conquest.

A relative latecomer to the imperial game in Asia, France's push up the Mekong was driven by the lure of profit: in particular, the prospect of opening a lucrative backdoor trade route to China's vast markets. This was compounded by its obsessive rivalry with Great Britain, then prospecting north into China from its newly conquered territories in Lower Burma. If de Lagrée's mission could establish a viable commercial trade route from Cochinchina to Yunnan, it would help check the British advance and lay the foundation for France's own rich empire in the east. The French Admiral Paul Reveillère later described the navigation of the Mekong as "a task worthy of raising the passions of our century, with its love for great undertakings."[3]

Within a few weeks of its departure from Saigon, however, the Mekong expedition ran into trouble. Instead of a placid broad Mississippi, the Frenchmen encountered a dizzying concatenation of spumes, rapids, and cataracts. On July 16, when the explorers' progress was halted at the frothing Sambor rapids in what is today northern Cambodia, Garnier reluctantly confided to his journal that his dream of establishing a trade route between Saigon and southern China had been "gravely compromised."[4] More impassable rapids in Laos, including the raging Khone falls just north of the Cambodian border, ended any realistic chance of opening the Mekong River to large-scale commerce.

Nonetheless, the mission pressed on through northern Laos and into China's Yunnan province, fighting chaotic swells and portaging along muddy mountain trails. De Lagrée soon fell gravely ill. On March 12, 1868, he succumbed to a badly afflicted liver and was buried in the Yunnanese town of Dongchuan.[5] Led now by Garnier, the expedition came to its end at Wuhan, two years to the day after its departure from Saigon. Exhausted and worn down by tropical disease, the remaining members of the Mekong Exploration Commission returned to France at the end of 1868.

Though it had failed at its principal aim, the president of London's Royal Geographical Society would later hail the Mekong Exploration Commission as "one of the most remarkable and successful expeditions of the nineteenth century."[6] In two years, de Lagrée and his men had traversed more than

3. The Mekong Region

9,000 kilometers of jungles, mountains, and rebellious borderlands, charting remote reaches of the Mekong and its tributaries. In so doing, they hastened the extension of French rule over the full extent of what Paris would later call "Indochina," an agglomeration of present-day Vietnam, Cambodia, and Laos. The French government would henceforth turn its imperial attentions to Tonkin (northern Vietnam), which it conquered in 1885, and, at a colossal cost in money and lives, linked to Yunnan by rail in 1910. The Mekong, however, remained untamed. Despite the French construction of a miniature rail line to circumvent the Khone falls in southern Laos, a British wartime naval handbook observed that it still took longer to travel from Saigon to Luang Prabang by river in 1937 than it did to travel by sea from Saigon to Marseille.[7]

A century and a half on, the French Mekong expedition is mostly forgotten, but the European colonial dream of linking China with the lands to its south has been taken up by a new generation of hard-hatted empire builders. Embarking on its own era of great undertakings, a resurgent China is spearheading the construction of a network of infrastructure links that has penetrated the isolated tracts of highland Southeast Asia once crisscrossed by European adventurers. New highways have supercharged ancient caravan routes and opium-smuggling trails, and Chinese engineers have opened the upper Mekong to large-scale commercial trade. Chinese state firms have even begun construction of a high-speed railway connecting the Chinese city of Kunming to the Lao capital Vientiane (see Chapter 4), an icon of Chinese engineering prowess that marks a step toward the fulfillment of another imperial dream: the linking of China to Singapore by rail.

These new physical connections are in many ways unprecedented. For centuries, the rugged mountains and deep forests of the Southeast Asian borderlands provided a natural barrier between the Chinese empire and the Indianized civilizations lying to its south. Indeed, until relatively recent times, this rambling upland region, which stretches from the eastern hill states of India to the reaches of northern Vietnam, lay beyond the effective control of any lowland state. While the chieftains and petty princes of the highlands often rendered tribute to lowland Southeast Asian courts or the Chinese emperor (or sometimes both simultaneously), they accepted the authority of neither. The upland peoples may have donned Shan, Burmese, or Chinese dress, or wielded titles bestowed by lowland kingdoms, but as the British anthropologist Edmund Leach observed of highland Burma in the 1950s, they "claimed to be lords in their own right, subject to no outside authority."[8] Later, James C. Scott would give this elevated region the name "Zomia," from *zomi*, a term for highlander common to several Tibeto-Burman languages spoken in the India–Bangladesh–Burma border area. Scott described Zomia as "the largest remaining region of the world whose peoples have not yet been fully incorporated into nation-states."[9]

Despite the region's resistance to central state control, China and mainland Southeast Asia have historically been bound by a rich and complex pattern of overland interactions. In precolonial times, the region was a realm of vassalage and a greensward of Chinese expansion. Many of its peoples originated in what is now Chinese territory, pressed south over the centuries by the pressure of the expanding Han Chinese into the fertile and sparsely populated valleys of the Mekong, the Irrawaddy, the Salween, and the Chao Phraya.

The new kingdoms that they established paid tribute to the Chinese empire, and traded with it via the Southern Silk Road: a network of mountain caravan trails running from the kingdoms of Yunnan and Tibet down into the northern hills of India and what are now Thailand, Laos, Vietnam, and Burma. Along these precipitous paths, Yunnanese muleteers lugged in copper pots, silks, rock salt, tinsel, and the gold leaf used to decorate Buddhist wats and other religious shrines; they returned with the exotic forest products like aromatic woods, ivory, and iridescent kingfisher feathers, much in demand at the imperial court.[10] Yet with the exception of Vietnam, which fate placed in smothering proximity to Chinese power, the forbidding terrain limited contact with the Chinese state; the amount of overland commerce was far eclipsed by the trade that took place by sea.

This ancient geographic barrier is now beginning to collapse. After a century and a half of weakness and internal discord, China has the financial resources to invest heavily in what John Garver has termed the "technological subjugation" of terrain.[11] These revolutionary transport networks have far surpassed the failed dream of the old French explorers, opening the thinly populated reaches of Upper Burma and Laos to unprecedented flows of Chinese capital, labor, migration, and tourism. This has precipitated a broad economic reorientation of the Mekong region away from its southern coasts and river deltas, traditionally its main outlet of trade and contact with the outside world, toward the colossal economy to the north. Buy a bottle of water or a pair of chopsticks in Lashio or Luang Namtha or Lang Son, and it is more likely to have come from China than anywhere else. Traveling through north-eastern Burma, where border enclaves glow with Chinese-powered prosperity, the historian Thant Myint-U marveled at the "stunning reversal" in the country's geography. "What had been remote is now closer to the new center," he wrote. "What were muddy mountain hamlets are now more modern than Rangoon."[12]

As the Mekong River approaches the small Chinese city of Jinghong, about halfway on its meandering 4,350-kilometer journey from the icy uplands of Tibet to the warm waters of the South China Sea, it widens into a broad course. As evening falls, tourists and residents gather at the water's edge to skim stones and pose for photos in front of the imposing suspension bridge that arches through the night sky. Pleasure boats ply the placid waters, their bright lights staining the glassy waters pink.

Spread along the Mekong in a pocket of rolling, mist-shrouded hills close to the border with Laos and Burma, Jinghong is the largest Chinese settlement on the upper Mekong, known in China as the Lancang. The city of 500,000 exudes a palpable thrum. Its boulevards, lined with colossal palm trees, are a jumble of shopping centers, fast-food outlets, and neon advertising. In a shaded quarter near the river, barbecue restaurants and beer stalls spill over into the lantern-strung streets. Nearby is a strip of small jade boutiques, many run by betel-chewing Rohingya Muslims from western Burma, and souvenir stores selling ethnic minority outfits and hard-packed discs of smoky *pu'er* tea. On each bank of the river, high-rise hotels and apartments press skyward, proclaiming the arrival of China's economic miracle on what was once a remote frontier.

When the French Mekong expedition passed through Jinghong in 1867, it was the central settlement of the Sipsong Panna (literally, "12 rice fields"), a loose confederation of statelets ruled by Tai-speaking chieftains, who pledged allegiance not just to China, but also to the royal courts of Burma and Siam. Most of the population were ethnic Tai, upland cousins of the Thai, Lao, and Shan peoples to the south; others belonged to a smattering of mountain-dwelling minority groups such as the Akha, Yi, and Lahu. While an Anglo-French compromise had left Jinghong under theoretical Qing control, the Han Chinese presence was sparse, and an American Protestant missionary who traveled through Jinghong in 1919 noted that "there are only the officials, the soldiers and a few merchants."[13] One impediment to colonization was the virulent strain of malaria that lurked in the hills, which the few hardy Han settlers tried to stave off by smoking opium. As one Chinese traveler drily observed in the 1930s, "The non-smokers are the exceptions."[14]

What was true of Jinghong was largely true of Yunnan as a whole. For most of its history, the region sat outside the Chinese imperial domain, the home of alien and often hostile peoples. Set on a high plateau fretted with great mountain ranges, Yunnan is hard to access from China's Yellow River heartland. In the northern part of the province, three of Asia's great rivers—the Mekong, Salween, and Yangzi—run in tremendous parallel valleys for hundreds of miles, separated by high mountain ranges, before diverging wildly and snaking out to the ocean. Sealed in by its terrain, Yunnan was populated by upland tribal peoples who discouraged exploration or settlement by outsiders. The independent states that arose on Yunnan's fertile plateaus—the kingdoms of Nanzhao (738–937) and Dali (937–1253)—were therefore much closer, in terms of culture and geography, to Indianized Southeast Asia than to the traditional locus of Chinese civilization.

Yunnan—literally, "south of the clouds"—was not decisively conquered until the Mongols swept through China in the mid-thirteenth century, toppling the Song dynasty and uniting China under the rule of the great Kublai Khan. When this short-lived dynasty collapsed in 1368, the successor Ming dynasty invaded Yunnan and grafted it permanently onto the empire, seeding the region with military garrisons and large populations of settlers. Instead of administering the new province directly, the Ming revived an old policy of "using barbarians to rule barbarians," ruling through local intermediaries, whom they gradually replaced with Han Chinese as the imperial administration rolled south. In some far-flung locales, this form of native rule, known as the *tusi* system, persisted well into the twentieth century.[15]

The Chinese conquest of Yunnan altered forever the relationship between China and mainland Southeast Asia. As Martin Stuart-Fox writes, the region's absorption projected Chinese culture and power far to the south and west, bringing it into direct contact with kingdoms and peoples with whom it had previously had little or no intercourse. As trade and other contacts increased, Burmese, Tai, and Lao principalities were drawn fitfully into China's tributary system, initiating a history of complex political relations that continues to the present day.[16]

While mainland Southeast Asian rulers dispatched regular gift-bearing tribute missions to the Chinese imperial court, Yunnan's rugged topography continued to keep the Chinese state at arm's length. Direct military intervention was rare, and Qing banner armies sent through the mountain passes to Burma and Vietnam in the eighteenth century fared poorly in the humid, malarial climate. As one of the last territorial additions to the Chinese empire, Yunnan was among the first to slip from central control when Qing power weakened in the mid-nineteenth century. In 1856, Yunnan's Muslim population rebelled and declared an independent sultanate, a revolt that was only put down with savage violence in 1873, sending waves of Yunnanese Muslims fleeing south into what are now Laos, Burma, and Thailand. Even after order was restored, Yunnan passed into the control of a succession of military governors and opium-smoking warlords, who ruled the region more or less autonomously until the communist victory of 1949.

In the context of the brewing Cold War, the new communist government moved to lock down what was now a strategic and sensitive frontier. At the end of the Chinese civil war, the last remnants of Chiang Kai-shek's defeated Nationalist Eighth Army had fled over the border into northern Burma. Here they regrouped and, with American and Taiwanese support, launched several failed incursions into Yunnan in 1951 and 1952. In response, Beijing reinforced its military presence, built up local industry, and opened the spigot of immigration. Between 1950 and 1958, nearly half a million Han Chinese moved or were transferred to Yunnan, many to work on state rubber plantations.[17] For the next few decades, the southwest frontier would become the conduit for a new Chinese export—revolution—in the form of aid, arms, and propaganda broadcasts that fortified communist insurgencies in Burma, Thailand, and Indochina.

By the 1980s, after Mao had died and China dropped its support of foreign revolutionaries in favor of trade and economic development, Yunnan assumed a new economic and strategic importance. As China's economy began to grow, planners grew concerned about the development gap that was opening up between the booming eastern seaboard and the provinces further west, which remained mired in poverty. What China lacked was a western ocean, which would give these landlocked regions much-needed access to the world's markets. Such an outward corridor would also help relieve China's heavy dependence on the Straits of Malacca. By utilizing Yunnan as a bridge to mainland Southeast Asia, they could achieve both of these aims: pump-priming China's underdeveloped western provinces, and creating an alternative overland route to the Indian Ocean.

As China's economy approached take-off in the 1990s, officials in Yunnan began lobbying Beijing for the revival and development of the province's historic connections with the lands to the south. They emphasized the region's non-Han ethnic identity, all the better to depict Yunnan as a natural partner of Southeast Asia. As one provincial official put it in 1993, quoting a Chinese saying, "Close neighbors are better than distant relatives."[18] Central support wasn't far behind. To open its poor southwest provinces, the government began upgrading the highways and rail networks connecting Yunnan to the rest of China, and onward to Burma, Laos, and Vietnam. On a visit to Yunnan in 2009, Hu Jintao declared that the province should work to become a "bridgehead for China's opening towards the southwest."[19]

Yunnan's newfound status was a throwback to the brief but important role it had played during World War II, when the Allies had used the famous Burma Road to supply Chiang Kai-shek's Chinese republican armies, then besieged in China's interior by the legions of imperial Japan. Slicing its way through more than a thousand kilometers of dense jungles and precipitous mountains, the Burma Road connected Lashio, a railhead in eastern Burma, to Kunming, the capital of Yunnan. Although the road was cut after the Japanese invasion of Burma in 1942, the strategic importance of this "back-door to China" prompted Owen Lattimore, the renowned American sinologist, to describe Yunnan as the future "pivot of Southeast Asia."[20] As the first modern transport link that China pushed beyond its national boundaries, the serpentine, single-lane motorway anticipated Xi Jinping's Belt and Road Initiative (BRI) by seven decades.

To realize its ambitions, China has piggy-backed on regional integration schemes, particularly the Asian Development Bank's (ADB's) Greater Mekong Subregion (GMS) program. Launched in 1992, with the five Mekong countries and Yunnan as initial members (Guangxi region joined a few years later), the GMS scheme aimed to construct a networks of roads, ports, railways, industrial zones, and power transmission grids that would help turn the region "from a battlefield into a marketplace" after decades of Cold War turmoil.[21] Spurred on by the introduction of market reforms in communist Vietnam and Laos, the Japanese-dominated ADB has since spent billions of dollars on the construction of two "economic corridors"—one running north–south, the other east–west—designed to lubricate the flow of trade, investment, and technology throughout the region.

Initially a backseat participant in the GMS, China was soon taking the financial lead on ADB projects, especially on infrastructure connections that deepened the integration of its southern provinces with mainland Southeast Asia. The Chinese government built bridges and river ports, and helped finance highways through Laos and Burma; it also funded the refurbishment of the old Burma Road. Beijing "used the ADB as a sort of neutral agency," said a logistics consultant who has worked extensively with the bank, "but it was really Chinese money." The combined effect of these various schemes has been dramatic: in 1991, it took six weeks for Yunnan's exports to reach Thailand by sea via the Chinese coast; with the completion of the Kunming–Bangkok Expressway in 2013, direct road travel time between the two cities had been cut to less than 24 hours. Primed by these new infrastructure links, Yunnan's trade with ASEAN rose from a few hundred million dollars per year in the 1990s to $13.2 billion in 2018.[22]

With a population of 47 million people and a $22 billion economy, Yunnan today functions as the forward operating base of China's renewed push to the south. In Kunming, a thriving metropolis of 6.6 million, old neighborhoods have been flattened as the city seeks to reinvent itself as the new economic mainspring of mainland Southeast Asia: a hub of belts, roads, railways, and oil pipelines fanning out to the Gulf of Thailand and the Andaman Sea. In 2016, city authorities unveiled the giant Kunming South railway station, where it could soon be possible to board a bullet train to Bangkok—and beyond.

Regional integration efforts have brought a jolt of energy to Jinghong, the capital of what is officially known as the Xishuangbanna Dai Autonomous Prefecture. Photos of the city from a 1981 publication show sleepy, palm-shaded streets lined with widely spaced buildings.[23] Since then, the population of Xishuangbanna—a Chinese gloss on its Tai name, Sipsong Panna—has swelled with an influx of Han migrants from other parts of China, including middle-class "smog refugees" from polluted metropolises like Beijing and Tianjin. Han Chinese make up more than a third of the population in Xishuangbanna today, with the remainder split roughly between the Tai and the smaller upland minority groups. Once an isolated frontier station, Jinghong now occupies a strategic position at the junction of two new highways running south to Thailand, via Laos and Burma. At the long-distance bus station in central Jinghong, buses leave every few hours for Vientiane and Bangkok, packed with tourists, migrant workers, and businesspeople.

As infrastructure has improved, and regions like Xishuangbanna have grown, China's economic miracle has started to spill southward, in the form of surplus Chinese capital and labor. Since the launch in 2001 of China's Going Out policy, which encouraged Chinese firms to invest in extending their operations abroad, private businesses and state-run enterprises—many from Yunnan and other southern provinces—have ventured out into the Mekong region, building roads, hotels, mines, agricultural plantations, and hydropower dams.

Like earlier flows of trade, the movement of Chinese capital has also been accompanied by a new mobile generation of laborers, entrepreneurs, traders, and illegal migrants who have headed south in the hope of making their fortunes on the new silk roads of Southeast Asia. These *xin yimin*, or "new migrants," are a global phenomenon: an overspill from China's great internal rural-to-urban migrations. But they are notably present in Southeast Asia, especially in the regions directly bordering China. The exact numbers of *xin yimin* are hard to determine. Zhuang Guotu of Xiamen University estimates that between 2.3 million and 2.7 million Chinese nationals emigrated to Southeast Asia in the two decades after 1990, many overland, but given the region's porous borders and the time that has elapsed since, the real figure is likely much higher.[24]

Today the furrowed highlands of Burma and Laos are dotted with new Chinese communities that look and feel like displaced extensions of urban China, down to the simplified Mandarin signage, concrete shop-houses, and dangling red plastic lanterns. Chinese expatriates and businesspeople are also an increasingly visible presence in the larger cities of the region, from Mandalay to Chiang Mai to Phnom Penh (though they are notably less visible in Vietnam).

While the *xin yimin* are just the latest generation of Chinese to make new homes in Southeast Asia, they differ from their predecessors in crucial ways. Previous generations of Chinese settlers were usually cast-offs from the southern fringes of the empire, and for long stretches of history were viewed by Chinese officialdom as renegade subjects, if not criminals. In contrast, today's migrants hail from every province in China, and have ventured abroad in an era of Chinese ascent, backed by a strong state's blessing. They view themselves not just as *huaren*—which is to say, ethnically or culturally Chinese—but as *zhongguo ren*, citizens of a united and newly powerful Chinese nation. The difference is symbolized by language. Where the old migrants spoke a rich stew of southern regional languages, including Cantonese, Teochew, Hakka, and Hokkien, the new migrants are united in their use of *putonghua*—the Mandarin Chinese of the new PRC imperium. Supported by their government, and aided by the improved communication links with their homeland, they have become key players in the economies—legal and otherwise—of the Mekong region.

The Chinese presence in upland Southeast Asia was predicted long ago by Chen Bisheng, a Chinese scholar who traveled through the southern border regions in the 1930s, and published his account in 1941 in a short book entitled *Miscellaneous Recollections of the Yunnan Frontier*. Looking forward to the day when southern Yunnan was again under firm central control, he predicted that the energetic and industrious Han Chinese would naturally seek greener pastures in the sparsely populated hills of Burma and Indochina. The overland movement of the Chinese into Southeast Asia, a continuation of China's historic push to the south, was "inevitable," Chen wrote, "no more possible to stem than the waters of a river."[25]

For the Mekong nations, this new phase of Chinese emigration has far-reaching implications. In his landmark 1972 study *The Southern Expansion of the Chinese People*, the British historian C.P. Fitzgerald pointed out that the Chinese empire's annexation of new southern territories was typically only the final step in a gradual movement of settlers, merchants, refugees, and exiles, "a pattern of seepage, of slow overspill from the great reservoir which was China."[26] Today, the presence of international borders rules out the formal conquests of the past, but it nonetheless remains hard to disentangle the outward flow of the Chinese people from the long-term strategic goals of the Chinese state. In the twenty-first century, a quickening movement of money and migration is helping to extend China's economic and political presence down the Mekong and out toward the sea.

Just before midday on October 5, 2011, a group of Thai soldiers boarded two Chinese barges that were seen floating listlessly in the Mekong River, a few miles upstream of the drowsy river town of Chiang Saen. The vessels were loaded with Chinese goods bound for the Thai market: the *Hua Ping* carried fuel oil; the *Yu Xing 8*, crates of apples and garlic. The soldiers found the former vessel deserted. The bridge of the latter was covered in blood, where, slumped over an AK-47 assault rifle, was a dead man later identified as Yang Deyi, the boat's Chinese captain. Stashed aboard the two vessels were clear plastic bags containing 920,000 methamphetamine pills, a haul with an estimated Thai street value of $6 million. In the following days, the corpses of the remaining 12 crewmembers were scooped from the milky-brown waters of the Mekong. The victims had been gagged with duct tape and blindfolded, with their hands bound or handcuffed behind their backs. Some had been stabbed. Others had gaping head wounds, suggesting that they had been shot at close range.[27]

The grisly murders had occurred just a few miles downstream from the center of the Golden Triangle, the rugged and impoverished region where the borders of Thailand, Laos, and Burma converge. For most of its history, this had been a zone of pristine lawlessness, a cauldron of bandits, drug smugglers, tribal chieftains, ethnic militias, and corrupt government functionaries where the writ of lowland states ran thin. Opium poppies were first cultivated in the region's hills on a large scale in the nineteenth century; by the 1960s, the region had become synonymous with narcotics production. Until the early 2000s, the Golden Triangle was the world's leading source of heroin. It still produces most of the methamphetamine consumed today in China and Southeast Asia.

The circumstances surrounding the murder of the Chinese sailors were foggy. Some witnesses claimed the murders had happened on the open water; others said the boats had docked before the shots were fired. The Thai authorities immediately arrested the nine soldiers who had boarded the boats, members of an elite anti-narcotics detachment known as the Pha Muang Taskforce. But it remained unclear if the Chinese sailors had been shipping the drugs themselves, or if the drugs had been planted afterward to deflect attention from the real culprits, whoever they were.

Back in China, the Mekong murders magnetized the public's attention. In the wake of "10/5," as the killings came to be known, gruesome photos of the sailors' corpses circulated online. Nationalistic internet users accused their government of failing to protect Chinese citizens abroad. In response, the authorities immediately suspended all Chinese traffic on the Mekong and summoned senior officials from the Golden Triangle nations to Beijing. There Chinese officials pressed them to participate in a new series of Chinese-led river patrols to ensure security along the middle Mekong. The governments of Thailand, Burma, and Laos also took the unprecedented step of allowing Chinese law enforcement to operate in their territory for as long as it took to bring the killers to justice.

As the investigation began, Thai authorities offered up a suspect: a notorious outlaw named Naw Kham, whom the media quickly dubbed the "freshwater pirate" of the Mekong. A stocky ethnic Shan born in 1969, Naw Kham had begun his criminal career working for a narco-militia run by Khun Sa, a flamboyant Shan-Chinese drug lord who established a powerful heroin empire in the Golden Triangle. As Alfred McCoy writes in his landmark book *The Politics of Heroin in Southeast Asia*, at the apex of his power in the late 1980s, Khun Sa controlled an army of 20,000 soldiers and half the globe's heroin supply: "a market share never equaled before or since."[28] In 1996, Khun Sa brokered a deal with Burma's military government: he agreed to surrender in exchange for amnesty and a quiet villa retirement in the capital Rangoon. At this point the young Naw Kham struck out on his own. Setting up his operation in Tachilek, a dusty smuggling hub on the Thai–Burma border, he started running heroin; later, he branched out into the production of methamphetamine, a cheap and highly addictive drug that the Thais called *yaba*, or "crazy medicine." .

After a raid in 2006, Naw Kham shifted his base to Sam Puu Island, a lozenge of land in the loosely policed stretch of the Mekong that forms the border between Burma and Laos. There he turned to piracy, imposing a "tax" on drug traffickers of about $160 for every kilogram of heroin and 10 cents for every methamphetamine pill.[29] His men prowled the riverbanks in sleek speedboats, swooping around the river's bends to snare unsuspecting vessels. Khuensai Jaiyen, a journalist who runs the Shan Herald Agency for News, a leading source of news from Burma's isolated Shan State, told me that Naw Kham got a cut of everything that moved through his territory: "He was making money out of the drug smugglers, he was giving protection."

To lead its manhunt, Beijing appointed Liu Yuejin, the director of the Narcotics Control Bureau, a subsidiary of China's powerful Ministry of Public Security. A hard-bitten anti-drug veteran, Liu followed his quarry with beady resolve. But the manhunt was far from straightforward. Naw Kham was known to enjoy protection from security forces throughout the Golden Triangle, and twice evaded capture after being tipped off by sympathetic locals. At one point Chinese officials even considered assassinating him with a drone.[30] Then, on April 25, 2012, Liu received a tip that Naw Kham planned to cross the Mekong into Laos. He passed word to his Lao counterparts, and when Naw Kham slipped ashore that night, the police were waiting.

The Thai village of Sop Ruak sits a few kilometers upstream from where the bodies of the Chinese sailors were pulled from the river, at the exact point where the borders of the three Golden Triangle nations converge. Here, the area's reputation for danger and opulence has been compressed into a harmless tourist display, a ribbon of 7-Elevens, opium museums, and souvenir encampments that unspools in a colorful line along the Mekong waterfront. Tourists, these days many of them from China, pose for photos in front of the tri-border confluence where the Mekong intersects with its tributary, the Ruak, looping down out of the Shan hills from the west. On a hill sits a quiet Buddhist pagoda and a couple of graves of Japanese soldiers, killed during World War II. Nearby, a large golden Buddha directs its serene gaze over to the Lao side of the river, where an enormous jewel-encrusted crown shimmers against a backdrop of hazy green hills.

The crown belongs to the Kings Romans Casino, the centerpiece of a Chinese-owned tourism and gambling enclave known as the Golden Triangle Special Economic Zone (GTSEZ). Over the past decade, Kings Romans Group—its Chinese name *jinmumian* means "golden kapok," after the trees that blanket the area with flame-red flowers—has spent hundreds of millions of dollars transforming this far-flung corner of Laos into a palm-fringed pleasure zone on the Mekong. The casino attracts hundreds of visitors each week from mainland China, where gambling is banned outside Macao. Most come down the new highways from Yunnan, or fly to northern Thailand and cross the Mekong on speedboats operated by Kings Romans.

The GTSEZ looks and feels like China: clocks display Beijing time, an hour ahead of Laos, and shops expect payment in Chinese yuan—even the street signage affects the municipal house-style of mainland China. The casino itself is a riot of rococo excess. A seated statue of Neptune presides in the entrance hall, raising his trident over gilded surfaces and marble floors. Inside, gamblers sit at green baize tables, cigarettes poised on moistened ashtrays, impatiently squaring stacks of Chinese and Thai bills. An ornate gate behind the casino announces a special "Chinatown" district of boutiques and restaurants, built in a kitschy transplanted style that can only be described as Forbidden City Lite. Nearby there is a depressing zoo filled with caged tigers and peacocks, and a golf driving range massed with black four-wheel drives.

The Kings Romans Casino and the enclave in which it sits are ruled by a fifty-something Chinese entrepreneur named Zhao Wei, originally from Heilongjiang in China's frigid northeast. Tall and gaunt, with drooping eyes and slicked-back hair—one local journalist who met the businessman told me to imagine "a Chinese Christopher Walken"—Zhao has spent most of his career haunting the murkier crannies of the Asian casino business. He first operated casinos in Macao, where he holds permanent residency, and then in Mong La, a notorious gambling enclave just over the Chinese border in the Burmese section of the Golden Triangle (see Chapter 6). In 2007, Zhao convinced the Lao government to let him export the casino model to their country, and it granted him a 99-year lease on 10,000 hectares of prime agricultural land along the Mekong. "The Lao government gives us the sky," he told an interviewer in a 2011 CCTV special titled *Zhao Wei: Kapok in My Heart.* "In return we will build a beautiful city as a gratitude to the Lao people." A few hundred Lao villagers were evicted, and Zhao's dreamland began to rise from the paddy fields.

While the GTSEZ remains under nominal Lao sovereignty—the government holds a 20 percent stake and former government officials sit on the zone's management committee—the area is reportedly free of direct government control.[31] Stuart Ling, a Lao-speaking Australian agricultural consultant based in the town of Huay Xai, about 50 kilometers downstream on the Lao side of the Mekong, described it as a "special zone" outside the jurisdiction of the local authorities. "Nobody collects statistics on it," he told me. "Even on paper it's not really part of Laos." Like Mong La to the north, which is controlled by a small rebel militia, the GTSEZ maintains its own security force, and Zhao wields such power over this outpost of Greater Yunnan that its Chinese residents refer to him as *tu huangdi*—"the local emperor."[32] "For me, he's a big guy," Shi Feng, a Chinese businessman who owns a restaurant near the casino, said over tea one afternoon in the Lao capital Vientiane. "In 2007 there was nothing there but mountains and forest. But now it's like a modern city."

Today, the Kings Romans Casino is the most garish signpost of China's rising presence on the Mekong. As part of its southward push from Yunnan, Beijing has spent the past two decades dredging sections of the river to deepen navigation channels, streamlining import and export procedures, and refurbishing port facilities. As a result, the river has grown into a burgeoning trade route, dominated by 200-ton Chinese barges like the *Hua Ping* and the *Yu Xing 8*, which ply the 265 kilometers between Guanlei, the main Mekong port in southern Yunnan, and Chiang Saen, where an expanded commercial port opened in 2011. Between 2004 and 2010, Mekong cargo volumes between Yunnan and Thailand tripled to more than 300,000 tons per year.[33] But the Chinese cargo boats passed through long stretches of the Mekong that were basically unpoliced, making them easy prey for freshwater pirates like Naw Kham. In 2008, unknown assailants attacked a Chinese patrol boat, injuring three Chinese police officers; the following year, a firefight on the Mekong between ethnic rebels and the Burmese army resulted in the death of a Chinese sailor.

Moreover, the illicit trades of the Golden Triangle were also rebounding back onto China itself. The same changes that had boosted legitimate trade since the late 1980s—the opening of borders and the improvement of overland transport links—also gave drug trafficking syndicates easy access to cheap Chinese-made precursor chemicals, and a gigantic new market for their product. By the mid-1990s, Golden Triangle narcotics had turned Kunming into the heroin capital of China, resulting in spiraling rates of drug addiction and HIV/AIDS. In 1996, more than 70 percent of China's reported HIV cases were from Yunnan.[34]

Narcotics were just the beginning. By the time of Naw Kham's arrest in Laos in April 2012, the new silk roads of the Golden Triangle were awash with weapons, stolen vehicles, exotic hardwoods, Burmese jade, and endangered animal products for use as aphrodisiacs and medicines—black markets primed by the rising demand of China's nouveaux riches. Sadly, this illicit traffic also included people: manual laborers, sex workers, and village women from Burma, Vietnam, and Laos, who were trafficked over the border by special brokers for marriage to men in rural China. As Ruth Banomyong, a logistics expert at Thammasat University in Bangkok, put it, "If you are a smuggler or you're doing something illicit, better roads are something fantastic." To Beijing's consternation, an increasing amount of this contraband was flowing directly into China.

With Naw Kham in custody, the Chinese authorities had the opportunity to make a strong statement. In November 2012, the Kunming Intermediate People's Court found the "freshwater pirate" and three accomplices guilty of the Mekong murders and sentenced them to death by lethal injection. Throughout the trial, the case was given front-page prominence in the state-run media. On the day of the executions, Naw Kham's final moments were captured in a two-hour television broadcast in which the cameras followed the four defendants on their forced march to the execution chamber, their faces blank with shock. The chilling live feed ran right up until the moment before doctors administered the fatal injections.

Interviewed during the coverage, Liu, the anti-drug czar, cast the executions as a pivotal moment for China and for ethnic Chinese around the world. "In the past, Overseas Chinese dared not say they were of Chinese origin," Liu told a presenter. "Now they can hold their heads high and be themselves."[35] This narrative was dramatized in a 2016 Hong Kong action movie, *Operation Mekong*, a feast of carnage and car-chases that ends with the villain—Naw Kham, played with sinister relish by the Thai actor Pawarith Monkolpisit— safely in the hands of the Chinese Ministry of Public Security. (Liu served as a special consultant on the production.) Beijing had used the case to send a message to its southern neighbors: it would go to great lengths to protect its economic interests on the Mekong.

However, the court's verdict failed to bring much clarity to the case. Chinese prosecutors never established a solid motive to explain why Naw Kham would have committed the murders. Moreover, speakers of Shan, a close cousin of the Thai language, reported that his "confession," aired on Chinese television, resulted from a mistranslation. Kheunsai Jaiyen said, "It was a kangaroo court. He was saying one thing, and they were translating another." Questions were also raised in Thailand, where an extensive police investigation had followed the arrest of the nine Thai soldiers. It concluded that the shots fired at the Chinese crewmembers came not from outlaws or drug gangs, but from weapons used by the Thai military. A Thai parliamentary committee later concurred, concluding that "circumstantial evidence suggests that Thai officials were involved in the sailors' deaths."[36] It was easy to see how Naw Kham's capture and execution was convenient for the Thai military: by pointing the finger at Naw Kham, it had successfully deflected attention away from the possible involvement of its own personnel.

In a detailed investigation into the Mekong killings published in 2013, the American journalist Jeff Howe identified another potential culprit: Zhao Wei, the chairman of Kings Romans Group. Unlike the harmless theme-park displays over the river in Sop Ruak, the casino was widely suspected of involvement in the region's illicit commerce. Campaigners working for the London-based Environmental Investigation Agency claimed that boutiques behind the casino sold illegal wildlife products, including ivory and tiger meat, allegedly smuggled in from Mong La on Chinese cargo boats.[37] During my visit to the zone in 2016, I picked up a casino brochure that featured the ghastly spectacle of *hugujiu*—a tiger skeleton floating in a tank of rice wine—and a shooting range where visitors could fire M16 assault rifles and Uzi submachine guns. Later, the US government imposed sanctions on Zhao Wei and three associates, accusing Kings Romans of involvement in "drug trafficking, human trafficking, money laundering, bribery, and wildlife trafficking."[38]

Howe concluded that Zhao's entry into the region's vice trade had entangled him in a turf war with Naw Kham, a struggle that continued right up until the killings in October 2011. It remained unclear whether Zhao was directly responsible for the sailors' murders, but the timing of events raised enough questions for Howe to conclude that Naw Kham's importance had been greatly exaggerated. He had become "a convenient legend," Howe wrote, "and, in the end, a scapegoat who allowed the real business of the Mekong to continue running smoothly."[39]

Whatever the truth of the matter, Naw Kham's capture and trial was a powerful expression of China's intensifying clout in mainland Southeast Asia. The expansion of its Mekong patrols, ostensibly conducted in concert with the governments of Burma, Thailand, and Laos, marked a major expansion of its role in regional security. Paul Chambers, a Thailand-based expert on the Golden Triangle economy, compared the hunt for Naw Kham to US General John J. Pershing's expedition to capture Pancho Villa, the gun-slinging Mexican revolutionary leader accused of killing 18 Americans in New Mexico in 1916. For the US government, then on the cusp of global power, the hunt for Pancho Villa represented more than the pursuit of a wanted criminal: it also symbolized a fledgling superpower's ability to assert control over its immediate neighborhood.[40] For Khuensai Jaiyen, Naw Kham's capture demonstrated how China has altered the power dynamics in the Golden Triangle. "He was paying the Burmese army, paying the Lao army, paying the Thais.

That's how he survived, and that's how he believed he would survive," he said of Naw Kham. "But in the end, no one could resist the Chinese."

Even as China's economic and political influence flows down the Mekong River into Southeast Asia, the most consequential long-term developments may be those taking place upstream. In the first half of 2016, the lower Mekong countries were hit by one of the worst droughts in living memory. In central Thailand, reservoirs dropped to unprecedented levels, forcing authorities to pump 49 million cubic meters of water out of the Mekong to relieve farmers living along its tributaries.[41] Downstream in Cambodia, farmers lost entire rice and cassava crops due to delayed monsoon rains. Further on, in the marshy flatlands of southern Vietnam, where the river splits into nine deltaic arms before merging with the South China Sea, the river sat at its lowest level since 1926.[42] Environmentalists put the drought down to a severe El Niño weather pattern, and the creeping effects of global climate change. But a crucial compounding factor was the years of man-made alterations to the river—particularly upstream in China.

As China's ambitions have grown in the Mekong region, it has shaped the Mekong to serve the needs of the Chinese economy. It has dynamited sections of the waterway to open it up to trade, and built a slew of large hydropower dams on the upper reaches of the Mekong, to power the industrialization of southwest China. Eleven mega-dams have been completed so far, with several more slated for construction by 2030. Because of conflict and the mountainous terrain along its upper reaches, development came late to the Mekong; it wasn't until 1994 that the first bridge spanned the Southeast Asian stretch of the river. But China's current ambitions for the Mekong, in tandem with a host of planned dams in Laos, Thailand, and Cambodia, amount to one of the largest artificial alterations to a river's course in human history—one that environmentalists fear could profoundly alter the river's ecology.

For centuries, the people of the lower Mekong have had a symbiotic relationship with the river and its resources. What begins as a freshet of snowmelt on the Tibetan plateau cascades into a mighty waterway that nourishes the world's largest inland fishery. Between the border of Yunnan and the Mekong Delta in southern Vietnam, some 66 million people depend on the river for their day-to-day subsistence. According to the Mekong River

Commission, the river yields around 2.6 million tons of wild fish each year. In Cambodia, this provides around four-fifths of the population with their main source of protein. The Mekong basin is also Asia's rice bowl: in 2014, Burma, Laos, Cambodia, Thailand, and Vietnam collectively produced more than 100 million tons of rice, around 15 percent of the world's total.[43]

Environmentalists worry that if current development plans go ahead, this life-giving channel will effectively be divided into a series of lakes and canals optimized for power generation and shipping, but otherwise ruinous for the fishermen and farmers that rely on the Mekong for their livelihoods. According to the non-governmental organization International Rivers, Beijing's dam-building spree, conducted without consultations with downstream nations, "threatens the natural flow cycle of the Lancang–Mekong ecosystem and downstream communities that depend on the vital sources of this mighty river."[44]

The potential danger has long been evident in the fertile flatlands of southern Vietnam, where the Mekong meets the sea. Here the great river is known as *cuu long*—the "nine dragons"—a reference to the snaking channels that enclose one of Southeast Asia's most fertile rice-producing regions. Centuries of human cultivation have threaded the delta region with a meshwork of canals and marshes, studded here and there with the eaves of Khmer Theravada temples and the rainbow hallucinations of the Cao Dai, a syncretic religious sect native to southern Vietnam that reveres Victor Hugo and Sun Yat-sen as saints. This rural cornucopia, roughly the size of Denmark, provides most of Vietnam's fish and fruit, as well as half its rice—all from just 12 percent of its land area.[45]

The 2016 drought had devastating effects in the Mekong Delta. In Soc Trang province, one observer wrote, the usually green landscape was reduced to "a desert of dry fields. Some were tilled in preparation for a season that had yet to come and others laid unprepared covered with dried, leftover stalks of previous harvests. Far off on the horizon, a fence row of hardy palm trees formed the only living vegetation in sight."[46] The drought forced thousands of Vietnamese farmers off the land, and into fast-growing centers like Cantho and Ho Chi Minh City.

The delta's problems have many interacting causes. These include over-cultivation, excess groundwater extraction, and encroaching salinity due to climate change. But according to Nguyen Minh Quang, a lecturer at Can Tho University, China's upstream dams are acting as a potent multiplier, compounding and magnifying these various environmental problems. Quang said the Chinese dams played an ominous, and avoidable, role in reducing the "beautiful floods" that replenish the delta's nutrient-rich sediment, which enriches farmers' crops while helping to stave off coastal erosion. "If the dam-building continues," he said, "the Mekong Delta will disappear in the near future." This is no exaggeration: at current rates, one recent study predicted, the entire delta will be under water by the year 2100.[47]

The environmental challenges facing the Mekong Delta demonstrate how China's control of the river's headwaters has magnified its power over the countries downstream. The geography of the Mekong River reflects the region's geopolitical hierarchy: a powerful China at the top and smaller, less developed nations below. The Chinese stretch of the river is narrow, deep, and thinly populated, unsuitable for fishing and farming but, unlike the wide stretches further south, ideally suited to dam-building. This has allowed China to reap the benefits of hydropower generation, while exporting most of the environmental costs downstream. Brian Eyler, an expert on transboundary issues at the Stimson Center in Washington, DC, and author of *The Last Days of the Mighty Mekong*, explained to me that the flow of water beneath China's Lancang dam cascade resembled "an erratic stock chart with random peaks and nadirs," indicating unpredictable rises and falls in the dry season water level. This has had serious impacts on agriculture, fish catches, and the riverside habitats of migratory birds.

All this gives Beijing considerable control over the southward flow of the Mekong. While China does not quite have the ability to "turn off the tap" to downstream countries, as some of its critics have suggested, Eyler pointed out that during the dry season about 40 percent of all the water in the Mekong basin comes from north of the Chinese border. "This means China has control over a large amount of dry season flow and could use it for its own purposes first before considering the usage needs of downstream countries," he said. Eyler predicted that the most likely future purpose would be the diversion of water resources to relieve China's chronic water shortages, especially if climate change begins to undermine the Himalayan glaciers that feed most of Asia's major rivers.

In March 2016, at the height of the drought, the Chinese government announced a "gift" for its parched downstream neighbors: a release of emergency water reserves from the Jinghong dam, the southernmost of the upper

Mekong cascade. At first glance this gift looked much like Chinese state media depicted it, as a gesture of friendship to its downstream neighbors. But it was a gift that came wrapped in a subtle reminder to the governments of Vietnam, Laos, Thailand, and Cambodia: that they now relied on the Chinese government for access to a life-giving resource.

This new reality was sketched with alarming clarity in research published by two American climate scientists in April 2020. Alan Basist and Claude Williams conducted their research during another record spell of drought in the lower Mekong region: one so severe that stretches of the river along the border with Laos and Thailand dried up entirely, leaving riverbeds cracked and exposed to the sun.[48] In previous years, the scientists observed, there was a rough correlation between water flows on the upper Mekong and water levels downstream, despite occasional dips and rises when dam reservoirs in China were being filled or released. In 2019, however, things changed dramatically. Between May and September of that year, Basist and Williams noticed that China's section of the Mekong welcomed an above-average volume of rainfall and snowmelt, but that its Lancang dam cascade prevented nearly all of this surplus water from flowing southward.[49] In other words, Chinese dam engineers were directly responsible for exacerbating the drought conditions downstream.

China's valve-like control of the upper Mekong has made downstream nations reluctant to criticize Chinese dam-building plans, all the more since some—notably Laos and Cambodia—have hydropower ambitions of their own, for which they rely on Chinese funding and support.[50] As the region's most robust opponent of China, as well as the nation with the most to lose and least to gain from Mekong hydropower, Vietnam has been the most outspoken about China's dam construction. Nguyen Truong Giang, a former Vietnamese ambassador to Brunei who now works for the Center for Strategic Studies and International Development in Hanoi, was blunt when I asked him about the issue: "China is using the Mekong as a weapon to control the countries in the lower Mekong River basin."

At the same time, China is seeking a more active role in regional institutions governing the use of the river's resources. In 2014, it inaugurated the Lancang–Mekong Cooperation (LMC) mechanism, which counts China, Burma, Thailand, Vietnam, Cambodia, and Laos as members. Coming after years of mounting criticism for its Mekong dam projects, the formation of the

LMC was a sign that China intends to become more proactive in promoting regional cooperation in the lower Mekong. As the first Chinese-built Southeast Asian institution, the LMC is also broadly consistent with Beijing's aim of creating new global and regional institutions in which it exercises clout commensurate with its increasing wealth and power.

It is hard not to view the LMC as a competitor to the existing US-supported regional institutional architecture: the mostly toothless Mekong River Commission (MRC), founded in 1995; and the Lower Mekong Initiative, established by the Obama administration in 2009 as part of its "rebalance" to Asia. Given the importance of the region, this Chinese undertaking is no surprise. The first Mekong Committee, set up in 1954 as a weapon in the struggle against communism, deliberately excluded China; nor did China become a member of the MRC, its successor organization, in large part because it had no wish to accept scrutiny of its own dam-building activities.

Moreover, the Chinese-led LMC mechanism is about much more than just water management. It is shaping up as a full-blown sub-pillar of the BRI, characterized by funding for infrastructure developments and economic zones that will further enmesh the two regions. In January 2018, Chinese Premier Li Keqiang likened the LMC initiative to the engine of a bullet train, pushing the integration and cooperation between China and the five Mekong countries into "the age of high-speed rail." China's Foreign Minister Wang Yi has used the metaphor of a "bulldozer."[51]

At first glance, things look impressive. At the inaugural LMC summit in 2016, China promised $1.6 billion in preferential loans and $10 billion in credit to the five Mekong countries. The next summit came with more eye-popping announcements. In total, China claims to have made financial commitments for 132 separate infrastructure projects. How many will see the light of day is unclear, given China's penchant for "sign-first-talk-later" diplomacy.[52] Nevertheless, Beijing's commitment to the LMC signifies the importance it places on consolidating the Mekong region as a Chinese sphere of influence: stable, prosperous, and tightly aligned with China's wider strategic interests.

To counter China's influence in the Mekong region, the US, India, and South Korea have all established or enhanced competing Mekong initiatives. The most active has been Japan. Anxious about China's growing clout in mainland Southeast Asia, a region that has seen vast injections of Japanese capital since the 1970s, the government of Prime Minister Shinzo Abe has poured billions of yen into the region. Japan first reached out to the Mekong countries in 2007 through the Japan–Mekong Regional Partnership Program; two years later, it convened the first Mekong–Japan Summit. Where Western nations have balked at engagement in the face of the region's sorry human rights situation, Abe's government has pragmatically bankrolled highways, bridges, and other large-scale infrastructure developments under the slogan "Partnership for Quality Infrastructure"—a sly dig at the poor reputation of Chinese-backed projects in the region.

The lower Mekong countries have much to gain from what one observer has described as the "infrastructure arms race" between Beijing and Tokyo.[53] Having spent much of the twentieth century consumed by conflict, Cambodia, Laos, Vietnam, and Burma lag far behind the most developed states in ASEAN. In 2017, their combined GDP made up just 11.7 percent of the bloc's total, and they desperately need investment and infrastructure financing to stoke up their economies. As one Cambodian government advisor put it to me, "It's good for us to have these two giants competing for subregional attention. Our region has become a beautiful lady again."

Nowhere is this competition more apparent than in the Cambodian capital Phnom Penh, where a new Chinese bridge has been built over the Tonlé Sap River. The New Chroy Changvar Bridge, completed in 2015 with a concessional loan from China, runs directly alongside the "old" Chroy Changvar Bridge—also known as the Cambodia–Japan Friendship Bridge—which was built with Japanese assistance in 1966, blown up during the Cambodian Civil War in the early 1970s, and then rebuilt with Japanese donations in 1994. Of the five bridges crossing the Mekong River in Cambodia, three were funded by China (including one currently under construction), and two by Japan. A similar pattern can be seen next door in Vietnam, where a Chinese-funded metro project in the capital Hanoi competes with a Japanese-funded metro in Ho Chi Minh City.

A strategic tug-of-war of sorts is even taking place within the ADB itself. Ruth Banomyong of Thammasat University said that since the 1990s, the Japanese have "totally cooled off" on the GMS's North–South Economic Corridor (NSEC), which links China with the Mekong region. Instead, they have focused their efforts on the East–West Economic Corridor linking Vietnam to Burma. "They see [the NSEC] as a way of China coming down, and that they need to build their own Wall of China," he said. As far back as 2007, Bronson Percival noted the irony in the fact that "Japan and the ADB, in which Japan has great influence, are paying the bulk of the costs for a massive development scheme that primarily benefits China."[54]

As economic integration and infrastructure development supercharge old smuggling routes and caravan trails, mainland Southeast Asia is being drawn closer to China than at any point in history. For the region and its peoples, this is a development that cuts both ways. Chinese trade and capital have done much to buoy the Mekong economies, turning once-quiet border regions into restless conduits of trade. China's economic vibrancy has given many Mekong citizens new educational opportunities and avenues for advancement. At the same time, the flow of Chinese state financing and investment has tended to amplify the governance problems that already plague much of the region. Chinese BRI infrastructure projects, legally bound to respect local laws that are either inadequate or weakly enforced, often proceed without proper social and environmental safeguards, nor much in the way of competitive open bidding processes.

To these effects must be added the unintended consequences of economic integration, leveraged up by the massive scale of China's economy. Given its size, even a proportionally small Chinese demand for products like rosewood, jade, or endangered animal products can translate into devastating impacts in the smaller countries to its south, an asymmetry vividly captured by an oft-quoted Burmese aphorism: "When China spits, Burma swims."[55] Despite the common image of China as a ruthlessly centralizing power, the Chinese state still has considerable difficulty in securing its winding, mountainous borders with Burma, Laos, and Vietnam, or controlling the people and goods that flow across them. This Zomian echo is a reminder of the sheer multitude of Chinese influences now flowing over its land borders with Southeast Asia, and the fact that much of the Chinese engagement with the region takes place outside the effective control of the Chinese state.

While all Southeast Asian nations face the challenge of living in China's shadow, it is in the mainland countries that the dilemma is most acute. More exposed to cultural and political influence from China than the comparatively distant maritime nations of the Malay archipelago, and more closely enmeshed with China's booming economy, it is here that China's rise has elicited the deepest fears and the most strident reactions. Conversely, it is also where Asia's new superpower has found its fastest friends and allies.

3
VIETNAM
DIFFERENT SHADES OF RED

Shortly before dawn on February 17, 1979, as the morning mist clung to the hills and jagged karst formations of the Sino-Vietnamese border, more than 200,000 soldiers of the Chinese People's Liberation Army swept into northern Vietnam. Asleep in her home in the countryside outside the city of Cao Bang, Nong Thi Linh first thought the distant artillery was drumming rain. "Then at 6 a.m., I heard people shouting, 'the Chinese are coming!'" she said. Linh joined a chaotic flood of soldiers and citizens evacuating southward. When she returned six weeks later, she beheld a devastated scene. "In Cao Bang, the town was heavily affected," she recalled, "and the Chinese threw people's corpses into wells."

Intended to teach Vietnam a "lesson" for its January 1979 overthrow of the Khmer Rouge regime in Cambodia, a close ally of Beijing, China's invasion of northern Vietnam immediately gave way to a bitter month-long struggle. Chinese soldiers were instructed to be merciless and worked themselves into a frenzy of "extreme emotions," according to military historian Edward O'Dowd. They were told to look upon the enemy "with the 'three looks': contempt, disdain, and hostility."[1] The invasion was met with ferocious resistance from the Vietnamese army, occupying mountain redoubts that had been utilized for centuries against invaders from the north. Their "lesson" duly administered, the Chinese troops withdrew on March 16, leaving large parts of the border in ruins. This forgotten sequel to the Vietnam War claimed the lives of tens of thousands of troops on both sides, along with unknown numbers of civilians.[2]

In Vietnam, most of the fallen soldiers came to rest in military cemeteries dotted throughout the northern mountains. In late 2018, a few months before the 40th anniversary of the conflict, I visited one such graveyard 20 kilometers south of the town of Lang Son, perched on a hillside at the top of a granite stairway. The graves were laid around a white monument topped with a five-sided star that pointed to a bright blue meridian. Each bore the inscription *liet si* ("martyr") above the name of the fallen, and a vase of fluorescent plastic lotus flowers. Many dated from February and March 1979. "The Vietnamese people honor those who have sacrificed for the country," said Chu Son, a gravel-voiced 51-year-old who manages the cemetery from a small office at the foot of the hill.

Memories of the border war remain especially vivid around Lang Son, where some of the heaviest fighting took place. Before the Chinese withdrew, they brought in military engineers to level the city, in what one Chinese official later described as a "goodbye kiss."[3] Tran Van Su, a retired railway engineer in his eighties who was evacuated during the war and returned to Lang Son a month after the Chinese withdrawal, recalled a city of empty streets, where buildings had been blown up or flattened by artillery. Dead bodies lay here and there. "Overall it looked like a ghost town," he said.

Lang Son has since been rebuilt into a pleasant town of tree-lined avenues and convivial roadside eateries. Shops and markets overflow with Chinese goods shipped through the incongruously named Friendship Pass border gate 12 kilometers to the north. Decorations are strung across the major roads: illuminated peonies, swooping doves, symbols of peace. One morning in September 2018, I went to visit Nong Van Phiao, a decorated veteran of the 1979 war, at his narrow two-story home in a leafy quarter of Lang Son. Phiao is an unusual name in Vietnam, a mark of the 60-year-old's origins as an ethnic Nung, a Tai-speaking people scattered across northern Vietnam and southern China. After exchanging our initial pleasantries, Phiao told me that his friends jokingly call him Michael Phelps, after the American swimmer. "His name sounds similar in Vietnamese," Phiao joked. He offered me a seat in front of a polished wood table. Next to us, a flat-screen TV and stereo system were set in a wooden case with mother-of-pearl inlay. Military portraits hung high on the wall.

Phiao retired from the military in 2016, after four decades of service. A stocky figure with a neat bowl-cut and pronounced limp—the result of a recent stroke—he signed up at the age of 18, shortly after the fall of Saigon to the communists in April 1975. After six months' basic training, he was posted to the border town of Dong Dang, just as Vietnam's relationship with its communist ally China was beginning to deteriorate. When the invasion came, his unit was holed up in a crumbling French fort, built on a hillside in Dong Dang to guard against Chinese incursions in the late nineteenth century. Phiao recalled fighting so fierce that the barrel of his AK-47 glowed red. "It was very brutal. The noise was unbearable, and there was smoke all around us," he said. His unit managed to hold off the invaders for a full week before, their supplies dwindling, the surviving men dug their way through a collapsed tunnel and escaped back to the Vietnamese lines.

After spending an hour or so recounting this tale, Phiao went upstairs and returned with a plastic bag filled with medals, which he emptied on the glass table-top. From the pile he picked out a simple gold star stamped with a Vietnamese flag, its red faded to gold: the Hero of the People's Armed Forces, one of Vietnam's highest military honors. In total, Phiao estimates that he killed thirty Chinese soldiers.

When China invaded, the Vietnamese state media declared that February 17, 1979 would "go down in history as a severe verdict of the 'Great Han' expansionists' crimes in trying to subdue and annex Vietnam."[4] Four decades on, however, Vietnam's government rarely talks publicly about the war. After Hanoi and Beijing normalized relations in 1991, ties between the two communist parties improved, the border was flung open to trade, and mentions of the 1979 conflict became politically taboo. In contrast to the copious memorials to Vietnam's wars against the French and the Americans—two victorious conflicts in which China was a vital partner—the question of how to remember Vietnam's most recent war is an awkward one for the Vietnamese Communist Party (VCP). As it works to maintain good relations with China, many ordinary Vietnamese hear echoes of 1979 in Beijing's current actions, including its assertive push into the South China Sea. "China used to be an enemy, and now they are considered a friend," Phiao said, echoing many ordinary Vietnamese I spoke to, "but this is not the kind of friend we can trust. We always have to be careful and wary of their intentions. China is a two-faced friend. Anytime Vietnam is not alert, China will strangle Vietnam."

It is impossible to detach Vietnam's long history from that of its northern neighbor. As one popular joke puts it, the country's S-shaped bend resembles an old woman straining under China's weight. Because of this "tyranny of geography," as Carlyle Thayer has termed it,[5] no other nation in Southeast Asia has been so exposed to China's expansionary tendencies, nor bears so strongly the stamp of Chinese civilization. For nearly a millennium until 938,

China ruled northern Vietnam as an imperial appendage, subjecting its people to a slow process of social, political, and cultural assimilation. Ever since, Vietnamese kings have fought off repeated invasions from the various states occupying the present territory of China.

This national memory is inscribed in the towns and cities of Vietnam, whose streets bear the names of the semi-mythical national heroes who battled against the Chinese. They include Hai Ba Trung, the two Trung sisters, who resisted Chinese rule in the first century and are often depicted riding into battle atop elephants; Le Loi, who fought off a short occupation by the Ming dynasty in the 1400s; and Nguyen Hue, who trounced an invading Qing army in 1789. At the Vietnam Military History Museum in Hanoi, a repository of the official narrative, a display lists 13 "Vietnamese Resistance Wars Against Invaders." Until the twentieth-century wars against the French and Americans, all came from the north. "Throughout thousands of years of history," a caption explains, "Vietnamese people have fought bravely, resiliently and continuously to conquer the harsh nature and against the invasion of foreign forces for survival and development."

However, the official story downplays the many ways in which China's proximity has benefited Vietnam. As the historian Keith Taylor has written, China's contributions to Vietnam cover "all aspects of culture, society, and government, from chopsticks wielded by peasants to writing brushes wielded by scholars and officials."[6] Over the centuries, the Vietnamese language absorbed huge quantities of Chinese vocabulary. Vietnam's monarchs took on the trappings of the Chinese emperors to whom they paid tribute, and Confucian morality shaped Vietnamese society. The ruling elite modeled itself as a meritocracy in the Chinese mold, its members selected via a rigorous drilling in the Confucian classics. At the Temple of Literature in Hanoi, built by King Ly Thanh Tong in 1070 to honor Confucius, visitors can still see weighty stone steles inscribed, in Chinese characters, with the names of those who scored most highly in the examinations. Indeed, Vietnam retained the Mandarin examinations even after they were abolished in China itself.

At the same time, Vietnam was no mere copy; Chinese tools were almost always turned to distinctly Vietnamese ends. Pham Xuan Nguyen, the chairman of the Vietnam Institute of Literature in Hanoi, explained that the adoption of Chinese cultural artefacts proceeded in parallel with a process that the Vietnamese call *thoat Trung*—"exiting" or "departing" from China's orbit.

"There have been two movements," he said one afternoon over tea in a book-lined room at the institute. "One is that we have copied from them; the other is that we have tried to depart from them."

This pinpoints the cardinal irony of Vietnamese history: namely, that political structures borrowed from China gave Vietnamese kingdoms the strength and cohesion to avoid reabsorption by the Chinese empire. Chinese bureaucratic practice, military technology, social and familial norms, imperial ideologies: all were taken and bent toward the goal of securing Vietnam's continued existence as an independent state.

These inheritances also gave the Vietnamese the means to launch their own southward expansion from the seventeenth century. Despite civil war and internal division, Vietnamese culture and political power moved steadily south, defeating the Indianized kingdom of Champa and displacing the Khmers from the Mekong Delta. By the time that the Nguyen dynasty unified Vietnam in 1802, its power extended all the way to the Gulf of Siam. Vietnam's southern march, or *nam tien*, not only recreated in miniature China's imperial march toward the tropics; it also reproduced the hierarchies of the Chinese tributary system, in which the Vietnamese imperial court was seen to represent the apex of a civilizational gradient that receded as it ran out toward the barbarian margins. Just as the Chinese viewed the Vietnamese as uppity "barbarians" in need of a firm civilizing hand, Christopher Goscha writes, the Vietnamese applied the same assumptions to neighboring people like the Khmer and Lao, "forgetting conveniently that they themselves had sprung from this barbarian world."[7]

The fact that Vietnam's absorption of the south owed much to the efforts of Chinese immigrants added a further layer of irony. After the collapse of the Ming dynasty in the mid-seventeenth century, a wave of Ming loyalists and refugees washed up in southern Vietnam. These *minh huong*—"keepers of the Ming incense"—settled in the region and helped the Vietnamese state extend its control over the unruly Mekong Delta frontier. By 1700, a Cantonese adventurer named Mac Cuu had founded an autonomous Ming-style port-state at Ha Tien, close to the present-day Cambodian border, which he and his descendants ruled for more than a century, loosening further the Cambodian hold over the area. The graves of these local "kings" sit today in a leafy compound in the placid coastal town, their tombs elaborately decorated with lions, dragons, and phoenixes—testaments to their former wealth and prominence.[8]

By moving south, the Vietnamese could emerge—at least temporarily—from life in China's shadow. Facing north, they "needed fixed concentration, steady nerves, and unfathomable resolve," Taylor writes. "However, when they turned south, it was possible to relax somewhat and indulge the senses."[9] Today, southern Vietnam presents the more capitalistic and outward-facing side of the Vietnamese national character. The south is the dynamo of the Vietnamese economy. In some intangible sense, it also looks and feels distinctly more "Southeast Asian," from styles of food and dress to the spoken language, which preserves more pre-Sinitic usages than the northern dialect.

The unification of Vietnam by the Nguyens in 1802 had momentous historical effects, effectively halting China's expansion down the coast of the South China Sea into today's Southeast Asia. Yet the country's fate remained yoked to that of its northern neighbor. Despite repelling repeated Chinese invasions, the threat from the north remained. The only choice was to find some way of coexisting with China. Accordingly, each Vietnamese victory of arms was followed by a pilgrimage to the imperial court to pay tribute and ritually reaffirm Vietnam's re-entry into the Chinese world order. By making these symbolic gestures, Vietnamese rulers managed to buy themselves long periods of peace and security.[10]

The legacies of geographic proximity and massive asymmetries of power continue to condition Sino-Vietnamese relations in the current age of renascent Chinese power. For China, Vietnam remains "the southern boundary stone of its grand notions of itself," in historian Brantly Womack's evocative phrase, a civilizational offspring that is expected to make regular gestures of gratitude toward its benevolent parent.[11] For Vietnam, China remains a subject of perennial concern, its size and power making Vietnamese leaders eager for peace, yet ever alert to any hint of impingement on their sovereignty and independence.

On May 2, 2014, China deployed a deep-water oil rig in contested waters 222 kilometers off the coast of central Vietnam. The installment of the colossal *Haiyang Shiyou 981*, owned by the state-owned China National Offshore Oil Corporation, made little economic sense, given the small size of the known oil reserves in the area. Its placement was rather an act of brinkmanship, designed to assert China's claims to the majority of the South China Sea. Predictably, Vietnam's government protested the placement of the rig, which fell within its 200-mile Exclusive Economic Zone, and dispatched both a coastguard force and a Maritime Surveillance Force to disrupt its operations. In the ensuing fracas, a Chinese flotilla rammed at least one Vietnamese ship and fired high-powered water cannons at several others, in a bid to cripple their communications capabilities. The belligerent Chinese state mouthpiece *Global Times* suggested that if Vietnam continued to challenge Chinese claims, China should give it a "lesson it deserves."[12] To many Vietnamese, the echo of Deng Xiaoping's "lesson"—the invasion of 1979—was unmistakable.

The oil rig's placement set off a rare surge of public unrest in Vietnam. Protesters converged in urban centers across the country, waving Vietnam's national flag, a yellow star emblazoned on red. Some wore T-shirts reading "No-U," in reference to China's U-shaped claims in the South China Sea; others bore the slogan "Say No to the Ox-Tongue Line." The demonstrations quickly spiraled into violent attacks on Chinese-owned businesses and factories in Vietnam. On the industrial outskirts of Ho Chi Minh City, workers on motorbikes smashed windows and lobbed gasoline-soaked rags into factory buildings. Ironically, most of the damage was borne by Taiwanese firms, which the rioters mistook for mainland Chinese. By mid-May, according to one estimate, the riots had killed 21 people. Hundreds were arrested.[13] On July 15, China announced that the *Haiyang Shiyou 981* had completed its work and withdrew it—a month earlier than it had previously stated.

As in the past, Vietnam finds itself on the front line of China's expanding power in Southeast Asia—this time at sea. The *Haiyang Shiyou 981* was installed 17 nautical miles south of Triton Island, the southwestern-most land feature of the Paracel Islands. The islands are claimed by Vietnam but have been under de facto Chinese control since January 1974, when China seized three islands following a battle with the teetering South Vietnamese republic. The two countries also assert competing claims to the Spratly Islands, which lie to the south of the Paracels. In 1988, Chinese forces displaced Vietnamese forces from Johnson South Reef and established Beijing's first foothold in the archipelago. During the operation, Chinese sailors methodically gunned down as many as 64 lightly armed Vietnamese military engineers who found themselves stranded on a reef during high tide.[14] In the Spratlys, China has since built uninhabitable maritime features into artificial islands complete with harbors, radar emplacements, and military-grade runways. On the features it occupies, Vietnam maintains a series of smaller fortified emplacements.

Vietnam claims sovereignty over both groups of islands based on historical contacts dating back to at least the seventeenth century, dismissing Beijing's own claims as "stories about fishermen," as one Vietnamese official put it to me. There is more to the dispute than simple nationalist posturing. A third of Vietnam's population lives along the coast of the South China Sea, and the latter's deposits of oil and natural gas could be potentially beneficial for the country's future development. Given its sinewy resilience, Vietnam stands as the Southeast Asian nation perhaps most able to stand up to Beijing's maritime claims, a consideration that has underpinned the recent warming of relations with its one-time enemy, the United States.

As the 2014 oil rig protests showed, the South China Sea disputes have also revealed the deep strain of anti-Chinese sentiment that courses beneath the surface of Vietnamese society, from the cyclo drivers of Ho Chi Minh City to the highest echelons of politics and business. In my conversations with ordinary Vietnamese, talk of China was sprinkled liberally with the word *tham*, meaning "greedy" or "avaricious." Nguyen Thi Li, an 82-year-old Lang Son resident, said China would always want to expand. "Because they're a big country, they'll always want to be bigger," she said. Similar sentiments are commonplace on Facebook, where nationalistic netizens frequently denounce China's actions in the East Sea, as the Vietnamese term it, and myriad other Chinese plots to swallow Vietnamese territory or impinge on its sovereignty.

Nguyen Tan Dung, the economically liberal southerner who served as prime minister from 2006 until 2016, deployed anti-Chinese rhetoric to telegraph his nationalist credentials, and to subtly criticize conservative opponents in the VCP who favored stronger ties to China and a greater state role in the economy. In modern times, the journalist Bill Hayton writes, the China question has become a "live issue in all the major debates about the future of Vietnam—a cypher through which other battles are fought."[15]

In recent years, as anti-China protests have become a regular occurrence in Vietnam's major cities, they have created headaches for the party. Despite the offshore tensions, Hanoi maintains good relations with Beijing, while economic ties with China play an important role in sustaining the prosperity that undergirds the legitimacy of communist rule. Dung Truong Quoc, an historian and member of Vietnam's National Assembly who edits the magazine *Past & Present*, said that the party is now struggling to balance popular suspicions of China against the need for productive relations. "If we're hostile to each other, it's not good, but if we're too close or too friendly, it's not easy either," he said. "The Vietnamese leaders are pressed between these two lines: pressed by the Vietnamese people, and pressed by the Chinese."

The VCP's position is complicated by its historical ties to the Chinese Communist Party (CCP). During the 1950s and 1960s, the two communist parties were as close as "lips and teeth," as the old socialist bloc phrase went. The Vietnamese revolution would probably not have succeeded without the Chinese aid and supplies—everything from arms and ammunition to ping-pong balls and soy sauce—that flowed south to support its struggles against the French and Americans. Chinese support was so important that Vietnam's communist leader Ho Chi Minh once described his country's relationship with China as being like "one hundred favors, a thousand loyal affections, and ten thousand loves."[16]

Ho encapsulated his country's ambivalent view of China. Like most educated Vietnamese of his generation, he read and spoke Chinese, and expressed frequent admiration for the CCP. He even translated Mao's study *On Protracted War* from Chinese into French.[17] But beneath his paeans to socialist brotherhood, traditional suspicions smoldered. When Chinese forces arrived in northern Vietnam in 1945 to supervise the post-World War II armistice, he told anxious colleagues that it was better to put up with French rule for a few more years than to endure another Chinese occupation. As Ho reputedly said, "I prefer to sniff French shit for five years than eat Chinese shit for the rest of my life."[18]

In reality, the brotherly relations between the two communist parties were based on a temporary convergence of interests. For the Vietnamese, Chinese support and sanctuary was vital in their fight against the French and American imperialists. For Mao and the Chinese leadership, communist Vietnam served as a proxy with which to attack the US and advance broader revolutionary aims. When these interests started to diverge in the 1960s, a by-product of the wider falling-out between China and the Soviet Union, old enmities resurfaced. By the time North Vietnam's Soviet-built T-54 tanks smashed through the gates of Saigon's Presidential Palace on April 30, 1975, bringing the Vietnam War to an end, the relationship verged on open enmity. The Chinese saw their southern allies as ungrateful Confucian-Leninist vassals who had rebuffed the CCP's benevolence. The Vietnamese, freshly victorious in a three-decade struggle against foreign occupation, heard echoes of an old imperial mindset.

Relations finally broke down over events in Cambodia, where the communist Khmer Rouge had marched to power in April 1975, two weeks ahead of Saigon's fall. Led by Pol Pot, the regime's faceless "Brother Number One," who enjoyed strong backing from Beijing, the new regime set the dials toward pure agrarian utopia. It immediately sealed off Cambodia from the world, evacuated the cities, and put much of the Cambodian population to work on vast labor communes. In time, Pol Pot also turned against Vietnam, his onetime ally, launching a series of increasingly deadly cross-border incursions designed to regain long-lost Khmer territories in southern Vietnam. Hanoi eventually lost patience. In December 1978, it invaded Cambodia, removed the Khmer Rouge administration from power, and installed a faction of more pliant Cambodian communists in its place. When China responded to the toppling of its client by launching its pedagogical invasion of northern Vietnam, the two former allies found themselves at war.

Sino-Vietnamese acrimony took a particularly bitter toll on Vietnam's ethnic Chinese, who were targeted by "anti-capitalist" campaigns and forced from the country en masse. Thousands of Sino-Vietnamese were expelled across the northern border, while others boarded leaky and overladen boats and drifted out into the South China Sea, where unknown numbers of them perished. To outside observers, the disintegration of Ho's "ten thousand loves" into nationalist hostility was so striking as to prompt the scholar Benedict Anderson to write *Imagined Communities*, his influential study into the origins of nationalism. As Anderson noted, neither side made any more than the most perfunctory attempts to justify the bloodshed in terms of Marxist–Leninist ideology.[19]

The 1979 border invasion plunged relations to a nadir that lasted through the 1980s. Referring to Vietnam as "the Cuba of the East," Deng Xiaoping assembled a regional coalition to isolate Hanoi, which included the US, the anti-communist nations of ASEAN, and an assortment of anti-government Cambodian and Lao rebels. Frequent skirmishes took place along the Sino-Vietnamese border, which was closed to trade. In Vietnam, hostility toward China was so pervasive that it was elevated into a constitutional principle. "No sooner had they emerged from thirty years of fighting a war of liberation," the preamble to Vietnam's 1980 constitution stated, "than our people, who were longing for peace to rebuild their homeland, were confronted with the Chinese hegemonist aggressors and their henchmen in Kampuchea."[20] On a trip to northern Vietnam in 2003, I came across an old mural outside the town of Sapa that showed Vietnamese soldiers beating back Chinese troops with bayonets.

With the end of the Cold War, however, the interests of Vietnam and China started to realign. As communist states in a post-communist world, they shared the goal of modernizing their economies and avoiding being swept, like their Soviet counterpart, into the dustbin of history. In 1990, Vietnamese leaders traveled to the southwestern Chinese city of Chengdu for bilateral talks, a summit that paved the way for the resumption of normal diplomatic relations the following year. For the Vietnamese leadership, it was a humbling end to a decade of defiance. Throughout the 1980s, Soviet support had helped sustain the illusion that Vietnam could live in the shadow of a hostile China. But in the end, Vietnam followed the old pattern: it "won" the war, and then, to secure the peace, made a pilgrimage to China to symbolically reaffirm Chinese superiority. The war drove home an age-old lesson: as a Vietnamese general later put it, "we must learn how to live with our big neighbor."[21]

Learning to live with the People's Republic of China (PRC) meant learning to forget. In the name of the "16 golden words" adopted by the two governments in 1999—"long-term stability and future orientation, friendly neighborhood, comprehensive cooperation," in their English translation—the 1979 war and other recent clashes have been blotted from official memory. On the Chinese side, too, silence prevails: the war, fought entirely on Vietnamese territory, contradicts Beijing's repeated claims that it has never threatened or attacked its neighbors. Ostensibly, this willed amnesia is motivated by the need to maintain amity with China. But to the VCP's critics, it looks a lot like capitulation. "We should not incite hatred concerning the war, but to completely forget it?" said Nguyen Quang A, an outspoken dissident. "It's totally wrong. History is history: you cannot redo history."

I met Nguyen Quang A on a rainy September afternoon in 2018, at an outdoor café in central Hanoi, not far from Ho Chi Minh's granite mausoleum, the high temple of communist historiography. The mausoleum was closed for Uncle Ho's periodic re-embalming. At the nearby Vietnam Military History Museum, tourists filed past displays of faded black-and-white photos and other revolutionary relics, and wandered around a sculpture made from the wreckage of downed American aircraft. In a park across the road stood a statue of Lenin, a vestige of a vanished age, casting a metallic gaze through the blur of traffic.

Nguyen Quang A, 71, has an unusual profile for a dissident. A former party member, he ran a successful IT company for years before making a late-career change to outspoken critic of communist rule. His politics were informed by his time studying telecommunications in Hungary in the 1960s and 1970s, when he came into contact with the intellectual currents of East European reform communism. As Vietnam opened its economy in the 1980s, Quang A began translating books by intellectuals including Adam Michnik and the Hungarian economist János Kornai. He also translated Leszek Kolakowski's 1971 essay "Theses on hope and despair," in which the Polish philosopher argued that the wide gap between communist dogma and reality opened up terrain for self-organized groups to carve out an independent sphere of political action—what we would today term "civil society." In 2013, Quang A and a group of like-minded scholars and writers founded the Civil Society Forum, a group dedicated to promoting gradual political reform; it even made a puckish bid to run independent candidates for Vietnam's National Assembly in 2016. Quang A told me that if the party doesn't reform itself, it will ultimately collapse. As he put it, "evolution is unstoppable. The question you have to face is, do you want a violent evolution?"

Like many Vietnamese pro-democracy activists, Quang A is highly suspicious of the government's swing from official hostility toward China to official silence, a move he put down to "pressure from the Chinese side." A significant slice of the Vietnamese public seems to agree. Each year on February 17, Vietnamese patriots take to social media to commemorate the "martyrs" and civilians who died in the 1979 war, and to attack their government for its reticence. At military cemeteries across the north, veterans and members of the public hold low-profile ceremonies. Quang A frequently joins unauthorized memorial events in Hanoi, where participants don headbands with nationalistic slogans and march solemnly along the shores of Hoan Kiem Lake. Similar tributes are held to mark the naval clashes with China in 1974 and 1988.

The problem for the government is that whenever people gather to vent their anger about China, criticisms of communist rule are usually not far behind. In fact, as Bill Hayton writes, in a country where open criticism of the authorities can lead to a lengthy prison term, anti-Chinese protests give people a patriotic outlet through which they can indirectly question communist rule.[22] It is here that the "China question" intersects with wider concerns about corruption and the influence of *nhom loi ich*: the "interest groups" that have used their connections to senior party officials to enrich themselves at the public's expense. For the past decade, high-profile corruption scandals involving the friends and "red offspring" of powerful party members have been commonplace. To many government detractors, Chinese support is crucial in keeping a corrupt and unpopular party in power. "Without the backup of the Chinese communists, the Vietnamese communists could not rule Vietnam any longer, so they kowtow to them," said Nguyen Tuong Thuy, the vice president of the Independent Journalists Association of Vietnam, and a vocal opponent of both China and communist rule.

The party has often used heavy-handed tactics to quash such challenges to its political monopoly. Critics and dissident bloggers are frequently sentenced to protracted prison terms on charges of "conducting propaganda against the state" or "abusing democratic freedoms." Others are detained or held under house arrest to prevent them from attending public events. Some report being beaten up while in custody. Quang A told me that he has been detained 19 times, usually to prevent him attending rallies or human rights seminars abroad, or, as on one occasion in May 2016, to stop him taking up a US embassy invitation to meet visiting President Barack Obama. A few hours after our meeting, Quang A texted me that he had been picked up by state security, for the twentieth time, just moments after we parted, on the busy street under Lenin's eye. As far as he could determine, the authorities feared he was planning to fly to Brussels to testify against a planned European free-trade pact with Vietnam.

With a miasma of official silence clouding most things related to China, netizens are all too ready to advance their own theories. Dissident Facebook discussions are rife with talk about secret pacts and political debts incurred during the Cold War. One common claim is that the authorities are quietly removing anti-Chinese monuments built in the 1980s. Party critics I spoke to made much of the fact that some war cemeteries list fallen soldiers as having been martyred in the "struggle against France" or "the struggle against America," whereas those killed in the war with China are simply listed as having died "defending the border" (*bao ve bien gioi*). The reason for this is hard to determine. Since many northern war cemeteries were built in the 1980s, when official anti-Chinese hostility was at its height, the different terminologies could be coincidental. But as Hayton argues, this is exactly the problem facing the party: "when it comes to China, few people believe them anymore."[23]

One challenge for the Vietnamese government, said Dien Luong, a Columbia-educated journalist based in Ho Chi Minh City, is its wooden approach to communication in the digital era. By the end of 2018, 60 million Vietnamese were on Facebook, giving it the seventh-largest pool of users in the world. Since Vietnam is unwilling, and probably unable, to adopt China's "Great Firewall" of internet controls, the authorities continue to use antiquated methods to shape public opinion. The editors of the state-run press are told when they can take a hard line on China, and when to back off—a contradiction noted by a savvy public. "They are not up to speed in the way that they convey their message to the masses," said Dien, the former managing editor of *VnExpress*, an online newspaper that publishes in Vietnamese and English. "There were times when the government's message was quite legitimate and correct, but it was conveyed so clumsily, it looked ridiculous."

In mid-2018, the Vietnamese National Assembly approved a new draft law setting up three new Special Economic Zones (SEZs) in north, central, and south Vietnam. Immediately, Vietnamese Facebook lit up with claims that the SEZs would help China to infiltrate Vietnam and colonize its territory under the cover of foreign investment. Protesters took to the streets in Hanoi and other Vietnamese cities, waving national flags and holding placards reading, "Down with those who sell our country." In central Vietnam, riot police clashed with demonstrators, who responded with a barrage of rocks. The unexpected backlash forced the government to delay the adoption of the SEZ legislation. In the aftermath, government officials pointed out that the word "China" appeared nowhere in the text of the draft law. They were right— but many ordinary Vietnamese were no longer listening.

These nationalistic spot-fires are an unwelcome complication for a party and government occupied with maintaining the galloping economic growth that undergirds the legitimacy of communist rule. By the end of the Cold War, the Vietnamese economy was shattered. Its people were impoverished and weary of war, and Hanoi had little choice but to hitch itself to the rising dragon's tail. Since the introduction in 1986 of the economic reforms known as *doi moi*, or "renovation," trade with China has boomed. Surging economic growth has created breakneck urbanization, a burgeoning consumer class, and a young generation with little memory of the war and its deprivations.

The freewheeling face of modern Vietnam is most on display in the southern metropolis of Ho Chi Minh City, which generates a third of the country's GDP from just a ninth of its population. Here the contradictions of Vietnam's socialist market economy are dialed up to a high pitch. Advertisements for designer fashion brands like Lancôme and Burberry sit jarringly alongside the party's socialist propaganda: images of swooping doves and charging tanks, and the ubiquitous Uncle Ho, beaming out from billboards like a Marxist-Leninist Colonel Sanders. Far from a monument to its austere namesake, the city of Ho Chi Minh has become a place of wild economic energy: the hub and pulsating heart of a great Vietnamese Capitalist Party.

The economic transformation is also apparent at the opposite end of the country, where former invasion routes now function as busy arteries of trade. At Friendship Pass north of Lang Son, the road is well-sealed, with a median of neatly tended gardens. From a billboard above the road, a hammer-and-sickle beams out, urging the populace to greater heights of socialist construction. Approaching the border, semi-trailers rumble past on their way to the Chinese customs building, two swooping eaves of red steel enclosing the official crest of the People's Republic. At a new bus terminal, Chinese traders smoke and stamp their feet.

Friendship Pass has changed considerably in forty years. In mid-1978, as relations between China and Vietnam collapsed, the border saw scenes of chaos as Hanoi forcefully expelled tens of thousands of ethnic Chinese, claiming that they were acting as a fifth column for Beijing. (China also encouraged the exodus, warning of anti-Chinese pogroms to come.) Throughout the 1980s, the border was heavily militarized and closed to trade. In those years, one local restaurant owner recalled, many locals survived by smuggling: "We had to trade illegally to obtain normal amenities that we didn't have, like blankets, flashlights, things like that. After a while, even soldiers would do illegal crossings." On these perilous border runs, many local people lost lives or limbs to landmines.

These days, the cross-border trade is thriving. In the border town of Dong Dang, the central market overflows with Chinese goods: everything from kettles and fans and rice-cookers to clothes and pesticides to blizzards of plastic ephemera. Trade has transformed the northern border region from an isolated upland—the end of the road in northern Vietnam—to the main conduit of a trade relationship now worth upward of $100 billion per year. For many people in Dong Dang, the usual suspicions of China are moderated by the frequent economic interactions. "It's relatively easy to work with Chinese companies," said Tran Thi Tuyet, 30, the local representative of a Haiphong-based transport company who works from a small office a few hundred meters from the border gate. "In fact," she added, "I sometimes trust them even more than Vietnamese companies, because they keep their word."

Still, there are few outward signs of the Chinese presence along the border—surprisingly so, given the volume of trade. While parts of northern Burma and Laos have taken on the unmistakable contours of urban China, even Chinese-language signage is rare in northern Vietnam, aside from the odd restaurant menu. Mainland traders seem to keep a low profile—a sign of the extreme sensitivity that still surrounds the issue of Chinese investment, and probably always will. As one market vendor in Dong Dang told me, "We trade with each other, but not to the extent of friendship."

Over the past two decades, alongside the reawakening of dormant sovereignty disputes, Vietnam's economy has become intertwined with China's. While the US is its largest export market, Vietnam now imports more from China than from any other country: everything from machine tools, fabrics, and electronic gizmos to iron and steel, chemicals, and consumer goods. Vietnam is particularly dependent on China for components needed for the manufacture of its key exports: the textiles it sews into shirts and sneakers, and the electronic parts it assembles into Samsung smartphones and flat-screen TVs. China has also become increasingly important to Vietnam's tourist trade: in 2017, nearly a third of the 12.9 million foreigners who visited Vietnam hailed from north of the border.[24]

In recent years, this dependence has manifested in a ballooning trade deficit with China, which amounted to a whopping $34 billion in 2019.[25] One reason for the deficit is that while China exports many high-value goods to Vietnam, most of Vietnam's exports to China are low-value primary goods like rubber, crude oil, coal, rice, and tropical fruits. Another reason is the large number of Chinese state contractors that have won tenders to build projects such as factories and power plants in Vietnam. Funded by preferential loans from Chinese state banks, these projects use Chinese technology, equipment, labor, and other services, the import of which adds to the deficit.

This economic mismatch poses a strategic conundrum for Hanoi, ensuring that any disruption in the trade relationship would impact Vietnam to an exponentially greater degree than China. One Vietnamese official has estimated that if China cut off trade to Vietnam, the latter's GDP would contract by as much as 10 percent.[26] This is not an unreasonable fear, given that China has shown its willingness to use trade as a coercive diplomatic tool, as when it halted banana imports from the Philippines in 2012 in connection with the disputes in the South China Sea. Beijing's control of the headwaters of the Mekong River, via its cascade of upstream dams, also makes Chinese cooperation important for the future of Vietnam's most productive agricultural region: the Mekong Delta.

As the 2018 SEZ protests showed, Vietnam's economic linkage with China is now an issue of both popular and elite concern. One particular gripe has been the influx of large numbers of Chinese laborers to work on Chinese engineering projects and infrastructure investments.[27] In 2009, populist fury erupted over a planned Chinese bauxite mining enterprise in the Central Highlands, with some activists claiming that the natural result would be a "quiet Chinese invasion" of the region. The protests received support from the revered war hero General Vo Nguyen Giap, then 97 years of age, and General Nguyen Trong Vinh, a former ambassador to China, who asserted that the presence of "up to 10,000 Chinese workers" posed an "unacceptable" national security threat.[28]

This accounts for the decidedly cool position that Hanoi has taken on the Belt and Road Initiative (BRI). Despite officially endorsing Xi Jinping's headline policy, and agreeing to improve connectivity between southern China and northern Vietnam, Vietnam remains cautious about the strategic implications of the BRI. It is wary of increasing its dependence on China by taking on additional debt—especially when similar funding is easily available from partners like Japan, who offer higher quality infrastructure and lower concessional interest rates, minus the historical baggage.

Offsetting its security fears and economic dependence on China has evolved into Vietnam's highest foreign policy priority. It has pursued this strategy by engaging China on a broad front, effectively quarantining the two nations' economic relationship from the South China Sea disputes, while building trade and security ties with as many other powers as possible. In the 1990s, Vietnam emerged from the Cold War embracing a new "multidirectional foreign policy" that prioritized multilateral diplomacy and the diversification of its relations with the major powers. This strategy took a major step forward in 1995, the year in which Vietnam joined ASEAN and normalized its diplomatic relations with the US. The country has since established "strategic partnerships" with 16 nations, including Australia, India, Japan, Russia, South Korea, and the United Kingdom, and "comprehensive partnerships" with 12 more. Hanoi has also embraced ASEAN, both to cushion its engagements with China and other major powers, and to underline its identity as a Southeast Asian—as opposed to "Chinese"—nation.

Vietnam's greatest hedge against China, however, remains its former wartime enemy. For a long time after normalization in 1995, Vietnam–US relations were marred by a deep mutual mistrust. On the Vietnamese side, there was the legacy of the calamitous American involvement in Vietnam, including the birth defects caused by the dropping of defoliants like Agent Orange across swathes of southern Vietnam. On the American side, there was unease about Vietnam's harsh persecution of political dissidents and religious minorities. But China's recent assertiveness in the South China Sea has prompted a rapid expansion of trade, investment, and defense ties between the two nations. The US is now the most important market for Vietnamese exports, and Vietnamese leaders have visited the White House under three US administrations. When President Truong Tan Sang visited Washington in 2013, the two countries raised their relationship to a "comprehensive partnership."

It is not hard to understand Vietnam's importance to policymakers in Washington. Were Vietnam to capitulate in the South China Sea, it would become much more difficult for other Southeast Asian claimants to hold the line. "If China can break off Vietnam," a US official told the writer Robert Kaplan, "they've won the South China Sea."[29] As a result, the US has tried to enlist Hanoi in its efforts to help preserve the current security order in the Indo-Pacific. In 2010, during a meeting of the ASEAN Regional Forum in Hanoi, Secretary of State Hillary Clinton declared for the first time that the US had a direct national interest in the South China Sea, and that it opposed "the use or threat of force by any claimant"—an obvious reference to China.

The 2014 oil rig crisis and China's colossal land reclamations in the Spratly Islands have prodded Vietnam ever further in the direction of Washington. In 2015, Nguyen Phu Trong, the general secretary of the VCP, visited the US and, remarkably, was received in the Oval Office by President Obama with the pomp usually reserved for a head of government. The following May, Obama announced the lifting of the American arms embargo on Vietnam, justifying it as an attempt to "ensure that Vietnam has access to the equipment it needs to defend itself." Most importantly for the hardliners in Hanoi, when President Sang visited Washington in 2013 to broker the "comprehensive partnership," the two sides made a commitment to "respect each other's political system"—what amounted to an official US commitment that it would not try to overthrow Vietnam's communist regime.[30]

Relations deepened further under the Trump administration, as the US pivoted toward a more confrontational China policy. Vietnam features as a potential strategic partner in all of the administration's key policy documents, from the National Security Strategy (2017) to the Indo-Pacific Strategy Report (2019). Before the Trans-Pacific Partnership (TPP) trade deal was scuttled by President Trump, Hanoi was an enthusiastic participant in the agreement, which would have helped diversify its economy away from its heavy reliance on China. The American withdrawal from the TPP was met with "frustration" and "disappointment" in Hanoi, said Do Thanh Hai, a senior fellow at the Diplomatic Academy of Vietnam and the author of a book on the disputes in the South China Sea. As he put it when we met in late 2017, the TPP "represented our zealous desire to become a part of the international community." Vietnam has since been energetic in pushing the Comprehensive and Progressive Agreement for Trans-Pacific Partnership, the successor version of the TPP agreement.

While Hanoi cherishes good relations with Washington, geography militates against Vietnam ever becoming a fully fledged American treaty ally. As Brantly Womack has observed, Vietnam has historically seemed most threatening to China when perceived as a proxy for wider global forces, fears that an open US–Vietnam alliance would almost certainly provoke.[31] In its 1998 defense white paper, to reassure Beijing that it had no hostile intent, Vietnam formulated the so-called "Three Nos" policy: namely, no foreign military bases; no foreign military alliances; and no using a third country to oppose another.[32] For this reason, too, Vietnamese strategists have been lukewarm about recent American initiatives like the Free and Open Indo-Pacific strategy, which the Chinese government understandably perceives as an attempt at containment. A looming China has thus both motivated Vietnam's tilt toward the US and constrained it; each step toward Washington has been accompanied by anxious glances in the direction of Beijing.

Furthermore, China and Vietnam are bound by a vestigial mistrust of American intentions. Conservative figures in both nations continue to harbor fears that the US, through the use of Facebook and American consumer culture, is plotting to undermine communist rule; the two governments even give this supposed plot the same name: "peaceful evolution." This is a timely reminder that whatever their past and present differences, much unites the two communist parties. They share the same goal of containing the contradictions of their socialist market economies; they also face similar challenges from a mounting popular nationalism, which both have stoked for their own gains, but which always threatens to escape their control. In 2017, a senior Chinese official declared that the two parties were united by "a shared destiny": a mutual interest in preserving communist rule.[33]

In 2020, a delicate status quo pertains, as Vietnam pursues a balance between the two superpowers that one of its diplomats once referred to as a "Goldilocks solution: not too hot, not too cold."[34] Despite another round of tense naval confrontation in 2019 at Vanguard Bank, southwest of the Spratly Islands, the Vietnamese government has managed effectively to sequester the South China Sea disputes and prevent them from contaminating other productive parts of the relationship. Trade continues to flow, despite the periodic fracas offshore, and the sensitive question of Vietnam's ethnic Chinese population remains dormant, in likely recognition of how combustive the issue could become. Hanoi continues to employ a time-tested pattern of working to assuage Chinese fears, while steeling itself to respond forcefully to any impingement on its sovereignty.

There are some senses in which a degree of superpower tension works to Vietnam's advantage. The greatest fear of Vietnamese strategists is that the US and China might one day cut a deal that leaves them stranded at the heart of a Chinese sphere of influence. In 2009, Vietnam bought six Kilo-class submarines from Russia, as an added deterrent to Chinese maritime adventurism. Nguyen Truong Giang, a former ambassador to Brunei, told me: "If you're afraid of the tiger, of course the tiger will swallow you." But as popular sentiment becomes inflamed, and the US moves more forcefully to contain Chinese ambitions in the Indo-Pacific, the stakes of Vietnam's balancing act are rising.

Walking through the military graveyards around Lang Son, I was conscious of China's looming presence just over the hazy rim of hills to the north, and the crushing burden that this represented for Vietnam and its people. For centuries, Vietnamese political and cultural life had been governed by a fraught dialectic of eager emulation of and fierce resistance to China. The national spirit of the Vietnamese had been hardened on the horns of this contradiction, each sentiment feeding algorithmically into the other, every iteration reinforcing their particular fate: to be bound to a hated enemy without whom they would be nothing.

Today's Vietnam stands at the confluence of the various strategic challenges pressing in on Southeast Asia. It faces China's expanding power both on land and on water, and is impacted by its stranglehold on the upper Mekong River and its actions in the South China Sea. In many senses, its fate reflects, in highly concentrated form, that of Southeast Asia as a whole: a region destined to sit in disconcerting propinquity to the world's most populous nation. "It's God's creation, unfortunately," the government critic Nguyen Quang A said. "We have a very big and powerful neighbor and we have to live peacefully with them. The one solution is that we find some island and move all our population there," he added, "but that's nonsense."

4

CAMBODIA AND LAOS
PHOBOS AND DEIMOS

A short drive outside the river town of Kampong Chhnang in central Cambodia lies a large military airfield. Its vast concrete runway sprawls out in breezy silence, untroubled by any sign of aircraft. Here and there half-finished roads lose themselves in fields of sugar palms. In a green grid of rice paddies, an empty control tower stands sentinel.

Abandoned in 1979, shortly before its completion, the airfield was built by the communist Khmer Rouge, whose mad dash toward agrarian utopia led to the deaths of an estimated 1.7 million Cambodians—about a quarter of the country's population at the time. According to prosecutors working at a United Nations-backed war crimes tribunal in the capital Phnom Penh, set up to try a handful of the regime's surviving leaders, the manpower was supplied by prisoners—most of them purged members of the Khmer Rouge military. They used basic tools to uproot trees, scrape the land clean, and pour thick slabs of cement. Many were worked to death or accused of sabotage and executed as traitors. Thousands perished.

The airport's 2.4-kilometer runway—still in fine condition despite four decades of neglect—is also evidence of the strong support the Khmer Rouge received from China. As Andrew Mertha writes in his book *Brothers in Arms: Chinese Aid to the Khmer Rouge, 1975–1979*, Beijing dispatched hundreds of engineers to oversee the construction of the airport, and the excavation of an underground command complex—a dank catacomb of reinforced concrete bunkers stretching hundreds of meters into the nearby hills.[1] Shattered out-buildings and support facilities still lie scattered across the surrounding area. Exploring in the woods nearby, I came across four empty water tanks, great industrial caverns that pinged with otherworldly echoes. Phat Bora, a 53-year-old woman who worked on a Khmer Rouge road-building brigade as a teenager, remembered the Chinese experts well; they were easily recognizable by their blue trousers and collared shirts. (The prisoners all wore black.) "Their skin was very white and beautiful," she said.

Between April 1975, when it seized power, and January 1979, when it was driven from Phnom Penh by a Vietnamese invasion, the Khmer Rouge regime cut Cambodia off from the world and embarked on a "super great leap forward" to communism. While China had no direct hand in the purges and killings, it was the only country to give Democratic Kampuchea (as the regime called itself) significant support. According to Youk Chhang, the director of the Documentation Center of Cambodia, which researches the regime's crimes, "Chinese support went from the village level all the way up to the highest level of the Khmer Rouge leadership." Within days of the Khmer Rouge seizing power, China extended aid and technical assistance to the new government. In June 1975, the regime's leader, "Brother Number One" Pol Pot, made a secret trip to Beijing to meet with Chairman Mao, who offered him $1 billion in aid—China's largest aid pledge up to that point. China sent everything from military materiel and radio transmitters to agricultural implements and food aid. A weekly flight from Beijing was one of Democratic Kampuchea's few links to the outside world.

The documentary evidence of Chinese support to the Khmer Rouge is preserved in the National Archives of Cambodia, which are housed in a mustard-colored French colonial building close to Wat Phnom, the fourteenth-century hillside pagoda that gives the Cambodian capital its name. During a visit to the archive in 2018, I spent two days sitting beneath the ceiling fans, poring through stacks of warped files held together with string. They included reams of Chinese blueprints and schematics, printed on waxy paper in astringent purple ink. These outlined plans for a variety of Chinese projects: radar stations, a thermal energy plant, and an oil refinery in Kampong Som, today known as Sihanoukville, which was halfway to completion when the regime fell. There were also bills of lading for Chinese shipments to the Khmer Rouge, many of them for military supplies, and a few hand-written Chinese notes, inscribed in a spidery hand.

Despite the common zeal and excess of Khmer Rouge rule and Mao's Cultural Revolution, Chinese support to Democratic Kampuchea was driven less by ideological affinity than by strategic imperatives: in particular, China's desire to counter the Soviet Union and its regional client, Vietnam. For similar reasons, China continued its support of the Khmer Rouge after they were driven from power in 1979. Along with diplomatic backing from the US and the anti-communist Association of Southeast Asian Nations (ASEAN), and logistical support from the Thai army, Chinese aid allowed Pol Pot's army to regroup in jungle camps along the Thai border and launch a civil war against the new Vietnam-installed government in Phnom Penh. Right up until their terminal collapse in the late 1990s, the Khmer Rouge wore olive-green Chinese military uniforms and communicated on Chinese-made radio transmitters. The role of China in keeping the Khmer Rouge alive was so pivotal that Hun Sen, appointed prime minister of Cambodia in 1985, described it during this period as "the root of everything that was evil" in his country.[2]

Three decades on, however, Cambodia is once again ensconced in Beijing's widening orbit. China is now the country's most important international backer, its main trade partner, and its primary source of tourism and foreign investment. Hun Sen, still in power, no longer denounces China's support for the people who ravaged his country. Instead, he praises its "no-strings" injections of capital. No country in Southeast Asia is closer to China than Cambodia, and none better demonstrates the extent to which China's economic and political re-emergence has altered the dynamics of aid and development in the region. History looked set to come full circle in 2015, when Cambodian state media reported that a Chinese firm was in negotiation to refurbish the old Khmer Rouge airfield in Kampong Chhnang—and finally press into service a runway laid with the bones of the dead.

The story of how Beijing so quickly swung from prime enemy to "iron-clad friend," as Xi Jinping declared in 2016, has its roots in Cambodia's unique political trajectory since the end of the Cold War. On October 23, 1991, less than three months before the collapse of the Soviet Union, four Cambodian armed factions, including the Khmer Rouge and Hun Sen's Cambodian People's Party (CPP), came together to sign the Paris Peace Agreements, an international peace treaty intended to end the civil war that had ravaged the country since 1979. To implement its terms, Paris created the United Nations Transitional Authority in Cambodia (UNTAC), then the most expensive and ambitious peacekeeping mission ever mounted. (It would eventually cost more than $2 billion.) Staffed by a multinational force of 26,000, including 18,000 blue-helmeted soldiers, it was tasked with disarming and demobilizing the four Cambodian factions, and repatriating some 300,000 refugees from camps along the Thai border. More ambitiously, it was also responsible for organizing free and fair elections, with the aim of turning a war-scarred nation with a creaking communist government into a liberal democratic state—a Denmark of the Far East.

This project was infused with the liberal ideological triumphalism that followed the conclusion of the Cold War. To many outside observers, Cambodia presented an appealing moral symmetry. For several decades, the country had been shattered by the conflict between the US, China, and the Soviet Union: pummeled by American B-52 Stratofortesses in the closing phases of the Vietnam War, razed by the mad designs of the Khmer Rouge, and then consumed by a further round of civil war in the 1980s. Now, with the Cold War at an end, Cambodia would be granted a dividend of peace. The same "international community" that had fueled Cambodia's civil wars would close ranks to shepherd a long-suffering people toward the promised land of democracy, free market prosperity, and human rights.

UNTAC's avowed aims were never that realistic. When the first UN peace-keepers arrived in Cambodia in 1992, the country was impoverished, reeling from a generation of conflict, with virtually no history of democratic politics. Perhaps more importantly, it was ruled by an entrenched quasi-communist party—the CPP—which viewed the West's liberal proclamations with skepticism. For the previous decade, the CPP (known until 1991 as the Kampuchean People's Revolutionary Party) had been on the wrong end of a cynical Cold War accommodation in which China, the US, and their ASEAN allies had backed a coalition of three armed rebel factions, including what was left of the Khmer Rouge, in an attempt to bleed Soviet-backed Vietnam and its client regime in Phnom Penh. This experience led senior CPP leaders, including Hun Sen, to see the coming of democracy not as a new dawn but simply as a more sophisticated means of removing their party from power. Far from ending, the civil war evolved into a new phase.

The UNTAC-organized election took place over a week in May 1993, in an atmosphere of keen anticipation. Huge numbers of Cambodians turned out for the first real democratic election in their nation's history, some traveling many hours to complete their ballot. The CPP lost to a royalist faction known as FUNCINPEC, led by the Francophile son of the charismatic Prince Norodom Sihanouk, who had ruled Cambodia in the 1950s and 1960s. But senior CPP officials refused to accept the result. Threatening a secession of the country's eastern provinces, they bluffed their way into an equal share of power in an unstable new coalition government. The UN dithered. Eager to declare Cambodia a success, it signed off on the result and left, as the two coalition partners began vying for power within the government. In July 1997, armed forces loyal to Hun Sen launched a lightning strike on FUNCINPEC's military wing and effectively seized power. In response, Western governments suspended aid, and Cambodia's UN seat was vacated. Under outside pressure, Hun Sen acceded to a new election in 1998, which the CPP won easily in a climate of fear and intimidation. The Western powers signed off on the results and resumed their aid. Hun Sen again became sole prime minister—a position he has held ever since.

While Hun Sen's Cambodia remained a multi-party democracy in name, real power resided in the loyalties and obligations that bound together a trellis-like network of tycoons, CPP officials, military commanders, and local big-men (and women) distributed throughout the provinces. These traditional patron–client ties, known in Khmer as *ksae*, or "strings," ran from the villages right up to the top levels of the Cambodian cabinet, bypassing or infiltrating the country's formal political institutions. Cambodian democracy thus came to have a curiously superficial quality: nominally pluralistic, but never really changing, as the CPP used intimidation, patronage, and occasional lethal violence to prevent the emergence of any serious threat to its power.

Despite piling up domestic victories, international legitimacy eluded Hun Sen. In the Western narrative of redemption that came to dominate views of Cambodia in the early 1990s, the one-eyed, belligerent former Khmer Rouge commander was the perfect villain—an authoritarian bogeyman who had thwarted history's grand democratic design. This view was particularly strong in the US, where a lobby of conservative Republican congressmen, some representing large Cambodian-American constituencies, denounced the Cambodian leader as a "new Pol Pot" and threw their support behind Sam Rainsy, a polished former financier who had spent most of his life in France. Where Hun Sen struggled to shed Cambodia's status as a special international "project," Rainsy labored to reinforce it, circulating through the capitals of the West, portraying himself as the one figure who could bring democracy to Cambodia. To domestic audiences, meanwhile, he usually focused on historic animosities toward Vietnam.

If Western governments balked at legitimizing Hun Sen's rule, however, there was a resurgent Asian power that had no such qualms. Throughout the

1980s, China had been enemy number one in Cambodia, but its support for the Khmer Rouge after 1979 was pragmatic. After cutting off funding to Pol Pot in 1990, it had no problem supporting whichever Cambodian leader could bring stability and support Chinese aims in the region. Initially, Chinese leaders invested their hopes in Prince Ranariddh. Since the 1950s, China had been close to the Cambodian royal family, a relationship anchored in the personal friendship between Zhou Enlai and Ranariddh's father Sihanouk, who had first met each other at the Bandung Conference of non-aligned nations in Indonesia in 1955. When Sihanouk was removed from power in a coup in 1970 and sought refuge in China, Zhou arranged financial support and a comfortable residence for him in Beijing, which he retained until his death in 2012.

Once in power, however, Ranariddh proved feckless and vain; worse, from Beijing's perspective, were his close ties to Taiwanese business interests. After his coup de force in July 1997, Hun Sen vaguely intimated that Ranariddh had received covert support from Taiwan, and shut Taipei's trade office in Phnom Penh. Chinese leaders were pleased. A few months later, China gave Cambodia a $10 million loan to replace the Western aid suspended following the violence; it also sent a $2.8 million shipment of military trucks and jeeps, which were used to equip security forces loyal to Hun Sen. These included his well-armed personal bodyguard unit, a private army that existed outside the normal military chain of command. The Cambodian leader praised the fact that, unlike Western countries, China "does not poke its nose into Cambodia's internal affairs."[3]

In this new convergence of interests, old enmities were laid aside. When Jiang Zemin paid a state visit to Cambodia in November 2000—the first by a Chinese leader since 1963—neither he nor Hun Sen made any public mention of China's past support for the Khmer Rouge. The only reminder was the small cluster of protesters who hoisted banners reading "China is a bad friend" and "Cambodia is not a Chinese province," before being bundled out of sight by police.[4] Hun Sen told Jiang that Cambodia's relations with China were "a precious gift."[5]

Chinese capital and investors started trickling into the country. In the 1990s, mainland wags had jokingly referred to Cambodia as "*qian buzai*": a pun on *jianpuzhai*, the Chinese name for the country, meaning that there was "no money" to be made there.[6] But as the bilateral relationship bloomed, the country saw the largest influx of Chinese citizens since the Khmer Rouge years. Between 2011 and 2015, Beijing funneled nearly $5 billion in loans and investment into Cambodia, for the construction of roads, bridges, and hydropower dams.[7] The fruits of this relationship could be seen in the gleaming new bridges spanning Cambodia's milky-brown rivers; the imported Chinese products that filled the stalls at Phnom Penh's modernist Central Market; and the high-rises that were altering the capital's skyline, ziggurats of blue-green gauze and scaffolding. China also offered military support, including uniforms, trucks, loans to buy helicopters, and a training facility in southern Cambodia.

In return, the Cambodian government supported key Chinese interests. It barred the Dalai Lama from traveling to Cambodia, and forcibly sent Falun Gong activists back to China. In December 2009, the government deported 20 ethnic Uighur Muslims, who had arrived in Cambodia seeking asylum after a long and perilous journey from China's Xinjiang region, where ethnic riots had broken out earlier that year. When the US government responded to the deportation by canceling a planned shipment of military trucks, China offered a larger shipment of Dongfeng trucks in its place.

Most controversially, Cambodia sided with China in the competing maritime claims over the South China Sea, a dispute in which it had no direct interests. In July 2012, during its chairmanship of ASEAN, Cambodian officials worked behind the scenes to veto mild criticisms of China's recent seizure of the Scarborough Shoal, following its protracted standoff with the Philippines. Unable to agree on language for the South China Sea disputes, the bloc failed to issue a joint communiqué for the first time in its 45-year history.[8] A few weeks earlier, Chinese President Hu Jintao had visited Phnom Penh, promising millions of dollars in investment and assistance. Cambodia would play a similar blocking role at an ASEAN meeting in Laos in July 2016.[9]

When Xi Jinping paid a state visit to Cambodia in October 2016, the two sides issued a joint statement endorsing Beijing's long-standing position: that the South China Sea disputes were not an issue between China and ASEAN, and that they should be resolved via bilateral talks: negotiations in which China would naturally enjoy the upper hand. Xi offered Cambodia a fresh tranche of Chinese funding and described the two countries as "good neighbors, real friends who are loyal to each other."[10]

Over time, Chinese "no-strings" support gave Hun Sen's government an escape hatch from the conditions that were often attached to Western aid money. Since the early 1990s, the CPP government had seethed at Cambodia's status as an international "project" and resented the fact that the country was held to higher standards than most of its neighbors. This was bitter medicine for Hun Sen, who fancied himself as a great peacemaker who had presided over a period of unprecedented economic growth and political stability. Left out of the Obama administration's "rebalance" to Asia, Hun Sen was forced to watch on as rights-abusing leaders like President Thein Sein of Burma and Nguyen Phu Trong, the head of the Vietnamese Communist Party (VCP), were ushered into the White House. The Philippines' Rodrigo Duterte and Thailand's junta leader Prayuth Chan-ocha would be invited to Washington in due course under President Trump.

These resentments came together in the run-up to the national elections of July 2018. The previous election five years before had veered unexpectedly off-script, when millions of discontented Cambodians threw their support behind the Cambodia National Rescue Party (CNRP), a new unified opposition party led by Sam Rainsy, Hun Sen's long-time rival. Across the country, huge crowds turned out to see Rainsy and his deputy Kem Sokha, who promised a new dawn for Cambodia after years of cronyism and corruption. While the CPP scraped through the election with its parliamentary majority intact (claims of electoral fraud notwithstanding), Hun Sen was shaken by the loss of support. Embracing Facebook, he unfurled a populist platform that included wage-hikes for civil servants, teachers, and soldiers. He also made clear that reform would happen on his own terms.

As the 2018 election approached, the Cambodian authorities launched a wide-ranging crackdown. Political figures and human rights defenders were arrested and beaten up in the street. Rainsy was forced into exile overseas on a raft of bogus criminal charges. In September 2017, Kem Sokha, who had replaced Rainsy as CNRP president, was arrested and charged with treason, on the grounds that he had conspired with foreign governments to topple the CPP. Two months later, the Supreme Court banned the CNRP altogether. The *Cambodia Daily*, a fearless English-language newspaper that had symbolized the promise of UNTAC, was also forced to close after being presented with a $6.3 million bill for unpaid tax. The paper's last front page, on September 4, carried a picture of Sokha being taken into custody under the headline, "Descent Into Outright Dictatorship."

Cambodia had never been a fully functioning democracy; in a sense, Hun Sen was simply bringing appearance into closer alignment with reality. But the fact that he no longer felt the need to offer democratic gestures to the West was a startling sign of how Chinese support had altered the status quo. In Beijing, a Foreign Ministry spokesperson responded to Sokha's arrest by saying that China supported "the Cambodian government's effort to uphold national security and stability."[11] This support allowed the CPP to sideline political enemies and extend its hold on power. It also enabled Hun Sen's final reckoning, a quarter-century on, with an unwanted intervention in his country's affairs. Cambodia's days as an international "project" appeared over.

When Washington complained about the crackdown, Hun Sen gave his resentments a full airing. He criticized Washington for its bombings of Cambodia during the Vietnam War, for supporting the Khmer Rouge through the 1980s, and for refusing to waive more than $500 million in "bloody" debt from the civil war of the early 1970s. Cambodia also suspended its participation in Angkor Sentinel, a military exercise it had held with the US Army since 2010, a month after holding—for the first time—a similar exercise with China. After Western nations withheld their support for the 2018 election, China donated laptops, computers, and voting booths to the Cambodian election authority; when the election campaign began in May 2018, Chinese Ambassador Xiong Bo was a guest at a big CPP rally in Phnom Penh.[12]

Election day came and went. The CPP sailed through unopposed, except for a handful of miniature Potemkin parties, and claimed all 125 seats in the National Assembly. The resulting pressure from the US and other Western governments, still measuring Cambodia by a 1991 baseline, simply pushed Hun Sen's government closer to China. Officials now described the two countries' bonds as "unbreakable," "all-weather," and "iron-clad." The Sino-Cambodian friendship was "like wine," Ambassador Xiong declared in 2018. "The longer it is, the better taste it has."[13]

Hun Sen's Chinese embrace, like that of Pol Pot, had deeper historical precedents. For most of Cambodia's history, the greatest threat to its survival had come not from a distant China, but from the two kingdoms to its east and west. Following the decline of the Angkorian Empire in the fifteenth century, a shrinking Cambodian realm found itself sandwiched between Siam and Vietnam (Annam), two rising powers that meddled in its politics and slowly encroached on its territories. To survive and prosper, Cambodian leaders frequently sought outside protection. In 1863, King Norodom welcomed the establishment of a French protectorate that probably saved his kingdom from being partitioned by its traditional foes. After independence from the French, his great-grandson Prince Sihanouk looked to communist China. "If we move away from China," he warned in 1965, "we will be devoured by the vultures."[14]

Like its predecessors, Cambodia's current government is keenly aware of the two larger countries pressing in from each side. Pou Sothirak, a former minister and ambassador to Japan who heads the Cambodian Institute for Cooperation and Peace, said that the government sees China as a better guarantor of Cambodia's independence and sovereignty than any other outside power, including ASEAN.

When Cambodia joined ASEAN in 1999, policymakers hoped that it would offer an enduring solution to the country's external security threats. But they grew disillusioned at ASEAN's perceived ineffectiveness in resolving the nationalistic spat that broke out in 2008 between Cambodia and Thailand over Preah Vihear, an eleventh-century Angkorian temple perched on a cliff along their shared border. ASEAN told Cambodia and Thailand to negotiate the border dispute bilaterally, and did not table it as a formal agenda item, until Hun Sen broke with protocol and raised it during a summit meeting in Jakarta in 2011. A subsequent agreement to dispatch Indonesian civilian observers along the border was never implemented.[15] The episode left many Cambodian policymakers with the view that, as Sothirak told me, "ASEAN is good, but maybe China is a little bit better."

Tilting toward China has also allowed Hun Sen to distance himself somewhat from his former patron Vietnam, the primary wellspring of Khmer nationalist angst. Cambodians have never forgotten Vietnam's slow absorption of the former Khmer territories in the Mekong Delta, and many believe it is still plotting to swallow what remains of their country. Like anti-Chinese sentiment in Vietnam, hostility toward the Vietnamese permeates the Khmer national consciousness, bridging every social and political divide. Given the CPP's historical association with Vietnam, which placed it in power in 1979, this has also been a fruitful line of attack for Cambodian opposition figures, who have long sought to portray Hun Sen and his cronies as "puppets" of Hanoi. In a 2014 speech, Sam Rainsy even declared that the CNRP supported China's claims in the South China Sea, on the logic that anyone opposing Vietnam must be Cambodia's friend. "The islands belong to China," he told a crowd of CNRP supporters.[16]

The CPP government maintains tight political ties to the VCP, especially in the realms of defense and border security, but Chinese largesse has allowed it to maintain a healthier balance of patrons. Hanoi is not overly happy with Hun Sen's Chinese love affair, but its leaders are pragmatic. "We recognize Cambodia and Laos's concerns and their need for development," one Vietnamese Foreign Ministry official told me, "so we don't want [them] to have to choose sides."

On the economic development front, too, China's Belt and Road Initiative (BRI) offers Cambodia a fast way to improve the electricity grids and transportation networks necessary to support its nascent manufacturing industry. Over pizza at an Italian bistro in Phnom Penh, Sok Siphana, a lawyer and government advisor who helped negotiate Cambodia's accession to the World Trade Organization in 2004, explained that the present government welcomed support from any source, but that China moved quickly compared to the traditional donors. "The World Bank, the ADB [Asian Development Bank] will take one year to send one or two guys to do a feasibility study. The Japanese will take God knows how long," he said, "and the need is there."

The most striking evidence of China's presence in Cambodia can be seen in the city bearing the name of Beijing's old friend. Until recently, Sihanoukville was a sleepy beach resort set on a promontory jutting into the Gulf of Thailand, popular with Cambodian holidaymakers and Western backpackers. In just a few years, Chinese investment has turned the small city, home to Cambodia's only deep-water port, into a roaring gambling and tourism center—a budget Macao by the sea. When I visited Sihanoukville in late 2018, I was astonished at how it had changed from my last visit eight years earlier. High-rise hotels and apartment buildings pressed up into the evening sky. City streets crumbled under the weight of cranes and cement trucks, and rainwater pooled in the ruts. Driving down from Phnom Penh on National Road 4, traffic slowed to a crawl behind lines of trucks hauling gravel, bricks, and other construction materials down to the coast.

Sihanoukville's development centered on its multitude of Chinese-run casinos, whose illuminated facades now dominated the city center. More than twenty had opened in the two years prior to my visit, with a dozen more reportedly on the way. Peeking inside the New MGM Casino, I saw Chinese gamblers in black T-shirts nervously fingering stacks of C-notes at baccarat tables, riding each flip of the cards in tense silence. Cambodian waitresses slid silently by with carts filled with teacups and plates of sliced mango. Outside, the dusty main roads were lined with Chinese restaurants and nightclubs. Construction hoardings bore Chinese-language advertisements for tattoo parlors and personal loans. On nearby O'Chheuteal Beach, as the sun sank below a bank of salmon-pink clouds, Chinese tourists haggled for skewers of barbecued squid and roared through the surf on jet-skis. The Western backpackers who once packed O'Chheuteal's bars had largely been replaced.

In 2017, China surpassed Vietnam to become the leading source of tourists to Cambodia; the same year, Chinese arrivals to Sihanoukville rose by nearly 200 percent. Sihanoukville International Airport is now directly linked to 27 cities in mainland China. The Chinese boom in *xigang*, or "Westport," as the town is known in Chinese, appears to have started shortly after Xi Jinping's visit to Cambodia in October 2016. "The relationship is very good," a restaurant owner from Hangzhou said. "As a result, many Chinese people have come." In addition to the casinos, many Chinese entrepreneurs have come to set up online gambling operations—part of a billion-dollar industry that allows Chinese citizens to place bets over the internet without traveling to Macao or Las Vegas. In 2018, it was reported that companies from China made up 104 of the 121 firms operating out of the nearby Sihanoukville Special Economic Zone (SEZ).[17] In mid-2019, the provincial authorities revealed that as many as 90 percent of Sihanoukville's businesses were owned by mainland Chinese.[18]

The coastal swell has drawn unemployed Cambodian youth from across the surrounding countryside. Some get jobs cleaning hotel rooms or dealing cards, others working on the construction sites that dot the center of town. On the beach, I met So Pheaktra, a 23-year-old from nearby Kampot, who was training as a casino dealer. She said the job paid $350 per month, more than she could earn in most other jobs. "Everything, including accommodation, is included. It's convenient work," she said.

But the freewheeling casino economy, absent much government oversight, has also been accompanied by a steep rise in drug use, violence, prostitution, and other social problems. Local newspapers are filled with reports of money laundering, online telecoms scams, illegal gambling, and drunk driving. "There is a lot of money coming in, but the Chinese also give our authorities headaches," said Seng Nim, the chief of Commune No. 4, which includes most of Sihanoukville's casinos. When I asked him about specific issues, he reeled off a list: "Beating, hitting, hacking, arguing, shooting, using drugs . . ."

Around town, I noticed Chinese adverts for a brothel calling itself the "Fairy International Leisure Club." Reports have emerged of visitors being detained in hotel rooms and tortured into repaying gambling debts. The Cambodian government's unpreparedness for the speed and extent of the development in Sihanoukville became tragically evident in June 2019, when a half-completed condo building collapsed, killing 28 Cambodian construction workers who were asleep inside. The Chinese owner had undertaken the construction without the required permit, and defied orders to cease work. Five Chinese nationals were later arrested over the collapse.

While much international media coverage has depicted Sihanoukville as a beachside paradise trampled by uncouth Chinese gamblers, the town has long had a sleazy edge. When Italian journalist Tiziano Terzani visited during the UN mission in 1993, he found "bars open until all hours, and a big discotheque where scores of girls flocked from the nearby villages, dressed like dolls and made up like kabuki masks."[19] Later, it became a playground of Russian oligarchs, including the fugitive billionaire Sergei Polonsky, a louche figure who maintained a Bond villain's mansion on Koh Dek Koul, a tiny private island off Sihanoukville's coast. As the Chinese presence began to grow, expats joked that "Sihanoukgrad" was turning into "Xi-anoukville."

As with many things concerning China, the devil was in the scale. People I interviewed said that the Chinese revolution had happened so quickly it set off sharp increases in the cost of everything from housing and petrol to cooking oil, mangoes, and chili peppers. "Before the Chinese came, my rent was $30 per month; now it's $100," said Phat, 52, a woman selling barbecued octopus on O'Chheuteal Beach.

At the same time, many see business drying up, as Chinese visitors predominantly patronize Chinese-owned businesses. Paying for packets of Hongtashan cigarettes and bowls of noodles via WeChat or Alipay, the money effectively never leaves China. Sam Rim, a 63-year-old woman running a fruit stand across the street from the Golden Sands Hotel and Casino, hacked away at a jackfruit and vented: "When the *barang* [Westerners] came we earned a lot. When the Chinese came, they sold a lot of the same things as us, so how can we earn a living? They only buy their own products." Displaced from the center of town by rising rents, locals have begun clearing forest on the outskirts of town—far from schools and most moneymaking opportunities. Since forests have traditionally been seen as the domain of ghosts and other spirits, this has given rise to a bitter local saying: "The Chinese kick out the Cambodians, the Cambodians kick out the ghosts."

Sihanoukville's ugly realities demonstrate the ad hoc nature of Chinese initiatives like the BRI, and the way in which "official" BRI projects, like the SEZ located next to the city's port, can be overwhelmed by private interests—in this case, low-rent gambling concessionaires and organized crime syndicates—that ultimately cut against the strategic goals of the Chinese state. By the time of my visit in 2018, the Chinese presence in Sihanoukville, coupled with land evictions associated with Chinese hydropower dams and real-estate projects elsewhere in the country, had given rise to something rare in Cambodian history: anti-Chinese sentiment.

With nationalists' fears laser-focused on Vietnam, Cambodia has generally been a friendly place for the Chinese, a fact that has been noted by outside observers since the early twentieth century.[20] Indeed, interactions between the two countries date back to China's earliest contacts with Southeast Asia. When Chinese emissary Zhou Daguan made his celebrated journey to the kingdom of Angkor in 1296–7, he was surprised to find settlers from his own country. "Chinese sailors do well by the fact that in this country you can go without clothes. Food is easy to come by, women are easy to get, housing is easy to deal with, it is easy to make do with a few utensils, and it is easy to do trade," Zhou observed, echoing the present. "They often run away here."[21]

Since then, ethnic Chinese have been a continuous feature of Cambodian life. A wave of immigrants arrived following the collapse of the Ming dynasty in the mid-1600s (via what is now southern Vietnam) and another came under the French. Their presence has peppered the Khmer language and diet with Chinese borrowings. Phnom Penh's Duanhua School, founded in 1937, remains the largest Chinese school in Southeast Asia, with more than ten thousand students. High levels of intermarriage and assimilation mean that a huge proportion of Phnom Penh's residents can claim some degree of Chinese descent, as indicated by the ancestral shrines that sit on the floors of many homes and businesses, piled with offerings of fruit, cans of soft drink, and packets of instant noodles. Some Cambodian friends have told me that these traditions are even being adopted by people with no Chinese ancestry whatsoever. "The Khmer are prone to accept Chinese culture," said Ou Virak, the director of Future Forum, a policy institute in Phnom Penh, "because there's an association with success."

Despite a period of harsh persecution in the 1970s and 1980s, Sino-Cambodians remain prominent in business, and now form the key economic props of CPP rule. In a 2007 diplomatic cable from the US embassy profiling Cambodia's "top ten tycoons," five were described as having Chinese ancestry.[22] One notable example is Choeung Sopheap, known commonly as "Grandma Phu," a Mandarin- and Teochew-speaking businesswoman who has used Chinese connections to build her firm Pheapimex into one of the largest conglomerates in Cambodia. (It helps that she is married to a prominent CPP senator.) Each Chinese New Year, hundreds of private security guards and other staff crowd in the street outside Grandma Phu's mansion in Phnom Penh to receive red *angpao* (*hongbao* in Mandarin): Chinese New Year envelopes stuffed with Cambodian riels and US dollars.

However, the recent inflow of Chinese tourists, migrants, and investors—very different in language, manners, and appearance from Cambodia's old Chinese—has begun to strain this traditional amity. As the casinos lit up in Sihanoukville, Cambodian social media was swamped with videos of Chinese drivers roaring through red lights or committing other acts of public nuisance. Before long, the public anger at the Chinese presence threatened to boomerang on Hun Sen's administration. In January 2018, Yun Min, the governor of Preah Sihanouk province, of which Sihanoukville is the capital, wrote a report to the Ministry of the Interior warning of the economic and social effects of the city's Chinese investment boom. The new Chinese arrivals "get drunk, yell, have arguments, and are fighting each other at restaurants and in public places," Yun Min wrote. The presence of so many foreigners "gives opportunity to the Chinese mafia to commit crimes and kidnap Chinese investors due to increased insecurity in the province." Worse still, he cautioned, "some mischievous people" might use Sihanoukville's makeover "to attack and influence the Cambodia–China relationship."[23]

Whether anti-Chinese sentiment will ever rival the reflexive hostility many Cambodians feel toward Vietnam is hard to say. Cambodia has experienced sudden influxes of outsiders before. Ou Virak of the Future Forum drew a comparison with the massive military and civilian contingent that accompanied the UNTAC mission, which brought its own share of troubles, including spiraling inflation and the scourge of HIV/AIDS. "In some strange way, Cambodians were taught to tolerate external people that they're not comfortable with," Virak said. "I'm pretty sure that the Cambodians will learn to live with the Chinese."

In any case, the gathering public backlash soon pushed the Cambodian government to rein in the unbounded Chinese developments in Sihanoukville. In August 2019, Hun Sen announced a ban on online gambling operations, effective January 1, 2020. The ban was introduced at the urging of the Chinese government, which had grown frustrated with how far Phnom Penh had let the situation on the coast deteriorate. As soon as the ban came into force, the city's development was thrown into reverse. Thousands of Chinese nationals left the city, and property prices started to deflate. Whether or not the ban is sustained—and Sihanoukville's long history of evading regulations gives ample grounds for skepticism—it highlights the fact that Phnom Penh and Beijing have a shared interest in curbing the spread of anti-Chinese sentiment among the Cambodian population.

More dangerous, perhaps, is the prospect of Cambodia getting tangled up in the mounting tensions between China and the US. By the time of the 2018 election, Hun Sen's embrace of all things Chinese had begun to attract attention in Washington. Particular concern focused on a Chinese tourism development in Koh Kong province, across the bay from Sihanoukville. Here the Tianjin-based Union Development Group (UDG) had been granted a colossal 36,000-hectare concession that included a fifth of Cambodia's coastline. The firm had grand plans: its five-star Dara Sakor Resort would include power stations, a golf course, water treatment plants, an industrial park, and medical facilities. To provide access, a highway was struck through virgin rainforest.

Most controversially, UDG's plans included a deep-water seaport able to berth bulk carriers and cruise ships, and potentially, Chinese naval vessels. According to a 2017 report published by the Washington-based C4ADS research group, the port would be large enough to house Chinese frigates and destroyers and their crews, or to provide logistical support to nearby warships.[24] Similar questions were asked about a nearby international airport that, some analysts observed, featured runways the same length as the military airfields China had built on three of its artificial islands in the South China Sea, complete with the tight turning bays favored by fighter jet pilots.[25]

The Cambodian government flatly denied that it intended to permit a Chinese military presence on its soil, but the story refused to go away. In July 2019, the *Wall Street Journal* reported that the two countries had signed a secret agreement granting China exclusive access rights to the Ream Naval

Base near Sihanoukville. Quoting unnamed American officials, the report claimed that the agreement would allow China to use the base for 30 years, with automatic renewals every 10 years thereafter. After the publication of the *Journal*'s article, the US State Department expressed concern that a Chinese military presence would threaten the centrality and coherence of ASEAN and "disturb peace and stability in Southeast Asia."[26]

These concerns were fanned by exiled opposition members, including Sam Rainsy, who lobbied Western governments to take a hard line on Hun Sen. He warned of China's "invasion" of Cambodia and the perils of the nation being snared "by massive, opaque debts to China, which it cannot repay."[27] In reality, Cambodia's level of external debt remained moderate, amounting to a manageable 32 percent of GDP in 2016. Even factoring in planned BRI projects, the Washington-based Center for Global Development concluded that Cambodia remained unlikely to be forced into default due to Chinese loans.[28] Nevertheless, as in the past, Rainsy told a simple story that many in Washington and Brussels wanted to hear.

As Hun Sen's crackdown deepened, Western governments ramped up the pressure on Phnom Penh. The European Union threatened to suspend Cambodia's tariff-free access to its markets, the destination for more than a third of Cambodia's exports. US congressmen tabled several bills levying sanctions on senior Cambodian officials. One of them, the Cambodia Accountability and Return on Investment Act of 2019, called for Cambodia to release Kem Sokha, now under house arrest, and dismiss the charges against him. It also demanded that the government "protect its sovereignty from interference" from China. Hun Sen showed no sign of budging. He told Western countries to "stop treating Cambodia as a toy" and announced he was "done taking orders" from foreigners.[29] He also praised Japan, which continued to offer ample infrastructure funding, despite the political conditions inside Cambodia.

To many American observers, Hun Sen's authoritarianism was now indistinguishable from his embrace of China. Both were proof of just how bad he was, and why he needed to go. But Western policy bore some share of the blame for Cambodia's eastward drift. Since the 1990s, the country had been seen as small and strategically unimportant, and therefore a place where human rights and democratic issues could take precedence over Western economic or security interests. From Phnom Penh's perspective, the apparent closeness between Western governments and the Cambodian opposition, and the more lenient treatment given to its rights-abusing neighbors, made Western "democracy promotion" seem awfully close to a policy of regime change. Far from halting Cambodia's move toward China, threats of sanctions only stoked Hun Sen's paranoia and pushed him further down the pariah's path to Beijing. Nevertheless, the Cambodian leader was playing a dangerous game, letting his resentments and fears lead him into a worrying over-reliance on China. As Washington and Beijing settled into a period of protracted tension, Cambodia risked once again being trapped between the pestle and mortar of dueling superpowers.

Although Cambodia presents an extreme case compared to the other Southeast Asian countries, it showcases China's main appeals to the region's governments: its deep pockets and broad adherence to the norms of national sovereignty and "non-interference." This is especially the case for small developing nations, which often fail to command much attention in far-off Western capitals. The Sino-Cambodian relationship also highlights the divergent ways in which ASEAN states see China. What for one is a threatening presence is for another a protective giant from the distant north. For small countries like Cambodia, for which dependency has been an historical norm, choosing the form of one's dependency—one's patron—was one way of exercising agency in a dangerous world. With some notable differences, much the same is also true for Laos, the other small satellite being drawn into close orbit around the red planet.

In mid-2016, the town of Boten in northern Laos was falling apart. On the main drag, weeds rose where bustling shops and restaurants once stood. Old nightclub signs blistered and peeled in the tropical climate. Around town, abandoned multi-story hotels rose into the mist: totems of this small town's rapid rise, and equally sudden fall.

Enfolded by the Chinese border in a landscape of jungle-clad hills, Boten has spent most of its history cut off from the outside world. Even when the border with China was opened in 1993, to reach the town required a bone-rattling two-day drive from the capital Vientiane. One journalist who braved the journey in 1995 described it as a "village of thatched huts and wooden shacks" where traders smuggled second-hand Japanese cars over the border into China.[30]

In 2003, however, change came to Boten, in the form of a Hong Kong-registered company, which signed a deal with the government of Laos to set up a tourism development zone called Boten Golden City. Concrete was poured and colorful buildings rose in the hills. Virtually overnight, the small Lao village became a gambling boomtown, drawing in thousands of visitors a month from across the border in Yunnan. Casinos and gaming rooms, run by mainland Chinese concessionaires, spawned a satellite economy of brothels and nightclubs, and even a cabaret show featuring *kathoey*, transgender performers from Thailand. With the Lao customs office placed a few miles inside Laos to make crossings easier, Boten became a 1,640-hectare entertainment annex, running on Chinese time, Chinese electricity, and Chinese money.

Before long, lurid reports about Boten were surfacing in the Chinese press, foreshadowing those that would later emerge from Sihanoukville. They detailed how casino owners had imprisoned and tortured visitors who racked up massive gambling debts. Chinese officials were sent to Boten to negotiate the release of several "hostages." Shortly afterward, China's Ministry of Foreign Affairs tightened border controls and cut the power supply. Deprived of its lifeline to China, the casinos closed. Boten went into steep decline.

When I visited the town in June 2016, it was home to just a few hundred hardy souls, scraping a living amid the collapsing infrastructure of its gold-rush years. At the Jingland Hotel, formerly the Royal, and once the showcase development of Boten Golden City, most of the 271 rooms were vacant. Tropical damp spread through the upper floors, and the hallways were scattered with translucent insect wings. A jagged hole gaped behind the lobby: the former entrance to a now-demolished gambling annex.

As a gray twilight settled in, orange streetlights caught falling rain, expanses of wet concrete, forlorn empty buildings. Deng Jie, 25, the Chinese owner of a bare-walled restaurant and karaoke bar on a strip of shuttered stores, lamented the lack of passing trade. "I've been here a year, but business isn't great," Deng said. In fact, it was so bad that he was now thinking of selling out and moving back to Mengla, his hometown in southern Yunnan. He added, "I can't keep going on like this."

Deng might not have realized it, but Boten's fortunes were already starting to turn once again. In 2011, investors from Yunnan announced a plan to plow more than $1.5 billion into a new development that they called the Beautiful Boten Specific Economic Zone (BBSEZ). This time, the plans were all about connectivity. Once an isolated backwater, Boten now occupies a strategic position as the border crossing for the Kunming–Bangkok Expressway, completed in 2013, which arrows south from Jinghong through a landscape of crumpled green mountains. It will also be the crossing for a planned $6 billion high-speed railway linking Vientiane to Kunming—the largest infrastructure project in Laos's history.

Boten is "like the door to China," said Vixay Homsombath, a Lao official who sits on the board of the BBSEZ development. Marooned in a mildewed office building near a shuttered duty-free mall, Vixay was happy to discuss the project that occupied most of his waking hours. He predicted that the railway would jolt Boten back to life. "It will create a lot of jobs," he said. A prospectus for the Boten project showed renditions of sleek bullet trains nosing into a modern town bristling with office buildings, apartments, hotels, and duty-free arcades.

The plans have been slow to eventuate, but by the time I visited in 2016 there were some stirrings of recovery amid the decay. Construction had begun on a series of 18-story towers along the highway through town, which was lined with billboards of Xi Jinping shaking hands with Choummaly Sayasone, then president of Laos. Not far away, an old casino was being converted into a jade emporium, its chandeliers aglow as workers in flip-flops hauled cans of paint. Even the *kathoey* cabaret was preparing for a grand reopening. Ai Hanyen, the head of the Vientiane office of Yunnan's Haicheng Group, which is coordinating the BBSEZ development, was full of confidence when we met a few days later in Vientiane. "In ten or twenty years we'll make Boten into a small Hong Kong," he predicted.

Boten's rise, fall, and impending resurrection is indicative of the rapid changes being wrought by Chinese investment in this small, communist-ruled nation of 7 million. Since the early twenty-first century, sleek new roadways have breached the northern mountains that once kept the Chinese empire far away. As Laos has gone from "landlocked" to "land-linked," as the Lao government likes to say, Chinese money has poured over the border, into mining, hydropower dams, massive agricultural plantations, and skyline-altering real-estate developments. This investment has drawn in tens of thousands of workers and "new migrants" from China, whose presence has transformed the face of Vientiane and the northern provinces, and is slowly spreading south.

Not long after my visit to Boten, billboards started appearing across the north of Laos. They were white and blue, inscribed with Chinese characters and lines of curving Lao script. Some featured a futuristic emblem of a high-speed locomotive; others bore slogans like "China–Laos friendship is everlasting" and "The Belt and Road will be built into a road of peace." Within the year, more substantial developments were underway. A concrete rail bridge was extended over the Mekong River outside Luang Prabang, the serene former royal capital. Chinese earth-boring machines set to work beneath the northern mountains. In the dusty flatlands north of Vientiane, concrete pylons marched through an ocher landscape of fallow paddy fields.

"More than any other technical design or social institution," the late historian Tony Judt once wrote, "the railway stands for modernity."[31] And nothing symbolizes China's vision of modernity quite like the technology of high-speed rail, or HSR. Since the construction of its first HSR line ahead of the 2008 Beijing Olympics, China has installed 25,000 kilometers of track, a network projected to expand to 38,000 kilometers by 2025.[32] Since then, the export of HSR technology has become a key pillar of the BRI. HSR lines have been proposed for at least six Southeast Asian countries, and Chinese officials frequently use the bullet train as a metaphor for the benefits of economic partnership with Beijing.

While the Laos–China railway project, which broke ground in December 2016, is not technically a "high-speed" line—passenger services will have a top speed of 160 kilometers per hour, well below that of standard HSR systems—it is nevertheless a striking example of Chinese technical prowess. The standard gauge single-track line will slice through 417 kilometers of rugged terrain from Boten to Vientiane, including 198 kilometers of tunnels and 61 kilometers of bridges.[33] These engineering challenges have done much to contribute to its controversial $6.2 billion price tag, equivalent to around 37 percent of Laos's GDP in 2016—or around $15 million per kilometer.

In its overweening ambition and tremendous cost, the rail project, scheduled for completion in late 2021, encapsulates the promise and peril of China's brash arrival in Laos. On the one hand, Chinese investment could bring prosperity to one of Asia's most impoverished countries; on the other, it could turn Laos into a mere outpost of a new Greater Yunnan, a way-station on China's long march to the sea. In Boten, the town's few remaining Lao residents were undecided. "I'm not sure," said Chanphon, 49, a Lao restaurant owner. "If it just passes through, we don't know if it will be any good for us."

Laos is the quintessential land between. It is landlocked and mountainous, except for a ribbon of rich alluvial terrain running along the Mekong River, which forms most of its border with Thailand. Like Cambodia, it has always found itself pressed between more powerful neighbors: China to the north, Vietnam to the east, and Siam and Burma to the west. The nation that came to fill this negative space was imagined by the French, who created a unified Lao state in the 1890s to act as a buffer between their territorial claims in Vietnam and those of Siam and British Burma. So constructed, Laos was "more a cartographic reality than a social or historical one."[34] Even today, many more ethnic Lao live in Thailand's northeast than live in Laos itself.

Before the arrival of the Europeans, the kingdoms of mainland Southeast Asia existed not as delineated territorial entities, but as blurry constellations of power lacking fixed boundaries. The historian O.W. Wolters described them as *mandalas*. In this system, smaller *mandalas* paid tribute to larger ones by providing them with resources like food and soldiers to fight the region's endemic wars; in return, the larger *mandalas* offered them protection from rival powers. These states existed in a constantly shifting tributary relationship, and "would expand and contract in concertina-like fashion" as the regional balance of power changed.[35] The historian Victor Lieberman referred to them similarly as "solar polities," in which "provincial planets" revolved around a "sun" whose gravitational pull diminished with distance.[36]

Laos's closest pre-modern progenitor was the Buddhist kingdom of Lan Xang, founded by the semi-mythical King Fa Ngum in 1353. Sitting at the crossroads of the region's caravan trade, the "Land of a Million Elephants and the White Parasol" flourished. At its sixteenth-century height, it exercised power over most of Laos's present-day riparian provinces—a period in which its kings constructed the jewels of classical Lao culture, including the golden-spired That Luang stupa in Vientiane, the country's most important Buddhist monument. Thirty-four kings ruled Lan Xang before it divided in the early eighteenth century into three small *mandalas*—the kingdoms of Vientiane, Luang Prabang, and Champassak—that the French eventually patched together and called "Laos." Whereas in Cambodia the French safeguarded a kingdom from the incursions of its neighbors, in Laos, they effectively conjured a new nation into being.

Laos has never quite shed its *mandala* heritage. Despite possessing all the accoutrements of modern nationhood, the country has remained weak and vulnerable to outside encroachment, especially along its porous periphery. At no time was this truer than during the Cold War, when, like Cambodia, Laos was sucked into the war in neighboring Vietnam. During the conflict, Vietnamese communist insurgents roamed the nation's eastern provinces at will, and the US dropped more bombs on the country than it dropped on Germany and Japan combined during World War II. This included an estimated 270 million cluster munitions, around a third of which failed to detonate, leaving the Mekong hinterland scattered with deadly unexploded ordnance (UXO). At the top of Phou Si hill, which rises over the spires and tumbling foliage of Luang Prabang, flowers sprout from rusted rocket cartridges. Nearly 30,000 people have been killed by UXO since the war.[37]

Despite sharing a modern border with China, dense geography meant that the empire's proximity historically weighed less heavily on Laos than it did on neighboring Vietnam, with its inviting mountain passes. Chinese chroniclers claimed Lan Xang as a vassal from the late fourteenth century, but in practice it was a land "secluded at the edge of the sky," as the Yongzheng Emperor put it in 1730, too weak and remote to command much attention from the imperial center.[38] To be sure, the Lao kingdoms engaged in constant trade with China, especially in valuable forest products like ivory, aromatic woods, sticklac, and benzoin. But, as in Cambodia, the main threats to its survival traditionally came from countries closer to hand—from the powerful neighboring kingdoms of what are today Vietnam, Thailand, and Burma.

The Cold War drew China more directly into Lao affairs. After Laos gained its independence in 1954, the new People's Republic threw its support behind the communist Pathet Lao (PL) in what became its "Thirty-Year Struggle" to topple the US-backed Lao constitutional monarchy. Kaysone Phomvihane, the young leader of the PL, first visited China in 1959, and from 1967 until 1976, the children of PL leaders (more than 1,000 in total) were educated at a school in Nanning, the capital of Guangxi province. Later, China sent in construction crews to build roads through the northern mountains, down which flowed Chinese economic and military support that helped secure the Lao communist victory of December 1975. In terms of material aid and political influence, however, China always came a distant second to Vietnam. Throughout the war, Vietnamese communist troops fought side by side with their Lao counterparts, and most of the PL's senior cadres, including Kaysone, received military and ideological training in North Vietnam.

The "special relationship" persisted beyond the PL victory. When relations between Vietnam and China soured in the late 1970s, the new communist government led by the Lao People's Revolutionary Party (LPRP) dutifully mirrored Hanoi's anti-Chinese line, purging suspected pro-Beijing elements from its senior leadership. But the break with China was never total. The two sides quietly reopened talks, and in October 1989, Kaysone paid a state visit to Beijing, the first foreign leader to do so following the Tiananmen crackdown. As relations warmed, senior Chinese officials started showing up in Vientiane, often with large business delegations in tow. In the 2000s, Beijing opened the "soft power" spigot. LPRP cadres started being invited to attend trainings and seminars in China, and the children of high-ranking Lao officials were granted scholarships for postgraduate degrees, which were awarded in suspiciously short order. Beijing bankrolled the construction of the Lao National Cultural Hall in Vientiane, where the LPRP celebrates important anniversaries, and even splashed out for a musical fountain in front of the Patuxai, Vientiane's imposing *arc de triomphe*.

The flowering of Lao–Chinese relations took place against a backdrop of increasing economic integration. At the end of the Cold War, the Lao communist leadership saw an opportunity to escape their country's landlocked geography and become "land-linked," capitalizing on its position at the crossroads of the Southeast Asian subcontinent. In 1993, the Boten border crossing with China was opened to trade; 15 years later, in March 2008, Laos unveiled Route 3, a 197-kilometer section of the Kunming–Bangkok Expressway linking Xishuangbanna to Thailand, via northern Laos. Previously, traveling overland from China to northern Thailand required negotiating snaking dirt roads that turned into impassable channels of mud during the monsoons. The new roadway slashed travel times to a matter of hours.

The result was a sharp increase in trade, migration, and investment from China. Cash-strapped Laos encouraged Chinese investment by offering "land for capital," leveraging access to its bounteous natural resources. Chinese firms started exploiting Laos's mineral deposits, and state-owned companies offered support for dozens of hydropower dam projects, furthering Vientiane's goal of turning itself into the "battery of Southeast Asia." SEZs mushroomed along the borders, including the casino enclaves in Boten and the Golden Triangle, where the government farmed out Lao sovereignty to foreign companies (often Chinese) in order to fire up development in remote regions of the country. Parts of the north were soon carpeted with plantations of bananas, watermelons, corn, and cassava—produce destined mostly for the Chinese market.

Plantation contract farming saw a marked spike in 2012, the year that China halted banana imports from the Philippines in retaliation for its standoff over the Scarborough Shoal (see Chapter 10).

As in Cambodia, China's rapid progress in Laos has been aided by a symbiotic relationship to those in power. While hammer-and-sickle party flags still flutter above Lao government offices, Marxist–Leninist doctrines have been shunted aside in favor of older patterns of patron–client relations. With the party needing money to grease the gears of patronage and sustain the economic growth necessary to shore up communist rule, China stands apart both for the depth of its pockets and the appeal of its "no-strings" approach to governance and human rights issues. Unlike the US, which did not restore normal trading relations with Laos until 2009, Beijing has been ready to offer financing without conditions, helping ensure that economic liberalization does nothing to threaten the party's position as the "leading nucleus" (as the country's constitution puts it) of the Lao state.

By 2013, China's economic gravity had begun to draw Laos out of its tight Vietnamese orbit. That year the cumulative value of Chinese investments in Laos topped $5 billion, exceeding for the first time that of its traditional patron.[39] Where once Vietnam was the "older brother," one Asian diplomat explained, "now things have changed. China is the older brother, and Vietnam is maybe the second brother."

The inflow of Chinese money has profoundly altered the physical landscape of northern Laos. Throughout the hills, quiet roads are now dotted with Chinese-run restaurants, hotels, vehicle repair shops, and furniture stores. In northern towns like Udomxai and Luang Namtha, Chinese nationals make up as much as a fifth of the population. The pull of Chinese migration is so strong, Brian Eyler writes, that new arrivals "need not learn to speak Lao. Upon arrival in northern Laos, Chinese immigrants can interact in a closed-loop system with their compatriots."[40]

The first of the "new migrants" to Laos arrived in the 1990s as workers or technicians on Chinese infrastructure projects, and then decided to stay. As connections with China improved, they were joined by a flow of traders and entrepreneurs, many pressed south by the increasing economic competition at home. As Ding Guojiang, the head of the China Chamber of Commerce in Laos, explained to me one morning at his office in Vientiane, "In China, there are so many companies doing the same thing, so you can't make much money."

Ding put the number of *xin yimin* in Laos at around 100,000, although lax regulation and porous borders mean that the real number is almost certainly higher; some estimates run as high as 300,000.[41]

Historically, few Han Chinese came to Laos. The distances were great; the terrain was unforgiving; the economic temptations were small. By 1960, just 30,000 ethnic Chinese were present there, less than a tenth the number in Cambodia.[42] Aside from a small number of Yunnanese Muslims who entered Laos overland and settled in the northern provinces, the Chinese immigrants who ended up in the country were mostly those who had "failed to prosper in Thailand, Vietnam, or Cambodia."[43] As in many parts of Southeast Asia, they nevertheless occupied a dominant position in the economy. "You saw them everywhere," one American writer noted of Vientiane's Chinese in the 1950s, "clopping along on clogs at the market, or smoking outside their small shops and restaurants which never seemed to close."[44] As in Vietnam, the communist takeover in 1975 was followed by the persecution of the Lao-Chinese, who bore a double stigma: Chinese *and* capitalist. A significant number fled the country, especially those with the closest business ties to the old monarchical regime. By 1997, as few as ten thousand remained.[45]

It was around this time that Ding Guojiang first visited the country. A soft-spoken, fastidious native of Zhejiang province on China's prosperous east coast, Ding recalled a time when there were "very few" Chinese in Vientiane, and many of the city's streets were still unpaved. Ding started buying cheap property around the city, and, in 2007, opened the Sanjiang Market in the western suburbs. Sanjiang—its name means "three rivers" in Mandarin—has since become the center of the city's burgeoning new Chinese community.

Entering the Sanjiang district is like stepping into a large town in Yunnan or Guangxi. Mandarin is the lingua franca. The market is packed with goods from mainland China, everything from clothing and karaoke machines to children's toys and *baijiu* firewater. Travel agents hawk bus tickets to Jinghong and Kunming. The Chinese presence is so strong that signs around the market remind visitors, "When in Laos make your payment in kip." Ding has since invested more than $100 million in Sanjiang. With upward of 1,000 shops employing 5,000 people, it is reputed to be the largest Chinese market in Asia outside of China. "It's like a small world. You can find everything here," he said. When the main market building was destroyed by fire in mid-2017, Ding opened a new multi-story mall complex on an adjoining plot. Business is as good as ever.

Chinese businesspeople with whom I spoke in Vientiane told me that Laos's current economic condition resembled their own two or three decades ago, and expressed their desire to help raise it up to China's level. "I really liked the people around here," said the owner of a Chinese restaurant group, "and wanted my generation to do something to help them." The flip side of this is a paternalistic perception of the Lao people as too relaxed to meet the demands of a modern market economy. In 1999, a Chinese report on Laos's economy noted that a "sense of urgency is wanting; the signature phrase of many [Lao] is, 'no hurry, take it easy.'" Or as Ding put it to me, "Lao people are pretty lazy." Views like this offer striking echoes of common Chinese perceptions of the ethnic minority peoples of Yunnan and other parts of southern China.[46] As in China, they diagnose a problem—economic "backwardness"—and prescribe a remedy: state-led modernization.

Popular anti-Chinese sentiment has generally been muted in Laos, a reflection both of the extremely repressive nature of LPRP rule, and the fact that the main threats to the country have historically come from elsewhere. But, as in Cambodia, things are starting to change. Many Chinese projects have come at a significant cost for local communities. "Land for capital" schemes like dams and SEZs have evicted thousands from their land. Chinese monoculture plantations involving the intensive use of pesticides have polluted water sources and impacted the health of thousands of workers, many from upland minority groups. When new roads were built into China, one of the first things that rolled over the border were trucks carrying illegally cut rosewood, destined to be carved into furniture and other luxury tchotchkes for the Chinese market. In Luang Prabang, many local people express fears that the Chinese tourist boom may permanently alter the town's otherworldly charm, and even imperil its UNESCO World Heritage Status. Luang Prabang is now linked by air to a number of destinations in southern China; its new international airport was built and financed by a Chinese contractor, and the town will soon be a major stop on the Laos–China railway.

Criticisms of China are now commonly heard in Vientiane. In 2008, many locals voiced discontent about a planned Chinese real-estate project in the city's That Luang marshlands. Granted to a Suzhou-based firm in exchange for building a 25,000-seat national stadium for the 2009 Southeast Asian Games, the concession was intended to turn 20 square kilometers of rice fields and peri-urban wetlands into "a modern city."[47] Rumors quickly spread that the project would become a gated preserve for thousands of Chinese immigrants—a question of added sensitivity given the project's close proximity to the golden That Luang stupa, a key symbol of Lao sovereignty. In the end, the That Luang Marsh development faltered and construction slowed to a crawl. Today, its rows of hollow concrete towers stand empty, looking out onto an artificial lake and a half-completed marina.

Similar concerns have crystallized around the Laos–China railway project. First proposed by Beijing in 2006, the enterprise was subject to nearly a decade of delays, as the two governments grappled with the terms of the financing, and whether such a costly venture really made sense for a country as poor as Laos. In December 2015, a deal was finally brokered: China agreed to pay for 70 percent of the project, issuing Laos a $480 million loan to help pay the remaining 30 percent, with five potash mines put up as collateral. Soon afterward, the blue and white billboards began appearing along the planned rail route.

The moving force behind the railway was Deputy Prime Minister Somsavat Lengsavad, believed to be Beijing's point man on the LPRP Politburo. A relatively urbane figure, Somsavad stood apart from the party's cloistered gray collective. Born in Luang Prabang in 1945 to parents of Hainanese ancestry, he joined the Lao revolution as a teenager, and served for three years in the ranks before joining the Communist Party. As a protégé of Kaysone, he quickly clambered up the leadership ladder. By 1991, he had gained a position on the party's Central Committee. Two years later, he was named foreign minister, an appointment symbolizing the revival of Laos's Chinese community after the hiatus of the 1980s.

Fluent in Mandarin, Somsavad became one of the most vocal advocates of Chinese investment in Laos. He met frequently with senior officials from Beijing and was closely involved in brokering a range of large projects, including Zhao Wei's Golden Triangle empire, the National Stadium in Vientiane, and the That Luang Marsh project. He oversaw the party's special Laos–China Cooperation Committee, established in 1996, and chaired it from 2007 to 2015. From its inception, he was also the main advocate of the railway to China, championing its benefits within the Politburo and helping usher the project to fruition.

From the beginning, however, there have been major questions about the railway's utility for Laos. The line forms just one small section of the Pan-Asia railway, a planned network that will stretch from Kunming to Singapore. The idea of a trans-Asian rail project dates back to 1993, and, in some senses, to the high imperial era of the late nineteenth century, when European powers dreamt of linking China by rail with the colonial possessions to its south. The project has since been absorbed into the BRI. For Beijing the benefits of the scheme are obvious: the rail line will connect China's underdeveloped south-west to the markets, ports, and industrial zones of Thailand and Malaysia, as well as giving it much-needed access to the sea. It will also strengthen China's economic hold over the northern provinces of Laos.

For Laos the equation is less straightforward. Proponents argue that the railway will help fulfill the government's "land-linked" goal, freeing it from the prison of its geography. As Ai Hanyen, the Chinese businessman leading the development of Boten, put it when we met for dinner, "Everything will change after the Laos–China train: transport, trade, everything." Others worry that the railway might one day be used by China for military purposes, maybe even to annex parts of northern Laos, while offering the country few economic benefits in return. Kasit Piromya, a former Thai foreign minister, was more blunt. He said, Laos "is going to be a transit country, passing through, a bus station on the way."

Given its cost and scale, the project has prompted comparisons with Sri Lanka's Hambantota port, signed over to a Chinese firm in 2017 after the government failed to meet debt repayments. Indeed, according to the Washington-based Center for Global Development, Laos was the one Southeast Asian country risking significant debt distress as a result of BRI loans from China, in large part because of the railway scheme.[48] There are also worries about the social impact of the project, which has already brought in an estimated 50,000 Chinese workers—many of whom, like their predecessors, could well decide to stay.

In January 2016, two weeks after the railway agreement was signed, Somsavad Lengsavad was removed from the Politburo, and immediately went into seclusion in a monastery in Luang Prabang. Over the years, the 72-year-old had leveraged his Chinese connections to become one of Laos's richest men; some interpreted his religious turn as an attempt to assuage a guilty conscience (though he has since returned to the business fold).[49] Outside the country, the removal of Somsavad and a wider series of LPRP leadership changes—which also saw the replacement of president and party chief Choummaly Sayasone with Bounnhang Vorachith, who underwent military and political training in Vietnam—was widely interpreted as marking a swing away from China, toward more pro-Hanoi elements in the party.

However, the situation was probably more complex. One source with close links to the Lao leadership described Somsavad's removal as the outcome of internal party politicking. Another person said that he had angered his Politburo colleagues with his tendency to go it alone in brokering investment deals. Still, the leadership change was a reminder that China was far from the only outside influence in Laos. Unlike in Cambodia, pulled into an international orbit by the UNTAC mission in the early 1990s, Vietnam retained much of its former clout in Laos, nourished by the umbilical relationship between the two countries' communist parties. Ian Baird, a professor of geography at the University of Wisconsin–Madison who specializes in Laos, told me that despite China's widening footprint, Vietnam retains considerable political influence. Most of Laos's current leadership studied or trained in Vietnam, and some harbor acrid memories of China's support for anti-government ethnic Hmong rebels during the 1980s. While China has excelled with its red-carpet diplomacy at the national level, Vietnam retains robust ties with provincial and district authorities, where a lot of power resides in the *mandala*-like Lao communist system. "The Lao are taking their money," he said of the Chinese, "but the level of political influence—you don't see it."

Shortly after taking office in 2016, the new government under Prime Minister Thongloun Sisoulith announced a campaign against corruption and party extravagance. Thongloun promised to rein in "land for capital" deals, and issued a ban on the establishment of new banana plantations, citing their impact on workers' health. Laos's new leader also moved to diversify his nation's foreign policy away from Vietnam and China by building better relationships with its ASEAN neighbors, Japan, and the US.

Against the backdrop of the LPRP leadership changes and the Obama administration's "rebalance" to Asia, US–Laos relations began to improve after decades of mutual suspicion. In 2009, the administration removed Laos from a Cold War-era blacklist that imposed a ban on Lao companies receiving financing from the US Export–Import Bank. In September 2016, President

Obama traveled to Vientiane for that year's ASEAN Summit, becoming the first sitting American president to visit the country. He was also the first to formally acknowledge the impact of the millions of cluster munitions dropped on Laos by US warplanes between 1964 and 1973. Announcing a $90 million tranche of funding for UXO removal, Obama declared, "I believe that the United States has a moral obligation to help Laos heal."[50] The year before, his Deputy National Security Advisor Ben Rhodes had told an audience in Washington that there was "a sense of potential" in the relationship with Laos "for the first time in a long time."[51]

All this indicated that, far from being a passive subject of outside encroachments, Laos's communist collective was seeking to maintain an active balance of dependencies between China, Vietnam, the US, and other powers. Tellingly, the Chinese railway project gained final Politburo approval only after Laos signed off on a separate Vietnamese railway link across the southern Lao panhandle: a Vietnamese railway to counterbalance the Chinese one.[52] During its 2016 chairmanship of ASEAN, Laos also avoided taking sides in the South China Sea disputes, balancing delicately between the positions of Hanoi and Beijing.

Nevertheless, Laos today remains very much open to Chinese investment. Having long jettisoned its Marxist–Leninist ideology for a more appealing form of crony capitalism, the 2016 leadership changes were more about curbing the worst excesses of corruption and mismanagement than they were about China's encroaching influence per se. "The party leaders in Laos are mostly interested in getting cash without strings, be it in the form of grants or zero interest loans or big brown paper bags," said the source with close ties to the Lao leadership. "They don't really care about the provenance as long as they can pocket a large sum for their families and another large chunk for the party coffers." Deep pockets, geographic proximity, and the sheer scale of China's economy—some 700 times the size of Laos's—ensure that Beijing's footprint will remain considerable over the long term.

Laos's future may come to resemble its past. As it becomes more tightly integrated into the Southeast Asian subcontinent, the country is reverting to its origins as an amalgam of weak *mandala* kingdoms. Tethered to southern China by road, river, and rail connections, the old northern kingdom of Luang Prabang has already fallen under a strong Chinese influence. Meanwhile, Vietnamese influence will continue to predominate in the southern half of the country, alongside that of Thailand, which is bound to Laos by strong cultural and religious affinities.

For a perspective on Laos's recent history, I arranged to meet in Luang Prabang with Prince Nithakhong Somsanith, a scion of the nation's former royal family, abolished by the Pathet Lao government in 1975. We met in the high-ceilinged library annex of a high-end luxury hotel, where he was now employed as a cultural consultant. Reflecting on his country's turbulent history, the prince predicted that, after centuries of foreign intrusions, Laos and its people would find a way to navigate China's ascent. "We saw the eagle come from the US during the Vietnam War, we had the bear from Moscow, we had the dragon from Vietnam, we had the white elephant from Siam, and we also had the French colonials," Prince Nithakhong said, as the ceiling fans turned above. "Adaptation is our politics."

5

THAILAND
BAMBOO IN THE WIND

One of Thailand's holiest Buddhist sites is Wat Phra That Doi Suthep, a temple perched on a mountainside overlooking the northern city of Chiang Mai. According to local legend, the temple was built in 1383 to house a precious relic: a fragment of bone belonging to the Buddha. To determine where the precious shard should be housed, the king of the Lanna Kingdom, which then ruled over northern Thailand, resorted to an elaborate expedient: he ordered the relic strapped to the back of a sacred white elephant, which was then released into the wilderness. When the beast expired from exhaustion, workers were brought in and a temple was erected on the site.

Today, Wat Phra That Doi Suthep commands soaring views over Chiang Mai and the surrounding countryside, and is thronged with pilgrims on Buddhist festival days. Its cultural significance and impressive vistas have also made it a must-see tourist attraction. Each day hundreds of visitors take taxis or tour buses up the winding road from Chiang Mai. From there, a 309-step staircase with banisters of bejeweled nagas leads up to the temple, where visitors can watch aircraft soar off the tarmac at Chiang Mai International Airport and walk around the temple's axis, a 24-meter-high gold-plated *chedi* (stupa) topped by a five-tiered umbrella.

In February 2015, a short video circulated on Facebook, showing a tourist—apparently Asian—kicking one of the iron bells arrayed along the temple walls. The disrespectful act set off a storm of indignation on social media. There were calls for the culprit to be hunted down and deported—even arrested. The Suthep kicker was never identified, but few Thai netizens had any doubt about his nationality. For the past few years, social media had buzzed with complaints about the rude behavior of tourists from China, visiting Thailand in greater numbers than ever before. Facebook ran hot with stories of Chinese mainlanders spitting, littering, cutting into lines, or allowing their children to relieve themselves in public pools. In March 2015, after witnessing Chinese tourists cutting an airport queue in South Korea, a Thai model named Duangjai Phichitamphon filmed a video rant, in which she complained of the Chinese, "Didn't their parents teach them any manners?"[1]

In less than a decade, China has revolutionized Thailand's tourism industry. Facilitated by rising incomes, cheap direct flights, and increased overland connectivity, Chinese arrivals to the country rocketed from 2.7 million in 2012 to 7.9 million in 2015 to more than 10 million in 2018.[2] Today nearly one in three international arrivals are from mainland China. The impact has been especially noticeable in Chiang Mai, a cosmopolitan northern city of 1 million famous for its temperate climate, buzzing night-markets, and the delicacy *khao soi*, a rich noodle soup made with coconut milk, curry paste, and tamarind.

In mid-2018, I moved to Chiang Mai with my wife and son and was immediately struck by the changes. Within the crumbling walls of the Old City, erected by the Lanna kings to guard against Burmese attacks, simplified Mandarin had become the mandatory third language on restaurant menus, alongside Thai and English. Chinese tourists now made up a large proportion of the visitors clambering up Doi Suthep or taking cruises on the Ping River. On Nimmanhaemin Road, a fashionable strip of cafés, expat eateries, and souvenir boutiques, they now outnumbered the *farang* (Westerners), and the windows of shops were filled with Chinese signs advertising local products— freeze-dried durian, natural latex pillows, tiger balm—popular with mainland visitors. Later, I heard that it was possible to hire a driver in Chiang Mai, without knowledge of either Thai or English.

Many attributed the boom to the Chinese road comedy *Lost in Thailand*, which, upon its release in late 2012, shattered box-office records in China. Partially shot on location in Chiang Mai, the film sent thousands of Chinese sightseers flocking to the city to retrace the steps of its comedic duo: the scientist Xu Lang and his sidekick Wang Bao, a Beijing scallion-pancake seller. Organized tours ferried visitors around the various locations from the film, from Buddhist wats to Muay Thai boxing arenas to the verdant campus of Chiang Mai University, which was so overrun by camera-toting mainlanders that it eventually started charging admission. "The landscape has completely changed," said Dr. Chayan Vaddhanaphuti, the director of the university's Regional Center for Social Science and Sustainable Development.

China's tourism clout forms an important, though under-appreciated, part of its emergence as a global power. As Elizabeth Becker writes in *Overbooked: The Exploding Business of Travel and Tourism*, Deng Xiaoping gave a series of lectures in late 1978 and early 1979 in which he emphasized the importance of tourism in China's economic opening. Deng not only argued that tourism was a good potential source of revenue; it was also essential to China's attempt to rejoin the world and become respected again as a major power.[3] Although Deng's initial focus was on attracting foreigners to China, it wasn't long before the opposite was happening—and in mind-boggling numbers. Since 2014, Chinese citizens have been the world's largest group of international travelers, taking 145 million international trips in 2017. That figure is projected to jump to more than 400 million per year by 2030, according to the China Outbound Tourism Research Institute.[4]

The upsurge in Chinese tourism has sent economic ripples across Southeast Asia. China is now the number one source of foreign arrivals to the region: in 2017, around 28 million Chinese citizens traveled to the ten ASEAN countries (up from 2.2 million in 2000), most of them arriving on the 2,700-odd weekly flights linking the two regions.[5] In addition to Thailand, mainland Chinese are the top visitors to Vietnam, Cambodia, and Singapore, and recently surpassed Australians to become the number one nationality visiting the Indonesian island of Bali. As the Thai experience suggests, the adjustment hasn't always been smooth. From Singapore to Sihanoukville to Seminyak, Chinese tourists have become the subject of many a sharp complaint. In 2013, in a bid to improve the bad reputation of Chinese tourists abroad, China's National Tourism Administration released a 64-page *Guidebook for Civilized Tourism*. The guidebook warned travelers, among other things, to refrain from picking their noses in public, to keep their nose-hair neatly trimmed, and not to steal life-jackets from airplanes.

These official efforts have apparently had little purchase in Chiang Mai, where locals voluntarily vent about the "noisy" and disrespectful habits of Chinese tour groups. But the criticisms of Chinese tourists in Thailand seem slightly overblown, especially when compared to the drunken, loutish behavior of Western and other Asian tourists in the seedy red-light districts of Bangkok and Pattaya. Nusara Thaitawat, a former journalist who owns a restaurant and hotel in Chiang Mai's Old City, told me that while the initial surge of Chinese visitors had overwhelmed the local tourist industry, their bad behavior had been greatly exaggerated by the Thai press. She put most of it down to technology: the fact that the Chinese boom, unlike past scandals involving Japanese or European tourists, has coincided with the advent of smartphone cameras and Facebook, which makes it easier to record and share incidents online. "I think that their timing is right to go viral," she said.

The negative reaction also reflects deeper concerns about the economic structure of Chinese tourism in Thailand: in particular, the scourge of so-called "zero-dollar" tours. Organized by proxy companies based in Thailand, these operations attract visitors from mainland China with cut-price travel packages promising free food and accommodation. Once in Thailand, the hapless tour-goers are pressured into buying goods and services at exorbitant rates from Chinese-run operations, at the expense of Thai hotel- and restaurant-owners.

While it is hard to know the current extent of "zero-dollar" scams—the Thai government announced a crackdown on the practice in 2016, shutting down three tour companies and impounding more than 2,000 tour buses—Nusara said she has noticed increasing numbers of independent Chinese travelers in Chiang Mai, who seem to be growing more attuned to local cultural sensitivities. "A lot of the Chinese genuinely like this place," she said.

Whatever the views of locals, the reality is that the Thai tourist industry has become highly dependent on a continued flow of visitors from China. When mainland arrivals dropped off in late 2018, after 35 Chinese tourists died in a boat sinking off the southern resort island of Phuket, local operators panicked. In response, the Thai government introduced tax breaks, free flights, and visa waivers in a bid to pump up the arrival numbers. Abhisit Vejjajiva, Thailand's prime minister from 2008 to 2011, described it as a classic case of can't live with them, can't live without them. "There are times when there are tensions between Chinese tourists and locals, and then there's a strong reaction when tourists disappear," he said. "They say, we can't go on, we need them back."

In a broader sense, the reaction to Thailand's Chinese tourism boom is one more reflection of the mixed feelings that have accompanied China's re-emergence as the dominant foreign presence in Southeast Asia. In just a few decades, the great dragon to the north has evolved from a hostile adversary of Thailand to a vital economic and strategic partner, threatening to displace its traditional ally, the United States. In 2007, China surpassed the US and became the country's second-largest trade partner; in 2014, it displaced Japan to become number one. Over the same period, it vaulted from being an insignificant investor to Thailand's second-largest source of foreign investment.[6]

As elsewhere in Southeast Asia, the past foreshadows the present. The kingdoms of old Siam sat within the Sinocentric Asian order, tethered to the imperial center by reciprocal ties of tribute and trade. Now, after an intermission of a century and a half in which the Western powers reigned supreme, China is once again a power that cannot be ignored. "They are an 800-pound gorilla," Panitan Wattanayagorn, a security advisor to the Thai government, said of the Chinese. "When they move, the earth shakes."

On the evening of May 22, 2014, Thailand's television stations cut abruptly to a feed of the army chief, General Prayuth Chan-ocha, flanked by a line of military officers. Reading from a prepared statement, he announced to the nation that the Royal Thai Army had taken control of the country. The takeover, Prayuth said, was necessary to end an ongoing political crisis and "reform the political structure, the economy, and the society" of the country. The new junta called itself the National Council for Peace and Order (NCPO); it immediately suspended most of the constitution, banned gatherings of more than five people, and imposed a curfew. Television stations blared patriotic anthems.

As Thailand's coup d'état unfolded, I watched from a one-star hotel in Rangoon, where I was reporting on Burma's halting transition out of military rule. It was hard not to note the ironic reversal in the two countries' political situations. For as long as anyone could remember, junta-run Burma had occupied a special category of international opprobrium, alongside Iran and North Korea. Now, right at the moment that it appeared to be making a startling move toward democracy and international acceptance, modern, Westernized Thailand was going the other way. Looks, of course, could be deceiving: the 2014 coup was the twelfth since the end of Thailand's absolute monarchy in 1932 (the nineteenth if you included failed attempts). Such interventions had become so commonplace that Thai society registered little outward disturbance. The bloodless takeover left the economy humming along like normal. Tourists kept flocking to the beaches of Phuket and Koh Samui, and factories kept churning out digital cameras, cars, and hard-drives for American and Japanese firms.

The 2014 coup capped a spiraling political crisis that had consumed Thai politics for more than a decade. This pitted the supporters of the exiled former prime minister Thaksin Shinawatra against the old-school political elite clustered around the nation's military and royal establishment. A former police lieutenant colonel who had amassed a huge fortune thanks to a near-monopolistic telecoms concession, Thaksin had won a landslide election in 2001, on a platform promising universal health care and easy access to micro-loans. His political success quickly came to be seen as a threat to the wealth and power of Thailand's urban, royalist elites, who employed increasingly anti-democratic tactics to undermine Thaksin's power. A coup in 2006 chased Thaksin from office and into a luxurious exile in Dubai, but failed to curtail his wild popularity, especially in parts of rural Thailand. After his removal from power, Thaksin's supporters poured into the streets wearing red T-shirts. They helped his proxies to victory in national elections in 2007, and then again in 2011, when Yingluck Shinawatra, Thaksin's younger sister, was elected prime minister.

Unable to prevail at the ballot box, Thaksin's opponents also turned to the street, dressed in royal yellow. They established the misnamed People's Democratic Reform Committee (PDRC), backed by elements in the military and the Thai business elite, which sought the permanent extirpation of Thaksin and his allies from political life. In late 2013, the PDRC launched a wave of anti-government rallies that forced Yingluck to dissolve parliament. It then boycotted the resulting snap election, which was declared invalid. With Thai politics snarled in an acrimonious gridlock, and some "yellow shirts" agitating openly for a coup, the military intervened to end the political impasse—one that it had a significant hand in creating. Looming above this crisis was the failing health of 86-year-old King Bhumibol Adulyadej, then in such poor health that he hardly ever appeared in public.[7]

The 2014 coup gave way to an unusually protracted spell of military rule. Instead of following the usual routine of appointing a pliable civilian government and then returning to barracks, the promised return to democratic rule was repeatedly postponed. In its first year in power, the NCPO detained more than a thousand politicians, academics, and journalists, and forced them to sign promises to cease political activity. It also presided over a spike in prosecutions under Thailand's harsh *lèse-majesté* laws. Designed to forestall criticisms of the monarchy, these were now employed to quash criticisms of military rule. The flip side to the crackdown was a widely ridiculed "happiness" campaign, promoted by public concerts featuring svelte young women in camouflage miniskirts. The campaign's centerpiece was a pop song titled "Returning Happiness to Thailand," supposedly written by Prayuth himself, which defended the military's seizure of power and promised to "bring back the love."

The military's seizure of power immediately soured Thailand's relationship with its long-standing ally, the United States. As it had done in 2006, the US responded to the coup by suspending millions of dollars of security assistance—a requirement under American law. This time Washington's response went further. High-level military engagements, including training exercises, were canceled or scaled back. Scot Marciel, a Deputy Assistant Secretary for East Asian and Pacific Affairs, warned that the post-coup repression made it impossible for the US to proceed with "business as usual," a message that was echoed by diplomatic personnel inside the country.[8]

Thailand's conservative elite reacted strongly to the American criticisms. When US Ambassador Glyn Davies expressed concerns about the misuse of lèse-majesté laws, Prayuth said that his opinion was "biased and not impartial," and could "lead to the deterioration of our long-term friendship."[9] Op-ed columnists denounced the US for its apparent double-standards in tacitly supporting a recent coup in Egypt while condemning Thailand's—to say nothing of Washington's active support for military rule in Thailand during the Cold War. Songsuda Yodmani, the Harvard-educated daughter of Thanom Kittikachorn, the US-backed military strongman who ruled Thailand from 1963 to 1973, declared, "We are not a colony of the United States. We will defend the pride and dignity of the Thai nation."[10]

The American reaction to the coup contrasted starkly with the approach taken by Beijing. Chinese officials made it clear that they regarded Thailand's political problems as "an internal issue" and said they "would not interfere."[11] Three days after the coup, the Global Times expressed its oblique support for the new junta, asserting that "Western-style democracy" had led Thailand astray.[12] In December 2014, Premier Li Keqiang jetted into Bangkok, the first high-level foreign official to visit Thailand since the army's takeover. A few days later, Prime Minister Prayuth (as he now styled himself) made the return trip to meet with Xi Jinping. He praised the Belt and Road Initiative (BRI), and the two governments began discussing a range of ambitious infrastructure projects. In 2015, when China and Thailand marked 40 years of diplomatic relations, official statements spoke of a "close and cordial relationship, based on the solid foundation and deep bonds of affinity and cultural ties rooted since time immemorial."[13] The same year, the junta announced that it planned to buy three Chinese Yuan-class submarines, at a cost of just over $1 billion.

As elsewhere in Southeast Asia, the Chinese emphasis on sovereignty and "non-interference" was warmly received. It sent the message that China's friendship with Thailand was unconditional: that it transcended the rolling crises of Thai domestic politics. Unlike the US and other Western governments, China "doesn't preach," Korn Chatikavanij, a former finance minister, said. "It's entirely consistent and practical, and that makes them in many ways easier to deal with."

Of all the nations in mainland Southeast Asia, Thailand's tilt toward China is potentially the most significant. The nation sits at the geographic heart of Southeast Asia, extending like an orchid's stem south to the warm waters of the Andaman Sea and the Gulf of Thailand. Its $500 billion economy is the largest on the mainland, and the second largest in ASEAN. Most crucially, Thailand is a US treaty ally and an anchor of American influence in Southeast Asia. With diplomatic ties dating back to 1818, it represents Washington's oldest relationship in Asia—and one of its closest.

The special relationship between Thailand and the US dates back to the end of World War II, when American officials intervened to prevent British demands for reparations and Thai territory in retribution for Thailand's wartime collaboration with imperial Japan. Over the subsequent decade, the two nations were pushed together by the gathering tension of the Cold War. The US allied with Thai conservatives to fashion the country's monarchy into a sturdy bulwark against communist expansion in Southeast Asia, and in 1954, the two nations became formal treaty allies. At the height of the Vietnam War, nearly 50,000 US servicemen and women were stationed on Thai soil and the country was covered with a grid of American military bases, from which bombing raids were flown into Vietnam, Laos, and Cambodia. The Thai army sent officers to the US for training and units to fight in the jungles of Vietnam. The US presence, in tandem with large injections of Japanese capital, brought breakneck growth and modernization of a distinctly American hue. Young Thais swilled Pepsi, listened to rock music, and went in their thousands to study in the US. To a generation of Thais, Washington was *maha mitr*: the "great friend."

The American security presence also offered Thailand a measure of protection from communist China, then a menacing presence to the north. By the 1960s, Beijing was openly backing the Communist Party of Thailand (CPT), which launched an armed struggle against the Bangkok government in 1965, and supported it with propaganda beamed into Thailand from a radio transmitter in Yunnan. However, Thailand's view of China began to shift toward the end of the decade, as the US began its staged withdrawal from Indochina. At the time, Thai leaders feared that the American military drawdown would leave Thailand exposed to retribution from the Vietnamese communists. "We have let the US forces use our country to bomb Hanoi," two-time prime minister Seni Pramoj warned in 1969. "When the Americans go away, they won't take that little bit of history with them."[14] The Thai response was to open back-channel talks with the Chinese government—even as the latter maintained its robust support to the CPT rebels in the northern hills.

In pursuing an opening with China, Thailand closely followed the lead of US President Richard Nixon, who made his milestone visit to Beijing in February 1972. Before Nixon's trip, "we were anti-China, we were fighting in the Vietnam War," said Kobsak Chutikul, a retired Thai diplomat involved in the normalization talks of the early 1970s. Afterward, "everyone had to move, everyone had to shift." In May 1975, a few weeks after the fall of Saigon to the Vietnamese communists, Prime Minister Kukrit Pramoj flew to Beijing, where he met an ailing Chairman Mao and signed an agreement formally establishing diplomatic relations.

The new relationship between Beijing and Bangkok was cemented when Vietnam invaded Cambodia to overthrow the Khmer Rouge regime in late 1978, bringing Vietnamese army divisions to Thailand's eastern border. In exchange for China cutting off its support to the CPT, the Thai government agreed to join Beijing and Washington in opposing Vietnam's occupation of Cambodia. Deprived of Chinese backing, and induced to surrender by Thai government amnesties, the CPT withered. At the same time, the Thai military helped funnel Chinese aid and military supplies to Cambodia's deposed Khmer Rouge, with diplomatic cover from the US and its fellow ASEAN member-states. In return, it profited handsomely from the trade of gems and timber from the Khmer Rouge strongholds dotted along the Thai–Cambodian border.

Cooperation on the Cambodia question established a firm basis for the improvement of ties between Thailand and China after the end of the

Cold War. The next breakthrough moment was the Asian financial crash of 1997, which began in Thailand and had particularly dire impacts on the country's economy. The baht shed half its value and the Crown Property Bureau, the body that manages the royal family's massive wealth, suffered grievous losses. Hundreds of firms collapsed, and millions were cast out of work. In return for its assistance, the International Monetary Fund (IMF) demanded that Thailand sharply deflate its economy. The US government insisted that Thailand comply with the harsh IMF measures but declined to contribute to the bailout fund. When asked why Washington had recently supported a similar bailout for Mexico but not for its Southeast Asian ally, a senior Treasury Department official explained, "Thailand is not on our border."[15]

China immediately offered Thailand its support, which included a $1 billion injection into the IMF's relief fund. As elsewhere in Southeast Asia, China's response to the crisis contrasted sharply with Washington's apparent unconcern —a foreshadowing of the discontent that would emerge in the aftermath of the 2014 coup. "We got nothing from the US," a former Foreign Ministry official told me. Beijing's actions, on the other hand, "contributed to the belief that in terms of help, China will always be forthcoming."

The Thai leader who did the most to accelerate relations with China was Thaksin Shinawatra, who took office following a landslide election victory in 2001. Thaksin harnessed the resentment that many people felt in the after-math of the economic crisis: that the financial "cure" pushed on Thailand by the IMF had been worse than the disease. Declaring that he would not be "a poodle to Western interests," he pledged to build up the economy and restore Thailand's self-confidence and international image.[16]

A descendant of Hakka immigrants from Guangdong province, Thaksin immediately deepened economic, political, and security ties with China. He chose the country for his first foreign visit after taking office, and made seven more trips there during his five years in power.[17] Describing Thailand as Beijing's "closest" and "most sincere" friend, he began joint Thai–Chinese military exercises and started purchasing Chinese arms.[18] Thaksin negotiated a free-trade agreement with China, which came into effect in 2003; during his time in office, trade with China quadrupled. Like his political opponents, Thaksin also appreciated the Chinese government's non-judgmental form of engagement, especially when he came under Western pressure in 2003 during his "war on drugs," a blood-soaked campaign that saw thousands of suspected drug-pushers shot by police. As Thaksin later attested of the Chinese, "Whoever becomes the government, they do business with them. They are like entrepreneurs, they do business, they don't do politics."[19]

Beijing's regional charm offensive—its battery of "soft power" exchanges with academics, journalists, Chinese friendship associations, and ethnic Chinese clan organizations—was particularly marked in Thailand. The nation would eventually host 15 Confucius Institutes, the most of any Southeast Asian country.[20] The Chinese Communist Party (CCP) established "party-to-party" ties with both sides of Thai politics, and the government made special efforts to cultivate Thailand's royal family, especially King Bhumibol's daughter, Princess Sirindhorn. A fluent Mandarin-speaker, the princess had been visiting China for more than twenty years, during which time she had reportedly set foot in every Chinese province. In 2004, the Chinese People's Association for Friendship with Foreign Countries awarded her the title of "friendship ambassador."[21]

This "soft power" onslaught coincided with the period of US distraction that followed the terrorist attacks of 9/11. As American attention was drawn toward the Middle East, the old "Thailand hands" that had once served as American ambassadors—who boasted an intimate familiarity with the country and deep contacts there—were replaced by less experienced officers on shorter rotations, right at the moment when China was upping the quality of its diplomatic engagement with Thailand.[22] The former US consulate in the southern Thai city of Songkhla, closed in 1993, later housed a Chinese consulate: a transfer, one American official lamented, that was "symbolic of our deteriorated public image in southern Thailand."[23]

The American relationship remained important for Thailand, but it increasingly seemed to be coasting on a fading nostalgia for the golden era of the 1950s and 1960s. The Obama administration's "rebalance" to Asia, designed to redress the neglect of the Bush years, was widely seen as amounting to words rather than action, even before it foundered on the 2014 coup. For Thai policymakers, it was hard to avoid the conclusion that Thailand was simply not as important to Washington as was once the case. In 2018, The Asia Foundation published a report on the state of Thai–US relations, based on in-depth interviews with 50 prominent Thais and Americans. It depicted a relationship in a state of drift. One of the factors underlying the state of US–Thai relations, it concluded, was "a decline in the number and depth of personal relationships." While older Thais still had a deep reservoir of goodwill toward the US, younger generations were more ambivalent. This was reflected in the declining number of Thais studying at American universities, which fell from 11,187 in 2000–1 to just 6,893 in 2016–17. In contrast, there were by then around 27,000 Thai students enrolled at Chinese universities, in addition to some 37,000 Chinese nationals studying in Thailand.[24]

Meanwhile, a desire for good ties with China was one of the few things that united Thailand's fractious political elite. Despite Thaksin's removal from power in 2006, relations with China trended upward through the Thaksinite, "yellow," and military governments that dominoed through the subsequent decade. It has helped that Thailand has no direct interests in the South China Sea, and that successive Thai governments have adopted a studied neutrality on the disputes. Benjamin Zawacki writes that an accommodative position toward Beijing has "become an institutional, cultural, *national* consensus. It not only transcends Thailand's domestic 'Yellow v. Red' divide, but is a rare contract between them."[25] On diplomatic occasions, it has become almost customary for Thai and Chinese officials to describe their nations' relations using family metaphors: as "brothers" or "blood-bonded relatives."

While such rhetoric is standard diplomatic etiquette, it is not entirely misplaced: the ethnic Tai peoples trace their origins to what is now southern China. Starting in the first century CE, the Tai migrated south in successive waves, displaced by the southward expansion of the Han Chinese. When the first Tai states coalesced in the sparsely populated Chao Phraya River valley from the fourteenth century onward, they naturally looked to the north. By the 1400s, the kingdom of Ayutthaya, which the Chinese referred to as *xian*, or *xian-lo*, had emerged as the dominant center. It offered regular tribute to China to secure access to the lucrative Chinese junk trade, which at times provided up to a third of its revenues.[26] After an invading Burmese army sacked Ayutthaya in 1767, a new Siamese kingdom reconstituted itself and was able to return quickly to regional prominence largely due to its economic connections to China, which remained strong until the rise of the European empires in the nineteenth century.

In addition to playing a momentous role in Siam's overseas trade, Chinese also played an important role in its domestic economy. As in other parts of Southeast Asia, the China trade brought to Siam large numbers of merchants, sailors, and adventurers from southern China. Predominantly male, many married local women and assimilated over time into Thai society, to the point that they had become "as much a part of Thai national life as the growing of rice."[27] Some settlers traded rice and distilled liquor; others managed the king's junk fleet, ran his treasury, and even represented Siam on tributary missions to China. Chinese culture left a deep imprint on Siamese society. Nineteenth-century Siamese nobles draped themselves in Cantonese silks, and read translations of the Chinese literary classic, *The Romance of the Three Kingdoms.*[28] Bangkok's temples were tiled with shards of Qing dynasty porcelain used as ballast in Chinese junks. The Thai language absorbed hundreds of loanwords from Teochew and Hokkien.[29]

China's influence extended to the Royal Palace: King Rama I, who established the present Chakri dynasty in 1782, was a descendant of Teochew immigrants from Guangdong, and well into the nineteenth century, the Chakri monarchs continued to use the red seal of the Chinese Zheng clan for important state documents.[30] Larger waves of Chinese immigration took place in the late nineteenth and early twentieth centuries, and by the eve of World War I, key industries were in the hands of the various Chinese dialect groups. The Teochews were the preponderant dialect group in Bangkok, controlling most of the pawn shops, rice mills, and Chinese medicine shops. Sawmilling for the timber trade was run predominantly by Hainanese, while leatherwork and tailoring was mostly a Hakka enterprise. Nearly 90 percent of rubber exporters were Hokkien.[31]

The rise of Thai nationalism in the twentieth century complicated matters for the ethnic Chinese, casting them as outsiders for the first time. In 1910, when Chinese workers and merchants launched a massive general strike to protest new taxes imposed by King Vajiravudh (Rama VI), the monarch published a rambling pseudonymous pamphlet titled "the Jews of the East." Heavily influenced by the anti-Semitic tropes then dominant in Europe, Vajiravudh described the Chinese as possessing a "racial consciousness" that cast them as inherently disloyal and un-Thai.[32] Fearing their infection by ideas from China (whether nationalist or communist), Siamese governments imposed a range of restrictions on the Chinese. These fears intensified with the establishment of the People's Republic of China (PRC) in 1949. While retaining their dominant perch in business, ethnic Chinese were pushed to take Thai names, and were barred from the armed forces. Chinese schools were shuttered, as were some Chinese-language newspapers; as late as the 1980s, the only place in Thailand where it was possible to study Mandarin legally was in the northern villages settled by remnants of the old Kuomintang army.[33]

One effect of the improving ties with China in the 1980s was to resolve the political contradiction between "Chinese" and "Thai," and allow Sino-Thais once again to express pride in their heritage. When restrictions on education were lifted, Mandarin language classes proliferated. Bangkok's Chinatown held boisterous celebrations for the Chinese New Year. Sniffing out votes, politicians began to advertise their Chinese origins openly, and a trend developed of Sino-Thais making pilgrimages to their ancestral homes in southern China. In 2005, Thaksin visited his mother's resting place in Guangdong province, during which he described Thais and Chinese as "relatives" hailing "from one family."[34] Today, ethnic Chinese account for around 10 percent of Thailand's population, and a majority of the population of Bangkok, though the distinction between Thai and Chinese has become blurred.[35] "The assimilation of the Chinese in Thailand is very, very deep," said Jeffery Sng, a former Singaporean diplomat and co-author of a recent book on the history of the Sino-Thai community. "In fact, I often joke that you cannot find a 100 percent Thai today."

Just about everyone who is prominent in business and politics today is a *lukjin*—"a child of China." In addition to Thaksin, almost every Thai prime minister in the past fifty years has had Chinese ancestry, as did 78 percent of those elected to the Thai parliament in 2011.[36] Sino-Thais are thus equally distributed on both sides of Thailand's intra-elite divide. Sondhi Limthongkul, the leader of the anti-Thaksin yellow shirts and the grandson of a Hainanese immigrant, once assailed Thaksin by claiming that Sondhi and his followers were "better Chinese" than Thaksin was.[37] Unlike in nations such as Indonesia (see Chapter 9), Thai nationalism has shed most of its anti-Chinese attributes, partly due to the role of Buddhism in encouraging assimilation.

As in old Siam, ethnic Chinese Thais play prominent roles in the economic relationship between Thailand and China. The most obvious example is the Charoen Pokphand Group, a Sino-Thai agribusiness conglomerate headed by the ethnic Chinese businessman Dhanin Chearavanont. Established in 1921 as a Bangkok seed shop, CP Group enjoys the distinction of being the first foreign firm to invest in China after "reform and opening," when it established a feed subsidiary in the Shenzhen economic trade zone in 1979. CP Group continued to invest heavily in the Chinese market and, by 1997, was reportedly the only foreign company with investments in every Chinese province.[38] Sarasin Viraphol, a former academic and Foreign Ministry official who now serves as a vice president for CP, told me that cultural and historical ties created a "special environment" for the firm to advance its interests in China. As another executive explained to the *Far Eastern Economic Review* in 1996, "They don't see us as a Thai company, but as a Chinese company."[39] CP Group was just the first of many Sino-Thai firms to leverage their Chinese connections to cut business deals on the mainland.

As in Cambodia and Laos, economic connections have encouraged a flow of Chinese tourists, expats, investors, and students to follow in the footsteps of past generations of emigrants. Bangkok's new Chinatown in Huai Khwang boasts growing numbers of grocery stores, confectionery shops, beauty salons, and Yunnanese restaurants. Chiang Mai also has a bustling community of expatriates and small-business owners. Most are drawn to Thailand for the same reasons as their Western counterparts: its natural beauty, toothsome cuisine, and the lure of economic opportunity. "It's easy; it's very close; it's cheap," said Wang Yunmei, a thirty-something Anhui native who teaches marketing at Assumption University in Bangkok. Wang fell in love with Thailand on a holiday in 2013, and then chose it as a destination to undertake a PhD in philosophy and religion. She then decided to stay. "We have an impression that the Thai people are very friendly, *sabai sabai* [happy], that kind of attitude," she said. "We enjoy this slow lifestyle, because back in China everything is so fast, extremely fast."

Another transplant I met was Dai Qing, a Chinese journalist and environmental activist, who relocated to Chiang Mai permanently after visiting with friends in 2016. The 78-year-old, who became well-known in the West during the Chinese campaign against the Three Gorges Dam in the 1980s, now lives in a house set amid green rice paddies outside the city—a marked contrast to her smog-choked hometown of Beijing. "In China, everybody knows the air is not fresh, the water is not clean, and the food, and the medicine . . . not to talk of the political situation, and the blocking of the internet, the firewall!" she said. "I made the decision immediately, almost."

In addition to helping business, cultural ties have also helped soften the anxieties provoked by China's rising economic and military power. "When we receive European and American delegations, they will come up with this question about the 'China threat," said former prime minister Abhisit, a fifth-generation descendant of Hokkien immigrants. "For most of us it doesn't resonate, partly because Thai people have so much affinity to Chinese people. The diplomatic relationship goes back just over forty years, but this affinity goes back a lot longer."

Yet there is more to Thailand's move toward China than cultural affinities. It is also consistent with a Thai strategic culture that has managed for centuries to maintain a careful balance between rival outside forces, recalibrating its foreign alignments in response to shifting power relations. According to an old Siamese saying, the country's foreign policy resembled "bamboo in the wind": firmly rooted, yet "flexible enough to bend whichever way the wind blows in order to survive."[40] In 1855, Siam became the first Asian state to repudiate its tributary relationship with the Chinese empire, exiting the Sinocentric world order and embracing the Western system of sovereign, bounded nation-states. This agile shift, which involved the ceding of peripheral territories to the British and French, was a key reason why Siam, alone among Southeast Asian nations, avoided colonization by the West.

This diplomatic legacy also explains Thailand's frictionless transition from its opportunistic wartime alliance with imperial Japan to its profitable postwar alignment with the US, as well as its rapid normalization with China following the American withdrawal from Indochina. As "the region's most astute judges of pecking orders and power balances and its least remorseful bandwagoners," the veteran American diplomat Chas Freeman has argued, it is no surprise that the Thais have now sought a more proactive balance between China and the US.[41] Indeed, the metaphor of bamboo swaying in the wind underplays how conscious and strategic these shifts have often been.

At the same time, however, Thailand's tradition of strategic balancing limits how far it will go in embracing China. While sharing Laos and Cambodia's historically accommodative view of Chinese power, this diplomatic tradition offers a "set of security antibodies that mitigates Thailand's drift into a vassal state relationship with China."[42] The country's relative economic strength also gives Thai policymakers more scope for balancing its relationship with China with robust ties to the US and other regional powers like Japan and India. Contrary to its smaller neighbors, Thailand has the leverage to set the terms of its engagement with China, and avoid being drawn into a narrow orbital dependence.

On a steamy morning in April 2017, three small boats with outboard motors set out into the strong current of the Mekong River in the far north of Thailand. Flying red Chinese flags that snapped in the breeze, the vessels carried engineers and surveyors employed by Second Harbor Consultants, a subsidiary of the state-owned behemoth China Communications Construction Company. In late 2016, Prime Minister Prayuth's cabinet had given its approval for Second Harbor to begin surveying a 97-kilometer stretch of the river that forms the meandering border with Laos. The purpose of the survey was to draw up plans to remove a stretch of islets, rapids, and reefs that formed a bottleneck for commercial shipping. Similar sorts of natural obstacles had foiled French plans to turn the Mekong into a trade route to China in the 1860s, and from the perspective of Chinese planners, continued to inhibit the realization of the river's full economic potential.

The Mekong blasting plans dated back to 2000, when China, Thailand, Laos, and Burma signed an agreement to open the waterway to increased commercial navigation. Between 2000 and 2002, Chinese work teams cleared most of the major obstructions in the river between Guanlei in southern Yunnan and Chiang Saen in northern Thailand, opening up a thriving trade. But the Thai government suspended the planned clearance further downstream in 2003, concerned about possible alterations to its riverine border with Laos. Even now, the stretch of the Mekong between Yunnan and Thailand remains devilishly tricky to navigate. Natural hazards restrict it to vessels smaller than 250 tons, and when water levels drop during the annual dry season, commercial river traffic frequently grinds to a halt.

If implemented, the modifications would deepen and lengthen the Mekong navigation channel, effectively transforming the middle stretch of Southeast Asia's great river into a 650-kilometer cargo highway running from Yunnan to the former Lao royal capital of Luang Prabang. On paper, this initiative involves all four upper Mekong countries, but as Pattana Sittisombat, president of the Committee for the Economic Quadrangle in the northern Thai city of Chiang Rai, put it, "the main activity came from the China side."

Unsurprisingly, the blasting project has provoked strong opposition from local conservationists and villages situated along the river. These groups are particularly worried by plans to dynamite the Khon Pi Long rapids, a 1.6-kilometer stretch of rocks, cataracts, and submerged shoals lying between Thailand and a remote part of northern Laos. The rapids sit on one of the most beautiful stretches of the Mekong, on the northern edge of a great semi-circular bend that arcs north and west from the town of Chiang Khong. In late 2018, I hired a motorbike and drove up to Khon Pi Long, taking a well-surfaced road through a landscape of rolling verdant hills. For long stretches, the road hugged the riverbank, the walls of bamboo and banana trees giving way onto vistas of swirling brown water and half-submerged rocks. In Thai, Khon Pi Long means "where the ghost lost its way"—a reference, it is said, to the countless locals claimed over the decades by the river's undertow. According to conservationists, its string of sandbars and deep, swirling channels provide a sanctuary for numerous species of birds and fish, and support thousands of people living in the vicinity.

"Blasting the rapids is very dangerous. It can kill the Mekong River," said Niwat Roykaew, the head of the Rak Chiang Khong Conservation Group. A rake-thin former teacher with a wispy gray ponytail, Niwat is a legendary figure on this stretch of the Mekong, where most people refer to him respectfully as Khru Tee: "teacher Tee." His organization—its name means "Love Chiang Khong"—has led the fight against the channel clearance since the early 2000s, when he fought against the initial phase of blasting, at one stage forcibly boarding Chinese survey vessels in a bid to disrupt their work.

I met Khru Tee at his Mekong School, established three years ago to educate local schoolchildren about the heritage and ecology of the "mother of rivers." The schoolhouse is a two-story teak house in Chiang Khong, engulfed in a thicket of foliag, which commands views over the Mekong into Laos. Khru Tee said that for many local residents, the Mekong has an almost spiritual significance: it "lives in their hearts, their souls." From this verdant perch the stream glided by under the morning sun, ageless and seemingly unperturbed. But Khru Tee said that construction of upstream Chinese dams had produced significant changes in the river's flow, which veered between flash floods and record-low water levels.

The Chinese plan to dynamite Khon Pi Long and dredge sections of the river will only make things worse, affecting the spawning of many important fish species and undercutting local livelihoods still further. Khru Tee said that clearing the shoals and rapids would be akin to "taking the heart out of the

Mekong." When Second Harbor began its surveys in 2017, Khru Tee and his comrades mobilized, unfurling a large white banner on the bank near Khon Pi Long, reading "Mekong Not For Sale."

Before I took my leave of Khru Tee, I asked him about a small statue sitting at the back of the garden, looped with strings of beads and plastic flowers. He told me that it was a depiction of Bulaheng, a guardian spirit who is said to protect the mother of rivers from evil spirits and disruptive forces from the outside. The statue had large black eyes that stared straight ahead. One hand was clenched by its side, the other held out in front as if to say "stop."

Were it to proceed, the Chinese-led blasting scheme would magnify a river trade that has already brought significant changes to northern Thailand. Over the past 15 years, annual cargo volumes between Thai and Chinese river ports have boomed, aided by the signing of the China–ASEAN Free Trade Agreement of 2003—particularly a special "Early Harvest program" between Thailand and China that removed tariffs on a long list of agricultural products. Most of the Chinese boats dock in Chiang Saen, a drowsy river town 10 kilometers south of the Golden Triangle confluence, where an expanded port opened in 2011 to handle the increased traffic. After leaving Yunnan's Guanlei port in the morning, cargo boats typically arrive here at dusk. The goods are then loaded onto trucks and transported south, reaching Bangkok's Talat Thai wholesale market at dawn. As Nataphon Rajatasilpin, the port's manager, explained, "To do things by river is much cheaper than by road—ten times cheaper." In less than 24 hours, southern China's agricultural exports move from Yunnan to the markets of the Thai capital.

Down at the docks in Chiang Saen, a Chinese river boat was moored, with a sea-green hull and spotlights mounted on the bridge: the common pigeon of the Mekong trade. The vessel was weather-beaten and pitted with rust. A faded registration hinted that it originated in Simao, a town in southern Yunnan. In a cabin onboard a lone umbrella hung on the wall next to a colorful poster of Chairman Mao and China's communist pantheon. A group of Thai and Burmese stevedores wearing T-shirts and flip-flops loitered about in a sliver of shade next to the vessel, where signs in five languages warned against littering or the dumping of engine oil. They awaited the arrival of the day's load: an Isuzu truck full of Thai rice, bound for the Chinese market.

Together with the goods that flow in via the Bangkok–Kunming Expressway, which crosses into Thailand via a bridge over the Mekong south of Chiang

Khong, the overland trade with China has altered consumer habits across the country. Apples, a luxury product once imported from the US, are now Chinese, cheap, and widely available. The same is true of cut flowers, formerly imported from the Netherlands, now freighted in from Kunming. Across northern Thailand I heard people complain that Chinese garlic had edged out the smaller, more flavorful local varieties. Evidence of the new China trade can be seen along the riverside in Chiang Saen, where market stalls are piled with brightly colored boxes of Chinese apples and persimmons, alongside packets of jasmine tea, sesame brittle, soy sauce, dried squid, and salted plums—all shipped south on Chinese cargo boats.

These new trade and transport links have built on the connections that have long existed between northern Thailand and southern China. Yunnan is home to an ethnic Tai minority that speaks a language akin to modern Thai and worships at Thai-style Buddhist wats. Likewise, Yunnanese traders have for centuries hawked their wares in northern Thailand, and Chiang Mai is still home to a thriving *jinhaw* (Chinese Muslim) community. Elsewhere in the north are villages peopled by the descendants of the Kuomintang troops that fled into Burma in 1949, and were later offered Thai citizenship in exchange for helping to combat communist insurgents. Outside Chiang Khong sits a quiet Kuomintang graveyard where departed soldiers reside in elaborate tombs hand-painted with peonies and flaming phoenixes. These new, supercharged silk roads function as a reminder of China's proximity: as the crow flies, the city of Chiang Rai is closer to Kunming than to Bangkok.

Yet it remains unclear how much northern Thailand will benefit from any future expansion of the river trade. So far, given China's size and expertise in river transport, the overall impact has been vastly asymmetric. "There are no barges that are operated by Thais. It's all Chinese," said Ruth Banomyong, a logistics expert based at Bangkok's Thammasat University. (Part of the reason is China's long experience in inland river transport.) The Mekong trade has thus widened Thailand's already large trade deficit with China. Residents in Chiang Saen told me that the river commerce had created jobs for porters and dock workers, but that most of the cargo otherwise was trucked straight out to the highway, bypassing the town. When I asked Khru Tee whether the local economy would benefit from the increased flow of goods downriver, he was incredulous. "When you blast, what will the benefit be?" he said. "Everything will pass, everything will pass to Luang Prabang."

In March 2019, after months of protests, the Chinese government formally shelved its Mekong blasting plans, a recognition—at least for now—of the deleterious effects on local communities. But Beijing's ambitions for the Mekong pale in comparison to what could potentially be the largest and most disruptive Chinese-led infrastructure project in Southeast Asia. In late 2018, Prime Minister Prayuth ordered a national planning agency to begin researching the feasibility of striking a canal through the Isthmus of Kra, the narrow stem of southern Thailand that separates the Gulf of Thailand from the Andaman Sea. The project would be a mammoth undertaking, requiring the excavation of a 135-kilometer channel deep enough for the passage of container ships and oil tankers. While plans for a Kra Canal have existed in some form for more than two centuries, Chinese resources and willpower have resurrected hopes that it might one day become a reality.

The idea of the Kra Canal was first conceived during the reign of King Rama I in the late 1700s, as a means of defending Siam against Burmese attacks. Later, it sparked the interest of European imperialists. Returning from a mission to Siam in 1855, Sir John Bowring, the British governor of Hong Kong, wrote that a canal through the collar of Kra "would be next in importance to those which have been proposed to cross the Isthmus of Darien, in America, and that of Suez, in Egypt." He predicted that it would shorten the trip from India to Eastern Asia "not by days, but by weeks."[43] Plans for the canal have been mooted frequently in more recent times without ever amounting to anything. The Americans conducted a feasibility study for the project in 1972 before abandoning it. By one count, more than 25 such studies have been commissioned—the latest in 2005 under Thaksin's government—but none has advanced beyond the earliest stages.[44]

To learn more about the Kra Canal and its potential impact on Thailand, I went to speak with one of its most persistent cheerleaders. Pakdee Tanapura, an owl-like septuagenarian with tufts of white hair above each ear, has been lobbying for the project since the 1970s, shortly after graduating with a political science degree from the Sorbonne in Paris. Since then the Bangkok businessman has been engaged in a quixotic quest to realize the project. He has written books, organized conferences—one in 1983 featured a keynote address from the controversial US political hustler and eight-time presidential nominee Lyndon LaRouche—and lobbied tirelessly in his capacity as an advisor to the Thai Canal Association for Study and Development.

At his office in the Latphrao district of Bangkok, where he owns a large printing company, Pakdee clicked through a PowerPoint presentation laying out the case for the project. He argued that rising traffic and persistent piracy in the Straits of Malacca makes a Kra Canal not only logical, but inevitable. "The Kra will represent the shortest route between the Indian and Pacific Oceans," he said. One slide displayed statistics from the Malaysia Maritime Institute, pointing out that the Straits of Malacca have a passage limit of 122,600 vessels per year—a figure estimated to be reached by 2030 at the latest. Then came a map of Asia covered in swooping lines and arrows, suggestive of unimpeded flows of trade. Pakdee claimed that the canal would create jobs for 3 million people in southern Thailand, and raise the living standards of 7 million more; it would give Thailand a source of income for generations. "Infrastructure stock lasts hundreds of years," he said. "It is better than oil."

Previous plans for the canal have been stymied not just by its daunting scale, but also its disruptive regional implications. By providing a cheaper alternative to the busy Straits of Malacca, the Kra Canal would radically redraw the economic and strategic map of Southeast Asia, with consequences that are difficult to foresee. In the 1960s, Singapore's Prime Minister Lee Kuan Yew told a senior Thai diplomat that the prospect of a Kra Canal gave him nightmares, given its potential to undercut Singapore's main asset: its position at the crossroads of Asia's maritime trade routes.[45] Unsurprisingly, this is also what makes the project attractive to Chinese policymakers. By creating a new direct route between the Indian Ocean and the South China Sea, the Kra Canal would ameliorate one of Beijing's chief strategic vulnerabilities: its paralyzing reliance on the Malacca Straits. In October 2018, China's ambassador to Thailand raised the prospect of a Kra Canal being funded under the BRI scheme, leading Prayuth to order fresh research into the project.

Kra Canal boosters hope that China's substantial financial resources and engineering prowess can succeed where past attempts have failed. "They said they can do it in three years," said Pakdee, who also serves on the board of the Thai–Chinese Culture and Economy Association, an organization with close ties to Beijing. The walls of Pakdee's office were covered with artists' renditions of the canal produced by Chinese firms, which presented sci-fi visions of industrial zones and islands of excavated earth mushrooming from jade-green oceans. A map showed the Kra Canal fitting seamlessly into the BRI.

Despite Pakdee's grand vision, most Thai policymakers are leery of the Kra Canal project. The first barrier to credibility is that it would create a physical division between the majority of Thailand and the country's fractious south, where a Muslim separatist insurgency has simmered for decades. In the words of Kasit Piromya, a former foreign minister, "It will split the country." The second barrier is the bottom line. While the cost of the canal would be comparable to Panama or Suez, its potential benefits for Thailand—in terms of time and money saved—would be much smaller.

Thai diffidence about the Kra Canal shows that despite the nation's growing economic ties with China, the political and security establishment remains willing and able to push back against anything perceived to compromise Thai sovereignty. The arch-royalists in the upper echelons of the military remember China's support for communist insurgents during the Cold War, and retain a keen awareness of the 1.4 billion Chinese located just a few hours' drive from Thailand's northern border. When China pushed the countries of the Golden Triangle to accept Chinese-led security patrols down the Mekong River following the murders of 13 Chinese sailors in 2011, Thailand was the one country that refused to allow Chinese boats to enter its territory. As a result, Chinese Mekong patrol boats are forced to turn around at the Golden Triangle, just before reaching Thai waters.

Similar considerations may also explain the slow progress on a proposed Chinese high-speed rail project, running from Bangkok to the city of Nong Khai, which sits across the Mekong River from the Lao capital Vientiane. The 873-kilometer line is designed to link Thailand's east coast ports and industrial zones to Kunming, via the line currently tunneling its way across northern Laos. The Thai government has agreed to the project on several occasions, only to let construction deadlines lapse, due to various disagreements over financing, labor, design, and land rights along the proposed track.

The link was originally conceived by the Thai government as part of an intra-ASEAN railway project, but was sucked into the orbit of the BRI after the 2014 coup, when the Prayuth government found it harder to attract funding from Western countries. By signing the initial Memorandum of Understanding (MoU) for the $9.9 billion project in December 2014, the junta bolstered its international credibility; Prayuth even declared that he would use special powers granted under Article 44 of the Thai constitution to circumvent various technicalities and expedite construction.

While the Chinese government saw the MoU as an official green light, progress on the project dragged. In December 2017, Prayuth broke ground on a first phase of the rail line, a 250-kilometer link connecting Bangkok to the northeastern Thai city of Nakhon Ratchasima. But by late 2018, construction had yet to extend beyond a 2-kilometer stretch of track on the outskirts of Bangkok. According to a report in *Asia Times*, the Chinese government was so frustrated by the slow progress that its officials lobbied for the removal of Transport Minister Arkhom Termpittayapaisith, a technocrat whose finicky insistence on implementing the necessary regulations was contributing to the project's delays.[46] Ruth Banomyong of Thammasat University said that the Chinese seemed confused by the fact that, in Thailand, "when the leader says something, no one really follows." He added, "What they don't realize is that in Thailand the bureaucracy dominates everything."

As with the Chinese railway project in Laos, many people question the necessity of the Sino-Thai railway project. Thailand already has a single-track line running from Bangkok to Nong Khai, and is currently adding a second, undercutting the economic rationale of the Chinese project. One analyst calculated that to recoup the costs of the investment, the new rail line would have to run a full train roughly every 5 to 9 minutes on a 12-hour daily schedule for 20 years.[47] In a confidential report, the government itself recognized that the cost of the train would outweigh the economic benefits.

Whether or not the project eventuates, the nettlesome rail negotiations demonstrate once again the limits of China's influence in Thailand. While Thai and Chinese officials speak of each other in family terms, it is more a relationship of equals: Thailand is unlikely to follow Cambodia into a dutiful orbit around Beijing. On the economic front, China's heft is still offset by that of Japan, which has dominated foreign investment in Thailand since the 1980s. Between 1993 and 1996, a new Japanese factory opened in Thailand every three days,[48] and Japan remains the country's top source of foreign investment. In cultural terms, too, Thailand retains close affinities to the West. The country's elites may grumble about the liberal admonitions of the US and other Western governments, but few things occupy them more than wangling their children admission to Harvard, Yale, or Oxford.

Much the same pertains to Thailand's security relationships. As John Blaxland and Gregory Raymond of the Australian National University have argued, despite a spate of recent defense procurements from Beijing, the Thai military's use of the English language and American military doctrines both continue "to favor the US alliance rather than China."[49] In extensive surveys of the Thai political and security establishment, Blaxland and Raymond found that while the prominence of Sino-Thais in politics and business had done much to promote trade with and investment from China, it had had no appreciable impact on political and security links. Similarly, they discovered that on the whole, Sino-Thai government and defense personnel did not view China any more positively than Thais without Chinese ancestry.[50]

Sure enough, US–Thai relations began to rebound under the Trump administration, which downgraded the promotion of liberal values in favor of a more transactional form of engagement. In October 2017, Prayuth was invited to the White House, where Trump enthused of Thailand, "It's a great country to trade with." The Pentagon stepped up its relations with the Thai military. In February 2018, the US sent more than 6,000 troops to the Cobra Gold military exercise in Thailand, the largest contingent since the 2014 coup. Two months later, Thai Defense Minister Prawit Wongsuwon visited Washington. Obama's "rebalance" had finally come to Thailand—in the guise of Donald Trump. Given these security developments, Gregory Raymond predicted that 2018 might end up being seen as the "high-water mark" of Chinese influence before Thailand balanced back toward the US.[51]

Thailand's improving ties with Washington demonstrated how a cultivated flexibility and ambivalence could act as a reliable bulwark of Thai sovereignty. Chulacheeb Chinwanno, a professor and expert on Thai–Chinese relations at Thammasat University, said that Prayuth's turn toward China was designed "to show to the Americans that we still have friends, that we don't have to rely on you." He added, "and we can see that the Americans have already started to change their position."

On March 24, 2019, Thailand held elections that ended five years of military rule and nominally returned the country to civilian government. The process was tightly constrained. Prayuth maintained his hold on power, but only thanks to the torturing of electoral rules, some last-second redistricting, and a 2017 constitution drafted by the NCPO that allowed the military to appoint all 250 members of the Senate. In June, Prayuth was sworn into office, promising "love, unity, and compassion." From Hong Kong, Thaksin declared the election rigged, describing it as "a terrible, and sad, moment for my country."[52] There were grounds for thinking that a large swathe of the Thai population agreed with him. Far from marking a genuine return to democratic rule, the election cemented the military's dominant role in Thai politics.

The advent of a new "elected" government gave the US the pretext it needed to promote renewed investment and closer diplomatic engagement with Thailand. Yet Bangkok's relations with Washington and Beijing remained in a state of flux. At the same time as Thailand's tradition of agile diplomacy placed limits on Chinese influence, the country's troubled political realities augured future strains with the West. The 2019 election showed that five years of military rule justified as a means to "solve" Thailand's political crisis had merely perpetuated it. It thus ensured that the structural causes of Thailand's authoritarian drift—the unmet political aspirations of a large segment of the Thai population, and the elite counter-reaction that these popular demands provoked—would persist for the foreseeable future. Caught between two increasingly adversarial powers, the only future certainty was that Thailand would continue its muddling progress through the new century, leaning this way and that as the regional winds grew stronger.

6

BURMA
AMONG THE CACTUS

Few things encapsulated the bad old days in Burma quite like the Myitsone dam. The $3.6 billion hydropower project was conceived in secret by the country's military junta, and approved without public consultation. It envisioned the extension of a giant concrete wall across the frothing confluence where the waters of the Mali and N'Mai rivers unite in northern Burma to form the Irrawaddy, the nation's longest river, which flows south in wide stately bends before spilling into the Andaman Sea some 2,220 kilometers distant. This Three Gorges clone, intended as the first of a series of seven large dams along the headwaters of the Irrawaddy, was expected to displace more than ten thousand people and flood an area larger than Singapore—yet 90 percent of the power generated by the dam was earmarked for export over the border to Yunnan province.

From the moment the agreement for the dam was signed with a Chinese state-owned firm in 2006, opposition was nearly universal. In particular, for the Kachin, an upland people converted to Christianity by colonial missionaries in the late nineteenth and early twentieth centuries, the project manifested the political inequities between the country's ethnic Burman majority and the numerous ethnic minority groups that have spent decades struggling for greater autonomy.

The Myitsone dam also threatened to submerge a region of profound cultural importance. According to Kachin mythology, the Mali River was poured out by the Creator with a golden spoon, and the N'Mai with one of silver, and the confluence of the two rivers is celebrated in poems and songs. "It is like our lifeblood," said Mung Ra, a 55-year-old Kachin Baptist pastor from a village close to the confluence. The Kachins were joined in their opposition by many ethnic Burmans, for whom the dam became a flashpoint for building anti-Chinese and anti-military sentiment. Many feared that the

Myitsone project would permanently damage the flow of the Irrawaddy, the cradle of Burma's pre-modern kingdoms.

The hydro-project was so unpopular that in September 2011, the country's new president, Thein Sein, took the unprecedented step of suspending the dam's construction, citing the "wishes of the people." When I visited the site five years later, there was little to see of the Chinese firm's construction. Across the water, trees that were cleared had begun to grow back, and the confluence of the two rivers remained still and peaceful. Overlooking the water was a popular picnic spot shaded by tall trees, with a line of cafés and restaurants and a gold-painted stupa. Down by the water an old message was written on the rocks in red spray paint: "No Dam, No War." Off the road leading to the confluence was a checkpoint guarding access to what remained of the construction site. It was manned by a solitary soldier; an old calendar issued by the Chinese company was taped to the guardhouse wall.

The suspension of the Myitsone project catalyzed a remarkable program of political and economic reform in Burma. Six months earlier, a nominally civilian administration had replaced the nation's old clique of ruling generals. Few outside observers gave it much credence, but before long, Thein Sein's government appeared to chart a new course for one of the world's most repressive countries. The Myitsone suspension was followed by a freshet of previously unthinkable reforms. In 2012, the new administration released hundreds of political prisoners, loosened restrictions on the press, and made overtures to the West. Stern official rhetoric took on a lighter tone. The government sought to inject a dose of rationalism into the country's distorted and moribund economy, in which almost a quarter of the budget was gobbled up by the Burmese military, or Tatmadaw. It also announced new peace talks with Burma's profusion of armed rebel groups and ethnic militias in a bid to resolve the civil conflicts that had ravaged mountainous regions like Kachin State for most of Burma's modern history.

At street level, the most visible sign of Burma's *perestroika* was the sudden appearance of "The Lady." For many years, displaying a portrait of Aung San Suu Kyi—the country's world-renowned pro-democracy leader—was viewed as an act of rebellion, and often led to a lengthy prison sentence. Since nation-wide protests in 1988, Aung San Suu Kyi, the daughter of Burma's anti-colonial hero General Aung San, had become a resonant symbol of opposition to a hated military regime. In late 2010, a week after the rigged election that had

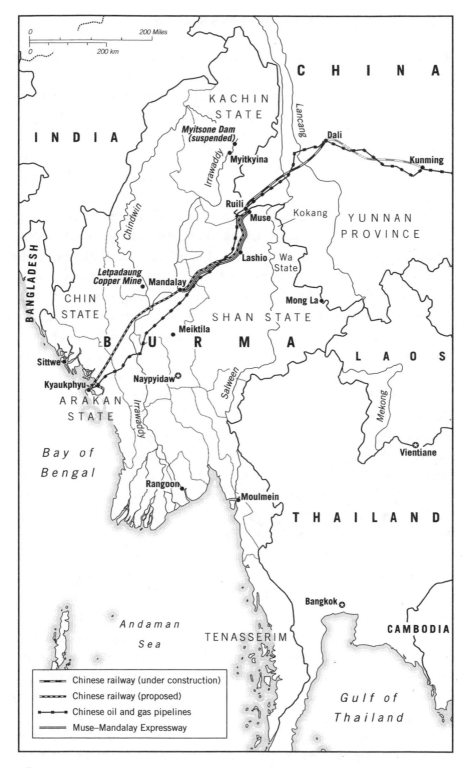

4. Burma

brought the new government to power, the generals had quietly released Aung San Suu Kyi from house arrest, and within a few months, the image of the Nobel laureate was everywhere: staring down from the walls of teashops, hanging on sun-dappled street corners, pasted on the windshields of the ramshackle Japanese sedans that thundered down Rangoon's potholed boulevards. Returning to the helm of her party, the National League for Democracy (NLD), for a by-election in April 2012, Aung San Suu Kyi was elected to parliament for the first time.

Aung San Suu Kyi's engagement with the new institutions established by the Burmese military gave Western nations the pretext they needed to phase out their ineffective sanctions regime and re-engage with the country. The Obama administration made normalization with Burma a centerpiece of its foreign policy "rebalance" to Asia. In December 2011, three months after the suspension of the Myitsone project, US Secretary of State Hillary Clinton visited the crumbling former capital Rangoon, and held landmark talks with Aung San Suu Kyi at her lakeside home, where she had spent much of the past two decades in junta-enforced isolation. It was the first such trip by a top-ranking Washington official in more than fifty years. The following year, Clinton was followed by President Obama himself, who hailed Burma's "flickers of progress" and spoke of "the power of a new beginning." Not long afterward, Thein Sein made the return trip to Washington. After decades of apparent stasis, the momentum in Burma's politics was dizzying.

Nobody was more disadvantaged by the changes than the Chinese. Beijing had been the dominant foreign presence in Burma since 1988, when the Tatmadaw's foot-soldiers had violently suppressed nationwide mass pro-democracy protests, killing an estimated 3,000 demonstrators and lacquering Rangoon's pavements with blood.[1] Two years later, the military government sealed its international pariah status when it rejected the result of national elections that returned an overwhelming victory for the NLD. From the late 1990s, Western countries, including the US, responded by erecting a wall of investment sanctions and trade bans. Like Cambodia, Burma evolved into an international cause, though for very different reasons. As a senior American diplomat posted in Rangoon had put it in 1989: "Since there are no US bases and very little strategic interest, Burma is one place where the United States has the luxury of living up to its principles."[2] Before long, the historian Thant Myint-U wrote, "the view of Burma in the West became fairly set—a timeless backwater, brutal and bankrupt, the realm of juntas and drug lords, as well as courageous pro-democracy activists, led by Aung San Suu Kyi. A place worthy of humanitarian attention, but unconnected to the much bigger story of Asia's global rise."[3]

The effect was a diplomatic vacuum that China quickly and happily filled. Sanctioned and isolated by the West, Burma's junta nuzzled up to Beijing for diplomatic protection and economic patronage. Throughout the 1990s and the first decade of the 2000s, China became Burma's staunchest defender at the UN Security Council, a leading supplier of loans and investment, and a customer for timber, jade, and other resources. Chinese guns and helicopters helped the Tatmadaw battle ethnic insurgents. Visiting Beijing in 2006, Burma's prime minister, General Soe Win, hailed China's "resolute support and selfless assistance."[4]

But this heavy reliance on China stoked both popular and elite anxiety. The opening of the two countries' long, meandering border in the late 1980s was followed by a flow of low-priced Chinese consumer products into Burma, which undermined local industries and contributed to the basket of economic grievances that underpinned the revolutionary mood of 1988.[5] Accompanying them came hundreds of thousands of economic immigrants from Yunnan. Moving in the other direction went jade, minerals, and logs of teakwood extracted from the scarred conflict zones of northern and eastern Burma. While the military profited from Chinese trade, both official and otherwise, it retained—like its Thai counterpart—a deep institutional suspicion of China. Many senior Tatmadaw officers began their careers fighting communist insurgents supported by Beijing, and saw comrades killed by Chinese arms. Even after the Communist Party of Burma collapsed in 1989, China's continuing connections to the four armed ethnic militias that succeeded it raised questions about its long-term intentions in Burma.

Concerns about China's overbearing presence was just one of the many factors that motivated Burma's reforms. The common denominator was the Burmese army's growing shame at the extent of their country's dysfunction, and the belief of Senior General Than Shwe, who headed the junta from 1992 to 2011, that the military's legacy and achievements should be enshrined within a looser and more popularly acceptable structure of control. An important part of this was the desire to rebalance Burma's lopsided foreign relations. These concerns were detailed in an internal document penned by Lt. Col. Aung Kyaw Hla, a researcher at Burma's Defense Services Academy, in

2004. The 346-page "master plan" asserted that the junta's reliance on China had created a "national emergency" that compromised Burma's traditional policy of neutralism, and hence its future independence.[6] As the veteran Singaporean diplomat Bilahari Kausikan put it, the West's "very moralistic" policies toward Burma had deprived the generals of any real options in their international alignments. "Part of the reason why they decided to civilianize themselves was to give themselves choice," he said.

Than Shwe's plan was unveiled in August 2003, in the form of a seven-step roadmap to what the junta called "discipline-flourishing democracy." The roadmap culminated in the creation of a new constitution, multi-party elections, and the establishment of "a modern, developed, and democratic nation." To safeguard its central role in political affairs, the Tatmadaw drafted a new constitution, passed by a bogus plebiscite in 2008, which roped off a quarter of the seats in parliament for military appointees. Since changes to the constitution required a three-quarters majority, this gave it an effective veto over future amendments. The constitution also preserved military control of the three most powerful ministries: Defense, Home Affairs, and Border Affairs.

The built-in limitations of Military Rule 2.0 would soon become apparent, but in the moment it was hard not to be swept up by the genuine excitement and international goodwill unleashed by the reforms. The enthusiasm crested in November 2015, when Burma's voters went to the polls for long-awaited elections and, in defiance of many predictions, handed an overwhelming victory to Aung San Suu Kyi and the NLD. I spent election day in Mandalay, the former royal capital in central Burma, where the atmosphere was electric with expectation. "This election has taken us straight to democracy," was the confident verdict of Maung Maung Gyi, a 56-year-old businessman whom I met casting his ballot at a Buddhist monastery near the moat of the old Mandalay palace. By dusk, supporters of Aung San Suu Kyi gathered around large projector screens, swathed in the NLD's red fighting peacock emblem, sending up cheers as the astonishing returns came in.

The NLD won lopsided majorities in both houses of the national legislature, consigning Thein Sein's military-backed Union Solidarity and Development Party to an ignominious defeat. Unlike in 1990, the military accepted the result. A few months later, the NLD entered government and Aung San Suu Kyi took what many in Burma and abroad saw as her rightful place as the nation's leader. Since the constitution barred Aung San Suu Kyi from becoming president—Article 59(f) ruled out anyone whose spouse, children, or parents were foreign citizens—she served as "state counselor," wielding de facto executive power while the presidency was filled by a loyal placeholder, Htin Kyaw. The following year, citing Burma's "substantial advances," President Obama lifted the remaining US sanctions on the country, which some were soon hailing as his administration's greatest foreign policy achievement. A nation once mentioned in the same breath as Iran and North Korea had seemingly flipped onto the right side of history.

Burma's reforms dealt a serious blow to China's privileged position in the country. For years, Chinese leaders had quietly urged the Burmese army to introduce reforms, repair ties to the West, and stabilize the economy, but they were unprepared for the speed and extent of the liberalization.[7] Suddenly, China faced competition from the US, Japan, the European Union, and a host of international organizations that rushed in as Burma opened its doors to the world. Emboldened by the relaxation of political control, local journalists, dissidents, and political cartoonists castigated China's overbearing role in their country's affairs. The public joined in, and anti-China sentiment rose to heights not seen since 1967, when the spread of Maoist zeal among the country's Sino-Burmese community touched off anti-Chinese riots in Rangoon and several other cities.

Nothing encapsulated Burma's perceived vassalage to Beijing more than the Myitsone project: a rare issue upon which both Burman and Kachin could agree. In 2016, locals in the Myitsone area were still bitter about China's involvement in the project. Kachin activists described it as yet another instance in which Beijing and Naypyidaw had colluded to strip the region's rich natural resources and send them over the border. Kachin State is "like an egg, inside the liquid is all gone, drained by China," said Steven Naw Awng of the Kachin Development Networking Group (KDNG), a civil society group based in Myitkyina, the capital of Kachin State. "We have no benefits," he added, "and the resources are all gone."

Other major Chinese investments also came under scrutiny. In late 2012, demonstrations erupted at a Chinese copper mine at Letpadaung in central Burma, run by China's Wanbao Mining Co. in partnership with the military-linked Myanmar Economic Holdings Limited, and it too was suspended; when anti-mine protesters gathered outside the Chinese embassy in Rangoon, one banner read, "This is our Country—Dracula China Get out!"[8] Investment from China fell. The government canceled a planned railway line from Yunnan, and backtracked on other ventures. After the NLD government took power, Yan Myo Thein, a Rangoon-based political analyst, said that for the Chinese government there was no going back to the way things were before. "They need to initiate reforms on doing business in Myanmar and engaging with the new government," he said over sweet Burmese tea on a sodden wet-season afternoon in the former capital. "They have to consider new strategies, new methods."

The rapid political changes in Burma threatened to disrupt what was perhaps China's most important strategic relationship in mainland Southeast Asia. For years, Burma's natural resources—particularly timber, natural gas, minerals, and jade—had flowed uninterrupted into China. Its 2,200-kilometer shared border, curling through some of the remotest parts of Asia, was vital to the security of southwestern China. Just as important as the country itself was what lay beyond. For more than three decades, Chinese thinkers had seen Burma as "China's California": a proxy for the western coast that it lacks.[9] As the most direct link between Yunnan and the sea, Burma was vital to China realizing two long-standing goals: opening its poor inland provinces to trade, and gaining unfettered overland access to the Bay of Bengal and the Indian Ocean.

This strategic goal was present in Chinese thinking as early as 1985, when a two-page article appeared in the official *Beijing Review*, titled "Opening to the southwest: An expert opinion." In the article, Pan Qi, a former Chinese vice minister of communications, argued for the construction of a network of highways connecting Yunnan to railways and river ports in Burma. These would provide a vital outlet for Chinese exports, and give landlocked Yunnan "more than one avenue to the outside world."[10] Pan's vision later helped address concerns about China's increasing reliance on imports of oil and other goods through the Straits of Malacca. Here, too, Burma was pivotal.

China's ambitions in Burma were symbolized by the construction of a large monument in 1993 in the Chinese enclave of Jiegao, just across from a bridge leading to the town of Muse in northern Shan State, the main gateway of trade between the two countries. The monument depicted four Chinese figures wheeling a large circular object, eyes narrowed and chiseled faces pointed determinedly to the south. At the base of the monument were six Chinese characters that read, "Unity, Development, Forge Ahead!"[11]

This Chinese vision of Burma as a corridor for the southward flow of goods reversed the nineteenth-century ambitions of the British, who, like their imperial rivals in Paris, plotted to gain access to China's huge market. Britain's conquest of Upper Burma was motivated in part by the desire to open a trading route into southwestern China, a plan advocated by the explorer Archibald Colquhoun and later adopted by British officials as a retroactive justification for the war that ousted Thibaw, Burma's last king, in 1885. "The wealth of Upper Burma and also the resources of western China and the Shan States are incalculable," Colquhoun wrote in 1898, "but they lie fallow at present for want of connections, both internal and with the outer world."[12]

Beijing's efforts to forge these connections and realize Pan's "opening to the southwest" were greatly aided by Burma's slide into international pariah status after 1988, and the sudden collapse in April 1989 of the Communist Party of Burma (CPB). While China had cut off effective aid to the CPB several years earlier, its disintegration removed one of the main sticking points in bilateral relations. It also helped stabilize a restive borderland that sat directly in the path of China's envisioned corridor to the sea. The CPB fractured into four well-armed rebel groups that inherited both its large "liberated zones" and close ties to Beijing, and quickly signed ceasefires with the central government in exchange for local autonomy.[13] As the borders opened up, trade between China and Burma began to flow.

By the time of Thein Sein's reforms, the southwest corridor was well on the way to becoming a reality. China had built new highways and refurbished the old Burma Road running from China into Shan State. It had constructed a pipeline that brought natural gas more than a thousand kilometers overland from offshore platforms in the Bay of Bengal deep into Yunnan's fast-growing interior. A second, parallel pipeline pumped tanker-loads of Persian Gulf and African crude oil from Burma's coast to refineries in Kunming. Under the Belt and Road Initiative (BRI), plans were in the works for a new expressway linking the Chinese border to the sea, and a $20 billion high-speed rail line following the same route—a project once envisioned by the British. All this would be capped off by a deep-water port and industrial zone at Kyaukphyu, where the Chinese pipelines terminated on the Bay of Bengal.

Here, too, geography cut both ways: just as proximity put Burma at the center of Chinese interests, it also fed Burmese misgivings about Chinese intentions. In precolonial times, a thick buffer of forested hills and mountains had mostly kept the Chinese imperial state at bay. Early Burmese encounters with northern power nonetheless left a deep impression. In 1271, Kublai Khan's Mongol armies swept into China, defeated the Song dynasty, and declared a new Yuan dynasty in its place. When the Burmese kingdom of Bagan refused to offer tribute, the Mongols launched a series of invasions, precipitating Bagan's defeat and collapse. Ever since, the Burmese have referred to the Chinese as *tayouk*, their term for the Mongols.[14]

The Burmese found themselves tangled up in Chinese affairs once again after the Ming dynasty fell to a series of Manchu invasions in 1644. After the fall of Beijing, Prince Yongli, the last successor to the Ming throne, retreated south to Yunnan, crossed into Burma with his dwindling army, and sought refuge in the Burmese capital of Ava, close to present-day Mandalay. The new Qing emperor promptly dispatched a military force to apprehend the pretender, who was captured in 1662, hauled with his remaining retinue back to Kunming, and executed by strangulation. The fighting devastated wide regions of northern Burma.[15] This pattern would recur three centuries later, when the victory of Mao's communists once again sent a defeated Chinese army—the Kuomintang—spilling into Burmese territory.

This history of turbulent encounters with Chinese power has shaped Burma's view on the challenges of living under China's shadow. The country's predicament was voiced in the mid-eighteenth century by a famous Burmese general following another series of wars between 1765 and 1769, when the Qianlong Emperor sent four well-equipped armies south to check Burma's burgeoning power. Each met ruin and defeat, and on the final occasion, when the Chinese commanders sued for terms, the Burmese generals refused to negotiate until Maha Thiha Thura, their commander-in-chief, intervened: "Comrades, unless we make peace, yet another invasion will come, and when we have defeated it yet another invasion will come," he said. "Our nation cannot go on just repelling invasion after invasion of the Chinese, for we have other things to do. Let us stop this slaughter and let their people and our people live and trade in peace."[16]

In conceding the stubborn fact of geography, Maha Thiha Thura foreshadowed the policy of neutralism that Burma would adopt in modern times. Following its independence from Britain in 1948, the new nation quickly found itself confronting a unified communist China to its north. With Cold

War tensions mounting, and their attention consumed by the eruption of a raft of civil conflicts soon after independence, Burma's leaders hoped that their neutralism would prevent the country from being sucked into the orbit of China or one of its rivals. In September 1950, Prime Minister U Nu described his country's vulnerabilities during a speech to Burma's parliament: "We are hemmed in like a tender gourd among the cactus," he declared. "We cannot move an inch. If we act irresponsibly . . . and thrust the Union of Burma into the arms of one bloc, the other bloc will not be contented to look on with folded arms. Oh, no!"[17]

Non-alignment both advanced and constrained Burma's ties with China. In 1950, it became the first non-communist state to recognize Mao's government, and later coined the special term *paukphaw* to describe the two countries' "fraternal" ties.[18] Yet the policy of non-alignment kept China at arm's length, frustrating the leadership in Beijing. Relations soured, reaching a low point with the outbreak of anti-Chinese rioting in several cities in 1967. This prompted China to bolster its support to the CPB, and to dispatch a heavily armed communist force, including hundreds of Chinese Red Guard "volunteers," which secured a "liberated zone" for the CPB along the Chinese border. In the 1970s and 1980s, Burma's neutralism was married to a policy of autarky and isolationism under the fatidic reign of General Ne Win. While Ne Win succeeded in sealing Burma off from the worst ravages of the Cold War, he did so at the cost of turning the country—once among the most economically advanced in Southeast Asia—into a repressive dictatorship and economic basket case.

In the late 1990s, Myanmar's neutralism was compromised by the imposition of Western sanctions and boycotts, which forced the country into a greater reliance on China. The two nations' snaking, porous border became an economic lifeline for the military government and an important source of products, including consumer goods, basic chemicals, and light machinery. When the junta began to relax economic restrictions in the 1990s, Chinese firms were among the main beneficiaries. From 1988 to 2013, China was the single largest foreign investor in Burma.[19]

During this period, a number of Sino-Burmese tycoons were able to amass huge fortunes by acting as bridges between the junta and its Chinese patron. The most curious case was that of Lo Hsing Han, an opium and heroin trafficker who rose to become one of Burma's richest men. Lo was born in 1935 in Kokang, an ethnically Chinese territory in northern Shan State inhabited by descendants of Ming refugees who fled to the remote region after the collapse of the dynasty in the mid-seventeenth century. By the 1960s, Lo had become a key player in the narco-economy of the Golden Triangle. At one stage he commanded a militia of 3,000 men that guarded multiple heroin refineries in remote and impoverished parts of Shan State, leading the Nixon administration to describe him as "kingpin of the heroin traffic in Southeast Asia."[20] After the collapse of the CPB in 1989, Lo played a central role in brokering the cease-fires between the government and the former communist armies occupying large territories along the Chinese border.

As Burma opened its economy in the early 1990s, Lo used his drug profits as seed capital to build a corporate empire named Asia World. Founded in 1992, Asia World would become a leading business partner of Burma's junta during the years of Western sanctions, as well as a conduit for Overseas Chinese investment from other parts of Southeast Asia. By the time of his death in 2013, Lo's commercial empire included a container shipping business, Rangoon port buildings, and concessions to import fuel and mine rubies and jade. Wherever China was active in Burma, Asia World was never far away. It was the local partner in the Myitsone dam project. It had a hand in the planned Chinese port in Kyaukphyu and the pipelines pumping oil and gas to Yunnan. In partnership with the Sino-Malaysian tycoon Robert Kuok, Lo built Rangoon's luxury Traders Hotel (now the Sule Shangri-La), and was a donor to the Myanmar China Chamber of Commerce. His firm was also one of the main contractors that built Naypyidaw, the junta's sprawling new capital in the flatlands of central Burma. During Lo's funeral in 2013, *The Economist* reported, "a cavalcade of cars, some carrying his portrait garlanded with flowers, processed through the streets of Yangon ... to his high-walled villa, right by the 16th tee of the city golf club."[21] Asia World remains one of Burma's largest and most prominent companies: an emblem both of the continuing economic dominance of ethnic Chinese tycoons in Burma, and the dense interleaving of the country's licit and illicit economies.

Today, the main economic gateway between China and Burma is the old Burma Road. Built before World War II to supply Chiang Kai-shek's embattled forces in the interior of China, and since extended south to the former royal capital of Mandalay, it has become a busy viaduct of trade. Each year, billions of dollars' worth of goods—more than half of Burma's overland trade—passes down this winding ribbon of tarmac from the wild frontier towns of Ruili and Muse. As far as anyone knows, this figure is exceeded by the illegal trade, which includes vast quantities of jade, timber, and animal parts, and coming the other way, Chinese precursor chemicals that feed the drug labs scattered across the rebel zones of eastern Shan State. Signs of China's presence are visible all along the Burma Road, from the lantern-adorned restaurants catering to Chinese traders to the semi-trailers rumbling north to the border, laden with logs of hardwood and other raw materials. In Lashio, the lowering hill town where American and British wartime supplies were once loaded from trains onto military lorries for the long journey up the Burma Road into Yunnan, the main drag is frequently jammed with trucks and motorcycles hauling Chinese goods. Today, Chinese migrants and traders make up around a third of the city's population.[22]

In 1998, the Burma Road was widened and resealed by none other than Asia World, which for years collected tolls along the road. But parts of the highway have since fallen into terrible disrepair, battered by heavily laden trucks and torrential monsoons. Accidents are frequent, as 22-wheeled Nissan diesels filled with watermelons and timber lurch around the hairpin bends. However, as a crucial link on China's planned economic corridor to the coast, several sections of the road are earmarked for improvements, and will in time become the final link in a new, expanded Burma Road running from Kunming to Mandalay—and onward to the sea.

The distance-demolishing effect of economic integration has amplified long-standing Burmese anxieties about China. Much of the angst fixates on the multitude of Chinese immigrants who have swept down the new high-ways from Yunnan. As in Laos, the thinly populated upland regions of Burma have exerted an almost irresistible pull on China's surplus population. As Archibald Colquhoun observed in the late nineteenth century, "Burma and its Shan States provide an admirable absorbing ground for the ever-increasing and dense populations of India and China. There is ample room for an increase of scores of millions to the present population of Burma."[23] By one estimate, as many as 2 million Chinese citizens have entered Burma since the 1980s.[24] Most are poor but entrepreneurial immigrants, some of whom have obtained identity papers through a variety of underhand means. According to one method described by Bertil Lintner in 1998, when a Burmese national died, their family were able to sell their identity card to a broker who would then pass it on to a foreign citizen, usually Chinese.[25]

While Chinese settlers, petty traders, and businesspeople can now be seen throughout the border regions, a particular angst surrounds the supposed Chinese "takeover" of Mandalay, an important cultural and religious center 450 kilometers—about a day's drive—down the highway from Yunnan. In recent decades, Chinese investors have bought up hotels, restaurants, karaoke bars, and commercial property in Mandalay's downtown. Shop signs abound in simplified Chinese, and the city's bustling jade market is frequented by snappily dressed Chinese dealers from the border town of Ruili opposite Muse. At first glance this city of wide boulevards and golden-spired *zedis* seems to be thriving on its proximity to China. New buildings stud the downtown and the streets are filled with new cars; by night, mobile phone shops and "beer stations" glow on the numbered city streets. But Mandalay's importance to Burmese Buddhism, and its status as the one-time seat of Burma's last royal house, makes the arrival of Chinese immigrants and expats an especially sensitive issue.

Chinese are hardly strangers to Mandalay society. A Yunnanese-style mosque, built in 1868, still rears its octagonal minaret over the traffic on 80th Street. But the new arrivals overwhelm past waves of migrants, both in their sheer numbers, and their marked cultural differences from the city's old Chinese. The complaints mirror those elsewhere in mainland Southeast Asia: locals blame Chinese migrants for spoiling the city's tranquil character, and for a steady rise in real-estate values that has forced many locals to relocate to scrubland and former paddy fields on the city's outskirts.

The new Chinese presence in Mandalay dates back to 1984, when a fire tore through the center of the city, destroying around 2,700 buildings and leaving more than 23,000 people homeless. Many locals, lacking the money to rebuild gutted homes, subsequently sold their land to newly arrived Chinese immigrants. In 1988, the local writer Nyi Pu Lay wrote a short story titled "The Python," which satirized how these Chinese arrivals were squeezing out the Burmese. A similar theme was taken up two decades later by the Burmese folk singer Lin Lin in a song titled "Death of Mandalay": "Who are they in this city? / Neighbors that arrive from northeast," he plaints over a simple guitar accompaniment. "I close both my ears in utter shame / Messed up with strangers / The death of our dear Mandalay."[26]

Nobody really knows how many *xin yimin* live in Mandalay today. Intermarriage and fraudulent papers make it hard to know who exactly counts as

Chinese. Some local estimates put the number as high as 50 percent of the city's population of 1.4 million.[27] While this is almost certainly a wild exaggeration, it points to the depth of the anxiety felt by many Burmans: the fear that their culture could be engulfed by a flood of outsiders from the north.

Despite all these signs of growing discontent, the Chinese government seemed surprised by the anti-Chinese sentiment that burst forth in 2011 and 2012. When Thein Sein announced the suspension of the Myitsone dam, Beijing responded at first with denial. Hinting at a conspiracy, Chinese analysts blamed Washington, which had given small grants to anti-dam groups. While years of Western sanctions on Burma had played to Beijing's advantage, the sudden shift demonstrated the downside to China's brand of pragmatic engagement: by using the junta to bulldoze through major infrastructure projects in the face of entrenched public opposition, it had become the predictable subject of popular anger.

The Chinese government had little choice but to adjust to the changing circumstances in Burma. As the scholar Enze Han observed, China faced much the same dilemma in Burma as the US did in Thailand after the 2014 coup: "neither side could afford to alienate the local government by exerting pressure that could push it into the embrace of its rival."[28] Beijing responded with a public relations offensive. Dignitaries, politicians, and journalists from across the political spectrum were invited on all-expenses-paid trips to China. The State Power Investment Corporation, the Chinese company building the Myitsone dam, set up a website debunking "myths" about the project and touting its benefits to Burma. The Chinese embassy appointed a new political counselor, who used Facebook (a service banned in China) to communicate more directly with the public. "If you don't walk the walk and just talk the talk, you won't win the hearts and minds of the local people," Counselor Gao Mingbo told *The New York Times*.[29] The handle of the embassy's Facebook page—@phaukpawfriendship—referenced a past era of Sino-Burmese amity.

China's most significant move was to begin courting the NLD. In June 2015, while the party was still in opposition, it invited Aung San Suu Kyi to Beijing for a meeting with President Xi Jinping, treating her to a reception befitting a visiting head of state. When the NLD government took office the following year, the first high-level diplomatic caller was Chinese Foreign Minister Wang Yi, who pledged renewed support, including backing for infrastructure development. A few months later, he was followed by an equally important though less well-known figure: Song Tao, the head of the Chinese Communist Party's (CCP's) International Liaison Department, which managed China's relations with Burma's profusion of armed rebel groups. In the euphoria of her party's massive election victory, many outside observers assumed that the Oxford-educated Aung San Suu Kyi would seal her country's embrace of the US and other Western democracies. But before long, the democratic idol, like Burmese leaders past, would find that China was too important to ignore.

In late August 2017, violence spread like a prairie fire across the swampy coastal littorals of Arakan State, a western region of Burma nestled against the British-drawn border with Bangladesh. The targets of the violence were the Rohingya, a mostly Muslim ethnic group who lived in villages concentrated in the northern part of the state. The perpetrator was Burma's military, backed by vigilantes from the state's Arakanese Buddhist populations. Although journalists and human rights workers were barred from the area, horrific reports quickly leaked out, of rape, torture, and extrajudicial killings of Rohingya civilians by soldiers and police. This was accompanied by a string of arson attacks, with satellite photos showing ash-colored blotches scarring the green rice paddies of northern Arakan. As the campaign advanced, hundreds of thousands of people fled over the Naf River into Bangladesh.

The military's "clearance operation" in northern Arakan was launched in response to a series of attacks by a ragtag Rohingya insurgent outfit calling itself the Arakan Rohingya Salvation Army (ARSA). The group was led by Ataullah abu Ammar Jununi, a half-Rohingya, half-Pakistani militant who grew up in Saudi Arabia and later received military training in Pakistan or Afghanistan. Jununi and a group of Rohingya exiles set up the ARSA in 2012, following an outbreak of communal violence between Rohingya Muslims and Arakanese Buddhists. ARSA had first attracted international attention on October 9, 2016, when a small force wielding mostly homemade weapons killed nine policemen during a surprise attack on three border posts in northern Arakan. The military responded with a fierce counterinsurgency operation involving the destruction of villages and the displacement of their inhabitants: an ominous foreshadowing of the ethnic cleansing to come.

Like many of Burma's ethnic conflicts, the Rohingya crisis was an outgrowth of the nation-building problems that had plagued the country since its independence in 1948. Many of these could be traced back to the colonial era, when

Great Britain, after seizing Burma in a series of conquests between 1824 and 1885, arranged the nation's ethnic and racial hierarchies in such a manner as to best facilitate the extraction of profit for shareholders in London and Glasgow. Importing institutions and methods from its Indian colony, to which Burma was administratively conjoined until 1937, the British placed different parts of the country under different forms of administration, while favoring certain ethnic minority groups over the majority ethnic Burmans. It also imported hundreds of thousands of Indian immigrants from the Raj, who, arriving with little more than the rags on their backs, squeezed the livelihoods of the Burmans. "Burma was born as a military occupation," Thant Myint-U writes, "and grew up as a racial hierarchy."[30]

At independence, the British handed the new Burmese state an histori-cally incongruous territory, in which around a third of the population belonged to a passel of non-Burman minority groups, many of them dwelling in outlying regions, like Kachin, Shan, and Arakan states, which had never been under effective central control. The British anthropologist Edmund Leach described the new nation as "a map maker's fiction": "Burma as repre-sented on a modern map is not a natural geographic or historical entity," he wrote in 1963. "It is a creation of the armed diplomacy and administrative convenience of late nineteenth-century British Imperialism."[31]

Moreover, since colonial policy had accorded many minority groups pref-erential treatment over the Burman majority, ethnic relations were poisoned from the outset. Immediately after independence, the Union of Burma was engulfed by ethnic and civil conflict, pitting the central government and the military, both dominated by ethnic Burmans, against ethnic minority groups seeking autonomy or independence from the central state. Things worsened after the military seized power in 1962, pursuing a chauvinistic Burman ethno-nationalism that inflamed opposition further.

The Rohingya crisis, in Martin Smith's words, represented Burma's various postcolonial failures "in microcosm."[32] Things there were complicated addi-tionally by the fact that the Buddhists of Arakan, the main local antagonists of the Rohingya, harbored their own host of grievances against the Burmese state. Many nurtured a distinct Arakanese identity linked to the independent kingdom of Mrauk U that was conquered and annexed by the Burmese state in the late eighteenth century, and defined itself against the influx of Bengali Muslims who entered the area during the British period.[33] In 2018, an armed group calling itself the Arakan Army began fighting government forces in northern Arakan State, further complicating any solution to the Rohingya crisis.

One of the few things Burman and Arakanese nationalists could agree upon was their distaste for the Rohingya. While many Rohingya claimed to have lived in Burma for generations, many within both communities had long viewed them as illegal "sneak-ins" from Bangladesh, whose creeping presence was eroding Burma's (and Arakan's) distinct Buddhist identity. Many refused even to utter the word "Rohingya," instead referring to them as "Bengalis" or *kala*, a derogatory word used to refer to foreigners who had an Indian appearance. Even though Burma's 1982 Citizenship Law gave the Rohingya a theoretical pathway to citizenship, prejudice in its enforcement rendered most effectively stateless.

Given this historical background, the military "clearance operation" of August 2017 seemed like an attempt to erase an unwanted community from Burma's territory once and for all. Within a year, around 800,000 terrified people had been forced over the border into Bangladesh. The aid group Médecins Sans Frontières estimated that 9,400 people were killed in the initial phase of the clearance campaign, including at least 730 children.[34] A UN fact-finding commission later concluded that the military's campaign amounted to possible genocide, crimes against humanity, and war crimes.

The resurgence of sectarian and ethnic violence in Burma formed a dark underside to Burma's reform drive. As in the former Yugoslavia in the 1990s, the loosening of political controls inflamed long-dormant disputes. As Thein Sein's government opened peace talks with some ethnic armed groups, fighting with others erupted in remote parts of Shan and Kachin states, reaching levels not seen in years. Anti-Muslim pogroms broke out in the central cities of Mandalay and Meiktila, leaving dozens dead. In May 2012, the trouble spread to Arakan State, where attacks by Buddhist vigilante groups left almost 200 people dead and drove around 140,000 Rohingya into internal displacement camps.

The spread of anti-Muslim and anti-Rohingya animus was aided by the sudden appearance of the internet and social media, particularly Facebook. Before 2011, these had barely existed in Burma. Under the junta's paranoid strictures, mobile SIM cards had cost thousands of dollars, and most people accessed the web at rickety internet cafés, where data dribbled in a few kilobytes at a time. When Burma opened its doors to foreign investment, two international telecoms firms built new mobile phone networks, bringing prices down sharply. By mid-2014, when the first 1,500-kyat ($1.60) SIMs went on sale, phone shops in Rangoon were mobbed by people eager to get their hands on the precious plastic chips. Nearly overnight, Burma leapfrogged from crackly landlines to web-enabled smartphones. In the two years after 2014, it saw one of the fastest surges in internet access of any country in history.[35]

Burma would turn out to be a signal lesson in the ambiguous effects of digital technologies. Among the savvier of Burma's new social media "influencers" was Ashin Wirathu, a monk from Mandalay. As the head of Burma's 969 movement, an ultra-nationalist Buddhist association, Wirathu peddled anti-Muslim poison perfumed with jasmine scent. On his Facebook page, he railed against the purported crimes of Muslims, and argued that their allegedly rapid demographic growth rate posed an existential threat to the country's Buddhist Burman identity. "The intention of Islam is to influence the whole world through rapid population [growth]," he said when I interviewed him in 2015, in the stuccoed monastery hall in which he instructed novice monks. If the Rohingya were accepted as citizens, Wirathu claimed, "Myanmar might become a wholly Muslim country, like Pakistan or Bangladesh." Outside the hall stood a billboard covered with gruesome images: acts of violence supposedly committed by Muslims in different parts of the world.

After the ARSA attacks of October 2016, Facebook helped fuel public vitriol against the Rohingya, conjoining them to broader fears of global Islamism. In March 2018, the UN reported that posts on Facebook had "substantively contributed to the level of acrimony and dissension and conflict" surrounding the Arakan crisis.[36] By this time, the NLD government had banned Wirathu from public preaching. Facebook had also canceled his account. But the damage had already been done.

The severe treatment of the Rohingya cracked the prevailing Western optimism about Burma. To outside observers, and many of us in the international press, the country's "transition to democracy" had had all the qualities of a fairytale, pitting the beautiful Aung San Suu Kyi and her downtrodden people against a villainous cast of generals and junta toadies. With the NLD's huge election victory in 2015, the story appeared to reach its happily-ever-after conclusion, as the heroine was borne into office on a wave of public adulation. One reason the story was so powerful was that it seemed to confirm the prevailing ideological assumptions of much of the Western media and policymaking elite: that the world was moving inexorably, if sometimes haltingly, in the direction of liberal values. Relying on international support to pressure the military, Aung San Suu Kyi did little to discourage this perception.

When it came to the Rohingya, however, Wirathu voiced a view that was disturbingly common among Burmans, including prominent NLD figures and pro-democracy activists. Many agreed with him that the Rohingya were a fake ethnic group, and supported the military's actions to expunge these "Bengalis" from Burmese soil. In May 2015, I attended an anti-Rohingya protest in Rangoon in which demonstrators, many of them supporters of the NLD, held banners denouncing the international press—the very same press that had once supported their struggle against military dictatorship. Banners and T-shirts described the Rohingya as "boat people" and called on the media to "stop blaming Myanmar."

Most deflating of all was the silence of Aung San Suu Kyi, an inspiring figure who had been garlanded by the world community for her brave opposition to military dictatorship. While the constitution gave the NLD government little direct power to restrain the military's actions in Arakan State, her State Counselor's Office took a leading role in trying to counter and discredit international reporting about the crisis. In September 2017, it blamed "terrorists" for "a huge iceberg of misinformation" around the Arakan crisis.[37] As 2018 dawned, pundits and journalists were calling for Aung San Suu Kyi to be stripped of her Nobel Peace Prize and other baubles of international recognition. A portrait of Aung San Suu Kyi was removed from the walls of St. Hugh's College at Oxford University, where she had studied as an undergraduate. Amnesty International withdrew its highest honor, telling her that "you no longer represent a symbol of hope, courage, and the undying defense of human rights."[38]

Before the reforms, Aung San Suu Kyi had dwelt in a realm beyond serious scrutiny. While some foreign officials who met the famous dissident commented on her apparent rigidity and intolerance for criticism, calling attention to these qualities was seen as carrying water for the junta. As Barbara Victor, one of her biographers, wrote in 1998, "deconstructing Aung San Suu Kyi is not part of the game."[39] But the elevation of "The Lady" into an emblem of liberal values had a distorting effect, flattening her country's complex realities into a simple redemptive struggle between a freedom-loving people and a heinous military dictatorship.

In reality, military rule was as much a symptom of Burma's problems as their cause. As the political scientist Mary Callahan argued in 2005, army rule was simply one solution—however baneful and self-defeating—to a centuries-old challenge: how to build a state in outlying regions of Burma that had rarely, if ever, been under effective central control. Presciently, Callahan argued that this would be a problem not only for the military junta of the time, "but also for any future regime, democratic or otherwise."[40] The election of Aung San Suu Kyi, an ethnic Burman politician who expressed affection for the Tatmadaw (her father Aung San had been central to its founding), did little to address these structural problems, nor to reconcile a chauvinistic Burman nationalism with Burma's multiethnic realities. Along the country's periphery, Aung San Suu Kyi was seen not as a goddess but as the least bad option—and sometimes regarded with open suspicion.

As international pressure mounted over the Rohingya crisis, and the US and European Union threatened to reimpose economic sanctions, "The Lady" turned in a familiar direction for support. China swiftly reassured the NLD leaders that it took a position of "non-interference" on the question of the Rohingya. When the UN Security Council drafted a statement condemning Burma's actions in 2017, Chinese diplomats vetoed its release. Indeed, they went further, echoing Naypyidaw's narrative justifying the attacks on the Rohingya on the grounds that the army was "fighting terrorism" and preserving "national security." Chinese Foreign Minister Wang Yi declared that the crisis was an issue between Burma and Bangladesh, and should not be "complicated" or "internationalized." On a visit to Beijing in April 2019, Senior General Min Aung Hlaing, the commander-in-chief of the Tatmadaw, praised China for its support and described it as an "eternal friend."[41]

As Burma's international isolation deepened, China took the opportunity to regain lost ground, pushing for the resumption of stalled infrastructure projects. In November 2017, the two countries signed an agreement on the construction of the China–Myanmar Economic Corridor (CMEC), a new catch-all for the raft of BRI infrastructure projects designed to connect Yunnan to the sea. China's proposed railway from Muse on the Chinese border to Kyaukphyu on the coast of Arakan State, shelved by Burma's government in 2014, was revived, and Chinese engineers began surveying a 431-kilometer stretch running from Muse to Mandalay.[42] Other projects under the CMEC included a strand of border trade zones in Kachin and Shan states opposite

Yunnan, and an ambitious plan to construct a "new city" in the outskirts of Rangoon. The linchpin of the CMEC was the deep-water port and Special Economic Zone at Kyaukphyu, not far from the conflict zones of Arakan State.

The Rohingya crisis aside, the NLD government had good reasons to maintain workable relations with Beijing. This was something that Aung San Suu Kyi had long recognized. "I have to be careful with China," she told an interviewer in March 2003, during a short interregnum between stretches of house arrest. "They are a big and important neighbor, and I cannot afford to offend them."[43] After taking office, Aung San Suu Kyi chose China as the destination for her first state visit and, to assuage the concerns of Chinese investors, approved the resumption of operations at the Letpadaung Copper Mine in central Burma. Aung San Suu Kyi's rebalancing was a recognition that she needed Chinese cooperation if she hoped to achieve her main domestic policy priority: forging peace and bringing development to Burma's restive periphery.

Shortly after entering office, Aung San Suu Kyi pushed for the completion of the national peace talks initiated by Thein Sein's government, convening a series of large summits that brought together leaders from most of Burma's thirty-odd armed ethnic groups. If her peace drive was to succeed, China's support would be pivotal: it had been involved in some of the conflicts since their inception, and retained close political and economic connections to the ethnic rebel statelets distributed across northern and eastern Shan State. Its relations were particularly close to those territories lying directly along the Chinese border, some of which had over the years grown into virtual Chinese annexes.

One of these was Mong La, the largest town in Special Region No. 4, a 4,946-square-kilometer crescent of autonomous territory along the Chinese border run by a militia calling itself the National Democratic Alliance Army (NDAA). For the past three decades, the leaders of this miniature Golden Triangle fiefdom had survived by attaching themselves like a limpet to the grimy underside of China's domestic tourist industry. Mong La's economy— the model for the casino tourism enclaves that would later sprout in Laos and Cambodia—revolved around gambling and its subsidiary ventures: night-clubs, brothels, restaurants, and massage joints. The NDAA's territory was especially notorious for its brazen trade in endangered wildlife products, including pangolins, ivory, and tiger bone wine, all of which were sold openly at boutiques and eateries around town. Many Chinese patrons crossed the border illegally. When I traveled up to Mong La in 2014 to research the illicit wildlife trade, a Burmese motorbike driver carried me over the border to China and back for about $20 worth of Chinese yuan.

The NDAA is led by the warlord Sai Leun, a former Maoist Red Guard who broke away from the CPB when it collapsed in 1989 and signed a cease-fire with the central government, in exchange for autonomy. While Sai Leun (Lin Mingxian in Mandarin) rules Mong La with little outside interference, protected by an army of 4,500 men that US officials have described as a "James Bondian private police force,"[44] it is an effective economic extension of China: a neon-lit island of Chinese urban modernity in a furrowed highland land-scape dotted with Akha and Lahu villages. It operates on China Standard Time and almost entirely on Chinese yuan. The NDAA leadership speak Mandarin and cooperate closely with local officials in Yunnan, which may account for the ease of illegal border runs. In fact, China probably has more say in what happens in Special Region No. 4 than Burma does.

Chinese officials have good reasons to keep a close eye on Burma's rebel groups and ethnic conflict zones, especially those abutting its sensitive southern border. For one thing, many of the peoples fighting for autonomy in Burma have ethnic brethren across the border, raising fears that instability there could spread into China itself. For another, China's planned corridor from Yunnan to the Indian Ocean runs directly through fractious regions contested between the Burmese government and a range of armed groups. Stability in these regions is a prerequisite to the fulfillment of China's broader strategic objectives in Burma.

Chinese fears of unrest flared in August 2009, when the Tatmadaw launched an offensive against Kokang, another autonomous "special region" bordering China in northern Shan State, and ousted its leader Pheung Kya-shin (Mandarin: Peng Jiasheng), a former communist and ethnic Chinese drug trafficker with close connections to China. The fighting caused around 30,000 people to flee into Yunnan. Beijing was jolted by the incident. As the International Crisis Group noted at the time, the Kokang conflict "dramatically changed China's view" of Burma's ethnic armed groups. Previously, Chinese officials saw them as buffers that could be played off against Naypyidaw for strategic gain. Once it became apparent that Burma was willing to use force to root out recalcitrant armed groups, Beijing began to see these rebel groups as a liability.[45]

Chinese concerns were exacerbated in 2011 and 2012, when political reforms coincided with the breakdown of old ceasefires and renewed fighting along its border with Burma. In June 2011, skirmishes in Kachin State broke a 17-year-old ceasefire between the Tatmadaw and the Kachin Independence Army (KIA). Late the following year, the escalation of the conflict led the Burmese military to bomb Chinese territory and sent thousands of refugees fleeing into China.

The renewed fighting drew China more deeply into Burma's ethnic armed conflicts. After the Kokang incident, China centralized control of Burma border policy, transferring responsibility from the Yunnan provincial government back to the capital. It also stepped up its involvement in the country's peace talks. In 2013, Beijing appointed Wang Yingfan, a veteran diplomat and former ambassador to the Philippines, as a special envoy to mediate armed conflicts in Burma. Shortly after Wang's appointment, China organized two rounds of dialog between KIA leaders and the Burmese government in Ruili.

The Chinese government claimed that its involvement in Burma's peace process was consistent with its principle of "non-interference." Sun Guoxiang, the current special envoy, argued that China was "only doing [its] duty as a friendly neighbor."[46] But the Chinese government's real aims were more nebulous. As mentioned, one pressing Chinese goal was to ensure the stability necessary for the completion of vital corridor infrastructure projects. Another was to neutralize the involvement of rival powers in the nationwide peace process initiated by Thein Sein's government. After 2011, outside powers, including Japan, the US, and Norway, had become active in the peace negotiations. Beijing had long viewed the Burmese border region as an exclusive sphere of influence, like the South China Sea. The prospect that competing powers were making inroads there was intolerable.

Chinese leaders were particularly alarmed when, in April 2014, General Gun Maw, the deputy commander-in-chief of the KIA, paid a visit to Washington, where he publicly called for the US government to deepen its involvement in Burma's peace talks. The following January, an American delegation traveled to Myitkyina for consultations with Kachin civil society organizations and political leaders. The delegation included General Anthony Crutchfield, the deputy commander of the US Pacific Command. At this point, Thant Myint-U writes, "the leadership in Beijing started to take notice: fighting was bad, but the wrong kind of peace could be worse."[47]

To secure its objectives, China has taken a dual-track approach to Burma's ethnic conflicts. On the one hand, it has used the peace negotiations to contain active conflicts along its border and push forward CMEC infrastructure projects. On the other, it has maintained close relationships with key ethnic armed groups, and used them to exert leverage over the government in Naypyidaw. The largest of these levers is the United Wa State Army (UWSA), Burma's most powerful rebel force, which occupies two expansive territories in Shan State guarded by a standing army of 30,000. Like minuscule Mong La, which borders its main territory to the south, the UWSA signed a ceasefire with the central government in 1989, and is led by an ageing ethnic Chinese former communist rebel, Bao Youxiang. The UWSA's economy is arranged around a network of industrial-scale drug labs, which for years have flooded mainland Southeast Asia with cheap *yaba* pills and crystal meth. Recognizing its importance, China has turned a blind eye to the UWSA's involvement in narcotics and other illicit trades, and has reportedly provided it with military equipment—including portable air-defense systems, armored vehicles, and heavy artillery—that have helped its leaders safeguard their autonomy from Naypyidaw.[48]

Beijing's relationship with the UWSA is a prime example of its approach to Burma's ethnic conflicts. As Yun Sun, a researcher at the Stimson Center in Washington, DC, argued in a 2017 report, the UWSA leads a coalition of ethnic armed groups that have been skeptical of taking part in nationwide peace talks. Given the Chinese influence over the UWSA, Beijing's cooperation is necessary if this coalition is ever to join a credible peace process—a sine qua non of any meaningful nationwide deal. This gives China considerable leverage over Burma's government. As Yun concludes, "China uses its involvement in that peace process as both a carrot to induce more cooperation from Myanmar and a stick when Myanmar appears to be deviating from the policy course that China desires."[49]

In late 2015, the stick was used to signal Beijing's displeasure at the creeping Japanese and Western inroads in the peace negotiations. In the run-up to the signing of the Nationwide Ceasefire Agreement that took place in October of that year, China's envoy Sun Guoxiang reportedly persuaded key armed organizations, including the KIA and UWSA, not to sign.[50] The following year, as relations improved under the NLD government, the stick was swapped out for the carrot. China not only supported the three large peace conferences organized by Aung San Suu Kyi's government; it also ensured that wavering insurgent armies fronted up, going so far as to force their representatives to board a chartered flight from Kunming to Naypyidaw to attend a key meeting in May 2017.[51] Instead of picking a side between Burma and the ethnic armed groups, Yun observes, Beijing "maintains good relations with both, and each serves a distinct purpose."[52]

A similar logic has guided China's approach to the Arakan crisis. In November 2017, three months after the military "clearance operations" against the Rohingya, Foreign Minister Wang Yi announced that the Chinese government was brokering a "three-phase plan" to bring about "a final and fundamental solution" to the humanitarian emergency in Bangladesh. The vaguely drawn plan involved a ceasefire, the repatriation of Rohingya refugees back to Burma, and unspecified measures to promote long-term economic development in Arakan State. Again, China's involvement was motivated less by humanitarian concerns than by the need to stabilize an area of strategic interest. Arakan, after all, is the site of the planned Kyaukphyu deep-water port: China's long-cherished outlet to the western sea.

Even as Burma's relations with China improved under the NLD, they remained hesitant and uneasy, feelings that have been encapsulated by Beijing's efforts to revive the Myitsone dam. After its suspension in 2011, the Chinese lobbied hard for the resumption of the project. When Burma's relations with the West deteriorated after 2017, they became pushier. In December 2018, Hong Liang, China's ambassador to Burma, flew to Kachin State and announced that further delays to the Myitsone project could hamper bilateral relations. "If this issue fails to be resolved," a statement published on the embassy's Facebook page quoted him as saying, "it will seriously hurt the confidence of Chinese entrepreneurs to invest in Myanmar."[53] For good measure, he warned Kachin political leaders against forging close relationships with Western diplomats, threatening unspecified "serious consequences."[54]

By leaving office without making a final decision on the Myitsone dam project, President Thein Sein had handed his successor a thorny dilemma: cancel the project and anger Beijing, or resume it and alienate a large slice of Burma's electorate. Aung San Suu Kyi's government chose Option C—none of the above—and left the Myitsone dam in a state of suspended animation, an unbuilt monument to Burma's eternal quandary: how to live with China?

During my visit to the Myitsone area in May 2016, I was surprised to find that anger at China had been partly displaced onto the NLD government for not canceling the project outright. One of the local residents I spoke to was Daw Kam, a 32-year-old Kachin shop owner evicted from her village by the dam's construction in 2010. Like most of her neighbors, she had voted for Aung San Suu Kyi in the 2015 election. "The people believed that she would stand for the people," she said, sitting under the eaves of the shop she ran in Aung Myin Thar, a relocation village set up to house the 2,500 people displaced by the project. Her shelves were a shrine to the thriving border trade, stacked with Chinese umbrellas, rubber shoes, backpacks with images of Disney princesses, crockery, plastic toys, insect poison. If the NLD government resumed the dam project, Daw Kam said, locals would "fight against Aung San Suu Kyi."

In January 2020, Xi Jinping paid a state visit to Burma, the first by a top Chinese leader in nearly two decades. He came bearing a bouquet of infrastructure funding commitments and memorandums of understanding. After meetings with Aung San Suu Kyi and Senior General Min Aung Hlaing, the two nations agreed to elevate their relationship to a "Sino-Myanmar Community of Common Destiny," Burma becoming the third nation, after Cambodia and Laos, to adopt this Chinese formulation officially. Despite China's unpopularity among the Burmese population, its no-questions-asked approach to the situation in Arakan State had won it a special pass to the chambers of power in Naypyidaw. Just the previous month, Aung San Suu Kyi had appeared at the International Court of Justice in The Hague to defend Burma from allegations of genocide in Arakan State, in a case brought by The Gambia.

But if a constructive relationship with China was vital for any government that ruled in Naypyidaw, old fears of overdependence were never far behind. Even as NLD and Tatmadaw leaders spouted paeans to Sino-Burmese amity, they whispered concerns about Chinese debt, and Beijing's ties to breakaway rebel groups in the borderlands. To address the debt issue, China and Burma renegotiated the Kyaukphyu deep-water port agreement, reducing its price tag from $7.3 billion to just $1.3 billion.[55] Burma set up a special committee chaired by Aung San Suu Kyi to scrutinize BRI infrastructure developments. As one Burmese diplomat told the academic J. Mohan Malik, "We don't want Myanmar interests trampled on by China on its road to greatness."[56] Xi's state visit in 2020 abounded in the usual frothy diplomatic language, but saw relatively scant progress on China's cherished infrastructure deals.

As the continuing opposition to the Myitsone dam indicates, China's new era of influence in Burma might once again contain the seeds of its own negation. In a March 2018 report, researchers from the London-based International Growth Centre argued that public trust in China remained as low as ever. "There is an explicit bias against Chinese investments in Myanmar," the researchers concluded, warning both governments of "the potential local resistance they may face if their investment strategies do not consider the local context carefully."[57] China's hectoring efforts to get the Myitsone dam project back on track suggested that its imperious brand of "great-state autism" remained firmly entrenched.

Like Thailand and Vietnam, Aung San Suu Kyi's Burma sought a judicious balance in its foreign relations, an update of its old neutralism for a new era of superpower competition. To offset China's looming presence, it sought closer economic and security relationships with the region's other major powers, including its traditionally close partners Japan and India, both of which harbored apprehensions about China's activities in Burma. At the same time, the nation's tortured ethnic relations, and the systematic human rights abuses that flowed from them, have made constructive relations with the US and other Western democracies difficult to sustain.

From the beginning of the reform period, many Western governments came to see Burma as a place where values and interests aligned: where advancing democracy would also yield a strategic dividend. In so doing, they allowed their hopes for Burma to outpace the country's realities. As Thant Myint-U argues, the West's nostrums of democracy and free markets did little to resolve the deep racial divisions bequeathed by British rule. Indeed, they merely served to widen existing economic disparities and to "inject a new layer of partisan competition on an already fractious landscape." At a time when this neoliberal package was increasingly being questioned in Europe and North America, he writes, it had become Burma's "only prescription for the future. Twentieth-century answers are being offered as the default answers to the country's 21st-century challenges."[58]

China isn't offering any better answers. Its plan of sluicing BRI money into the conflict zones of Shan and Arakan states is no solution to these regions' problems, and will in all likelihood inflame the situations there. Yet for all its deafness to Burmese concerns, the Chinese government remains keenly attuned to the intractability of the nation's problems. Unlike many Western governments, it is willing to engage Burma's troubled realities in order to push forward vital strategic interests. As long as they persist, Burma's dynamics of ethnic conflict and division will therefore continue to exert a steady pressure in China's direction. All this puts the Burmese government in a liminal bind. Apprehensive about China's intentions, yet unable to escape its magnetic power, it remains stuck partway between the poles of fear and attraction, moving only so far in one direction before events send it sliding back.

7

SINGAPORE
THE GREAT LEAP OUTWARD

Southeast Asia's oldest church sits on a low hill above the Malaysian city of Malacca, overlooking the famous neck of water that shares its name. The small chapel of St. Paul's was erected in 1521 by the Portuguese nobleman Duarte Coelho, as an act of gratitude after he made a miraculous escape from a storm in the South China Sea. Today, all that remains of the church is a shell of laterite walls, open to the sky, and a whitewashed bell tower with blue shutters. On a brick plinth outside, the Spanish missionary St. Francis Xavier gazes coastward, frozen in white marble. His left hand clutches a cross to his chest, but his right is missing, lopped off clean on a windy day in 1953, by a falling branch from a casuarina tree.[1] Unperturbed, St. Francis extends his stump toward the distant Straits of Malacca, where container ships hang suspended, melting into the haze.

At the time of St. Paul's consecration, Malacca was one of the largest emporiums in the Orient: a fulcrum of the first great era of globalization. Founded at the beginning of the fifteenth century by the Malay prince Parameswara, it quickly grew into the center of a prosperous Muslim sultanate whose power extended across the Malay Peninsula and large parts of northern Sumatra. In addition to controlling access to the straits—then, as now, an artery of international trade—Malacca was situated at the mid-point of the wind-driven maritime trade routes running from the Indian Ocean and the South China Sea.

At its height in the mid-1400s, Malacca's harbor was thick with Chinese junks and Arabian dhows, its bazaars alive with foreign tongues and an overflow of exotic merchandise: cloth and gemstones from Gujarat and Bengal; spices and sandalwood from Sulawesi and the Banda Islands. Malays hawked tin, gold, rattan, and tortoiseshell; Chinese sold silk, porcelain, and camphor. "No trading port as large as Malacca is known, nor any where they deal in such fine and highly prized merchandise," wrote the Portuguese apothecary Tomé Pires, who lived in Malacca in the early sixteenth century. So important was the city to international trade, he declared, that "whoever is lord of Malacca has his hand on the throat of Venice."[2] Coveting its control over global commerce, Portugal seized Malacca from its Muslim rulers in 1511, an event that marked the beginning of more than four centuries of European domination of Asia.

Malacca's subsequent history is a fable on the fickleness of globalization. By the middle of the nineteenth century, after periods under Dutch and then British rule, the town's port had silted up and the flows of commerce—now driven by coal and steam—had long passed it by. "The stillness of death reigns through the streets," one traveler wrote of Malacca in 1837, "and even the laborious Chinese, seem here to catch the general spirit of quiescence." A few decades later another described Malacca as "a town 'out of the running', utterly antiquated . . . a veritable Sleepy Hollow."[3] The trade that once made Malacca prosperous passed instead to the British settlements at Penang, further up the Peninsula, and Singapore, at the southern entrance to the straits. Singapore grew into a bustling town under British administration, and later, into a global trans-shipment hub and offshore financial center: a Malacca for the shipping container age.

Old Malacca, meanwhile, has settled into a sleepy afterlife as new Melaka, a provincial capital and tourist center trading on its association with a vanished era of globalization. At the bottom of its church-crowned hill, visitors can examine the last remaining section of the fortress erected by the Portuguese after their conquest of the city. Once nicknamed *A Famosa* because of the unusual size of its keep, the pockmarked stone structure seems to have diminished with time, an antique icon of Iberian prestige now dwarfed by the Dataran Pahlawan Melaka Megamall across the street. Another popular sightseeing spot is the old Dutch town square, dominated by a terracotta-colored church dated 1753 and a British fountain bubbling in honor of Queen Victoria. The surrounding streets are a warren of narrow Chinese shop-houses.

In particular, Malacca's tourist industry abounds in references to Admiral Zheng He, the seafaring explorer of China's Ming dynasty, who steered seven massive armadas through the Indian Ocean between 1405 and 1433, before the Ming emperors abandoned their maritime ventures and turned inward. While Zheng's "treasure fleets" ranged as far as the Arabian Peninsula and the

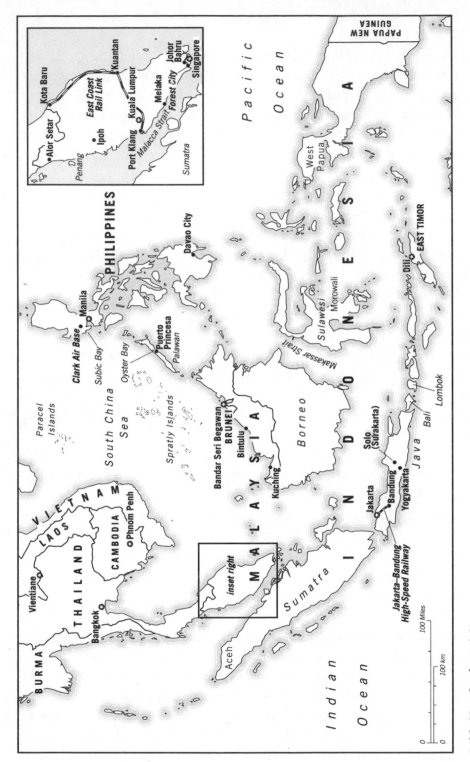

5. Maritime Southeast Asia

1. Chinese President Xi Jinping participates in a parade celebrating the 70th anniversary of the founding of the People's Republic of China in Beijing on October 1, 2019. Under Xi, the Chinese Communist Party (CCP) has tightened control at home and asserted its power abroad, seeking to recapture China's former status as the preeminent power in Asia.

2. A cartoon published in *Le Petit Journal* on January 16, 1898, depicting the Western powers and Japan scheming to partition a weakened imperial China. Memories of this "century of humiliation," inculcated by decades of state nationalism, have fueled the CCP's drive to restore China's wealth and power.

3. An engraving of the Mekong Exploration Commission at Angkor Wat in 1866, during its attempt to chart a viable commercial trade route from Saigon to southern China. Although the expedition failed in its aim, it helped extend French control over Indochina and foreshadowed China's current economic integration with the Mekong region. The mission's commander, Ernest Doudart de Lagrée, is at far right.

4. The Mekong River at Pakbeng, Laos. In recent years, Beijing has shaped the great river to serve its economy, damming its upper reaches and opening the waterway to large-scale cargo transport. China's control of the headwaters of the Mekong gives it increasing strategic leverage over the smaller nations downstream.

5. Ornamental gate at the Chinese-run Golden Triangle Special Economic Zone, a palm-fringed gambling enclave on the Mekong River in northwestern Laos. The zone and its crown-topped casino are among the most ostentatious signs of China's rising influence along Southeast Asia's great river.

6. Chinese police escort Naw Kham, an ethnic Shan bandit and drug-runner, to his execution in Kunming on March 1, 2013. Accused of masterminding the murder of 13 Chinese sailors in 2011, the hunt for Naw Kham marked a dramatic increase in Beijing's security presence in mainland Southeast Asia.

7. Zhao Wei, chairman of the Kings Romans Group, pictured in a promotional brochure produced by his company. Zhao's gambling operation in the Golden Triangle Special Economic Zone is believed to be deeply immersed in the region's illicit trades.

8. A Vietnamese infantryman beats back invading Chinese troops on a mural at a military cemetery outside the town of Sapa in northern Vietnam in March 2003. A 1979 border war with China cost tens of thousands of lives, but in the interest of good relations with Beijing is seldom mentioned by Vietnam's communist government.

9. Patriotic demonstrators take part in an unauthorized march in Hanoi on March 14, 2016, marking the anniversary of a 1988 naval clash with China in the Spratly Islands, in which Chinese sailors gunned down 64 Vietnamese personnel. Nurtured by centuries of tense relations, anti-Chinese sentiment cuts across every social divide in contemporary Vietnam.

10. Prime Minister Hun Sen of Cambodia attends a state funeral in the capital Phnom Penh in June 2015. During his 35 years in power, Hun Sen has gone from being one of China's harshest critics to its closest friend and client in Southeast Asia.

11. A Chinese-run casino in Sihanoukville, on the Cambodian coast. Since 2015, a wave of Chinese money has transformed this small port city, once popular with Western backpackers, into a tourism and gambling hub: a down-market Macao on the Gulf of Thailand.

12. A Chinese railway bridge under construction in the hills of China's Yunnan province, en route to the Lao border town of Boten and the capital Vientiane. The Laos–China railway, which will tunnel its way through 414 kilometers of rugged terrain, is a striking example of Chinese engineering prowess—but questions linger over its utility.

13. Chinese shops at the Sanjiang Market in Vientiane, Laos. Since the 1990s, Laos and other mainland Southeast Asian nations have become a magnet for traders and businesspeople from China. This wave of "new migrants" has transformed parts of Vientiane and northern Laos into facsimiles of urban China, right down to the dangling red plastic lanterns.

14. Thailand's Prime Minister Prayuth Chan-ocha attends a birthday ceremony for Princess Maha Chakri Sirindhorn in Bangkok in April 2015. When Western powers criticized the coup d'état that brought him to power in May 2014, Prayuth steered his nation into a closer partnership with China.

15. Yaowarat Road, the main thoroughfare in Bangkok's Chinatown, the largest in Southeast Asia. As elsewhere in Southeast Asia, ethnic Chinese predominate at the upper echelons of Thai politics and business, facilitating economic linkages with China and softening apprehensions of its waxing power.

16. Aung San Suu Kyi, Burma's de facto leader, speaks at an election campaign rally in Shan State on September 6, 2015. As the one-time human rights icon came under fierce Western criticism following the military's ethnic cleansing of Rohingya Muslims in late 2017, her government was pushed into an uneasy reliance on China.

17. A vista of Mong La, the capital of Special Region No. 4, a militia-run enclave perched on the border between Burma's Shan State and China's Yunnan province. An effective annex of southern China, the small settlement testifies to Beijing's strong presence in the ethnic rebel zones abutting its sensitive southwestern frontier.

18. A statue of Admiral Zheng He, who led the great Ming dynasty ocean voyages in the early fifteenth century, at the Tay Kak Sie Temple in Semarang, Indonesia. As China builds up its naval capacity, Zheng has been used to bolster Beijing's claim that its rise will be uniquely peaceful and beneficent.

19. Xi Jinping, then China's vice president (left), and Singapore's minister mentor Lee Kuan Yew unveil a commemorative bust of Deng Xiaoping in Singapore on November 14, 2010. Deng's visit to Singapore in 1978 laid the foundation for a special relationship between the two nations—one that is now coming under increased strain.

20. The showroom of Forest City, a major Chinese property development, in Johor Bahru, on the tip of peninsular Malaysia. Concern about China's expanding influence during the administration of Prime Minister Najib Razak played a significant role in the historic defeat of Najib's Barisan Nasional coalition at national elections in May 2018.

21. A cartoon published in May 2017 by the Malaysian cartoonist Zunar, accusing Najib of selling out Malaysia in exchange for Chinese largesse. Under political fire for receiving hundreds of millions in pilfered funds from the sovereign wealth fund 1MDB, Najib allegedly approved a raft of overpriced Chinese infrastructure deals.

22. The aftermath of riots in the Indonesian capital Jakarta on May 14, 1998, which ended Suharto's 31-year rule and saw violent pogroms against Chinese-Indonesians. Indonesia's relationship with China is impossible to detach from popular prejudices toward the country's small but economically dominant ethnic Chinese minority.

23. Kopi Es Tak Kie (est. 1927), the oldest café in Glodok, Jakarta's Chinatown. While Indonesia's Chinese community has come a long way since the fall of Suharto, it finds itself caught between China's increasing power and a rising tide of religious populism that casts ethnic Chinese as alien to Indonesian society.

24. Philippine President Rodrigo Duterte (holding sniper rifle) with outgoing national police chief Ronald "Bato" dela Rosa during a handover ceremony in Manila on April 19, 2018. After his shock election victory in May 2016, Duterte wrenched the Philippines' foreign policy away from the United States, its traditional ally, and embraced China.

25. An aerial view of Thitu Island—known as Pag-asa, or "hope" in Tagalog—taken on November 26, 2005. This isolated Filipino outpost in the Spratly Islands supports a population of 120 civilians, who dwell in the shadow of the imposing Chinese military installations on nearby Subi Reef.

east coast of Africa, the eunuch admiral is most closely associated with Malacca. He visited the entrepôt at least five times, during which he built godowns and stockades for use on subsequent voyages. His journeys also sealed Malacca's tributary relationship with the Ming: its first three leaders traveled to China for formal investiture by the emperor, and the sultanate dispatched regular missions of tribute.[4] In exchange, the Ming navy offered protection from Siam and the powerful kingdom of Majapahit on the island of Java, security that was pivotal to Malacca's commercial flowering.

Six centuries on, Zheng is once again a dominant presence in Malacca. A street, a gallery, and several hotels are named after Cheng Ho, as his name is rendered in Malaysia. He is commemorated by a statue and a plaque on the Malacca River that records where he first touched Malaccan soil in 1405. The most elaborate monument to Zheng's legacy is the Cheng Ho Cultural Museum, a narrow two-story building not far from the old Dutch square. Officially opened in 2005, on the 600th anniversary of his first voyage, the museum offers a detailed telling of Zheng's life and times, from his birth to a prominent Muslim family in Yunnan to his capture by an invading Ming army at the age of 13, when he was castrated to serve as a palace eunuch. It also describes the pioneering voyages that earned him his place in history.

For the museum's founder Tan Ta Sen, a Malaysian-born scholar and entrepreneur from Singapore who heads the International Zheng He Society, the famous voyager deserves credit for securing Malacca's independence, and bringing peace and prosperity to the region as a whole. "Zheng He is important history, not only to Malacca and Southeast Asia, but for the spirit itself," Tan, a salt-haired man in his seventies, said when we met in Singapore in late 2017. "When the Portuguese came, they slaughtered 15,000 people, but Zheng never killed anybody, never took one inch of territory."

For Tan, the Cheng Ho Cultural Museum is the culmination of a lifetime's fascination with Zheng and his voyages. A decade ago, he relinquished day-to-day control of Utraco, his successful construction firm, and returned to the scholarly career that he abandoned in the late 1970s to go into business. He has since written numerous books and monographs about the Ming dynasty and its ties to Malacca, and amassed an extensive private collection of Chinese antiquities, including Ming cannons and ceramics dating as far back as the Tang dynasty. Those not on display at the museum he stores on the second floor of his office, a boxy steel building in the Jurong industrial district of Singapore. During the construction of the museum in Malacca, workers found five ancient wells, and unearthed numerous fragments of Ming porcelain: proof, Tan said, of his theory that it occupies the site of a former warehouse complex built by Zheng six centuries ago. "It took many years. It's a passion," he said of the museum.

The museum's displays reflect Tan's view that the Ming ventured abroad to trade, but never to conquer. Captions describe Zheng as "a big-hearted peace ambassador" who exported "peace and fortune" to the world, teaching Vietnamese to make tofu and Africans to plant cotton. In a darkened room, a video shows CGI renditions of the Ming fleets and effuses on their contributions to culture and diplomacy. "Cheng Ho helped to acquaint the world with China," a stentorian voiceover intones, "and China with the world."

In the West, Zheng and his legacy have long been the subject of debate, especially since the publication in 2002 of *1421: The Year China Discovered the World*, by the former British submarine officer Gavin Menzies. In the book, Menzies asserted that Zheng's fleets rounded the Cape of Good Hope and visited South America, decades ahead of Columbus. The hypothesis is mostly dismissed by historians; one international group of experts called the book "a work of sheer fiction presented as revisionist history."[5]

Yet even by the light of the available evidence, the Zheng He voyages were remarkable endeavors. His "treasure ships" (*baochuan*) were some of the largest wooden vessels to take to the seas, each weighing 1,500 tons, five times the size of the battered caravel that the Portuguese explorer Vasco da Gama would coax around the Cape and on toward India at the end of the fifteenth century. Their hulls painted with dragons, their rigging snapping with pennants of colored silk, the treasure ships were imposing manifestations of the majesty of the Ming at the apogee of its power. Zheng's fleet is believed to have contained 250–300 *baochuan* accompanied by a flotilla of supply ships, warships, and patrol boats. In total they carried around 27,000 men, most of them soldiers. In its prime, Joseph Needham writes, "the Ming navy probably outclassed that of any other Asian nation at any time in history, and would have been more than a match for that of any contemporary European State or even a combination of them."[6]

Then, just as their naval power reached its height, the Ming rulers initiated a sudden inward turn. This followed the death in 1424 of Yongle, the first great emperor of the Ming, who had ordered Zheng's expeditions. His successors decreed a ban on all seafaring activities, dismantled Nanjing's mighty ship-yards, and shrank the imperial navy down to a small coastal defense force. China's maritime power rapidly declined, never fully to recover. Thus ensued one of the great contingencies of global history. The Ming withdrawal from the oceans halted the momentum of China's maritime development just as the Europeans were beginning to take to the seas. In 1498, Vasco da Gama dropped anchor on the Indian subcontinent, initiating an era of Western exploration and conquest. Deprived of Chinese naval protection, Malacca fell to the Portuguese in 1511, and the sultanate went into decline. For the Chinese empire, the ramifications of this retreat from the sea were less immediate, but ultimately sped it on a downward trajectory that led to the Opium Wars, the treaty ports, and its "century of humiliation" at the hands of the Western imperial powers and Japan—all of which fell upon China from the seas.

Historians have offered several theories as to why the Ming abandoned the ocean. One theory is that Yongle's successors saw the "treasure fleets" as a costly extravagance that they were unwilling to sustain. Another is that the renovation of the ancient Grand Canal in the early 1400s reduced China's need for an ocean-going fleet. Whatever the exact cause, the inward turn was consistent with the Chinese state's historically disdainful attitude toward the maritime world. Across the vast sweep of its history, the greatest threats to imperial China's survival had come not from the sea, but from the barren steppes to the north, home to nomadic "barbarian" warrior peoples like the Mongols and the Manchus. This continental focus, the historian Wensheng Wang writes, "pushed the seafaring world to the margins of the Chinese cognitive frame as though it stood outside and beyond history." Wild and incomprehensibly vast, the seas were viewed as an untamable realm, "a terror-filled world of disorder and unknown possibilities."[7] The concrete manifestation of this earthbound mentality was not the imperial armada, restlessly seeking out distant markets and colonies, but the Great Wall, a physical barrier against the barbarian realm.

To be sure, the oceans were hardly terra incognita to the Chinese. Dating back to the time of the Roman Empire, coastal peoples like the Hokkien had sailed widely through the south seas, and maintained enduring commercial connections across the waters. By the time of Zheng's voyages, southern Chinese had been dominant in the South China Sea trade for half a millen-nium, dealing in everything from silk and porcelain to sea cucumbers and edible birds' nests. Over time, the historian Wang Gungwu writes, the maritime expanses of the Nanyang "became to the southern Chinese what the land outside the Jade Gate was to the northern Chinese. Its waters and its island straits were the sands and the mountain passes of Central Asia; its ports were like the caravanserais."[8] Later, they emigrated in large numbers into the Nanyang, often in defiance of official bans: in fact, the Chinese state's turn from the seas in the fifteenth century coincided with the first significant movement of Chinese into Siam, Vietnam, and the Malay archipelago.

Despite the connection of China's coastal peoples with the sea, Zheng He's titanic "treasure fleet" was an exception to the continental rule: an ocean-going feat never matched by any Chinese state, before or since. Nearly 600 years on, however, China is embarking upon the most determined maritime push since the heyday of the Ming dynasty. As the country's economy has grown, the Chinese Communist Party (CCP) has engineered a "great leap outward" into the seas, building up a "blue-water" navy capable of projecting power deep into the Pacific and Indian oceans, and claiming sovereignty over vast swathes of ocean once traversed by Zheng's armadas.[9] For the first time in six centuries, Chinese officials are speaking of their country's destiny in explicitly maritime terms.

The hard edge of China's maritime leap is a military modernization drive that has focused on the navy and supporting air power and reconnaissance capabilities—all instruments of maritime power projection. Under Xi, the People's Liberation Army Navy (PLAN) has expanded rapidly in size and capability. Between 2014 and 2018, China launched more submarines, warships, amphibious vessels, and auxiliaries than the number of ships currently serving in the navies of Germany, India, Spain, and the United Kingdom, combined.[10] Many were new advanced classes of frigates, destroyers, and nuclear-powered submarines that have quickly closed the operational gap between the PLAN and the US and Japanese navies. In 2012, the Chinese navy commissioned its first aircraft carrier, the Liaoning, purchased from Ukraine in 1998 at a knock-down price and subsequently refitted in China. Two more domestically produced carriers—known as Type 001A and Type 002—are currently in production.

President Xi has also been more willing than his predecessors to deploy naval force in support of Chinese objectives, especially in the South China Sea. In late 2013, Chinese dredgers began creating facts on the ground in the disputed Spratly Islands, transforming reefs and barren maritime features into fortified islands complete with radar installations and airfields. These islands have provided refueling and resupply bases for the navy and coastguard vessels that China has used to extend its control over the critical waterway.

China's immediate goal is to protect the shipping lanes upon which its economy is heavily dependent. In practice, this means gaining unfettered control of the waters lying within what Chinese strategists refer to as the "first island chain," which traces an arc south from the Japanese archipelago to Taiwan, the Philippines, and the northern coast of Borneo. Unable for now to match the US Navy in a head-to-head confrontation, the Chinese have instead invested in what security boffins term "anti-access and area denial": an asymmetric strategy designed to incrementally raise the costs to American vessels of entering its desired zone of influence, with the eventual aim of evicting them from the area altogether. Ahead of his appointment as commander of the US Indo-Pacific Command in 2018, Admiral Philip Davidson told a congressional committee that China was now capable of controlling the South China Sea in all scenarios "short of war with the United States."[11] This strategy is informed by Beijing's ardent desire to reattach the island of Taiwan to the mainland, but also extends beyond it. As the naval scholar Toshi Yoshihara argues, Taiwan's totemic status for the CCP is matched by its importance as a potential springboard into the Pacific. He quotes a Chinese military strategist who describes the island as "a lock around the neck of a great dragon."[12]

Like his dynastic progenitors, Mao Zedong disdained the seas, opting for a small navy capable of controlling the waters immediately touching China's shores. Like much else in China, this emphasis began to shift under Deng Xiaoping in the 1980s. Just as some Chinese strategists were pushing for the creation of an overland corridor through mainland Southeast Asia to the Indian Ocean, others were directing their gaze offshore. Many absorbed the writings of Alfred Thayer Mahan, the nineteenth-century American evangelist of sea-power, who argued that control of the "wide common" of the ocean was the key to national survival and economic development. Mahan's greatest work, *The Influence of Sea Power upon History*, published in 1890, underpinned the American republic's colonial push into the Pacific, its seizure of Hawaii and the Philippines, and its development of a world-class navy. Now his teachings were helping China in its own maritime push.

The most prominent Chinese booster of Mahanian strategy was Admiral Liu Huaqing, a storied People's Liberation Army (PLA) veteran who had endured the Long March and fought in the war against the Nationalists. As PLAN commander from 1982 to 1987, Liu argued that as China became more reliant on trade and investment to modernize, it needed to strengthen its control over the seas. Wielding Mahan's writings against his bureaucratic opponents, he called for the nation to develop a "blue-water" capability that would secure the sea-lanes lying within the first island chain. "Without an aircraft carrier, I will die with my eyelids open," Liu told an interviewer in 1987.[13] Early the following year, the Chinese navy seized Johnson South Reef in the Spratly Islands, establishing its first beachhead in the archipelago. By the end of the year, China had occupied six reefs and atolls in the Spratlys. It was a dramatic display of Liu's doctrine in action.

Liu's naval advocacy took place around the same time that other Chinese intellectuals were scrutinizing the conservative, land-bound values of traditional Chinese civilization. One notable example was *River Elegy*, a six-part documentary series directed by the scholar and filmmaker Wang Luxiang, which was televised in June 1988, at the height of the pre-Tiananmen political ferment. The series depicted China's backwardness as an outgrowth of fundamental flaws in Chinese culture, arguing that the nation's revival would come not from the Yellow River—Wang's symbol for the ossified conservativism of old China—but from the oceans, which he used to embody the more open, explorative cultures of Europe, America, and Japan.[14]

Shortly after airing, *River Elegy* was banned by the CCP for its implied advocacy of political reform. Nevertheless, there was much in Deng's reforms that evinced its more open approach to the outside world. His decision to start by developing China's coastal provinces built on their long connections with the oceans, transforming the sites of the humiliating "unequal treaties" into engines of economic rejuvenation. He also negotiated the return of the former colonies of Hong Kong and Macao from Britain and Portugal: emblems of China's subjugation by the maritime empires of the West. In a final gesture before he died, Deng requested that his ashes be scattered over the seas.[15]

The oceans have since become central to China's re-emergence as a global power. Coastal provinces and cities account for a small fraction of its landmass, but more than half of its GDP.[16] Between 1980 and 2000, China built more than 184 new ports to support its rapidly expanding economy, and the country today boasts seven of the world's ten busiest container ports.[17] By 2018, Chinese companies had helped build or expand 42 ports in 34 countries, many under the aegis of the Belt and Road Initiative (BRI).[18] China's growing dependence on foreign supplies of oil, natural gas, and other commodities—transported predominantly by oil tanker and container ship—has made control of these routes vital to its continued growth. In 2015, a Chinese defense white paper urged that the "traditional mentality that land outweighs sea must be abandoned, and great importance has to be attached to managing the seas and oceans and protecting maritime rights and interests."[19]

The Chinese government's new seafaring focus is profoundly informed by the disasters of the past. During the giant naval regatta marking the 70th anniversary of the PLAN's founding in April 2019, state media commentaries were rich with references to old humiliations. "A strong navy is essential for a country to safeguard its national security," one Xinhua report declared. "From 1840 to 1949, China was invaded by foreign powers more than 470 times from the sea, which brought untold suffering to its people."[20] Like the British before them, and the Americans today, China aims to "rule the waves and waive the rules"—first in its backyard, and then beyond.

Unsurprisingly, China's oceanic push has created considerable friction with the five nations of maritime Southeast Asia, a dispersed island region that runs in a crescent from the balcony of Aceh at the tip of western Sumatra to the Banda Islands in the east of the Indonesian archipelago to Luzon island in the northern Philippines. To soothe the region's anxieties, Chinese leaders have reached back to the nation's last great era of sea-going endeavor: the "treasure fleet" voyages of the early fifteenth century. In recent years scholars and officials have repeatedly referenced Admiral Zheng He as an envoy of trade, brotherhood, and cultural exchange—a figure who, as a leading Chinese scholar of Southeast Asia has put it, made "outstanding contributions to global navigation and to the friendship between China and other countries."[21] Like the Cheng Ho Cultural Museum in Malacca, this view emphasizes the supposedly peaceful intent of Zheng's voyages, projecting them onto present maritime ambitions. Effectively, Zheng has been enlisted as the official mascot of China's new march to the sea.

For several centuries after his death, Admiral Zheng was all but forgotten in his homeland, even as memories endured in the Malay archipelago, where he passed into local folklore as the quasi-spiritual deity San Pao Kung, the "lord of three treasures," worshipped at mosques and temples throughout the islands.[22] It was only in the late nineteenth century that Zheng resurfaced in Chinese discourse, resurrected by reformers eager to stiffen an enfeebled China with a new sense of national pride. As Howard French relates, the story of China's pioneering admiral was quickly used to anchor a narrative of Chinese exceptionalism, which contrasted the peaceable Ming voyages with the aggression of the Western empires. The Chinese scholar-reformer Liang Qichao frequently invoked Zheng's exploits—in 1905, he published an essay titled "Zheng He: A great navigator of our homeland"—as did the republican leader Sun Yat-sen. Both looked to Zheng as a reminder of the grandeur of the past, and as "proof that China was different by nature and, by clear inference, morally superior to the West."[23]

Today, Chinese officials wield this exceptionalist narrative to buttress China's claim that its rise will be different—more peaceful, more "win–win"— to that of the great powers of the past. Among the most active retailers of the Zheng myth in the current Chinese administration is Premier Li Keqiang, who has referenced the famous admiral on state visits to the Philippines, Indonesia, and Singapore. During an official visit to Malaysia in late 2015, Li gave several speeches hailing Zheng as an example of the "invaluable bond of peace and friendship" between China and the maritime nations of Southeast Asia. "Instead of blood and fire, plundering and colonialism," Li told delegates to the 18th China–ASEAN Summit, "he brought with him Chinese porcelain, silk, and tea as well as friendship and goodwill from the Chinese people."[24] The following day, Li traveled to Malacca and visited the Cheng Ho Cultural Museum, where Tan Ta Sen gave him a private tour. (Photos from the visit are on display in the museum's lobby.)

Zheng's legacy also offers historical ballast for the softer edge of China's naval modernization drive: the 21st Century Maritime Silk Road (MSR), a scheme of port-building and ocean connectivity that forms the "road" component of the BRI. Xi launched the initiative in October 2013 in a speech to the Indonesian parliament rich with references to the "shared destiny" of China and maritime Southeast Asia. He included a customary mention of Zheng He, who, in Xi's words, "left nice stories of friendly exchanges between the Chinese and Indonesian peoples."[25] The MSR shows a keen awareness of historical precedents: maps of these maritime "roads" resemble closely the routes traveled by Zheng's fleets in the fifteenth century.

The problem is that Zheng He's voyages were never as peaceful or "win–win" as Chinese officials like to claim. The "treasure fleets" were one part of a policy of aggressive southern expansion undertaken by the Yongle Emperor in the early fifteenth century. During Yongle's 1402–24 reign, Chinese armies invaded and briefly annexed northern Vietnam, and undertook a concerted program of settler colonialism in recently conquered Yunnan. The historian Geoff Wade, a specialist on relations between Southeast Asia and the Ming, has argued that Zheng essentially carried this expansionist spirit to the seas: his fleets included large contingents of troops, and intervened openly in the disputes of the region. In what is now Sri Lanka, he even toppled a local ruler, Alaskawera, and hauled him back to the Ming court in Nanjing. The aim of Zheng's voyages, Wade writes, was "to achieve the recognition of Ming dominance of (or perhaps suzerainty over) all the polities of the known maritime world. To achieve this they used force, or the threat thereof."[26] As with Gavin Menzies's claim that the Chinese admiral voyaged to the Americas, the official narrative of Zheng's voyages does not stand up to close scrutiny.

That's not to say that this message will fail to resonate in maritime Southeast Asia, which, like China, experienced the contusions of Western and Japanese imperialism in the nineteenth and twentieth centuries. When I interviewed him in October 2017, Malaysia's two-time prime minister Mahathir Mohamad said that for all his concerns about Chinese power, "Malaysia has been dealing with China for 2,000 years. Somehow or other they have never conquered us." The problem is that Beijing's actions are increasingly undercutting its self-image as a fellow Asian victim of Western bullying. Three of the region's states—Malaysia, Brunei, and the Philippines— directly contest China's "nine-dash line" claim in the South China Sea, while the remaining two—Singapore and Indonesia—have spoken out strongly against it. This is not simply a question of dueling nationalistic traditions. At stake also is access to a share of the region's bountiful maritime resources, including large undersea deposits of oil and gas. In the sea-girt regions of Southeast Asia, including Vietnam, I have also heard concerns about the strain on vital fishery resources, and the adverse environmental impacts of Chinese land reclamation efforts.

As these sovereign clashes suggest, maritime Southeast Asia presents a much more formidable barrier to the extension of Chinese influence than the five mainland nations contiguous with China. Despite trading for centuries with China and absorbing huge numbers of its sons and daughters, the island region has had only glancing contact with the Chinese state. As Philip Bowring writes in his book *Empire of the Winds*, maritime Southeast Asia has historically been the domain of Austronesian peoples—the Malays—who share a common cultural, linguistic, and seafaring heritage. This unity has led Bowring to term the region "Nusantaria"—a derivation of *nusantara*, a Malay word meaning "island realm."

Contrary to Beijing's historical claims to most of the South China Sea, the Chinese state came late to "Nusantaria," just one in a succession of outside influences—Indian culture, Islamic religion, Western civilization—that washed through the region.[27] While the Malay peoples traded with and occasionally paid tribute to the Chinese empire, as in the case of the Malacca Sultanate, C.P. Fitzgerald writes that the archipelago was "only marginally concerned with China and only very occasionally affected by her power."[28]

Until the twentieth century, the region's main contact with China came via the peoples that flowed from China's shores, first as sailors and merchants, then as immigrants seeking refuge and prosperity across the warm, fertile arc of the Nanyang. In the nineteenth and early twentieth centuries, these immigrants set forth from the port cities of Fujian and Guangdong, boarding leaky steamships that bore them into new lives of toil on Javanese sugar plantations, in the tin mines of Malaya, and on the docks of Singapore. Here they joined an earlier wave of Chinese transplants—the Peranakans, or Straits Chinese—whose presence dated back to the time of the Zheng He voyages and earlier, and who had since intermarried with Malays and assimilated deeply into the local cultures.

While large-scale Chinese emigration to Southeast Asia was not the result of a conscious state policy—indeed, the inward-looking Chinese state frequently disdained those who left—these ethnic Chinese communities have had profound impacts on the ethnic composition and political life of maritime Southeast Asia. Today, three out of every four Singaporeans is of Chinese descent, and ethnic Chinese make up around a quarter of Malaysia's population. They also constitute smaller yet disproportionately wealthy and influential slices of the population in Indonesia and the Philippines.

The presence of these ethnic Chinese populations adds a further complicating layer to Beijing's bid for influence in maritime Southeast Asia. Anxieties about Chinese immigrants, long present across the region, have been especially acute in maritime Southeast Asia, where they have tended to fit most awkwardly into the prevailing national, ethnic, and religious categories. As mentioned in Chapter 1, these frictions originated in the late nineteenth century, when Chinese nationalism led to an awakening of Chinese identities across Southeast Asia, tainting overseas ethnic Chinese with the perception of divided loyalties. These worries intensified after 1949, when the People's Republic of China (PRC) began exporting revolution to the region, leading colonial governments and independent states to impose various discriminatory measures against those of Chinese extraction.

The "Chinese question" has been a constant thread in the modern history of maritime Southeast Asia. The question of racial parity determined the territorial shape of the Malaysian Federation established in 1963, and contributed in some measure to Chinese-majority Singapore's expulsion from it two years later. Anti-Chinese politics has left an especially toxic legacy in Indonesia, where a small, economically dominant Chinese minority, still somehow associated with the specter of a long-vanished communism, has frequently been subjected to violent pogroms—most recently in May 1998, during the upheavals that accompanied the fall of President Suharto. The situation is less serious in the Philippines, where ethnic Chinese have been deeply assimilated into the nation's polyglot mix, but even there, questions of dual loyalties have arisen over the recent discord in the South China Sea. For the nations of maritime Southeast Asia, perceptions of China's rising power are inextricably bound up with their own internal ethnic politics, and the fear, only partly assuaged by Beijing's rhetoric of "non-interference," that China might one day call upon the loyalty of the ethnic Chinese abroad.

On this count, there are legitimate causes for concern. In 1980, China renounced the principle of dual nationality in an attempt to reassure Southeast Asian nations that it drew a firm distinction between Chinese ethnicity and Chinese citizenship. Now, two forces are conspiring to muddy the distinction once again. From one side, an emboldened and confident China under Xi Jinping has cast off its old policy of restraint, ratcheting up its cultural and political outreach to the ethnic Chinese abroad, hailing them as "members of the Chinese family" and employing a more assertive rhetoric about the welfare of its "compatriots" abroad. From the other side, nationalist and religious firebrands in maritime Southeast Asia, especially in Muslim-majority Malaysia and Indonesia, are again playing on fears of the ethnic

Chinese for domestic political gain, bringing anxieties about a resurgent China, and dormant resentments of its prosperous offspring, back into worrying alignment.

All the factors that make China's power an issue of great apprehension in maritime Southeast Asia converge on the tiny island-nation of Singapore. Like the Malacca Sultanate that rose to short prominence six centuries ago, modern Singapore is an offspring of globalization, skimming prosperity from the trade that courses through the Malacca Straits. First founded as a modern seaport by Sir Thomas Stamford Raffles in 1819, on an island at the southern tip of the Malay Peninsula, it quickly grew into a thriving cosmopolitan settlement, and an important node of British imperial power. Accounting for the success of his new emporium, Raffles ascribed credit to "the simple but almost magic result of that perfect freedom of Trade which it has been my good fortune to establish."[29]

Swap out British sea-power for American, and much the same is true of Singapore today. Under the rule of the leonine Lee Kuan Yew and his People's Action Party (PAP), which has ruled Singapore since its accidental independence in 1965, the straits entrepôt has grown into the most economically advanced nation in Southeast Asia. What old Malacca was to the age of wind, Singapore is to the age of diesel and microchips: a critical seat of the global economy, boasting the world's second-largest container port after Shanghai. Its pearly skyscrapers house the regional headquarters of multinational corporations and a concentration of legal and financial services without peer in Southeast Asia. Singapore is also the region's premier offshore banking hub, and the preferred place for Burmese and Cambodian kleptocrats to stash their money. In 2018, Singapore's GDP was $364 billion, around the same as neighboring Malaysia, a nation with a population six times the size.[30]

As a wealthy island-nation reliant on a protective shade of Western power—first, the imperial *Pax Britannica*, now the regional security order undergirded by the US Navy—Singapore stands in unique relation to China's rising power. The city-state's pragmatic leaders see China as vital to their country's economic future, but their reliance on maritime trade has made them outspoken on the need for a stabilizing American military presence in the region. Singapore's position is complicated further by another artefact of British rule: its status as an ethnic Chinese-majority state.

The first Chinese arrivals to Singapore were Straits Chinese, who trickled down the peninsula from Malacca and Penang; later, they came directly from China itself. Within a few decades of its founding, Singapore had replaced Bangkok as the leading center for Chinese shipping in Asia, linked by a regular steamship service to the ports of Xiamen and Quanzhou in Fujian province.[31] "In going through one part of the town, during business hours, one feels himself to be in a Chinese city," one Western traveler wrote in 1837. "Almost every respectable native he sees is Chinese; almost every shop, ware-room, and trade, is carried on by the Chinese; the hucksters, coolies, traveling cooks, and cries common in a great city, are Chinese."[32] Today, ethnic Chinese make up nearly 75 percent of Singapore's population of 5.6 million—most of them descendants of Hokkien-speaking immigrants who came to work on the British docks.

If the ethnic Chinese have been seen at times as "the Jews of the East," as Thailand's King Vajiravudh infamously referred to them, Singapore has been viewed as something like the "Jew among nations" in Southeast Asia, its Chinese-majority status a persistent complication in its relations with its larger Malay neighbors. The city's ejection from Malaysia in 1965 was a direct result of bitter disputes over the preservation of rights for ethnic Chinese in the new Malay-dominated federation. Shot into an independence that few had anticipated or planned for, Singapore suddenly found itself sandwiched between two mostly Islamic Malay-speaking nations, which were inclined to view their small neighbor much as they viewed their own Chinese minorities: as a potential Chinese "fifth column."

In Singapore's case, the accusation never made much sense; Lee was always a strident anti-communist, as he had shown in February 1963, when he launched Operation Cold Store, a sweep of arrests that crippled Singapore's communist underground. The PAP nonetheless found it prudent to downplay their new nation's Chineseness in favor of a hybrid Singaporean identity based on multi-racialism and meritocracy. It adopted a Malay national anthem and later made English—the language of Singapore's elite since 1819—the country's official working language. To avoid discord between Singapore's three main ethnic groups—Chinese, Malays, and Indians—the PAP evolved an intricately engineered policy of multiracialism that held the various groups in steady proportion. To assuage its neighbors' fears that it was subordinate to China, Singapore also made it a point to refuse formal diplomatic relations with the PRC until 1990, after both Malaysia and Indonesia had done so.

The "Chinese question," along with Singapore's diminutive size and exposed strategic position, has contributed to the keen sense of insecurity that has accompanied, and in some senses driven, the nation's much-lionized journey "from third world to first."[33] While Singapore was far from a fishing village at independence, its survival in 1965 was no foregone conclusion. Severed from a Malayan mainland of which it had once formed an integral part, it faced a range of daunting challenges, from housing shortages to high unemployment. It had very few natural resources, aside from its magnificent deep-water port and serendipitous geographic location. In this vacuum, the PAP faced the challenge of creating a new Singaporean nation—and identity—from scratch. In light of its various handicaps, Sir Peter Hall, the British urbanist, described Singapore's success as "perhaps the most extraordinary case of economic development in the history of the world."[34]

Yet despite its almost miraculous thriving, Singaporean leaders have always been at pains to emphasize that their country is small and its future uncertain. In 2007, Lee told an interviewer that Singapore's modern urban superstructure rested on "a narrow base" that could easily disintegrate: "Can we survive? The question is still unanswered. We have survived so far, 42 years. Will we survive for another 42? It depends upon world conditions. It doesn't depend on us alone."[35] In 2015, the former Singaporean diplomat Kishore Mahbubani published a book entitled *Can Singapore Survive?*, in which he aired his worry that the country might one day go the way of Kodak: a once-successful company brought low by short-sightedness and complacency.

This sense of vulnerability has shaped Singapore's trajectory through the past half-century. It explained the PAP's decision to eschew the messiness of democratic politics for a sort of technocratic vanguardism led by a meticulously groomed meritocratic elite. It provided the rationale for its leashing of trade unions and the press. It inculcated an almost Darwinian focus on extending Singapore's extraordinary record of economic success. The city-state's guardians have striven tirelessly to develop new industries, from petrochemicals to advanced information and medical technologies. In 2013, tropical Singapore even became an observer on the Arctic Council, so that it might anticipate changes in global trade flows wrought by the melting of the polar icecaps.

Singapore's insecurity has also nurtured a ruthlessly practical and unsentimental approach to foreign relations. This amounts to something like the inverse of Edward Luttwak's "great-state autism": the small state's fine attunement to the interests and actions of larger powers. This distinctly Singaporean brand of realism has two main pillars. First, Singapore has built its armed forces into a cutting-edge military deterrent, fortified by mandatory national military service on the Israeli model, to compensate for its lack of strategic depth. Second, it has invested heavily in regional cooperation: it is active in ASEAN and other institutions like the Asia-Pacific Economic Cooperation (APEC) mechanism, hoping to bind the region in a mesh of norms and rules. The Lion City's approach has allowed it to sustain a singular distinction: as Gideon Rachman observes, Singapore is "perhaps the only country in the world to have a special relationship with both China and the United States."[36]

Singapore's tiny size and reliance on the unimpeded flow of trade have naturally made it an advocate for the continued forward deployment of US naval power in Southeast Asia. The PAP government strongly supported the American role in the region during the Cold War, and when the US Navy closed its base at Subic Bay in 1992, agreed to the relocation of a key naval command to Singapore. Later, Singapore commissioned the construction of a pier at Changi Naval Base specifically designed to accommodate port calls by the US Navy's Nimitz-class aircraft carriers. The US is a key supplier of weaponry to the Singapore Armed Forces, while the US Navy maintains a logistical command unit in Singapore from which it coordinates warship deployment throughout the region, including in the South China Sea. Although not a formal treaty ally, Singapore has been among Washington's most steadfast and reliable partners in Asia.

While looking to the US for security, Singapore has looked to China for trade. Though it did not formally recognize the PRC until 1990, relations between the two nations dated back to May 1976, when Lee flew to Beijing and met with a debilitated Mao Zedong. But it was Deng Xiaoping's return trip to Singapore in November 1978 which was to have the more lasting impact. Deng was greatly impressed by the clean, ordered city that he encountered. Lee likewise admired Deng's stated intention to pull China from the political chaos whipped up by Mao. As Ezra Vogel recounts in his magisterial biography of Deng, the meeting between the fastidious, Oxbridge-educated Lee and China's new paramount leader, a head shorter in his austere Zhongshan suit, marked the beginning of a long and productive relationship. "Before Deng's visit to Singapore," Vogel writes, "the Chinese press had referred to Singaporeans as the 'running dogs of American imperialism.' " A few weeks after Deng's visit to Singapore, however, this description disappeared from the Chinese press. Now, "Singapore was described as a place worth studying for its initiatives in environmental preservation, public housing, and tourism."[37]

Later, as a reforming Deng groped for the stones beneath his feet, Singapore provided a rough model for what he wanted to build in China. In a speech during his Southern Tour in early 1992, Deng praised Lee's achievements. "Singapore's social order is rather good. Its leaders exercise strict management," he told officials. "We should learn from their experience, and we should do a better job than they do."[38] It was not simply Singapore's success that attracted Deng, but its achievement (as he saw it) by fellow Chinese. As Lee reportedly told Deng during his 1978 visit, "If Singapore Chinese who were the descendants of poorly-educated coolies could make good, how much better mainland China could be if the right policies were adopted."[39]

Singapore's role in encouraging the PRC's economic opening extended its long history of involvement in mainland Chinese affairs. In the late nineteenth and early twentieth centuries, British Singapore had been the main center of Overseas Chinese activity in Southeast Asia. The reformers Liang Qichao and Kang Youwei spent time there, and Sun Yat-sen made the city a republican nerve center and fundraising base; he visited eight times in the early 1900s, staying in a double-story bungalow in Balestier owned by the Teochew rubber magnate Teo Eng Hock. Singaporean Chinese later played active roles in the conflicts roiling their homeland: they supported the Kuomintang and the CCP, established newspapers, and raised emergency relief funds during the war against the Japanese in the 1930s and 1940s. Some returned to China to serve the two regimes in various roles. Among the most prominent was Tan Kah Kee, the "Henry Ford of Malaya," a millionaire rubber baron and philanthropist who founded Xiamen University in his home province of Fujian in 1921, and later coordinated wartime relief efforts. After 1949, Tan returned to China from Singapore and served the PRC until his death in 1961. Today, he remains a revered figure in both nations.

By the 1980s, these dormant connections between Singapore and China were stirring back to life. Singapore and its people started investing and working on the mainland. For instance, when Kentucky Fried Chicken opened its first store in China in November 1987, its manager was a Chinese Singaporean.[40] Singaporean officials, including Lee's close associate Goh Keng

Swee, were enlisted as economic advisors to various Chinese cities and regions. At the same time, Chinese delegations began flying to Singapore to study its approach to issues as diverse as housing development, water treatment, and transport regulation. Between 1976 and 2015, Lee made 33 visits to China, and worked closely with a succession of Chinese leaders.[41] By the time of his death in 2015—after a political career spanning six decades, including 31 years as premier—China had become Singapore's leading trade partner and an increasingly important source of foreign investment, while Singapore supported key Chinese initiatives including the BRI and the Asian Infrastructure Investment Bank. Upon his passing, Chinese leaders queued to offer eulogies; Xi Jinping praised his "outstanding contributions" to peace and development in Asia.[42]

In November 2010, China and Singapore marked the twentieth anniversary of diplomatic relations by unveiling a small bronze bust of Deng Xiaoping in central Singapore. The statue is nestled on the bank of the Singapore River, a short walk from the spot where Raffles first disembarked on the island on January 28, 1819. From his perch under the trees, Deng looks across the water toward the historic Fullerton Hotel, an imposing neoclassical building that once served as colonial Singapore's Central Post Office, and the iron spans of the nineteenth-century Cavenagh Bridge, both now dwarfed by the glass and steel towers of Singapore's financial district. On the back of the statue is inscribed, in English and Mandarin, a slogan of Deng's: "Development is of overriding importance." It is a statement that could just as easily have come from Lee.

Despite its equally constructive relations with China and the US, Singapore has drawn its lines of interest with precision, never hesitating to stand up to one power or the other when necessary. Lee and his successors have made it clear that their nation's cooperation with the US was (and remains) a matter of shared interests rather than shared values. In 1988, the Singaporean government expelled an American diplomat, E. Mason Hendrickson, for meeting and allegedly cultivating opponents of the PAP, which Singapore claimed amounted to interference in its internal affairs. An official statement accused Hendrickson and his superiors of acting "as if they were the colonial power and Singapore their protectorate."[43] During the so-called "Asian values" debate of the 1990s, Lee and other Singaporean officials were forthright in challenging the principle that democratic freedoms and human rights were universal. "People may find us slightly prickly," said Chan Heng Chee, a former ambassador to Washington. "We're a bit too insistent on independence, on our own identity, on telling the Western press, you're not going to tell us what to think."

Singapore has taken the same approach to China, although geographic and cultural proximity makes it a much trickier challenge. In the early years of engagement, Singapore encouraged China to grow within the contours of the prevailing US-dominated regional order. In the 1990s, a full decade before then-US Under-Secretary of State Robert Zoellick announced that Washington should try to turn China into a "responsible stakeholder" in the international system, Singapore was already working to embed China into existing regional institutions and socialize it into the "ASEAN way." For a while it seemed to work. But China's expanding economic power and growing regional truculence now threatens to destabilize the American-backed security environment that has benefited Singapore for so long.

One fear, at least theoretically, is that large Chinese-backed infrastructure projects designed to alleviate the Chinese economy's heavy reliance on shipments through the Malacca Straits could redirect the flows of trade on which Singapore has historically relied. As Lee admitted to a Thai official in the 1960s, the possibility of Thailand building a canal across the Isthmus of Kra kept him awake at night.[44] By undermining Singapore's natural geographic advantage, it raised the possibility that Singapore might go the way of old Malacca: consigned to irrelevance by the shifting patterns of global trade. While this scenario is unlikely—Singapore has long ceased to rely on geography alone—China's newfound clout gives it the ability to exert considerable economic or military pressure on the city-state: the main reason that Singapore has been so outspoken on the need for a continued American military presence in Asia.

These frictions have been most evident on the question of the South China Sea. When Beijing formally asserted its "nine-dash line" claim in 2009, Singapore took the strongest stance of any non-claimant state, prompting then-Chinese Foreign Minister Yang Jiechi's frustrated remark about "big countries" and "small countries"—reportedly delivered while looking directly at his Singaporean counterpart George Yeo.[45]

Open disagreement flared in July 2016, after the Permanent Court of Arbitration in The Hague ruled against China's "nine-dash line" maritime claim in the South China Sea, in a case brought by the Philippines. After the ruling, which Beijing denounced as "null and void," Singapore issued a cautious statement urging "all parties" to the dispute, China included, "to fully respect legal and diplomatic processes," including the Hague ruling.[46] Two months later, the *Global Times*, the CCP's nationalistic tabloid mouthpiece, published a report claiming that, during a summit of the Non-Aligned Movement in Venezuela, Singapore had tried to insert an endorsement of the ruling into the meeting's final document. Stanley Loh, Singapore's ambassador to Beijing, subsequently wrote to Hu Xijin, the editor-in-chief of *Global Times*, decrying the report as "false and unfounded." Hu shot back: "I think Singapore should feel ashamed when you tried to trip up China, your largest trading partner."[47]

Feeding into the Chinese angst was Singapore's strong support for the Obama administration's "rebalance" to Asia. This included the deployment to Singapore in 2015 of the new P8 Poseidon aircraft, which was used (among other things) to track Chinese naval movements in the South China Sea. Visiting the White House in the final months of President Obama's second term, at the height of the strains with Beijing, Prime Minister Lee Hsien Loong declared that his focus on Southeast Asia had "won America new friends and strengthened old partnerships, including with Singapore."[48]

The war of words escalated. In October 2016, Professor Jin Yinan of the PLA's National Defense University, an influential Chinese security advisor, said that Singapore was "playing with fire" in seeking to play big countries off against one another, suggesting that Beijing should make it "pay the price for seriously damaging China's interests."[49] The following month, Hong Kong customs officials seized nine Singaporean Terrex armored personnel carriers en route from military exercises in Taiwan. Lee was also disinvited from the inaugural Belt and Road Forum in Beijing in May 2017. He was one of just two Southeast Asian heads of government not to hear President Xi reference Zheng He, "the famous Chinese navigator," in his keynote address. (The other absentee was Prime Minister Prayuth of Thailand.)

As relations with Beijing frayed, Singaporeans were treated to an unusually public debate on the question of how to handle Asia's rising superpower. In July 2017, *The Straits Times* published an article by the retired diplomat Kishore Mahbubani, then the dean of the Lee Kuan Yew School of Public Policy at the National University of Singapore (NUS), reflecting on the recent isolation of Qatar by a coalition of bigger Arab states. In the article, Mahbubani argued that Qatar offered Singapore an important lesson: "Small states should behave like small states." Referring to Singapore's outspoken stance on the South China Sea, he said the PAP government should be "very restrained in commenting on matters involving great powers." If not, Mahbubani warned, the Lion City risked a Qatar-like fate. "In the jungle, no small animal would stand in front of a charging elephant," he wrote, "no matter who has the right of way."[50]

The article touched several prominent nerves in the Singaporean governing establishment. K. Shanmugam, the Law and Home Affairs Minister, described Mahbubani's argument as "questionable intellectually," adding, "We have to be clear about our interests and go about it smartly. But not on bended knees and by kowtowing to others." Bilahari Kausikan, the retired former permanent secretary of the Foreign Ministry known for his candid views on foreign affairs, took to Facebook to rebut its "muddled, mendacious" argument. He wrote, "Of course we recognize asymmetries of size and power—we are not stupid—but that does not mean we must grovel or accept subordination as a norm of relationships."[51] Visiting Singapore shortly after the controversy broke, I went to see Mahbubani at his light-filled office at the Lee Kuan Yew School. He was in defensive mode, though refused to back down. "Singapore should recognize that when the world changes, it's got to change and adapt," he said, citing (as in his book) the case of Kodak. "We shouldn't go around as a small state making great powers angry. I know I trod on sensitive toes, but it's a fact of life."

China's vehemence toward Singapore was not only a question of size. It also grew from a common Chinese perception of the ethnic Chinese-majority city-state as a "Chinese" nation, and one that should therefore naturally defer to Beijing's wishes. As relations soured, Chinese internet forums brimmed with commentary accusing Singapore of "forgetting its origins" (*wangben*) or of being "a country of Han traitors" (*hanjianguo*)—a loaded epithet once used for Chinese collaborators during the "war of resistance" against Japan.[52] Kausikan explained to me that the perception was also widespread among PRC officials, who had difficulty in accepting Singapore's multiracial identity, and frequently asked for its "understanding" on the basis of shared cultural and ethnic affinities. Kausikan said that to accept such a characterization would strain Singapore's multiracial compact, and potentially, its social cohesion. "To be described as a Chinese country is not just a description," he said, "it also prescribes a norm of behavior."

These concerns have been brought into focus by a recent increase in Chinese outreach and influence efforts targeting Singaporean Chinese, part of Beijing's wider pitch to members of the "Chinese family" overseas. Over the past decade, the PRC has helped organize a range of people-to-people exchanges with Singapore. It has reached out to Singaporean Chinese business and clan associations, and convened conferences of ethnic Chinese entrepreneurs. It has put together *xungen* ("roots-seeking") camps, similar to Israel's Birthright program, where young Singaporeans are flown to China to practice calligraphy and tai chi, even to sing "red" songs from the Maoist era.[53] Ja Ian Chong, an associate professor at NUS, said that while the main purpose of these outreach efforts— often arranged and funded in part by state agencies like the Overseas Chinese Affairs Office—is to highlight shared ethnic and cultural origins, political questions are never entirely absent. He said, "Where culture and history stop, and state policy and intentions begin, is a very blurred line."

Singaporean officials I spoke to were sanguine about the threat posed by Chinese ports and canals, some of which may never eventuate. But they expressed apprehensions about the blurring of Singaporean Chinese identities under the pressure of Chinese cultural outreach and more covert influence operations designed to shape public opinion in China's favor. While the Singaporean government has yet to state these concerns openly, retired officials and ambassadors-at-large have given voice to the increasing official consternation. In a public lecture in June 2018, Kausikan warned that pro-China narratives were being seeded, through word of mouth and Chinese social media apps like WeChat, in a bid to sway Singaporean Chinese sentiments in Beijing's direction. He called on the country's citizens to resist any attempt to "impose a Chinese identity on Singapore."[54] China's ambassador to Singapore, Hong Xiaoyong, later wrote an op-ed rebutting Kausikan's remarks, arguing that China had "no intention of influencing Singaporeans' sense of their national identity and will never do so."[55]

Just how seriously the Singaporean authorities take this question became clear in August 2017, when the government expelled from the country Huang Jing, an American academic born in China, for what it said was his covert effort to influence Singapore's foreign policy on behalf of an unnamed foreign government, widely believed to be China. The PAP government has also tightened its laws to protect against "fake news" and false information. Sometimes Singapore has used subtler methods to telegraph its separateness from China.

During his talks with Deng Xiaoping in 1978, Lee Kuan Yew spoke in English, rather than Mandarin, and did so in all of his subsequent dealings with Chinese officials. Singapore also pointedly over-represents ethnic Malay and Indian officials in its delegations to China. When Beijing inaugurated a China Cultural Centre in Singapore in late 2015, the Singaporean government countered by building its own Singapore Chinese Cultural Centre in the middle of the financial district. In a speech given at the unveiling of the 11-story, $110 million project in 2017, Prime Minister Lee harped on Singapore's distinctiveness from China: "The Chinese Singaporean is proud of his Chinese culture," he said, "but also increasingly conscious that his 'Chineseness' is different from the Chineseness of Malaysian and Indonesian Chinese, or the Chineseness of people in China, Hong Kong or Taiwan."[56]

However, the issue has been complicated by the PAP's own contradictory attitude toward the idea of "Chineseness." While taking pains to assert a distinctly Singaporean—that is, non-Chinese—identity, it has selectively leveraged its historical and cultural connections to take advantage of China's economic growth. "In the '80s and '90s, as China was opening up, we were really pushing our Chinese identity," said P.J. Thum, a Singapore-born historian at the University of Oxford, who also hosts the *History of Singapore* podcast. "The government was telling us, oh you are Chinese, so you should behave certain ways, believe certain things, and eat certain foods, and speak Mandarin."

In 1979, the PAP government launched a campaign encouraging Singaporean Chinese to adopt Mandarin Chinese in place of the dialects spoken by their ancestors. The "Speak Mandarin" campaign saw regional languages like Hokkien and Teochew largely effaced from the media. Singaporeans who watched Cantonese-language soap operas from Hong Kong had to get used to seeing them dubbed into a tongue some could barely understand. At the same time, the complex traditional Chinese characters were replaced by the PRC's simplified form of written Chinese, which now features on all official signage in Singapore. The first decade of the campaign saw the number of dialect-speaking Chinese households drop from 76 percent to 48 percent; by 2015, it had fallen to just 12 percent.[57]

Initially, the campaign's goal was to create a unified "Chinese" community from the country's myriad dialect and clan allegiances. But by the 1990s, as China's economy began to take off, the Mandarin push had acquired an inexorable economic logic as well. Many Singaporean Chinese in their thirties and forties recall the pressures they came under to learn Mandarin at school. Kirsten Han, an independent journalist and editor-in-chief of *New Naratif*, a pioneering regional long-form journalism outlet, recalled, "What they said to us is, you guys need to go and do business in China, and it will be so much easier for you if you speak the language."

But the Speak Mandarin campaign constructed a linguistic bridge that now runs both ways, increasing the reach and penetration of Chinese broadcasting networks—particularly PRC-friendly television stations from Taiwan—which disseminate the official line of the Beijing government. As an indirect result of Singapore's efforts to engineer a nation of Mandarin-speakers, said Ja Ian Chong of NUS, "the narrative about a 'Greater China', this very racialized idea of the nation, well, Chinese-speaking Singapore audiences are getting more of that than before."

Singapore's Chinese community is far from homogeneous, and such efforts to exert influence are unlikely to have uniform effects. Younger Singaporeans raised in English, with only a vague notion of China, are less likely to take up Beijing's line unthinkingly. But older Singaporean citizens, especially those educated in Chinese, are potentially more susceptible to influence. "It's very unsettling," one Singaporean netizen wrote in a discussion of Chinese influence operations on Reddit in 2018. "My dad went from a Singapore patriot to a Chinese one after he got a smartphone and cable TV."[58]

Another factor in the equation is the huge numbers of mainland Chinese who have arrived in Singapore over the past two decades under a government-engineered immigration drive. Since PRC citizens are considered "Chinese" in Singapore's system of racial accounting, they have been a logical target for efforts to offset the city-state's famously low birthrates. (Earlier attempts to attract Hong Kong and Malaysian Chinese proved less successful.) Hundreds of thousands have arrived in the past 20 years, their presence visible in the Sichuanese restaurants that line New Bridge Road in Chinatown, the students filling the cafés at NUS, and the revelers knocking back cold bottles of Tiger Beer in the bars of Geylang, Singapore's red-light district.

This arrival of PRC nationals has had contradictory effects. On the one hand, it has widened the pool of citizens and permanent residents with a shallower sense of attachment to Singapore. In recent years, mainlanders have arrived in such numbers that they have less incentive to assimilate than the first trickle of PRC citizens who moved to Singapore in the 1980s and 1990s.

On the other hand, Chinese immigration has further heightened Singapore's distinct sense of national identity. This was illustrated in horrific fashion in May 2012, when a 31-year-old Chinese citizen named Ma Chi ran a red light in a $1.4 million Ferrari and slammed into a taxi in central Singapore, killing himself and two others. The accident undammed a pool of bitterness against cashed-up mainlanders like Ma, who had arrived in Singapore from Sichuan province in 2008, as well as the larger number of low-skilled Chinese arrivals, including bus drivers and construction workers, who were placing an increasing strain on public services. In online forums, PRC Chinese were blamed for driving up real-estate prices and snatching the best jobs—even for stealing husbands. Bloggers described Ma as "spoiled and corrupt"; detractors created a mock Facebook page, later removed, which quickly filled with ugly epithets.[59]

This anti-mainland China sentiment, part of a broader backlash against the PAP's immigration policies, showed how the visible influence of China in the everyday lives of Singaporeans had sharpened their sense of identity. "They're very foreign to us," said P.J. Thum of the mainland Chinese. "And that, more than anything else, has really driven a sense of Singaporean-ness among the Singapore Chinese. Before that, you could cling to this idea that we come from this civilization of thousands of years, but now you're actually seeing the civilization up close, and you're like: we're nothing like that."

For now, the PAP's ruling mandarins seem confident they can keep pace with the challenges thrown up by China's expanding military, economic, and cultural power. In September 2019, Singapore and the US renewed for a further 15 years the 1990 agreement facilitating the American use of defense-related facilities in Singapore. This took place a few months after Singapore indicated that it would move forward on a revised defense agreement with China, and less than a year after Singapore, as ASEAN chair, coordinated the first ever joint maritime exercise between China and the ASEAN countries.

Given its foreign policy pragmatism, Singapore has come closest to articulating a common Southeast Asian perspective on the growing Sino-American tensions. In his keynote speech to the Shangri-La Dialogue security conference in May 2019, Prime Minister Lee offered advice to both superpowers. While praising China's growth as "a tremendous boon, both to itself and to the world," he said that Beijing had to reconcile its victim complex with the reality of its own burgeoning power. China "can no longer expect to be treated in the same way as in the past, when it was much smaller and weaker," Lee said. He added that the Chinese leadership should seek to resolve maritime disputes "through diplomacy and compromise rather than force or the threat of force."

At the same time, Singapore has taken an agnostic view on the Trump administration's Free and Open Indo-Pacific strategy, fearing that its aggressive turn against China could dislodge ASEAN from its position of centrality and fracture the region. In his Shangri-La speech, Lee said that US policymakers had to accept that China would continue to grow, "and that it is neither possible nor wise for them to prevent this from happening." Instead, he called on Washington to forge "a new understanding that will integrate China's aspirations within the current system of rules and norms."[60] It was unclear whether either side was ready to heed Lee's advice—but Singapore will surely be energetic in navigating the transition from *Pax Americana* to whatever, if anything, comes next.

8

MALAYSIA
LORD OF THE RINGGITS

The showroom for Forest City, Malaysia's largest residential property development, looks less like an office than an airport hangar or a museum's atrium: a domed steel space filled with noise and light. Sprawling at the center of the hall is a scale model depicting the initial phase of the project. Here, illuminated towers rise like spacecraft from a field of roads, shopping malls, and residential high-rises, lined with the tiny streetlights and toothpick palms. Some buildings have miniature "SOLD OUT" labels attached. Groups of hopeful buyers—mostly mainland Chinese—crowd around the display as Chinese-speaking sales staff conjure a vision of the gleaming city of 700,000 that will one day rise from the southern tip of the Malay Peninsula.

Billed as "an exclusive island paradise" and a "magnet for global elites," Forest City will eventually encompass four artificial islands covering around 20 square kilometers in the Johor Strait, which divides Malaysia from Singapore. Standing behind the project is Country Garden, one of the largest private property developers in China, and a local investment entity led by Ibrahim Ismail, the Sultan of Johor, whose official portrait looms in medallioned splendor above the showroom entrance.

The Forest City showroom is so lavish that it has become an attraction in its own right. When I visited on a humid October morning in 2017, a band in the main atrium breezed through a set of pop standards. Children dashed through the model apartments, past marble counters and tables laden with bottles of Chilean Merlot. Outside, Indian and Malay families strolled along the man-made beach, where palm trees bent toward the distant cranes and smokestacks of Singapore's Tuas industrial zone. Two Malay women in *tudung* headscarves posed for a photo next to a 10-foot statue of the project's official mascot, Mr. Forest, a mustachioed grenadier sporting a white bearskin, green coat, and epaulettes.

Forest City sits at the heart of Iskandar Malaysia, a Special Economic Zone (SEZ) set up in Johor in 2006 in a bid to replicate the success of China's Pearl River Delta Economic Zone, which encloses the hi-tech manufacturing center of Shenzhen. Once complete—the target date is 2035—Forest City will be a self-contained island paradise of well-tended lawns, spacious shopping arcades, golf courses, and international schools, all swathed in vertical greenery.

Since its launch in 2014, Forest City has pitched itself mostly at affluent mainland Chinese, touting its "blue skies, white clouds, pure sea breeze" as a respite from polluted mega-cities like Shanghai and Beijing. Much of Country Garden's promotional material is in Chinese, and the firm has opened show-rooms across China. The pitch is straightforward: Singapore's lifestyle, at Malaysia's prices. "Our price is much cheaper than Singapore, but it's just 2 kilometers away," said Yu Ting, a 25-year-old English-speaking sales repre-sentative from Guangdong whom I met floating around the main reception desk, dressed in the official company uniform: striped shirt, red scarf, and white sailor cap. She told me that busloads of Chinese buyers were coming each day to tour the project. "It's very close to Singapore," she said, "just like Shenzhen is very close to Hong Kong."

Forest City's plans include its own customs and immigration checkpoint, facilitating quick access across the strait to Singapore. It offers buyers various tax breaks, full freehold titles, and a path to residency under the government's Malaysia My Second Home program. So far, two-thirds of the apartments have been purchased by mainland Chinese. "In Malaysia there's no winter— but China gets very cold in winter, which is no good for my body," Xing Hanjiang, a 62-year-old small businessman from Shanghai, told the *Financial Times*. "The distance isn't very far between Malaysia and China, and there's no language barrier."[1]

However, Forest City's plan to turn Johor into the "next Shenzhen" made the project a political lightning rod as Malaysia approached national elections in May 2018. In particular, it drew flaming salvoes from Mahathir Mohamad, Malaysia's two-time prime minister. From 1981 to 2003, Mahathir had ruled his country in brash, authoritarian fashion. In that time, he had done more than any other leader to modernize Malaysia, prompting comparisons with Singapore's Lee Kuan Yew (whom he reportedly detested). In 2016, Mahathir had come out of retirement, at the age of 91, to oppose Prime Minister Najib

Razak, his one-time protégé in the United Malays National Organisation (UMNO), which had ruled Malaysia since independence in 1957. In the run-up to the election, in which he would score an astonishing victory over his former party, catapulting him to a surprise second term in office, Mahathir frequently beat up on Forest City, warning that it would eventually become a "Chinese settlement" cut off from the rest of the country. At one point he said he would prefer that it revert to actual forest, whose residents "will consist of baboons, monkeys, and so on."[2]

Forest City thus became the focus of a broader debate about China's expanding economic presence in Malaysia. Under Najib, the country's already close relationship with China had reached dizzying new heights. No other country in the Association of Southeast Asian Nations (ASEAN) engaged in as much trade with China. The People's Republic of China (PRC) was also Malaysia's largest source of foreign investment in manufacturing and its third-largest source of foreign tourists, despite a downturn following the mysterious disappearance of Malaysia Airlines flight MH370 in 2014. In his farewell speech in 2017, Huang Huikang, China's outgoing ambassador, said the Sino-Malaysian relationship "should move up over the next 40 years to reach mutual dependency, like lips and teeth."[3] Mao had once used the phrase to refer to China's relationship with Kim Il-sung's North Korea.

In October 2017, I caught an express train to Putrajaya, the manicured administrative zone outside the capital Kuala Lumpur, to ask Mahathir about Forest City and China's growing economic prominence in Malaysia. Mahathir's office was located in the cockpit of the Perdana Institute, an organization dedicated to preserving the legacy of former prime ministers. Oil paintings of these distinguished gentlemen lined the cream walls of the institute; each wore a *songkok*, the Muslim cap common throughout the Malay archipelago. There was also a portrait of Mahathir on horseback, complete with jodhpurs, dress boots, and equestrian helmet.

In his office, Mahathir sat propped in an ergonomic chair, a large Quran opened on a stand behind him. A few months earlier, the ageing politician had led a small delegation out to the Forest City showroom. He said he was impressed with the project, though he doubted that many locals could afford to live there. "If the city is to be populated, and it must be populated, it is necessary to bring in foreigners, and the biggest source of foreign migrants would be China itself," he said.

For Mahathir, as for many Malay nationalists, this evoked uneasy memories of the waves of Chinese immigrants who swept into colonial Malaya in the late 1800s and early 1900s, drastically altering Malaysia's demographic balance, and helping feed a profound feeling of Malay impermanence: a sense that the country's "native" majority were becoming strangers in their own land. Mahathir compared the Forest City project to the island of Temasek—today's Singapore—which fell under British control in 1819 and quickly filled with Chinese immigrants, a fact that partly contributed to its expulsion from Malaysia in 1965. "Because the population was so different from the population of the countries originally owning Singapore, it became impossible for Singapore to return to become a part of the mainland," he said softly. "And as a result, Singapore became a foreign country."

Another of Mahathir's concerns was debt. Under Najib, Malaysia had become the largest recipient of Belt and Road Initiative (BRI) financing of any nation bar Pakistan, and some of the Chinese projects came with eye-watering price tags. The largest was the $16.1 billion East Coast Rail Link (ECRL), a project of the China Communications Construction Company. The planned rail line was slated to run from Port Klang, Malaysia's main port near Kuala Lumpur, to the border with Thailand, bisecting the peninsula's forested interior of tea plantations and former colonial hill stations. Then there was the Melaka Gateway project ($10.4 billion), which sought to revive the old city of Malacca as a global economic hub with the construction of a deep-sea port and maritime industrial park on three reclaimed islands offshore. This was backed by PowerChina International, a major Chinese utility, and two Chinese port developers. There were plans for another Chinese-backed industrial zone and port refurbishment in Kuantan, in Najib's home state of Pahang on the east coast, which also ran into the billions. While Forest City wasn't technically a BRI project, the line between the Chinese state and private business was characteristically vague: Country Garden's showroom in Johor featured an illuminated floor-to-ceiling map highlighting Forest City's "strategic location" at the center of the Belt and Road.

China isn't the first outside power to take an interest in Malaysia. The country has long been a prize of empire, with rich natural resources and a strategic location at the hinge of the Pacific and Indian oceans. Since the commercial heyday of the Malacca Sultanate at the turn of the sixteenth century, Malaysia has attracted waves of colonists—Portuguese, Dutch, and

British—all eager to control this fulcrum of global trade. In modern times, China's main connection with Malaysia came through the southern Chinese immigrants—mostly illiterate and male—who settled there in the nineteenth and early twentieth centuries. But for today's China, with its maritime ambitions, Malaysia has become a key piece of the jigsaw in Southeast Asia: less obstreperous than Singapore, more receptive to Chinese influence than Indonesia. And it isn't hard to connect the strategic dots of the BRI in Malaysia. By constructing deep-water ports on both sides of the Malay Peninsula and a railway running between them, Beijing was effectively planning a land bridge over the peninsula: another potential route around the Malacca Straits and Singapore.

But what was in it for Malaysia? Najib's critics pointed out that many of these BRI projects would be constructed by Chinese state-owned firms, using mostly Chinese labor and building materials, with loans from Chinese state banks. P. Gunasegaram, a veteran journalist with a regular column in the online newspaper *Malaysiakini*, questioned whether they could really be called "investments" at all. Given the financial opacity surrounding projects like the ECRL, he argued that there was no way of knowing whether they were economically viable: "The terms have not been disclosed, there's no feasibility study, there's no environmental impact study, nothing has been done, so nobody can see any of these figures as to the feasibility of the project." Gunasegaram drew a comparison to Sri Lanka's Hambantota port, which was signed over to a Chinese firm in 2017 after the government was unable to service the loan for its construction.

Many people that I spoke to in late 2017 suspected that Najib's Chinese embrace was intimately connected to his troubles on the home front—in particular, the radioactive scandal surrounding the sovereign wealth fund 1Malaysia Development Berhad (1MDB), which had been set up by Najib's government in 2009 to invest in green energy and tourism ventures. In July 2015, the *Wall Street Journal* reported that $681 million originating in the 1MDB fund had flowed into the prime minister's personal bank accounts. Rumors about mismanagement and financial shenanigans had surrounded 1MDB for some time, but this was the first time the allegations had been linked to Najib himself.

The revelation hit Malaysian politics like a tidal wave. For years, public anger had been simmering about corruption and Malaysia's widening inequities of wealth, which were the most lopsided in Asia. In 2006, a group of opposition members and anti-corruption activists had started a movement known as Bersih—the Malay word means "clean"—to call for fair elections and transparent government, holding large "yellow-shirt" rallies in 2007 and 2011. This anger contributed in part to UMNO's poor showing in the general election of 2008, when the ruling Barisan Nasional (BN) coalition, of which UMNO was the dominant part, failed to win a two-thirds majority for only the second time in its history.

Now Najib stood accused of involvement in a scheme of unprecedented scope and audacity. The 1MDB theft was "no run-of-the-mill corruption case in yet another developing country," Tom Wright and Bradley Hope wrote in *Billion Dollar Whale*, their riveting, novelistic account of the scandal. It was one of "the greatest financial heists in history."[4] Investigators would later learn that around $4.5 billion from the fund, raised from international financial markets and contributed directly by the Malaysian government, had been sluiced through a maze of offshore accounts and shell companies. Sitting at the center of this globe-spanning grift was Low Taek Jho—Jho Low to friends—a little-known Penang financier and associate of Najib who had encouraged him to set up the fund, and then allegedly stole several billion dollars for himself, his friends, and co-conspirators. These he used to build a Hollywood production company, amass luxury real estate, and throw wildly decadent parties featuring celebrity guests including Alicia Keys and Leonardo DiCaprio. Proceeds from 1MDB allegedly funded Najib's re-election in 2013, and furnished his wife Rosmah Mansor with tens of millions of dollars' worth of jewelry.

At first, Najib responded to the *Journal*'s report with denials. In a Facebook message posted the day after the article's publication, he denied taking any funds for personal gain and described the allegations as "part of a concerted campaign of political sabotage."[5] Then he went on the attack. Najib replaced Malaysia's attorney general just as he was getting ready to file criminal charges against him, and sacked cabinet members critical of the government's handling of the fund. Media outlets that reported on 1MDB had their licenses suspended. Najib found it harder to keep a lid on investigations abroad. In July 2016, the US Justice Department announced that it was seeking the seizure of more than $1 billion in assets bought in the US with money allegedly stolen from 1MDB. The assets included high-end real estate in New York and Los Angeles, a $35 million private jet, works of art by Van Gogh and Monet, a stake in EMI Music Publishing, and—ironically—a share of the profits from *The Wolf of Wall Street*, Martin Scorsese's 2013 film about a corrupt stockbroker. In its civil lawsuit, Justice Department officials alleged that some of the pilfered funds had flowed into the accounts of "Malaysian Official 1," a thin pseudonym for Najib. Similar investigations were also under way in eight other countries, including Switzerland, Abu Dhabi, and Singapore.

The American probe came as a heavy blow for Najib, a scion of one of Malaysia's most prominent political families, and an old boy of Britain's Malvern College and the University of Nottingham. He had come to office in 2009 promising reform and moderation, and quickly caught the attention of the Obama administration. An Anglophile who said all the right things about democracy and radical Islam, he seemed like the perfect partner for Obama's "rebalance" to Asia. In 2014, Obama visited Malaysia, the first US president to do so in half a century, and his deputy national security advisor Ben Rhodes referred to Malaysia a "pivotal state" in the region.[6] Obama and Najib later golfed together while on holiday in Hawaii. During the president's visit, Malaysia became one of four Southeast Asian countries to join the Trans-Pacific Partnership (TPP), the economic component of the "rebalance," before it was scuttled by President Donald Trump in early 2017.

The 1MDB scandal, and the government's heavy-handed response, sank Najib's reputation in the West. As financial probes fired up overseas, Najib turned to his country's main economic partner. In early 2016, China came to Najib's relief with a bailout plan for 1MDB. Chinese state-owned firms bought up shards of the toxic fund, including power plants and a large stake in Bandar Malaysia, a multibillion-dollar property and transportation project in Kuala Lumpur.[7] The Chinese government also reportedly helped Malaysia repay a $6.5 billion debt to a state-owned petroleum firm in Abu Dhabi.[8]

To many of his critics, the prime minister's desperation to plug the financial hole in 1MDB made him unable to refuse any Chinese request. "Najib is an international beggar now," said Zunar, a political cartoonist who was among the Malaysian leader's fiercest critics. Since the breaking of the 1MDB scandal, Zunar—real name Zulkiflee Anwar Haque—had frequently lampooned the prime minister, drawing him as "The Lord of the Ringgit" and the "Man of Steal," complete with Superman outfit and sack of misappropriated funds. "Foreign governments are very happy to deal with Najib, because he's very weak," Zunar said. Another of his cartoons showed a pair of Chinese chopsticks picking up the two halves of Malaysia like succulent dumplings.

Sure enough, in early 2019, the *Wall Street Journal* published another report revealing how the Chinese government had leveraged the 1MDB scandal to its advantage. The report, based on uncovered minutes from meetings between Najib's government and Chinese officials across several months in mid-2016—around the time the US Justice Department announced its asset seizures—claimed that certain Chinese infrastructure projects had been purposefully planned at "above market profitability," with the excess funds intended to relieve 1MDB's debts. The documents showed that the ECRL, valued at $16.1 billion, had been originally estimated by a Malaysian consultancy to cost just $7.25 billion. The other project mentioned was a $2.5 billion Trans-Sabah gas pipeline, which would be built partly on Malaysia's portion of the island of Borneo. According to notes of a discussion on September 22, Chinese and Malaysian officials agreed to move ahead with the infrastructure deals even though "they may not have strong project financials." There were further juicy revelations: Chinese officials told visiting Malaysians that China would use its influence to try to get the US and other countries to drop their 1MDB probes. Najib also opened secret talks to let Chinese navy vessels dock at two Malaysian ports.[9]

In November 2016, not long after the meetings reported by the *Journal*, Najib paid a state visit to China. While in Beijing, he wrote an editorial in the state mouthpiece *China Daily* slamming "former colonial powers" for "lecturing countries they once exploited on how to conduct their own internal affairs today."[10] He returned with commitments for $34 billion worth of trade and investment deals, including the agreement for the ECRL. As in Cambodia, Thailand, and Burma, Chinese officials, hoisting the banner of "non-interference," had capitalized on the souring relations between a Southeast Asian leader and the West.

But before long, it became apparent that China had taken a long position on an over-leveraged asset. As the full scope of the 1MDB scandal became public, Bersih organized new protests calling for Najib's resignation. On August 29 and 30, 2015, the center of Kuala Lumpur became an ocean of yellow as tens of thousands denounced the administration's corruption. It was one of the largest public demonstrations in Malaysia's history. Mahathir attended the second day of the rally, and soon thereafter quit UMNO and founded a new party, known as Parti Pribumi Bersatu Malaysia, which he aligned with the other parties opposing Najib's government.

The new multiethnic Pakatan Harapan (PH) opposition coalition—the name meant "Alliance of Hope"—was a nest of awkward bedfellows. Most notably, it united Mahathir with Anwar Ibrahim, a former deputy he had sacked and jailed on spurious charges in the 1990s. (After leading the opposition to its largest-ever electoral gain in 2013, Anwar had since been re-imprisoned by Najib.) Umapagan Ampikaipakan, a Malaysian radio broadcaster, noted that Mahathir now found himself "campaigning for the political party that was set up to fight injustices allegedly perpetrated while he was in power."[11] Similarly, former critics of Mahathir's cronyism, judicial meddling, and suppression of the press were forced into the strange position of defending his legacy. Those I spoke to offered a simple line of reasoning: under Mahathir, graft had been the hors d'oeuvres of government. Under Najib, it was the entire meal.

These strange alliances were on display at a PH rally I attended in October 2017. The gathering was held on a sodden field in Petaling Jaya, a residential city now subsumed within the widening penumbra of greater Kuala Lumpur. Among the colorful tents and pulled-tea vendors, the predominant theme was state corruption in general, and 1MDB in particular. People wore T-shirts that read, "Love Malaysia, remove kleptocracy," below an image of floating jewels, graphic shorthand for the prime minister's lavish spending. Others asked, "Where is the RM 2.6 billion?" referencing the $681 million that had materialized in Najib's bank accounts. In a surreal scene, Mahathir sat on stage as a monochrome "Free Anwar" appeal flashed on a video screen to a plaintive orchestral swell. As the rally reached its climax, Mahathir took the stage to the opening strains of "The Final Countdown." Picked out by the stage lighting, he appeared a shrunken figure, his red PH T-shirt tucked into loose black trousers. The crowd stilled to quiet as Mahathir's voice echoed out across the field. "Never before have we had a prime minister who is a thief. He steals so he can have a comfortable life," Mahathir said. "Najib's fate is in our hands. We can get rid of him."[12]

When I met him a few days later, Mahathir explained that Najib's corruption had begun to endanger Malaysia's sovereignty, particularly by pushing him into an unhealthy reliance on China. "We have benefited from being able to export goods and services to China," he said. "But in the process, China has become extremely rich, and with that wealth, it has shown that it can actually overcome other countries, not through war, but purely through its wealth."

There was much in Mahathir's background to make him wary of China's rising power. Born in 1925 in Alor Setar, the low-slung capital of Kedah state on the west coast of peninsular Malaya, he had come to adulthood at a time when most of Southeast Asia languished under some form of Western colonial rule. "Asia was a region without pride," he wrote in the 1990s, "and our economies were structured to serve the European demand for raw materials and natural resources."[13] While Mahathir could be prone to political hyperbole and conspiracy theories—he once blamed "Jewish" financiers for the 1997 Asian financial crisis—he was well-attuned to the ways that economic domination could generate imperial designs. He had experienced not only British colonial rule, but also Malaya's vicious wartime occupation by imperial Japan between 1942 and 1945. In China's "win–win" appeals, Mahathir heard the echoes of imperial projects past. If elected, he promised, Najib's Chinese deals—including Forest City—would face close scrutiny.

Three decades earlier, Mahathir had done much to lay the foundations of Malaysia's close economic relationship with China. In 1981, the year he became prime minister, ties between the two nations were permeated with mistrust. To Malaysia's frustration, China continued to offer moral support to the outlawed Communist Party of Malaya (CPM), then waging an insurgency from its remote jungle redoubts along the border with Thailand. Its ragtag army had long ceased to pose much threat, but the specter of Chinese subversion cast a dark shadow over Malaysia, a nation born into independence at the tail end of the Malayan Emergency, an insurgency launched in 1948 by the CPM against British rule. After its founding in 1949, the PRC had offered strong encouragement and backing to the Malayan communists. There is little evidence that Beijing sent military supplies to the CPM, but it welcomed its leaders to China for ideological mentoring and medical treatment, and established a radio station in Hunan—Suara Revolusi Malaya, the "Voice of the Malayan Revolution"—which relayed propaganda into Malaya and Singapore. The CPM's cadres were deeply impressed by Mao's revolution and dutifully followed the political line laid down in Beijing. As the CPM's leader Chin Peng later wrote, "Nothing could move forward without China's consent."[14]

Since the majority of the CPM's fighters were ethnic Chinese, many of them disaffected coolies and squatters from Malaya's tin mines and rubber plantations, China's support for the insurgency was inseparable from Malaysia's own tense ethnic politics. Since its colonial heyday, Malaysia had been haunted by racial divisions. In the mid-nineteenth century, as the American Civil War had sent global demand for tin soaring, wealthy Straits Chinese investors—and, later, Europeans—moved to develop the rich alluvial deposits of western Malaya. To work the mines of Perak, Ipoh, and Seremban, they imported hundreds of thousands of indentured laborers from southern China, who were fleeing poverty, famine, and the instability of the Taiping Rebellion. The British also imported large numbers of workers from southern India, who joined the Chinese in backbreaking labor on Malaya's sprawling rubber estates.

While ethnic Chinese had been present in Malaya in modest numbers since the time of the Malacca Sultanate, these new streams of southern Chinese immigrants had a profound effect on the colony's subsequent development. The mostly male immigrant workers—"lean, smooth-shaven, keen, industrious, self-reliant, sober, mercenary, reliable, mysterious, opium-smoking, gambling, hugging clan ties, forming no others, and managing their own matters," as one British traveler described them in 1883[15]—lived a parallel, separate existence from the Malays, whom the colonial authorities encouraged to remain planted in their rural *kampongs* (villages). During the colonial "tin rush," Malaya's economic center of gravity shifted from the old Malay towns to new urban centers dominated by the Chinese. By 1880, the town of Taiping, formerly a Malay village, had become "a thriving, increasing place, of over six thousand inhabitants, solely Chinese, with the exception of a small Kling [Indian] population" and "scarcely any Malays."[16] Between 1900 and 1941, the Chinese population of Malaya tripled from around 800,000 to more than 2.5 million, by which point they constituted close to half of Malaya's population.[17]

"The rich Malaysia of today," V.S. Naipaul wrote in 1982, "grows on colonial foundations and is a British-Chinese creation."[18] It was also marked deeply by the colonial racial divisions of labor: between the prosperous and overwhelmingly urban Chinese and the rural Malays, relegated to the lower rungs of the economic ladder. When the Union Jack came down for the last time in Kuala Lumpur on August 31, 1957, marking the birth of an independent Malaya, Malay nationalists and politicians had wrestled with the question of how to redress the imbalance. The new nation's constitution gave Malays a special status as *bumiputera*, a Sanskrit-derived word meaning "sons of the soil"; it also enshrined Malay as the national language, and İslam as the official religion.

When Malaya was folded into a larger Malaysian Federation in September 1963, racial considerations weighed heavily. The idea of a federation was first broached by Malayan Prime Minister Tunku Abdul Rahman in 1961, and later encouraged by the British, who hoped that fusing Malaya and Singapore into a new federation would help prevent communists from gaining the upper hand in the self-governing Lion City. Since this would make the Chinese a majority, however, the new state also incorporated the British Crown Colonies of Sabah and Sarawak, thousands of kilometers across the South China Sea on the island of Borneo, to dilute Chinese representation and preserve Malay predominance.[19] (London made sure to exclude the tiny, oil-glutted sultanate of Brunei, which would remain a British colony until 1984.) In this way, the Chinese helped determine the very shape of modern Malaysia.

In the years following Malaysia's creation in 1963, racial tensions occasionally flared into violence. For some Malay "ultras"—right-wing communal extremists—constitutional concessions weren't enough; they called for more radical measures to institutionalize *ketuanan Melayu*, or "Malay supremacy." In 1964, racial riots erupted in Singapore, a prelude to the city's expulsion from the Malaysian Federation the following year. Five years later, on May 13, 1969, the violence came to Kuala Lumpur. A *TIME* correspondent described the scene: "Malay mobs, wearing white headbands signifying an alliance with death, and brandishing swords and daggers, surged into Chinese areas in the capital, burning, looting, and killing. In retaliation, Chinese, sometimes aided by Indians, armed themselves with pistols and shotguns and struck at Malay *kampongs*. Huge pillars of smoke rose skyward as houses, shops, and autos burned."[20] The riots took place three days after a general election in which the governing Alliance Party coalition, of which UMNO was the dominant member, had lost significant support to its opponents, in particular two newly formed, and predominantly Chinese, opposition parties. An estimated 800 people were killed in the violence, which threw a long shadow over Malaysia's subsequent history.[21]

Against this backdrop of racial discord, China's support for the Malayan communist movement—and its ambiguous policy toward the nation's ethnic Chinese population—cast it as a serious security threat. In 1966, Tunku Abdul Rahman warned that Beijing's goal was to "carve up large parts of Asia, partition Southeast Asia, and draw the fragmented parts into the communist sphere of influence."[22] In the early 1970s, when the two nations began negotiations on the establishment of diplomatic relations, these two issues were among the most contentious. It was only after China promised to dial back its support to the CPM, and to refrain from tampering with ethnic Chinese loyalties, that normalization was able to proceed. In May 1974, Malaysia became the first ASEAN state to establish diplomatic relations with China. (Thailand and the Philippines would follow suit in 1975.)

When Mahathir entered office in 1981, China still insisted on continuing its "moral" support to what was left of the communist insurgency, but this would fall away as the Cold War neared its end. At a ceremony in December 1989, a month after the fall of the Berlin Wall, the Malayan comrades finally laid down their arms after more than four decades of struggle. Chin Peng, who had lived in exile in Beijing since 1961, ensconced in a state bungalow close to Tiananmen Square, signed a peace accord with the Malaysian government in Thailand. Refused entry to Malaysia, he retired to Bangkok, where he died in 2013. Thus a once-feared communist insurgency followed its Thai and Burmese counterparts through the trapdoor of history, removing the last obstacle to improved relations between Malaysia and China. Mahathir was quick to recognize China's economic potential, lifting restrictions on travel to the mainland that had been in place since the Emergency. "It is high time to stop seeing China through the lenses of threat," he said in 1995, "and view it as an economic opportunity."[23]

China became a crucial factor in Mahathir's ambition to propel Malaysia into the ranks of the developed world—a project he dubbed "Vision 2020." During his 22 years in power he visited the country seven times, and nine more times after his retirement. "Tun Mahathir broke the ice," said Abdul Majid bin Ahmad Khan, a former Malaysian ambassador to Beijing, when I met him at the Royal Selangor Golf Club in Kuala Lumpur, a bastion of old colonial Malaya set amid 348 hectares of lakes, gardens, and undulating fairways culminating in the shining chrome needles of the Petronas Towers. "To us, [1989] was the real beginning of relations with China," Abdul Majid said. "Mahathir took it a step forward and said, 'no more ideology. Now it's about economic opportunity.'" During Mahathir's time in power, Malaysia–China trade climbed steeply, from $307 million in 1982 to $14 billion in 2002.[24] China's money wasn't the only thing that appealed to Mahathir. An acerbic critic of Western attempts to promote democratic and liberal values in

developing countries—the subject of the "Asian values" debate of the 1990s—
he found a like-minded partner in China, which frequently emphasized its
commitment to national sovereignty and mutual non-interference.

Mahathir's good relations with China continued under his successors. Like
many Southeast Asian governments, UMNO and the BN coalition recognized
the importance of China's economy in sustaining the growth that buttressed
and legitimized their rule. After Najib took office in 2009, Malaysia's relationship with China became closer than ever. Both sides frequently and warmly
referenced the fact that Najib's father, Prime Minister Tun Abdul Razak, had
been the one to establish relations with the PRC in 1974—the first ASEAN
leader to do so. In 2009, China became Malaysia's largest trading partner
and has remained so ever since. Spurred by the China–ASEAN Free Trade
Agreement, which came into effect in 2010, bilateral trade reached an all-time
high of $124 billion in 2019, with a large surplus in Malaysia's favor.[25] In
October 2013, Xi Jinping visited Malaysia and the two nations elevated relations to a "comprehensive strategic partnership." When Najib came under fire
for cozying up to China, he asked, "What's wrong with us fostering closer ties
with China, which is expected to be the biggest economy in 2030?"[26]

As with Singapore, improved ties led to a reawakening of Malaysia's
centuries-old connections with mainland China. This was perhaps best epitomized by the opening in 2015 of the Malaysian campus of Xiamen University,
the first overseas campus established by a major Chinese university. Here, on
a hot plain in Selangor, 45 kilometers outside Kuala Lumpur, the entwined
relations between China and the Chinese Malaysians came full circle: Xiamen
University, the main institution of higher education in Fujian province, was
founded by the Chinese-Malayan rubber magnate Tan Kah Kee in 1921; now
a statue of Tan stood in front of a commanding suite of concrete buildings in
his adopted homeland—funded and built by the Chinese government.

Robust cultural and economic ties have shaped Malaysia's approach to its
conflicting territorial claims in the South China Sea. Malaysia claims 12 features
in the Spratly Islands group, all of which lie within China's "nine-dash line"
claim. It occupies five of them, including Swallow Reef, which includes a tourist
resort and popular dive spot. Some 80 kilometers from the Malaysian coast—
well inside its Exclusive Economic Zone—is James Shoal, which Beijing has
officially declared the southernmost point of its territory, despite it being
"22 meters below the sea surface and over 1,500 kilometers from China

'proper.'"[27] In 2013, China also began stationing coastguard vessels at the Luconia Shoals, which lie around 100 kilometers off the coast of Sarawak, and comprise one of the largest reef formations in the South China Sea, believed to contain significant oil and gas deposits. Since then, China has maintained a near-constant coastguard presence around the shoals, most of which are under water at high-tide.

Despite frequent Chinese incursions, however, Malaysia has generally eschewed the vocal approach of Vietnam and the Philippines to the disputes in the South China Sea. China, for its part, has responded to Malaysian activities in the Spratlys with restraint, compared to similar actions undertaken by Vietnam.[28] Kuala Lumpur has "consistently played down China's activities in our territories," said Wan Saiful Wan Jan, chief executive of the Institute for Democracy and Economic Affairs, a Malaysian think-tank.[29]

Of course, the Malaysian defense establishment has exercised justified caution about China's maritime designs. After China held military exercises around James Shoal in 2013 and 2014, Malaysia announced the construction of a new naval base in Bintulu, about 80 kilometers away on the coast of Sarawak. In a similar vein, Malaysia has strongly supported a US military presence in Asia, if in a more muted key than neighboring Singapore. US warships undertake dozens of port visits to Malaysia each year, and five of the past six chiefs of the Malaysian navy have been graduates of the US Naval War College in Newport, Rhode Island.[30] As Robert Kaplan writes, the US has given Malaysia tens of millions of dollars' worth of radar equipment for use in the South China Sea, under the pretext of the global "war on terror." In this way, American power "helps give Malaysia the luxury of its national ambiguity."[31]

In general, Malaysia aims to deter Chinese encroachments in the South China Sea, while avoiding a fight that would disrupt a lucrative bilateral relationship. It has been able to employ this strategy in large part because the South China Sea has not become the subject of popular mobilization to the extent that it has in Vietnam, with its strained history of relations with China, or even in the Philippines. According to the Pew Research Center, no other Southeast Asian country is more positively disposed toward China: in 2015, 78 percent of those surveyed in Malaysia reported a favorable view of China, compared to just 19 percent in Vietnam.[32] As Shahriman Lockman, a Senior Analyst in the Foreign Policy and Security Studies Programme at the Institute of Strategic and International Studies, put it, "It doesn't really matter to most of the populace right now."

Of greater concern to many Malaysians are the ways in which Chinese power may be affecting the country's fragile balance of ethnicities from within. On the afternoon of September 25, 2015, China's ambassador to Malaysia made his way to Petaling Street in the heart of Kuala Lumpur's Chinatown. Dressed in a psychedelic red batik shirt, Huang Huikang smiled for the cameras as he presented local traders with moon cakes for the approaching Mid-Autumn Festival and sampled Petaling Street's famous *air mata kucing*, a refreshing iced drink made from medicinal herbs and monk fruit.

Afterward, from a table at the back of a Chinese restaurant, he read a prepared statement to the press. Huang started by praising the multiracial culture of Malaysia's capital. He then went on to say that he did not want to see this harmony "destroyed by any people with ulterior motives." The ambassador issued a warning: "The Chinese government has always pursued peaceful co-existence in international relationships and non-interference in the internal affairs of other countries." But Beijing would "not sit idly by" over any "infringement on China's national interests, violations of legal rights, and interests of Chinese citizens and businesses which may damage the friendly relationship between China and the host country."[33]

Ambassador Huang's statement was a response to a large ultra-nationalist Malay "red shirt" rally that had taken place near Chinatown ten days before. On September 16, an estimated 30,000 people had flooded into central Kuala Lumpur in a show of support for "Malay supremacy" in general, and the administration of Prime Minister Najib in particular. Organized by Jamal Yunus, a pro-Najib UMNO leader, and a nationalistic martial arts group called Pesaka, this rally for "Malay dignity" was intended as a response to the massive yellow-shirt Bersih protests the previous month, which had called for Najib to step down over the 1MDB fiasco.

Under increasing pressure at home and abroad, Najib was doing what must have seemed like the logical thing: he was playing the race card. Swathed in red, protesters held signs reading "Don't insult Malays and Islam" and "#najibstays." Others chanted Islamic verses. The rally had a strong anti-Chinese undercurrent. According to witnesses, some demonstrators hurled racial abuse against ethnic Chinese and made references to the May 1969 riots.[34] Protesters were eventually dispersed by riot police with water cannons outside the large ornamental gate marking the entrance to Petaling Street. It was later reported that the "red shirts" were planning another demonstration in Chinatown on September 26—the pretext for Ambassador Huang's visit to Petaling Street.

Huang was no amateur. He had previously held diplomatic posts in the US and Canada, and served as China's special representative for climate change negotiations. Like other recent Chinese statements about the ethnic Chinese abroad, his comments were vague—perhaps intentionally so. In previous remarks, Huang had bundled Malaysian Chinese into the category of *haiwai qiaobao*, or "Chinese compatriots overseas."[35] It was similarly unclear whether his Petaling Street statement referred to Chinese expatriates, Malaysian Chinese, or, to the extent that there was a meaningful distinction to Malay radicals, both. Some speculated that Huang's statement was an oblique way of signaling Beijing's dissatisfaction over Najib's military cooperation with the US, or his support for the TPP trade agreement.

Whatever the ambassador's motivation, he was widely seen as having broken a decades-long taboo against Chinese interference in Malaysia's ethnic politics. Dennis Ignatius, a 36-year veteran of the Malaysian Foreign Service, described Huang's comments as "an unprecedented breach of a solemn undertaking" made in 1974. He asked, "How do tense race relations in Malaysia impinge on friendly relations with China, unless, of course, China still considers itself the overlord of all ethnic Chinese whatever their citizenship?"[36] As he and many others noted, China's insertion of itself into Malaysia's racial politics would do little to help the local Chinese: more likely, it would simply confirm the suspicions of the Malay right wing that they enjoyed the protection of a "big brother" in Beijing—that they were fundamentally foreign, disloyal, alien.

Ambassador Huang's Petaling Street outing demonstrated how China's economic, political, and cultural power is beginning to alter Malaysia's racial dynamics in subtle but significant ways. In the aftermath of the racial riots of 1969, UMNO introduced a far-reaching affirmative action scheme known as the New Economic Policy (NEP). The NEP was designed to close the economic gap between the Malays and the Chinese, which the government viewed as the root cause of the violence. It was the most explicit and aggressive attempt by any Southeast Asian nation to redress wealth imbalances between its ethnic Chinese and indigenous majority. It reserved university places for Malays, gave special financial handouts to *bumiputeras*, and favored Malay-owned companies for state contracts. At the same time, UMNO formed a new coalition—Barisan Nasional—that included distinct parties representing the ethnic Chinese and Indians. Their "controlled, and subordinate, political participation" achieved the political stability necessary to attract foreign investment and fuel Malaysia's sustained economic boom.[37]

The NEP succeeded in bolstering opportunities for rural Malays and increasing *bumiputeras'* share of the nation's capital, which rose tenfold between 1970 and 1991, from 3 percent to nearly a third.[38] But its side effect was the reinforcement of ethnic boundaries. These borders have only hardened further as Malay identity has come to be more widely identified in Islamic terms, making race and religion an ever-tempting play for Malay politicians. "Despite official integrative visions of 'One Malaysia,'" writes Michael Vatikiotis, "there is in reality virtual ethnic and religious segregation."[39] Faced with the 1MDB scandal, it was only natural that Najib would resort to the hoary trope of Malay impermanence, and try to paint the accusations as a "Chinese" plot.

While China's economic and political presence has teased out deep-rooted Malay insecurities, as evidenced by the controversy over Forest City, its impacts are most likely to be felt by Malaysia's Chinese. In broad terms, China's emergence has been good for the quarter or so of the Malaysian population who have Chinese ancestry. Improved bilateral relations have helped soothe racial tensions, and created business opportunities in mainland China. This was especially the case in the early years of the PRC's reform and opening, when Malaysian-Chinese industrialists gained a lucrative foothold in the Chinese market. The most prominent was Robert Kuok. Once described by *The Economist* as "the quintessential Asian tycoon," Kuok made his original fortune by cornering Malaysia's markets for flour, palm oil, and sugar.[40] He then branched out with canny investments in China, including his Shangri-La hotel group, which opened its first hotel in Hangzhou in 1984, and his tentacular transport conglomerate Kerry Logistics. Today, the media-averse 96-year-old, the son of a barefoot *fin-de-siècle* immigrant from Fujian, is the richest person in Malaysia, with an estimated net worth of $13.1 billion.[41]

However, not all Malaysian Chinese have benefited from increased economic relations with China. Malaysia's racial preferences have roped off key sectors of the economy for Malay entrepreneurs and the large government-linked companies (GLCs), dominated by Malays, which have been the biggest Malaysian investors in mainland China. Meanwhile, labor-reliant small- and medium-sized enterprises, the types of Malaysian businesses most likely to be owned by ethnic Chinese, are also the most vulnerable to competition from cheap Chinese-made imports, and the large Chinese state-owned firms that are increasingly investing in Malaysia.[42] When it comes to headline BRI and state-backed construction projects, "Chinese businessmen here have very little share in the projects involved," said Tony Pua, a parliamentarian for the Democratic Action Party (DAP), a member of the PH coalition. "They are essentially marginalized."

To some extent, this reflects a growing distance between the PRC and Malaysia's Chinese community. While domestic ethnic politics played into Tun Abdul Razak's decision to open diplomatic relations with Beijing in 1974—in particular, he hoped it would help him win Chinese votes ahead of that year's general election—younger generations are more culturally and emotionally removed from the land of their ancestors. "Malaysian Chinese are very proudly Malaysian," said Rita Sim, the fast-talking co-founder and director of the Centre for Strategic Engagement, a think-tank that studies the changing composition and attitudes of the Chinese community in Malaysia. "They don't want to be told that they are Chinese from China." In this context, ethnic and linguistic ties to China no longer give Chinese Malaysians any signficant advantage over the Malay-dominated firms and GLCs that enjoy strong state backing.

For Chinese Malaysians, China's expanding economic presence in Malaysia contrasts starkly with the disadvantages they face within the country's system of racial preferences. Steven Gan, the co-founder and editor-in-chief of *Malaysiakini*, observed that Najib peddled anti-Chinese politics while praising China and signing mammoth BRI infrastructure deals. "Suddenly you've got mainland Chinese coming here, and they've been treated better than the minority Chinese," he said.

Similar concerns arose in 2017, when the Chinese car manufacturer Geely purchased a 49.9 percent stake in Malaysia's national car company, Proton, and quickly appointed a mainland Chinese executive as CEO. This wasn't the first such case for a GLC—Malaysia Airlines had appointed a German chief executive in 2015—but many Malaysian Chinese were keenly aware that this was a position long barred to members of their own community. The fact that Geely's CEO was himself ethnic Chinese only deepened the sense of injustice. Before, said Tony Pua, "The Malays were first-class citizens, the Chinese were second-class citizens. But with foreign Chinese coming in, that has relegated the local Chinese to third-class."

Similar tensions are evident in the cultural sphere. As in Singapore, China's economic emergence has coincided with the increased use of Mandarin, and the fading of the Chinese regional tongues—Cantonese, Hokkien, and so forth—originally spoken by immigrants from southern China. In Kuala Lumpur, Mandarin TV series from the PRC are rapidly gaining in popularity at the expense of Hong Kong-produced Cantonese dramas that, until recently, dominated Chinese-language viewing in Malaysia.[43] The Chinese government has encouraged this trend as part of its "soft power" push in Malaysia. This has seen it offer donations to Chinese-language schools, and ramp up scholarships for Malaysian students to attend Chinese universities. By 2015, an estimated 7,500 were studying in China.[44] In 2009, it opened a Confucius Institute at the University of Malaya, and later, the large Malaysian campus of Xiamen University outside Kuala Lumpur. An outgrowth of this is that Mandarin proficiency is spreading not just among ethnic Chinese, but among Malays and Indians, too. According to Rita Sim, non-Chinese enrollment at Chinese primary schools is now at "an all-time high"; nearly one in five students hail from other ethnic groups.[45]

For Malaysia's Chinese education movement, which has fought for years to preserve the use of Chinese languages, this is a classic case of being careful what you wish for. While Beijing's efforts probably guarantee the survival of Mandarin Chinese in Malaysia (if not the dialects), its adoption by non-Chinese Malaysians threatens to erode the natural advantages that ethnic Chinese have long enjoyed. Historically, Sim pointed out, Malay ministers and politicians had to employ ethnic Chinese aides to liaise with the Chinese community. These positions are now filled increasingly by Chinese-speaking Malays. Similarly, the head of operations for the Chinese-language program at the government broadcaster Radio Television Malaysia—a position once reserved for ethnic Chinese—is now a Malay, as is the head of the Chinese-language program at Bernama, Malaysia's national news agency.[46] Sim said, "While this was once supposed to be your space that nobody could enter, the other races are coming in."

All this takes place against a backdrop of low birthrates and brain-drain emigration, the latter of which can be directly linked to Malaysia's system of institutionalized discrimination. Chinese Malaysians have steadily shrunk as a total share of the country's population, from 37.2 percent at independence in 1957 to 22.8 percent in 2019. The Asian Strategy and Leadership Institute, a local think-tank, predicts that if current trends hold, this figure will fall to 19.6 percent by 2030.[47] As time goes by, Malaysia's ethnic Chinese are becoming less politically salient and more economically confined, but no less convenient as a scapegoat for Malay politicians.

Shifting demographics and continued racial tensions explain the tenor of the reaction to Ambassador Huang's Petaling Street warning. As the Chinese government reaches out to ethnic Chinese in Malaysia, and adopts more vigorous rhetoric about the protection of its "compatriots" abroad, it risks becoming entangled in what Hishamuddin Rais, a Malay writer, filmmaker, and stand-up comic described to me as Malaysia's "unresolved national question." Rais said that for many Malay conservatives there was increasingly little distinction between being anti-China and being anti-Chinese. "The unresolved national question is now muddled with the arrival of the [mainland] Chinese here," he said over jet-black Malay coffee and chicken satay at a roadside market in central Kuala Lumpur. "When China interferes, the backlash will be on the local Chinese."

On May 9, 2018, Mahathir led Malaysia's opposition to a landslide election victory against Najib and the BN coalition. The following day, at the Istana Negara palace in Kuala Lumpur, Malaysia's sixth prime minister was succeeded by its fourth, as Mahathir was sworn back into office, two months shy of his 93rd birthday. Few people had given his rackety PH coalition much chance against the well-oiled patronage machinery of UMNO and the BN alliance. But UMNO's advantages masked the fact that support for the party had been waning for years. Increasing numbers of Malay voters had become fed up with corruption and widening income inequalities, while ethnic Chinese and Indians were tired of their perpetual second-class status. For the first time since independence, UMNO found itself in opposition. The novelist Tash Aw described it as "the end of the only government Malaysia has ever known."[48]

Mahathir immediately ordered a reopening of investigations into the 1MDB fund. On July 3, exactly three years after the *Wall Street Journal* scoop that sank his political career, anti-corruption officials arrested Najib at his mansion in Kuala Lumpur. The Attorney General's office subsequently charged the ex-prime minister, his wife, and a number of senior officials with corruption and money-laundering offenses related to 1MDB and other scandals. When police raided Kuala Lumpur apartments owned by Najib's family, they carted out $274 million worth of items, including 12,000 pieces of jewelry, 567 handbags, and 423 watches, as well as $28 million in cash.[49] Meanwhile, Jho Low, wanted by both the US government and the new Malaysian administration, had gone to ground, apparently in China. Many believed he was under Beijing's protection.

Mahathir followed through on his promise to review the Chinese infrastructure deals signed by the Najib government. In July, his government canceled the ECRL and froze several other projects, including the Melaka Gateway development and the natural gas pipeline in Sabah. The PH victory was also bad news for Forest City: in August, Mahathir announced that foreigners would be barred from buying residential units there. Later he backpedaled slightly, saying that those purchasing properties would not receive automatic Malaysian residency, but his comments cast the future of the project into serious doubt. At the same time, Mahathir adopted more muscular rhetoric about Chinese actions in the South China Sea and, during a visit to Beijing in August 2018, shocked his hosts by implying that the BRI could become a "a new version of colonialism."[50] China had been opportunistic in taking advantage of Najib's quandary. Now it was weathering the backlash.

Amid the souring relations between Washington and Beijing, Mahathir's turn against China prompted exuberant reactions from some American observers. "While Washington wasn't looking, democracy won a major battle over authoritarianism in Malaysia," one *Washington Post* columnist enthused. "The unexpected change has given the Trump administration a chance to reverse a policy of benign neglect toward the region, support democracy—and gain a rare win over China."[51] Yet, as elsewhere in Southeast Asia, Malaysia's cronyism and patronage could not so simply be put down to Chinese influence. UMNO's power had always been premised on a tight nexus between politics and business and the distribution of patronage along racial lines. Moreover, while the 2018 election represented a genuine breakthrough, it was easy to overlook the background of the leader it returned to power—one who had once meddled with the judiciary, imprisoned political opponents, and presided over a nested system of cronyism concealed under the cloak of Malay uplift. During the "Asian values" debate of the 1990s, Mahathir had been among most vociferous critics of Western-style liberal democracy.

It soon became clear that on the question of China, Mahathir differed from his predecessor in degree rather than in kind. While beating up on China had been an effective campaign strategy, once in power Mahathir began to moderate his rhetoric. In interviews he made it clear that he wanted Chinese investment, so long as Malaysia stood to benefit. Beijing seemed happy enough to meet Malaysia's new government halfway. In March 2019, Malaysia reversed its decision to terminate the ECRL project, after renegotiating the costs down by about a third, from $16.1 billion to $10.7 billion. Other projects were also given a reprieve. In April, the government resurrected the multibillion-dollar Bandar Malaysia project, with the involvement of the state-owned China Railway Engineering Corp. The same month Mahathir attended the second Belt and Road Forum gala in Beijing, his second visit to the Chinese capital in less than a year. There he gave a speech in which he said he was "fully in support" of Xi's headline initiative, though he offset this by underlining the importance for Malaysia of free passage through the South China Sea.[52]

In essence, Mahathir's pushback against China was more of a course correction than a fundamental shift. His view of China remained much as it had been in the 1990s, when he recognized that Chinese trade and investment were vital for Malaysia's economic advancement. His justified concerns about China's rising power, and the abject dependence of the Najib administration, were balanced by his engrained suspicion of Western—particularly American—intentions. If some US hawks sought an ally against China in Southeast Asia, they wouldn't find an easy one in Mahathir.

That is not to say that Chinese influence was likely to become an unimportant factor in Malaysian politics. During the 2018 election campaign, the question of China had figured prominently on both sides. While Mahathir and PH focused on the Chinese threat from without—the concerns of Chinese debt and immigration—UMNO focused on the threat from within. It painted the PH as a front for the DAP, whose membership is predominantly ethnic Chinese, and argued that an opposition victory would erode Malay Muslim privileges. In the run-up to the elections, pro-UMNO Islamist organizations labored to blur the boundary between the PRC and Malaysian Chinese. In March, the group Ikatan Muslimin Malaysia hosted a forum to promote the idea that the entire Chinese diaspora would eventually fall in line with Beijing. "Humans cannot run from a sense of belonging, of tribalism, the social connection," Abdul Rahman Mat Dali, the group's deputy president, said of Chinese Malaysians.[53]

After the election, similar racial tropes were mobilized to assail the new PH government. Politicians from UMNO and the Parti Islam Se-Malaysia (PAS), Malaysia's largest Islamist party, positioned themselves as defenders of ethnic Malay rights and Islam, which they claimed were threatened by the new government's reform agenda and the appointment of non-Malay politicians to prominent posts. During a by-election rally in Selangor, a senior UMNO official asserted that the new chief justice, attorney general, and finance minister—all non-Malays—had failed to complete their respective oaths of office because they had not been sworn in on a Quran.[54] In November 2018, pressure from UMNO and PAS—the country's two largest Malay parties—forced the government to abandon plans to ratify a UN convention against racial discrimination, which they feared would undermine Malay privileges and threaten Islam's status as Malaysia's official religion. The parties celebrated with a rally of more than 50,000 at Merdeka Square in central Kuala Lumpur, which was attended by a range of UMNO luminaries, including Najib and Rosmah. "People don't respect or care about our dignity. They insult our religion because we have lost power," UMNO deputy president Mohamad Hasan told the crowd. "For us to rise again, we must regain power."[55]

In the event, the perennial appeal to race and religion provided UMNO with a speedy path back to power. In February 2020, Malaysian politics was shaken by the sudden collapse of the PH coalition, the resignation of Mahathir, and the elevation of Najib's former deputy Muhyiddin Yassin to the prime ministership. The events, as remarkable in their own way as the election that had toppled UMNO 21 months earlier, originated in attempts to forestall Mahathir's promised handover of power to Anwar Ibrahim and marginalize the Chinese-dominated DAP.

In late 2019, senior officials of Mahathir's Parti Pribumi Bersatu Malaysia (PPBM) began reaching out to UMNO and PAS to explore the possibility of creating a new pan-Malay coalition that would exclude Anwar and the DAP. On February 24, Muhyiddin, a former deputy to Najib who served as president of PPBM, withdrew the party from the PH coalition and realigned it with UMNO, a move adamantly opposed by Mahathir, who blenched at joining hands with corrupt elements of his former party. The prime minister resigned in protest, hoping that it would open the way to the formation of a new national unity government under his own leadership. Instead, on March 1, Malaysia's king appointed Muhyiddin to form a new government bringing together UMNO, PAS, and PPBM. The result was that the most ethnically diverse cabinet in Malaysia's history was succeeded by an unelected alignment of the nation's three largest Malay parties. The sudden reversal showed that PH's era-ending victory had barely altered the racial identities and subterranean flows of patronage that had undergirded Malaysian politics since independence, and would likely continue to do so for the foreseeable future.

"Self-determination's a ridiculous idea in a mixed-up place like this," Anthony Burgess has a character remark in *The Long Day Wanes*, his trilogy of novels set in the dying years of British Malaya in the 1950s. "There's no nation. There's no common culture, language, literature, religion."[56] In many ways, the last half-century of Malaysian history belies such a jaded assessment. Compared to Burma, with its morass of ethnic conflicts, a hybrid nation has done well to create unity from heterogeneity. Yet for all this progress, race and religion remain the fundamental cleavages in Malaysian society, with complex implications for the future of Malaysia's relationship with China. Dating back to the Emergency, perceptions of China have been inseparable from Malaysia's own racial dynamics. In the years to come, Beijing will need to tread carefully to avoid awakening history's ghosts.

9

INDONESIA
A LONG SPOON

Twenty years on, the scars are still faintly visible. On busy Jalan Pintu Besar Selatan, in Glodok, Jakarta's Chinatown, a row of shop-houses lies abandoned, an octagonal *feng shui* tile still attached to a bricked-up window. Across the street, locked steel shutters offer a glimpse of charred beams and walls blackened by fire. A nearby three-story building stands in ruins, entwined with resurgent foliage, its inside walls scrawled with graffiti.

In May 1998, when angry mobs vented their rage against economic crisis and three decades of cronyism under President Suharto, much of the violence was directed at the nation's ethnic Chinese minority. Despite making up just a tiny slice of the country's population, Chinese Indonesians were widely perceived to have profited handsomely under Suharto's "New Order" regime. Over three days of rioting, hundreds of Chinese homes and businesses were destroyed. Dozens of Chinese women and girls were raped. More than 1,000 people were killed, many of them rioters who found themselves trapped in flaming shopping malls. Latif Yulus, 67, recalled a city on fire. "People were yelling, 'burn, burn, destroy!'" he told me. "It was chaos. There were fires everywhere."

Today, Yulus (Chinese name Liong Tjiang Joe) is the proprietor of Kopi Es Tak Kie, the oldest café in Glodok. Established by Yulus's grandfather in 1927, shortly after stepping off the boat from Guangdong, Tak Kie stands as an emblem of the enterprise and resilience of the *Tionghoa*, as Indonesia's Chinese are known locally. The café survived the conflagrations of 1998, and remains a thriving neighborhood hub, alive with the rat-a-tat of Hokkien dialect and the clatter of white Formica dishes. Framed photos of celebrities on the wall testify to the popularity of Tak Kie's chicken noodles, *nasi campur*, and sweet iced Java coffee, among them Jakarta's former governor Joko Widodo, now Indonesia's president.

Things have improved significantly for Sino-Indonesians since 1998, but memories of the riots still resonate. In May 2017, a few months before I spoke to Yulus, a Jakarta court sentenced the city's ethnic Chinese former governor Basuki Tjahaja Purnama, commonly known as Ahok, to two years' prison on charges of blasphemy, amid a campaign of public demonstrations with strong anti-Chinese overtones. For many of the traders and residents of Glodok, Ahok's downfall was a reminder that ethnic Chinese retained a precarious foothold in the Indonesian national community. "We are a minority," Yulus said. "We have to be aware, not be arrogant."

Nowhere else in Southeast Asia is a nation's relationship with China so closely entangled with the status of its ethnic Chinese minority. As in other parts of the Malay archipelago, Chinese traders and sojourners have been present across the Indonesian islands for more than a millennium. On the island of Borneo, archaeologists have unearthed caches of Song dynasty ceramics, carried by enterprising Chinese traders who ventured up the rivers to exchange their jars and beads for hornbill beaks, edible bird's nests, and other jungle products.[1] When the Dutch East India Company, or VOC, established its first outposts in the Malay archipelago in the seventeenth century, it encountered Chinese merchants who traded cargoes of tea, porcelain, and silk for local products like pepper, sandalwood, and *trepang* (sea cucumbers), then as now a prized delicacy. As early as the 1300s, some Chinese had settled permanently along the coasts of Java, where they assimilated, married local women, and occasionally rose to prominent positions in the precolonial sultanates. By the mid-1700s, the local rulers of at least four cities in Java were of Chinese descent.[2]

Chinese merchants came to occupy an important place in the VOC's commercial networks, and helped build Batavia (today's Jakarta) into a flourishing colonial entrepôt. "If there were no Chinese here," the Dutch minister and naturalist François Valentijn observed in the 1720s, "Batavia would be very dead and deprived of many necessities."[3] The VOC granted the Chinese economic and social privileges, including the right to collect taxes and control the official opium monopoly. Sitting in an elevated position halfway between the Dutch and the *pribumi*, or native Indonesians, the Chinese eventually came to be resented by both. Racial antagonisms exploded in 1740, when Chinese sugar mill workers revolted, prompting a pogrom by VOC troops and indigenous collaborators that took the lives of around ten thousand ethnic Chinese.[4]

The so-called "Batavia Fury" was just the first instance in which the ethnic Chinese would be scapegoated by local rulers seeking to defuse popular anger.

These colonial-era prejudices against the Chinese would outlive the Dutch, carrying over into the Indonesian nationalist movement and the independent republic to which it gave birth. At this point, latent anti-Chinese sentiments were magnified by the threat of communism. The Republic of Indonesia and the People's Republic of China (PRC) were founded within months of each other in late 1949, and established diplomatic relations in April 1950. However, it was a decision that was strongly opposed by Indonesian conservatives, particularly members of Muslim organizations and elements in the Indonesian army. These groups viewed the new regime in Beijing as an existential threat, due to its assumed influence over both the local Chinese and the Indonesian Communist Party—the Partai Komunis Indonesia (PKI)—which had launched a failed uprising in eastern Java in 1948, during the war of independence against the Dutch. Early PRC actions served to reinforce these perceptions. In the early 1950s, Wang Renshu, China's first ambassador to Indonesia, established close ties to the PKI and aggressively courted Indonesia's ethnic Chinese, hoping to swing their loyalty away from the Kuomintang regime on Taiwan. As an Indonesian-born former PKI member who had been exiled by the colonial authorities and now returned as a fanatical emissary of Mao's China, Wang's biography neatly embodied Indonesian fears of conflicting Chinese loyalties.[5]

Relations with China improved somewhat after 1957, when Sukarno, Indonesia's first president, did away with parliamentary politics and embarked upon a period of populist authoritarian rule known as "Guided Democracy." A flamboyant nationalist orator and hero of the independence struggle against the Dutch, Sukarno hoped to position Indonesia in the vanguard of the world's non-aligned and anti-colonial forces. Gradually, he began steering his country's foreign policy in a more radical direction. In speeches, he castigated the West and denounced the deepening US involvement in Vietnam. In 1963, Sukarno launched a political and military campaign called *Konfrontasi* (Confrontation) against the new Federation of Malaysia, which he derided as a puppet of British and American imperialism. All the while he tilted closer to China, culminating in the establishment in August 1965 of a "Jakarta–Beijing Axis," a partnership that threatened briefly to reshape the trajectory of the Cold War in Asia.

Sukarno's leftward turn disturbed the delicate balance between Indonesia's two most powerful political forces: the military, which enjoyed strong backing from the United States, and the PKI, which had links to China. In the early 1960s, Sukarno had managed to play the two hostile camps off against each other, while keeping both reliant on his patronage. But as he swung further to the left internationally, he also tilted toward the PKI domestically, tipping the scales against the military and other anti-communist forces. The situation came to a head in the early morning hours of October 1, 1965, when dissident army officers launched an abortive coup, kidnapping and killing six senior Indonesian army generals.

The circumstances surrounding the so-called September 30th Movement (known in Indonesia as Gerakan 30 September, or G30S) have never been fully illuminated. The participants claimed it was a response to a US-backed attempt to overthrow Sukarno, though such a plot was never definitively proven. Whatever its initial purpose, the G30S conspiracy provided a political opportunity for the army's Strategic Reserve Command (Kostrad), led by a little-known major general named Suharto. Pinning the plot on the PKI, Suharto and the army elbowed Sukarno out of power and, with the aid of local militias and conservative Muslim groups, set about systematically liquidating its communist arch-rival.

Over the months that followed, an estimated half-million people were butchered as the PKI—then the third-largest communist party in the world after those of China and the Soviet Union—was torn out by the roots.[6] The party's leaders were summarily executed, and around a million people were detained without charge, some for decades. The destruction of the PKI amounted, in Geoffrey Robinson's words, to "one of the largest and swiftest, yet least examined instances of mass killing and incarceration in the twentieth century."[7] It was also a major turning point of the Cold War, cheered by much of the American press.

From this bloodshed and upheaval, Suharto emerged in control of Indonesia. Appointed acting president in 1967, he proclaimed the *Orde Baru*, or New Order, and steered Indonesia into the anti-communist camp. Accusing Beijing of orchestrating the G30S plot, Jakarta severed relations in 1967 and wouldn't reestablish them until 1990, holding out even as Thailand, Malaysia, and the Philippines recognized the PRC in the mid-1970s. The reason was straightforward: having seized power to head off a supposed Chinese-backed coup attempt, the New Order had an interest in continuing to depict China as an existential threat. So central was this "red scare" to the regime, the historian Harold Crouch wrote, that it "felt that its legitimacy might be put at stake if it restored friendly relations with the power it had portrayed as the embodiment of evil."[8] Suharto's position only began to soften in the mid-1980s, when the economic benefit of engaging with China came to outweigh the political benefit of demonizing it.

While ethnic Chinese were not the main victims of the anti-communist purges of 1965–6, as is sometimes claimed, the toxic anti-China politics of the New Order quickly engulfed Indonesians of Chinese descent.[9] On high alert for any hint of Chinese subversion or infiltration, the Indonesian government banned Chinese schools and newspapers, and public displays of Chinese characters. Ethnic Chinese were forced to take more Indonesian-sounding names, as with the Glodok café-owner Latif Yulus. Unable to express their Chinese identity, the *Tionghoa* were also unable to shed it. They bore a special mark on their national ID cards, which effectively barred them from the military, the bureaucracy, and most areas of political life. In the region of Yogyakarta, they were even prevented from owning land, a stricture that remains on the books today.[10]

The effective outcome of these discriminatory policies was to reinforce the traditional ethnic Chinese dominance of the commercial sector: the one place where Chinese Indonesians faced few restrictions. The New Order regime thus paradoxically gave birth to the *cukong* ("bosses") a tiny clique of ethnic Chinese compradors who relied on Suharto's patronage and grew immensely rich when Indonesia opened its doors to foreign investment in the 1970s and 1980s. By the time of the 1998 riots, 13 of the country's top 15 taxpayers were Chinese Indonesians. (The remaining two were sons of Suharto.) While making up just 3.5 percent of the country's population, ethnic Chinese were estimated to control around a third of its wealth.[11]

Among the most prominent of these palace tycoons, and perhaps the closest to Suharto himself, was Liem Sioe Liong. Liem had arrived in the Dutch East Indies as a penniless Fujian immigrant in 1938, and befriended Suharto during the independence struggle. Once in power, Suharto granted Liem lucrative concessions; in return, Liem buttressed his rule financially. "One hankered after power, the other after money," wrote the tycoon's biographers. They "worked very closely together, building a symbiotic relationship that resulted in huge benefits for both."[12] Liem established partnerships with ethnic

Chinese tycoons elsewhere in Southeast Asia, including Malaysia's Robert Kuok and Thailand's Chin Sophonpanich. By 1997, his Salim Group—called after Sudono Salim, the Indonesian name that Liem adopted in 1967— was reportedly the largest Chinese-owned conglomerate in the world, with $20 billion in assets and some five hundred subsidiaries.[13] During the New Order, Salim and its affiliated companies dominated Indonesia. Bank Central Asia was the country's biggest private bank, and Indocement its dominant cement producer. Indofood was its leading manufacturer of instant noodles.[14]

Suharto's strategy of surrounding himself with ethnic Chinese cronies was politically astute. As Benedict Anderson writes, "The Chinese would have economic but not political power, while the indigenous Indonesians (among whom a rival or successor to Suharto might arise) would have political positions, but no concentrated independent sources of wealth."[15] But this racial division of labor had the malign effect of associating an already suspect ethnic Chinese minority with a crooked and increasingly despised regime. When the Asian financial crash buffeted Indonesia in 1997, setting off the economic and political aftershocks that eventually brought down the New Order, many turned on the familiar scapegoat. When violent riots that erupted across the archipelago in May 1998, some of Suharto's supporters, eager to deflect public rage away from the regime, directed it toward Chinese targets in Jakarta and other cities with significant ethnic Chinese populations. Needless to say, those Sino-Indonesians who fell victim to the riots were not the reviled *cukong*— those with the means fled Indonesia, along with billions of dollars in capital— but small business owners and other civilians. On May 21, amid continuing unrest, Suharto announced his resignation and handed power to his vice president, B.J. Habibie. The New Order thus ended much as it began: in paroxysms of violence.

Paradoxically, the 1998 riots marked a turning point both for Indonesia's relationship with China, and for the treatment of ethnic Chinese in Indonesia. Unlike in Malaysia, where racial riots in 1969 were followed by a tightening of discriminatory measures against those of Chinese descent, the early years of Indonesian democracy saw the relaxation of ethnic restrictions.[16] No longer reliant on the communist bogeyman to sustain their rule, and under pressure from Chinese community associations, Habibie and his successor Abdurrahman Wahid lifted the bans on expressions of Chinese culture. Chinese New Year returned, with its firecrackers and lion dances; so did Chinese newspapers and dialect associations. As Sino-Indonesians reconnected with Chinese culture at home, some forged closer cultural and commercial ties to the PRC.[17]

These developments paralleled Indonesia's warming relationship with China. While contacts had remained cautious since the reestablishment of diplomatic ties in 1990, China's image improved greatly following the Asian financial crisis in 1997. As in Thailand, the effects in Indonesia were severe, as was the anger at the high-handed response of the International Monetary Fund (IMF), which demanded a host of austere financial reforms in exchange for its bailout. To many Indonesians, a famous and widely circulated photograph of the IMF director Michel Camdessus, standing with arms crossed over a seated and clearly humbled Suharto as he signed off on the IMF's $40 billion bailout package, recalled the humiliations of the colonial era.[18] The Chinese government, in contrast, offered emergency medical aid, extended a $200 million credit line to Indonesia, and contributed $500 million to the IMF's bailout package.[19]

Another factor in the improved relations was Beijing's restrained response to the May 1998 riots. During past episodes of anti-Chinese violence, the Chinese government had railed and condemned, earning hostile rebukes from the Indonesian government. This time the Chinese handled the issue delicately, despite a public outcry at home. It left Hong Kong and Taiwan to register the loudest protests, and when forced to refer to those killed in the riots, it avoided using the term *huaqiao* (Overseas Chinese), and instead described them as *yinni huaren* (Indonesians of Chinese descent). Beijing's ambassador in Jakarta made it clear that China viewed the incident as Indonesia's "internal affair." As he put it, "The Chinese government must not act as if it could be the chef in somebody else's kitchen."[20]

By soothing a core Indonesian sensitivity, China's response allowed the two nations to begin working on issues of overlapping interest, from a shared opposition to regional separatism—Indonesia was then struggling to contain independence movements in the outlying regions of Aceh and West Papua— to a mutual interest in boosting investment and trade. Whatever their misgivings, Indonesian leaders were now awakening to the fact of China's economic emergence, and its potential benefits for their country. By the first decade of the 2000s, the roads of Indonesia's cities were teeming with Chinese motorbikes, which mixed with the Hondas and Yamahas that had been manufactured locally since the 1970s. Non-stop flights were established to China, and mainland tourists, scared off by the violence of 1998, began to return, as did much of the Overseas Chinese capital stashed abroad after the riots. Chinese state firms started to invest in Indonesia's rich deposits of coal, minerals, and natural gas. By 2007, China had become Indonesia's fifth-largest trading partner; ten years later, it had leapt into first place. By then, it was also the country's third-largest source of foreign investment. "There's real meat there," one prominent Chinese-Indonesian businessman told me. "You have Chinese who have lots of capital . . . and we need that capital to invest in infrastructure. Indonesia has so much to gain."

The same is true for China. Indonesia is an increasingly important source of raw materials for the Chinese economy, everything from wood pulp to mineral ores to palm oil. It is set to become the fourth-largest economy in the world by 2050, according to the global consulting firm PricewaterhouseCoopers, with a young population and an expanding middle class that makes it an attractive external market for Chinese consumer goods.[21] As the largest nation of maritime Southeast Asia, Indonesia is also central to China's seafaring ambitions. Its 17,000-odd islands bestride some of the world's most strategically important shipping lanes and chokepoints, including the Malacca, Sunda, Lombok, and Makassar straits. It was no accident that Xi Jinping chose the Indonesian House of Representatives as the venue in which to unveil the 21st Century Maritime Silk Road (MSR)—the maritime component of the Belt and Road Initiative—in October 2013. Xi's vision of a maritime "road" linking China to Europe is impossible to imagine without Indonesian support.

In fundamental ways, however, Indonesia is likely to remain resistant to Chinese influence. Partly, this reflects the history of mistrust dating back to the Cold War. Partly, too, it is a function of Indonesia's prominence and size. Encompassing the majority of the Austronesian realm that conjoins the Pacific and Indian oceans, Indonesia's 264 million people and $1 trillion economy give it a strong gravity of its own, and make it the only Southeast Asian nation that could potentially counterbalance China's power. In this respect China and Indonesia can be described as mirror images: both are large, multiethnic, inward-looking nations: "middle kingdoms" that share a sense of their own centrality to their respective regions.[22] In precolonial times, the Malay peoples of what is today Indonesia experienced limited intercourse with the Chinese state, despite their extensive trade with southern China. As in Malaysia, the arrival and spread of Islam through the archipelago—a process ironically furthered by the fifteenth-century maritime voyages of the Muslim Admiral Zheng He—only heightened the sense of cultural distance. If Indonesians look abroad today, writes Martin Stuart-Fox, they look to Mecca before they look to Beijing.[23]

Thriving economic interactions thus coexist with growing uneasiness about China's push into the oceans, particularly in the South China Sea, whose southern reaches lap at Indonesian shores. Shadowing this is the persistent question of China's relationship with Indonesia's small but economically prosperous ethnic Chinese community. For all the progress of the past two decades, many Indonesians take the view, as Michael Leifer phrased it in 1999, "that in supping with China, as with the devil, it is best to use a long spoon."[24]

The Natuna archipelago lies scattered across the southernmost rim of the South China Sea between Borneo and the Malay Peninsula, a group of islands ringed with sandy beaches and wooden fishing shacks raised on stilts. On June 17, 2016, a small Indonesian navy corvette, the KRI *Imam Bonjol*, was patrolling through waters north of the Natunas when it encountered a group of Chinese fishing boats and two much larger vessels from the Chinese Coast Guard. The boats had entered far inside Indonesia's 200-nautical-mile Exclusive Economic Zone (EEZ), and the *Imam Bonjol* gave chase. After firing a few warning shots, it seized one of the Chinese fishing boats and arrested its seven crewmembers, before towing them back to its ramshackle base on Natuna Besar, the main island in the Natuna chain.

The incident was just one of a series of recent confrontations between Indonesian and Chinese vessels in waters around the Natuna Islands. While Indonesia is not a formal claimant in the South China Sea, its EEZ overlaps with the southernmost part of China's "nine-dash line" claim, creating a zone of friction that encloses some of the world's most biodiverse oceans and largest untapped reserves of natural gas. Three months earlier, an Indonesian attempt to capture another Chinese boat in the area had been foiled by the intervention of a Chinese Coast Guard vessel, operating 1,500 kilometers from the nearest Chinese coast, which forcibly severed the towline connecting the impounded vessel to an Indonesian patrol boat.

These incidents grew out of a war on illegal fishing declared by President Joko Widodo, known often by the nickname Jokowi, shortly after he took office in 2014. Illegal fishing had long been a serious problem in Indonesia, costing the nation billions of dollars in lost revenue each year. Leading the crackdown was Susi Pudjiastuti, then Jokowi's Minister of Maritime Affairs and Fisheries. A chain-smoking divorcée and aviation magnate who was serving in political office for the first time, she oversaw a campaign in which Indonesian authorities seized dozens of foreign vessels found fishing without permission in Indonesian waters. After Susi's appointment in 2014, she promised, "We will track down and sink every single illegal fishing vessel we catch."[25] For the benefit of the press, some of the seized vessels were dramatically destroyed with explosives.

Few of the boats captured by the Indonesian navy were Chinese; most were from Vietnam or Malaysia. But given Beijing's notorious tendency of using its civilian fishing fleet to assert maritime sovereignty claims, Indonesia's willingness to impound even a few Chinese fishing trawlers strongly signaled its intention to defend its EEZ against Chinese incursions. In response to the June 2016 incident, the Chinese Foreign Ministry had denounced the Indonesian arrests, asserting that the region was part of China's "traditional fishing grounds."[26] A few days later, Jokowi flew to Natuna Besar. Dressed in a bomber jacket, he boarded the *Imam Bonjol* and inspected the warship's gun turrets as fighter jets roared overhead. Security Minister Luhut Panjaitan said Jokowi's visit was aimed at sending a "clear message" that Indonesia was "very serious in its effort to protect its sovereignty" around the islands.[27] In 2017, the Indonesian Foreign Ministry announced a high-profile press conference to unveil a new map that renamed the waters around the Natuna Islands the "North Natuna Sea," adding to the crowded catalog of patriotic nomenclature in the South China Sea. It also bolstered its military presence in the Natunas, and held military exercises in nearby waters.

During his campaign for president in 2014, Jokowi had promised to bolster Indonesia's status as a seafaring nation. He pledged to turn Indonesia into a "global maritime fulcrum": to build connectivity between its islands, and leverage the nation's enviable location at the hinge of the Pacific and Indian oceans. In October 2014, he delivered an inaugural speech crammed with maritime metaphor: "We have far too long turned our back on the seas, the oceans, the straits, and the bays," Jokowi declared. Describing himself as "the captain of the ship" of Indonesia, he promised that "we will raise the mast, a strong one. We will face the tides in the ocean with our own power."[28]

Once in office, Jokowi set out to implement this vision by establishing a Coordinating Ministry for Maritime Affairs, creating a unified coastguard, and empowering Susi's ministry to pursue illegal fishing boats.

Jokowi's maritime emphasis sought to correct a long period of Indonesian neglect. Despite being the world's largest archipelago, with around 93,000 square kilometers of inland waters, Indonesia had paid surprisingly little attention to securing and defending its ocean expanses. This was partly an outgrowth of the challenges bequeathed by Dutch colonialism. When Sukarno proclaimed Indonesia's independence in 1945, Elizabeth Pisani writes, "he was liberating a nation that didn't really exist, imposing a notional unity on a ragbag of islands that had only a veneer of shared history."[29] As a result, the new nation was preoccupied with creating "unity in diversity" (as Indonesia's official motto went) and suppressing the serious regional rebellions that flared up across the archipelago from the late 1950s. The Indonesian armed forces focused most of their attention inward, prioritizing internal security over the enforcement of external claims. For years, Indonesia's defense spending has been among the lowest in the Association of Southeast Asian Nations (ASEAN) relative to GDP; even then, most of this has gone to the land forces.[30] This left the Indonesian navy perilously ill-equipped to assert control over its maritime domain—a weakness revealed by China's burgeoning naval presence in the South China Sea.

While Jokowi's forceful actions around the Natuna Islands were viewed internationally as pushback against China's aggressive claims in the South China Sea, the Indonesian leader's views on China were more ambiguous. Indonesia's seventh president was a unique figure in his country's history: the first to hail from neither the military nor the established political elite. Raised in a riverside slum in the Javanese heartland city of Solo, Jokowi had run a furniture exporting business there before being elected the city's mayor in 2005. In that office he became known for his simple, unaffected demeanor and hands-on style of governance, characterized by frequent *blusukan*—impromptu field visits in which he bantered with his constituents, with aides and camera crews in tow. After becoming Jakarta's governor in 2012, he exported this energetic style to the capital, earning him a nationwide profile. Two years later, Jokowi surfed into national office on an Obama-like message of "hope and change," a can-do small-city politician who promised to curb corruption, fire up the economy, and overhaul Indonesia's woeful infrastructure.

Jokowi came to the presidency in 2014 without much interest in foreign affairs. Unlike his predecessor Susilo Bambang Yudhoyono, who had tried to raise Indonesia's international standing to one commensurate with its status as the world's fourth-most populous nation, Jokowi had no previous diplomatic or military experience, and was reportedly bored by the annual cycle of multi-lateral summitry.[31] Jokowi was therefore inclined to view China's rise through the lens of his domestic agenda: in particular, his promise to build up Indonesia's infrastructure, especially in the poorly developed eastern islands. On coming to office, Jokowi's administration announced plans for $355 billion worth of industrial parks, ports, and airports stretching from Sumatra to Sulawesi to Kalimantan. Unable to fund these projects from the national budget, Jokowi looked to China, viewing the 21st Century Maritime Silk Road and his own "global maritime fulcrum" as basically complementary enterprises.

Straight away, Jokowi established a good relationship with Xi Jinping, whom he reportedly saw as a fellow "results-oriented" leader.[32] During his first two years in office, he met Xi five times and joined the new China-led Asian Infrastructure Investment Bank. In September 2015, his government awarded the contract for a $6 billion high-speed rail line between Jakarta and Bandung to a consortium of Chinese and Indonesian state-owned enter-prises, a project that initially looked likely to go to a Japanese firm. In May 2017, Jokowi attended the first Belt and Road Forum in Beijing, where he praised the Belt and Road Initiative (BRI) as a "realistic" approach to devel-opment: "It is not merely talk, but it is about actually building something. From ports to railways, these are industries we can see and touch. This is exactly the sort of courage and real action the world needs right now."[33] The following year, China and Indonesia signed contracts for $23.3 billion worth of BRI infrastructure projects, including two hydropower plants in North Kalimantan on the island of Borneo, a power plant in Bali, and a steel smelting facility.[34]

Although progress on these projects would be sluggish, Jokowi's desire for Chinese financing played into his administration's approach to the tensions around the Natuna Islands. Its dramatic campaign of boat scuttling masked the fact that Chinese vessels were generally handled far more delicately than those belonging to other countries. In a 2016 report for Sydney's Lowy Institute for International Policy, Aaron Connelly observed that plans to sink several Chinese vessels along with dozens of other foreign vessels that year were canceled at the last minute, presumably due to the likely diplomatic ramifications. (The last Chinese fishing boat was blown up in May 2015.) Jokowi's "emphasis on delivering tangible domestic economic results and his associated skepticism of multilateral summit diplomacy" also led his administration to step back from Indonesia's previously active regional diplomacy aimed at building an ASEAN consensus on the South China Sea disputes.[35]

In some ways, Indonesia's approach to the Natuna Islands reflected its long-standing preference for maintaining an "independent and active" foreign policy. Before Suharto's takeover, this meant forging a middle path that would safeguard Indonesia's independence: what Sukarno's vice president Mohammad Hatta characterized in 1948, in another memorable Southeast Asian metaphor of balancing, as "rowing between two reefs."[36] In an age of escalating competition between China and the US, this has manifested as a hedging strategy that Evan A. Laksmana, a senior researcher at Jakarta's Centre for Strategic and International Studies (CSIS), has termed "pragmatic equidistance": a policy of engaging with the various great powers on a range of fronts while maintaining a careful balance between them.[37] Notwithstanding Jokowi's lack of interest in multilateral diplomacy, this approach is also inseparable from Indonesia's traditional leadership role within ASEAN, and its active participation in multilateral groupings from the G20 to the Asia-Pacific Economic Cooperation forum to the Organization of Islamic Cooperation.

Seen in this light, Jokowi's war on illegal fishing passed the Goldilocks test. Seizing a few Chinese boats helped quell criticisms from Jokowi's political opponents that he was soft on China. It also led to significant increases in fish catches, an important domestic issue for Indonesia's coastal communities. At the same time, by framing the Natuna dispute as one of law enforcement rather than maritime sovereignty, Indonesia could assert its own claims without risking a serious break with Beijing. Jakarta's official "non-claimant" status also allowed it to continue working for a peaceful resolution to the South China Sea disputes through ASEAN, even if less vigorously than previously.[38]

Despite Jokowi's shows of strength around the Natuna Islands, however, Indonesian control over its ocean expanses remains fragmented. Evan Laksmana said that despite Jokowi's best efforts, the country's maritime and coastguard forces are a chaos of overlapping mandates, under the nominal authority of the navy and around a dozen ministries and other bodies, making it difficult to coordinate policies. At times, even interpretations of maritime law differ from agency to agency. "Just because we come off as strong on some parts of the maritime domain," he said, "that's not necessarily the position of Indonesia in general."

If events near the Natuna Islands have yet to forestall healthy economic relations between China and Indonesia, those onshore portend greater difficulties. In May 2017, just days before Jokowi flew to Beijing for the first Belt and Road Forum, a court in Jakarta found his ally Basuki Tjahaja Purnama, the city's Chinese-Indonesian former governor, guilty of blasphemy. The public campaign for his jailing evinced worrying echoes of the past. Unabashed about his Chinese heritage, Basuki—known commonly as Ahok, from his Hokkien name Tjung Ban Hok—encapsulated the great strides that Chinese Indonesians had made since 1998. Elected in 2012 as Jokowi's deputy, and bumped up to the top job in 2014 after Jokowi was elected president, he was both ethnic Chinese and Christian—the first "double minority" to govern Indonesia's capital for a half-century. His downfall also indicated that old prejudices against the Chinese retained a poisonous political currency, with potential implications for Indonesia's future relations with China.

The blasphemy controversy originated in Ahok's gubernatorial re-election campaign in late 2016, when he referenced a passage of the Quran during a campaign speech. In essence, Ahok told voters to ignore political arguments that non-Muslims should not be allowed to govern Muslims. But when a selectively edited excerpt of the speech went viral, hardline Islamist vigilante groups, including the pugnacious Islamic Defenders Front (Front Pembela Islam, or FPI) rallied hundreds of thousands of protesters in central Jakarta calling for Ahok to be arrested for blasphemy. Amid rising public pressure, a court laid formal charges. After losing an April 2017 runoff election to his opponent Anies Baswedan, a former minister of education and culture who did not hesitate to play the religious card he had been so fortuitously dealt, Ahok was found guilty and sentenced to two years' prison.

The campaign against Ahok was underpinned by a current of Islamic conservatism that had gained considerable ground in the post-Suharto era. Strict, "modernist" interpretations of Islam have been part of Indonesia's religious mix since colonial times. The New Order had suppressed hardline fundamentalist groups as a possible threat to its hold on power, but the Suharto era was also a period of economic flux and urbanization that seeded a growing religious observance. Another crucial factor was the concurrent influx of Saudi petro-dollars into Indonesia, which went toward the construction of mosques and *pesantren* (Islamic boarding schools) promoting Saudi Arabia's exacting brand of *salafi* Islam. The trend of Islamization accelerated after 1998. It was visible in the adoption of more austere forms of dress by increasing numbers of Indonesian Muslims, including the *niqab*, a head-to-toe covering worn by women. It was also marked by the ascent of pressure groups like the FPI, which inveighed against any group deviating from the *salafi* norm, whether Christians and "heretical" minority Muslim sects like the Ahmadiyah, or progressive student groups and the LGBT community.

In the history of Indonesian populist nationalism, anti-Chinese sentiment has often accompanied expressions of Islamic identity. The country's first mass-based political organization, Sarekat Islam, was founded in 1911 by Javanese *batik* merchants fearful of competition from Chinese interlopers. As it grew and spread across the archipelago, Sarekat Islam embodied the idea that the nascent Indonesian national community it envisaged "was inspired by Islam and excluded Chinese."[39] This association was cemented after 1949, when Muslim concerns about the PRC's militant atheism were displaced onto Indonesia's ethnic Chinese, few of whom were Muslim.

From the beginning, the Ahok blasphemy campaign was marked by veiled (and not-so-veiled) anti-Chinese and anti-China rhetoric. Railing against Ahok's supposed crime, street demonstrators unfurled banners that read *Ganjang Cina* ("Crush the Chinese"). One protest in November 2016 turned violent, as demonstrators looted several Chinese-owned shops in an affluent suburb of North Jakarta. Facebook rumors claimed that Ahok's administration was reclaiming land in the capital to house 10 million mainland Chinese workers; another "fake news" item described a purported Chinese plot to import to Indonesia dried chilies infested with bacteria.[40] A 2017 survey conducted by Singapore's ISEAS–Yusof Ishak Institute found that 47.6 percent of Indonesian respondents agreed with the statement, "Chinese Indonesians may still harbor loyalty towards China."[41]

To be sure, Ahok had been a brash and polarizing figure. His critics blamed him for clearing thousands of urban poor from riverbanks in Jakarta, waving away the concerns of evicted residents and housing rights groups. He also angered devout Muslims when he prohibited Jakarta's public schools from requiring female Muslim students to wear a headscarf, likening the Islamic head coverings to "the napkin in my kitchen." Stanley Widianto, a 26-year-old Indonesian journalist of Chinese descent, said, "He's a flawed person. He's not really savvy politically; he ran his mouth at the crowd by saying that Quran verse. I'm not saying that he was wrong per se, but from a political standpoint that was bad. He was running for governor, for God's sake."

Ahok thus became the focus for converging streams of fundamentalist ideology, ethnic suspicion, and populist resentment linked to the widening inequalities of wealth in Indonesia's capital. Charlotte Setijadi, a fellow at the ISEAS–Yusof Ishak Institute who studies Indonesia's ethnic Chinese minority, explained that Ahok came to epitomize many of the traditional stereotypes about the Chinese. "He was kind of like the perfect embodiment of all of that," she said, "a Chinese Christian, an impolite man in a position of power, who insulted the faith of the majority of Indonesians." In Jakarta's ethnic Chinese community, I heard varying opinions about Ahok. While some people expressed pride that one of their own could rise so high, others accused the governor of disturbing the city's precarious ethnic balance. "It's better to stay quiet," said Ie Tiat Fo, 57, a Hokkien textile merchant in Glodok. "When he chose to be quiet, everything was okay."

If Ahok's rise showed how far Indonesian democracy had advanced since 1998, his fall highlighted the worrying extent to which old attitudes and personalities held sway. Behind the anti-Ahok campaign lay a pernicious alliance between religious fundamentalists and conservative politicians, some with roots deep in the New Order. Bonnie Triyana, an historian who edits the monthly magazine *Historia*, said that the swirl of Islamic and anti-Chinese rhetoric had been whipped up by these conservative forces to discredit avowed reformists like Ahok and Jokowi. He described the affair as "a moment when historical memories came together with political vested interests."

The power of this old guard is one key reason why Indonesia has yet to pursue accountability for the New Order's founding atrocity: the anti-communist massacres of 1965–6. Scholars and human rights groups attempting to explore the episode have been branded "communists" and had their meetings broken up by police or Islamic vigilantes. In 2016, when activists convened a "people's tribunal" in The Hague that found the Indonesian government guilty of genocide over the killings, Defense Minister Ryamizard Ryacudu denounced it as "the work of the PKI"—a party that hadn't existed for 50 years and was still officially outlawed, along with Marxist teachings more generally.[42] More than two decades after the fall of Suharto, Indonesian museums and schoolbooks still propagate the era's line: that the New Order delivered Indonesia from the jaws of the PKI and the Chinese communists.

This New Order hangover was embodied in the gruff, stocky figure of Prabowo Subianto, a former general who ran against Jokowi in the 2014 presidential election, and gave vocal support to the campaign against Ahok. A leading hardline general in the dying years of the New Order, and a former son-in-law of Suharto, Prabowo has been credibly implicated in a litany of human rights abuses, including atrocities committed in the conflict zones of East Timor and Aceh, and the abduction of pro-democracy activists in the regime's final months. After his March 1998 appointment as the head of Kostrad, the post that Suharto occupied on the eve of his own takeover in 1967, Prabowo was accused of joining with radical Islamic groups to fan anti-Chinese sentiment in the lead-up to the May riots. This is alleged to have been prompted by an internal power struggle between Prabowo and General Wiranto, the head of the armed forces, over who would succeed the ageing dictator.[43]

Prabowo's 2014 presidential run was shot through with nostalgia for the Suharto years and populist promises of a return to stable strongman rule. The scholar Edward Aspinall describes Prabowo as an "oligarchic populist" who mimicked Sukarno's barnstorming mass rallies and sartorial affectations— down to his white safari suits, black *peci* cap, and vintage microphones—and combined them with a raging sense of personal entitlement.[44] Prefiguring the later attacks on Jokowi's ally Ahok, Prabowo's campaign peddled the anti-Chinese tropes that have long been the handmaiden of reactionary politics in Indonesia. Some claimed that Jokowi was ethnically Chinese; others, that he was secretly pushing a communist agenda.

To get a handle on how anti-Chinese sentiment and conservative religious currents were feeding into perceptions of China's increasing power and influence in Indonesia, I set out on a steamy July afternoon for a musty office building in South Jakarta, to meet with Habib Muchsin Alatas, a senior member of the FPI. Set up by a group of generals to fight pro-democracy protesters in 1998, the FPI had developed into a potent force in Indonesian street politics, feared for its aggressive "sweeping" operations, in which swarms of wispy-bearded zealots shut down bars and clubs, or attempted to break up "un-Islamic" public events and film screenings. It had also played a central role in the campaign to bring down Ahok.

Alatas, the chairman of the FPI's shura council, its top decision-making body, was dressed in a white *salafi* robe and gray turban. With a wide face and booming voice, he struck an imposing figure, an impression accentuated by the perch he occupied behind a broad, glass-topped CEO desk. After the formal introductions, and the customary distribution of fried snacks and rice cakes, we got around to the topic of Ahok. For Alatas, the question was simple: Islam had been central to the nation since its founding. Ahok's "blasphemy" threatened to inspire similar sentiments elsewhere in Indonesia, precipitating a general breakdown in religious morality and, by extension, national unity. "If we are tolerant to Ahok, then other leaders will do the same. That's why Ahok was dangerous," he said.

The other key part of this equation was China. Alatas described Ahok as a "martyr for the grand designs of Chinese imperialism" in Indonesia, which included the alleged importation of millions of Chinese workers under the cover of BRI infrastructure investments. "And you know, China is communist, anti-religion, anti-God," he added, bringing the connections full circle. "It's like the opposite of Indonesia."

For the moment, this conflation of China and Indonesia's ethnic Chinese remains the view of a vocal minority. But as Indonesia moved toward presidential elections in 2019—another Jokowi vs. Prabowo battle—the China question again raised its head. This time, the concern surrounded China's economic footprint in Indonesia, which had expanded markedly during Jokowi's first term. Social media buzzed with stories about Chinese tour guides stealing jobs from locals in Bali, and mainland workers being shipped in to build roads and dams. Local media attention focused on a joint-venture industrial estate in Morowali in central Sulawesi, one of the largest Chinese investments in Indonesia. Although not officially a BRI project, the huge enterprise, which included a nickel smelter and mill capable of churning out 3 million tons of steel a year, was said to be employing thousands of mainlanders illegally on tourist visas.

In reality, few of the big BRI projects sought by Jokowi's administration had materialized. The Jakarta–Bandung high-speed railway had seen repeated delays due to funding disagreements, permit issues, and the glacial pace of land acquisition. Other projects languished at the planning stage. Meanwhile, official figures put the number of Chinese workers in Indonesia at just 32,000—orders of magnitude short of what rumor suggested. As Yose Rizal Damuri, an economist at CSIS, pointed out, "There are far more Indonesians working in Hong Kong than Chinese working in Indonesia."[45] Yet the salience of such rumors suggested the extreme sensitivity of even the slightest possibility that China was taking jobs from local workers.

Similar themes flowed into the election campaign proper. Hoping to replicate the strategy that had brought Mahathir Mohamad back to power in Malaysia the year before, Prabowo vowed a stringent review of Indonesia's BRI investments, including the Jakarta–Bandung railway, and (channeling Donald Trump) promised to "seek a better deal" in trade that would reduce Indonesia's large trade deficit with China.[46] As at the election five years earlier, the campaign played out against a backdrop of social media hoaxes and misinformation alleging the usual anti-Chinese outrages: that Jokowi was trying to infiltrate Chinese workers into Indonesia, that he was an agent of China, or the PKI, or both.

In the end, Jokowi won re-election, though not without significant challenge. Initially, Prabowo refused to accept the election result and the ensuing protests evolved into violent confrontations between police and pro-Prabowo demonstrators, some waving black Islamic flags. At least eight people were killed and hundreds injured in the post-election unrest. Again, the turmoil was colored by anti-Chinese rhetoric. Messages circulated on social media claiming that rioters killed in the melee had been shot by "police from China," who had arrived in Indonesia "disguised as foreign workers."[47] Even though Prabowo's macho posturing and authoritarian appeals failed once again to defeat the softer populism of Jokowi, who would later welcome Prabowo into his cabinet as Minister of Defense, it demonstrated that anti-Chinese populism remained a live current in Indonesian politics. While a repeat of May 1998 was unlikely anytime soon, Bonnie Triyana said, "The seeds of hatred are still there"—and seemingly no shortage of politicians and demagogues willing to tend them and bring them to flower.

As in the past, the "Chinese question" remains an acutely sensitive factor in Indonesia's already uneasy relationship with China, complicating the Chinese government's pursuit of its broader strategic goals in maritime Southeast Asia. In the words of Evan Laksmana of CSIS, "China will always be the most domestically combustible relationship we have with a foreign country." And just as Beijing will always struggle to transcend the acute suspicion that surrounds its relationship to the local Chinese, there is a danger that it could again worsen the situation through over-confident or ill-advised outreach to Chinese Indonesians.

Given Indonesia's long history of anti-Chinese discrimination, China's re-emergence as an economic, political, and cultural power poses greater complications for Indonesia's ethnic Chinese community than for its counterparts elsewhere in Southeast Asia. Those I spoke to registered a broad range of views about their ancestral homeland. Agus Hendry Susanto, 62, a Chinese-Indonesian businessman in Yogyakarta, whose family came from Fujian province during the Chinese Civil War in the 1930s, told me that he was "very proud" of China's newfound superpower status. He then hastened to add, "I am proud of both China and Indonesia." In Glodok, I interviewed the owner of a small restaurant selling *soto betawi*, a noodle soup made with beef and coconut milk. Giving his name only as Afung, the septuagenarian spoke about his parents' immigration from Guangdong in 1940. Afung said he was proud of his heritage—"everywhere we can see the sunrise, the Chinese are there," he said—but it was hard to feel much allegiance to a country that he had never seen with his own eyes. "I was born in Indonesia," he said, "and I will die in Indonesia." Others expressed the view that the increasing visibility of ethnic Chinese politicians and businesspeople in Indonesian life had drawn unwelcome attention to the community as a whole.

As Charlotte Setijadi argued in a 2017 paper, Sino-Indonesians' attitudes toward China divide along generational, linguistic, and economic lines. For some, China's rise and the more open climate for Chinese cultural expression have led to a process of "Sinification," in which they are "orientating themselves more to a Mainland Chinese version of Chineseness": speaking Mandarin, consuming mainland media, and so forth. Others continue to identify much more with their adopted homeland than their ancestral one. This roughly matches the old division between the *peranakan* Chinese, deeply acculturated and often no longer fluent in any Chinese language, and *totoks*, more recent Mandarin-speaking immigrants with closer affinities to the mainland.[48]

In recent years, as relations between Indonesia and China have improved, both governments have come to view Chinese Indonesians as a natural economic and cultural bridge. In encouraging them to play this role, however, they run the risk of reinforcing old suspicions of bifurcated loyalties. Given prevailing attitudes among *pribumi* Indonesians, Setijadi said that positive perceptions of mainland China rarely transfer to the local ethnic Chinese, "while negative stuff almost certainly gets connected to Chinese Indonesians."

There are some indications that the Chinese embassy in Jakarta recognizes the sensitivity of the "Chinese question" in Indonesia, focusing most of its educational and other people-to-people exchanges on Muslim *pribumi* Indonesians. But mainland officials have made comments that hint at a worrying muddying of the lines between Chinese heritage and Chinese citizenship. In April 2012, Li Yinze, the director of Beijing's Overseas Chinese Affairs Office (OCAO), gave a speech at the China Chamber of Commerce in Jakarta in which he urged young Chinese Indonesians to learn Mandarin "in order to strengthen their identification with the Chinese nation." Three years later, another senior OCAO official told an Indonesian-Chinese audience that "China will always be the strong backer of the people of Chinese descent overseas."[49] In their very ambiguity, these statements provided fertile soil for suspicion. While local anti-Chinese prejudice is yet to align with broader fears of China to the extent that it did under Suharto, heedlessly cultivating ties to Indonesia's ethnic Chinese, against a backdrop of maritime tensions and anti-Chinese religious demagoguery, could have dire consequences.

Further in the background looms the question of what the Chinese government might do in response to another outbreak of anti-Chinese violence in Indonesia. The riots of May 1998 prompted nationalist outrage on the Chinese mainland, where the incident is now remembered as "Black May." At the time, demonstrators in Beijing defied an official ban to protest both the Indonesian violence and what many saw as their own government's lukewarm response.[50] Christine Susanna Tjhin, a Chinese-Indonesian researcher who has done extensive research in mainland China, said the incident still resonates there. From taxi drivers to students to members of the business community, she said, "the image of May '98 is firmly ingrained in the minds of mainland Chinese." Though China's reaction was subdued in 1998, would it be willing or able to show such restraint today, in an age of ascendant Chinese nationalism, when events are broadcast and amplified in real time on social media? It is a hard question to answer; suffice to say, Beijing is watching developments in Indonesia closely.

As competition mounts between China and the US, Southeast Asia's largest nation once again finds itself "between the reefs," facing cross-pressures from two adversarial superpowers. Given Indonesia's size and prominence in Southeast Asia, and its traditionally active role within ASEAN, how it responds to these dynamics could help set the tone for the region as a whole. Surprisingly, given its complex and troubled history of ties with Beijing, Indonesia has remained skeptical about the adverse turn in US policy toward China, particularly the Free and Open Indo-Pacific (FOIP) strategy announced by the Trump administration in late 2017. While Indonesian policymakers, like many of their Southeast Asian counterparts, view US power as an important stabilizing force, they fear that aggressive American efforts to contain Chinese ambitions could undermine "ASEAN centrality" and polarize the bloc.

To a great extent, Washington's current policies toward China are anathema to Indonesia's "independent and active" foreign policy tradition, which prizes multilateralism and views open great power alignments with suspicion. Since its inception in 1967, ASEAN has been the primary vehicle through which Indonesia has pursued regional leadership, as symbolized by its hosting of the ASEAN Secretariat in Jakarta. Despite Jokowi's personal indifference, Indonesian diplomats and policymakers continue to view ASEAN as the best way of managing the region's security challenges.

As the bloc's largest member—and perhaps the quintessential "Indo-Pacific" nation—it is no surprise that Indonesia has led ASEAN's efforts to formulate a response to the FOIP, anchored squarely in ASEAN and its multilateral processes. In 2019, Jakarta played a key role in drafting the bloc's "Indo-Pacific Outlook," its first official response to the new American strategy. The "Outlook" steered a middle course between competing Chinese and American geopolitical visions in a bid to avoid any "zero-sum game" and to "continue being an honest broker within the strategic environment of competing interests."[51]

Indonesia's present approach has its limits, though. As Connelly writes, Indonesia's preference for balancing the great powers had sometimes led it to adopt positions that seem "inconsistent with its own self-interest" on certain issues, particularly in the South China Sea.[52] Similarly, its focus on sometimes toothless multilateralism has given rise to the perennial claim that Indonesia has failed to evolve into the regional power that its geographic and demographic size might suggest. To many outside observers—particularly in the US—it has long been conventional wisdom that Indonesia "punches below its weight" in world affairs.[53] Since the advent of the FOIP strategy, some outside analysts have expressed disappointment at Indonesia's apparent unwillingness to take a stronger stand against China.

Yet Indonesia's approach to the mounting regional tensions is unlikely to change for the foreseeable future. Despite its maritime geography, the orientation of the Indonesian state remains overwhelmingly inward-looking, consumed with the challenge of unifying its fissiparous regions and delivering prosperity to its 267 million citizens. In 2018, Indonesia's military spending remained the lowest in ASEAN relative to its size.[54] With most of its economic resources focused on domestic challenges, Indonesian leaders perceive, for better or worse, that the nation's "regional and global profiles are best served and amplified through the multilateral forums that it has invested in over the years."[55]

Until now, Indonesia's self-absorption may have redounded to the region's ultimate benefit. As Donald Emmerson writes, "If Indonesia had not punched *under* its 'weight' inside ASEAN—lowering its voice in foreign affairs, forsaking Sukarno's high-decibel rhetoric against Malaysia, accepting the need to cooperate with its 'underweight' neighbors—the organization would not have survived and the region might well have been less stable today."[56] How well this approach is suited to the coming century remains to be seen. In the end, it may well be decisions made in Beijing and Washington, rather than in Jakarta, that determine whether Indonesia holds to its middle path, or runs aground on the reefs.

10
THE PHILIPPINES
SLOUCHING TOWARD BEIJING

President Rodrigo Duterte is an unnerving presence in his hometown in the southern Philippines. He stares out from posters and bumper stickers, and lurks on life-size cardboard cutouts in restaurants and hotel lobbies. Since trolling his way into office in 2016, Duterte's squat bungalow in Davao City has become a place of pilgrimage for supporters, who pose for photos while making his trademark raised fist salute. In the surrounding streets, stalls run a hot trade in Duterte merchandise, including trucker hats, coffee mugs, and license plates. One T-shirt features Duterte in shades, in action hero pose, under the line #MyPresident. Another likens Duterte to The Punisher, a vigilante from Marvel Comics who wages a relentless one-man war on crime.

Before seizing international headlines with his vulgar comments about the Pope and his bloody battle against illegal drugs, Duterte served for more than two decades as mayor of this port city on the fractious southern island of Mindanao. During that time, he ran Davao City like a disheveled, hard-drinking Lee Kuan Yew. He banned smoking and the sale of liquor after 1 a.m. He legalized prostitution. Most importantly, local residents say, he turned Davao City into a refuge of order and stability in a region long known as the Philippines' "wild south." "People here were not safe," said Roda Ladera, 45, whom I met one evening while strolling through Davao City's Chinese Cemetery. But under Duterte, she said, "there was peace and order, bad people were minimized."

When Duterte was elected mayor in 1988, Davao was nearly lawless: assassinations by communist insurgents were common, and criminal gangs engaged in shootouts in the street. Ladera, who works as a caretaker at the cemetery, said that even the graves there were ransacked for valuables. While much of Mindanao is still plagued by communist and Islamic rebel groups, Davao City, now run by Duterte's daughter Sara, claims to be one of the safest cities in the Philippines. Rolan Ordinacion, a 35-year-old taxi driver, declared: "Everyone in Davao believes in Duterte."

Yet for some, admiration for the former mayor is tempered by unease at the hardline methods that would later earn him notoriety as president. Human rights groups claim that between 1998 and 2015, more than 1,400 poor Davaoeños were murdered by vigilante death squads. The victims included street kids and petty criminals, as well as addicts and dealers of crystal meth, a scourge that Filipinos call *shabu*.[1] "His strategy was to chase criminals and threaten them—with murder," said Virgilio "Ver" Bermudez, a Davao City-based journalist who covered Duterte for nearly three decades. "There was a general strategy to instill fear."

Most of the killings were blamed on "unknown vigilante killers," few of whom were ever brought to justice. Although Duterte has denied any direct knowledge of these death squads, he never shied away from using force. In 2009, he said that criminals were "a legitimate target of assassination."[2] The rest of the Philippines would soon become familiar with these methods. When Duterte made a run at the presidency in 2016, his pitch was simple: to expand his Davao City "model" nationwide, including his scorched-earth campaign against illegal drugs. "It's going to be bloody," he promised during the campaign. "People will die." Duterte even boasted that he had killed armed criminals himself, though no conclusive evidence ever emerged.

Although he looked and acted like an outsider, Duterte hailed from a well-established political family, with ties to powerful dynasties in Mindanao and the Visayas; his father once served as governor of Davao province. Nonetheless, his slouching presentation, casual dress, and promise to use extreme violence to solve the Philippines' endemic social problems set him apart from the rest of the national political elite. When Filipino voters went to the polls in May 2016, they handed Duterte a convincing victory. He won nearly 7 million votes more than his nearest rival.

Duterte didn't renege on his promise. Within days of his entering the Malacañang, the turreted Spanish colonial palace on the banks of Manila's Pasig River, the police were fanning out into the warren-like slums of Manila and Cebu. Led by Ronald "Bato" dela Rosa, who had served under Duterte as police chief of Davao City and now headed the Philippine National Police, law enforcement officers smashed in doors and shot alleged drug dealers, many of whom were simply addicts. Filipino journalists who covered the drug war compared it to working in a conflict zone. Luis Liwanag, a photo-journalist who co-produced a short film titled *Duterte's Hell*, recalled nights on end working from 10 p.m. until 4 a.m., following squad cars from crime scene to dimly lit crime scene. "When you get home all your flesh is tingling," he said when we met at a Starbucks in Quezon City, a prosperous suburb north of Manila. "You can have hallucinations, especially late at night."

The death tolls from Duterte's war were monstrous. Officially, the police declared 5,104 "drug personalities" killed as of January 2019; Duterte's critics claimed up to four times that number, including many innocents who were wrongly suspected of drug crimes. Within a few months, the war on drugs had killed at least three times as many Filipinos as had died in nearly a decade of martial law under the dictator Ferdinand Marcos during the 1970s and 1980s.[3]

The war on drugs soon bled into the Philippines' foreign policy. When Western nations criticized the violence, Duterte embraced Xi Jinping's China and Vladimir Putin's Russia. When the International Criminal Court opened a preliminary inquiry into the killings, he announced the Philippines' withdrawal from the court and warned UN human rights investigators, "do not fuck with me."[4] As the foreign affairs analyst Richard Javad Heydarian writes in his book *The Rise of Duterte*, the new president engineered a rapid and wrenching reorientation of the Philippines' domestic and international policies. In a matter of months, the island-nation "went from one of America's staunchest regional allies to one of its most vocal critics; it went from a bastion of human rights and liberal values in Southeast Asia to a new haven for 'Asian values' and strongman leadership."[5] But despite his use of violence—or perhaps because of it—Duterte remained hugely popular. According to surveys conducted by Social Weather Stations, a local polling agency, at no time between September 2016 and June 2019 did public approval of the "drug war" drop below 75 percent.[6]

Given the timing of his election, descriptions of Duterte as "the Donald Trump of the Philippines" fast became a US media cliché. But some of the parallels were undeniable. As with Trump, Duterte was canny in his manipulation of the media, and similarly instinctive in his grasp that outrageous public behavior guaranteed endless free coverage in the press. Both men were also lucky, prevailing over a divided field of lackluster candidates. Like Trump, too, Duterte was more symptom than disease. As Heydarian writes, the elevation of the trash-talking Davaoeño to the leadership of Southeast Asia's second-most populous nation grew directly from the manifold failures of the Philippines' liberal elite political class, which had spent three decades promising prosperity and inclusive development, and repeatedly failed to deliver.[7]

In February 1986, when a campaign of mass public demonstrations brought down the "conjugal dictatorship" of Ferdinand Marcos and his wife Imelda, Filipinos had good reason to hope for a better future. Thirty-one years of Marcos had left the nation in a dire state; its democratic institutions had atrophied, and the nation was saddled with $27 billion in foreign debt. To millions of devout Catholic Filipinos, the elevation of Corazon Aquino, the widow of Benigno "Ninoy" Aquino Jr., a rival of Marcos assassinated on his return from exile in 1983, was literally miraculous. In the West, the EDSA revolution—named after the Epifanio de los Santos Avenue, a major Manila thoroughfare that was the scene of mass demonstrations—was also viewed in quasi-messianic terms, as incarnating a sort of historical inevitability. As James Fallows summarized the prevailing wisdom in 1987, "The evil Marcos was out, the saintly Cory was in, the worldwide march of democracy went on."[8]

In reality, EDSA was less a revolution than a restoration of the old order. The fall of Marcos and his cronies was followed by the return of the country's old *mestizo* planter elite, which had risen under the Spanish, crystallized under the Americans, collaborated heartily with the Japanese during World War II, and more or less controlled the country since independence in 1946. Cory Aquino—*TIME* magazine's Woman of the Year for 1986—was very much part of this old ruling class. Her family, the Cojuangcos, were key members of the tiny Chinese-*mestizo* aristocracy, which traced its roots back to immigrants who had arrived from Fujian province in the eighteenth and nineteenth centuries.[9] She was the daughter of the wealthy sugar magnate Don José Cojuangco, and the cousin of Eduardo Cojuangco, one of the most notorious booty capitalists of the Marcos era. At one stage, it was estimated that Eduardo's business empire accounted for a quarter of the nation's GDP.[10]

As a result, the fall of Marcos did little to change the Philippines' skewed distributions of wealth and power. Although the 1987 constitution included a clause banning "political dynasties," the nation remained in the grip of a network of rich families, who as of 2013 still governed in 72 of the Philippines' 80 provinces.[11] This elite complacency was exemplified by Duterte's predecessor. President Benigno Aquino III, the son of the saintly Cory and the martyred Ninoy, was elected in 2010 on promises of hope, change, and clean government after the corruption scandals that had stained the previous administration of Gloria Macapagal Arroyo. Going by the numbers, his presidency was a success. The Philippines experienced its highest economic growth since the 1960s: from 2010 to 2017, GDP grew by an average of 6.4 percent a year, compared with 4.5 percent between 2000 and 2009.[12] As World Bank country director Motoo Konishi declared, the Philippines was "no longer the sick man of East Asia, but the rising tiger."[13]

But while poverty rates fell in the aggregate, few tangible benefits seemed to leak through to the bottom rungs of society. In 2011, the Filipino economist Cielito Habito calculated that 76.5 percent of the wealth generated that year had accrued to the nation's 40 richest people.[14] Meanwhile, millions of Filipinos remained mired in poverty and malnutrition, a reality that was closer to that of contemporary Cambodia than to South Korea—or even to Thailand. Nowhere was this more visible than in Manila's slums, a Hobbesian jumble of cinderblock and corrugated iron shacks that stretched for miles along littered streams. As Ver Bermudez told me in Davao City, the Philippines' impressive GDP figures reflected its high rate of population growth and remittances from the 10 percent of the population that worked abroad—themselves both reflections of serious governance problems. "GDP is really misleading," he said. "This society has failed—that is the truth."

By the time Duterte stepped onto the national political stage, a swathe of the voting population had become deeply disillusioned with the Philippines' political elite. There were a number of warning signs. One was the Reagan-like foreshadowing of Joseph Ejercito "Erap" Estrada, a former B-movie star who rode to the presidency by mimicking the gangsters he played on screen. (He served in office from 1998 to 2001.) Another was the growing nostalgia for the Marcos years, which some Filipinos now recalled as a golden age of stability and growth. During the 2016 election campaign, when Duterte proposed a plan to rebury Marcos, who had died in exile in Hawaii in 1989, with "official honors" at the Heroes' Cemetery in Manila, a survey found that 59 percent of Filipinos supported the idea.[15] (His remains were transferred there in late 2016.) On election day, the dictator's son, Ferdinand "Bongbong" Marcos Jr., came within a hair of winning the vice presidency.

All this ensured a broad customer base for Duterte's swaggering brand of law-and-order populism, and his pledge to franchise his "Davao model" nationwide. As Heydarian put it when we met for Japanese food at a mall in central Manila, "People were saying, like, if this is the best that our democracy can create since Marcos, then we want something else."

That something else involved a dramatic shift in the Philippines' foreign policy, away from the US, its former colonial ruler and main security partner, and toward China, until recently its main security threat. Under Aquino, relations with China had plunged following a series of tense skirmishes in the South China Sea, where Beijing's outlandish claims overlapped with large expanses of the Philippines' 200-nautical-mile Exclusive Economic Zone (EEZ). In 2012, the two nations engaged in a heated naval standoff over Scarborough Shoal, 198 kilometers due west of Subic Bay. In response, the Aquino administration took the unprecedented step of filing a formal complaint in the Permanent Court of Arbitration in The Hague, challenging a number of China's maritime claims and activities in the South China Sea. The Chinese government retaliated with a range of coercive economic measures. It introduced travel restrictions that drastically cut the number of Chinese tourists visiting the Philippines; it also carried out "health inspections" of Philippine pineapples and bananas, leaving them to rot at Chinese ports.

On coming to office in June 2016, Duterte junked this confrontational policy in favor of a more pragmatic, conciliatory approach. When the arbitral tribunal ruled in the Philippines' favor that July, determining that China's "nine-dash line" had no international legal standing and supporting most of Manila's legal claims, he set the victory aside and promised to talk directly with President Xi Jinping, hoping to tap Beijing for badly needed infrastructure funding. At the same time, Duterte lashed out at the US, particularly over criticisms of his drug war. When President Obama raised the issue, the Philippine leader told him to "go to hell." He shocked his own aides by threatening to expel US Special Forces operating in the southern Philippines, and end annual exercises with the US military.

Duterte's foreign policy pivot was crystallized during a remarkable state visit to Beijing in October 2016. "In this venue I announce my separation from the United States," he announced in the Great Hall of the People, promising his Chinese hosts that he had "realigned myself in your ideological flow."[16] The pomp and circumstance of Duterte's visit contrasted starkly with one Aquino had made in August 2011, when he was welcomed by overcast skies, a hostile editorial in the *Global Times*, and a scrupulously correct, yet palpably cool, official welcome. Manolo Quezon III, a columnist and former speechwriter for Aquino who accompanied him on his visit to Beijing in 2011, described the contrast between Aquino's reception and Duterte's. As an honor guard, "we had a detachment, and he had a battalion," Quezon said. "We were in an inner function room, he was on the front steps." Duterte came away from Beijing with $24 billion in promised business deals and infrastructure funding.

Stripped of his outrageous rhetoric, Duterte's "pivot to China" was neither as new, nor as irrational, as it seemed. Since Marcos had opened relations with China in 1975, economic and political ties had steadily improved, reaching a peak under the administration of President Arroyo (2001–10), who proclaimed a "golden age" of bilateral relations. The real outlier was Aquino, who, in response to Chinese maritime activities, had taken an unusually confrontational stance toward Xi's government, on several occasions comparing it to Nazi Germany. In the words of Jay Batongbacal, director of the University of the Philippines' Institute for Maritime Affairs and Law of the Sea, "There was really no way for Philippine–China relations to go but up."

Duterte's China policy was also inseparable from the Philippines' close and deeply unequal relationship with the US. After half a century of direct colonial rule, and seven decades of entwined relations, the US and the Philippines remained closely attached. The US embassy in Manila was still one of the largest American missions in the world, its colonnaded chancery facing onto Manila Bay, where the American Asiatic Squadron under Commodore George Dewey defeated a Spanish fleet on May 1, 1898, bringing the Philippine islands under US control. After independence in 1946, American control persisted in indirect form. The Philippines was granted preferential access to the US market, enriching and entrenching the rural *mestizo* oligarchs. In 1951, Washington and Manila signed a defense treaty that laid the foundation of a tight Cold War security pact, symbolized by the Clark Air Base and the colossal naval station at Subic Bay.

Political and security ties went hand in hand with cultural transmissions. Filipinos inherited the American passion for fast-food and firearms, and were bound closely to the US by marriage, migration, and barracks-room camaraderies. The US influence in the Philippines is so striking that Stanley Karnow likened the Filipinos to "some kind of lost American tribe that has somehow become detached from the US mainland and floated across the

Pacific."[17] According to surveys conducted by the Pew Research Center, no other nation in the world views the US more positively. In 2018, 83 percent of respondents in the Philippines said they had a favorable view of America—a higher proportion than in the US itself.[18] From a certain angle, it is not hard to see the American state that the Philippines might, but for a different twist of history, have become.[19]

Yet there has always been a constituency suspicious of the American presence in the Philippines. To some on the political left, the US security umbrella that protected the Philippines was also a humiliating reminder of the country's continuing colonial dependency. In 1991–2, this manifested in the successful movement for the closure of the military bases at Clark and Subic Bay—the most conspicuous sign of the US presence in the Philippine islands. At Subic today, this opposition is marked by a monument known as The Hands that Freed the Nation, which bears the hand prints of the 12 senators who voted against the renewal of the basing agreement in September 1991, spelling the end for Subic and Clark. The monument is topped by a Virgin Mary-like figure representing *Inang Laya*—the "mother country"—breaking her chains after "more than four centuries of foreign military presence."

Duterte's anti-Americanism drew deeply from this tradition. Like many Mindanaoans, he knew about the massacres and other atrocities committed by occupying US troops in the southern Philippines at the turn of the twentieth century. He also had close ties to left-wing intellectuals, the constituency traditionally most critical of American influence. For a time, Duterte was a student of José Maria Sison, who founded the Communist Party of the Philippines in 1968. Reports also suggested the salience of personal resentments. Duterte claimed that during his childhood he was abused by an American Jesuit priest; later, he was rejected for a visa to visit the US.[20] As mayor of Davao, Duterte made the unprecedented decision to block joint Philippine–American military exercises in 2007, and twice denied US armed forces access to the city's airport for drone operations.[21] Ahead of the 2016 presidential election, Duterte had promised to chart a new foreign course that would "not be dependent on the United States."[22] In doing so, he was greatly aided by the structural peculiarities of the Philippine political system, which granted the president considerable latitude to shape foreign policy.

In addition to its criticisms of his drug war, Duterte's pivot away from the US was also a reaction to the Obama administration's ambiguous stance toward its maritime disputes with China. In 2014, the Philippines and the US had signed an Enhanced Defense Cooperation Agreement (EDCA), which permitted the US to deploy conventional forces in the Philippines for the first time in decades—a key element of the Obama administration's strategic "rebalance" to Asia, which also saw American warships return to Subic Bay. Yet when things heated up in the South China Sea, the US had declined to confront China directly. Under the 1951 Mutual Defense Treaty (MDT) Manila and Washington promised to support each other in the event of an attack on either country, but its wording was vague: it was unclear whether the treaty applied to Philippine-claimed islands and reefs in the South China Sea, which were only officially incorporated in 1978.

This uncertainty suffused the tense ten-week standoff that took place between the Philippines and China at Scarborough Shoal in 2012. The triangle-shaped ring of reefs and rocks, named after a British East India Company tea-trade ship that ran aground there in 1784, had been a source of low-level tensions since China began its maritime build-up in the 1990s. In April 2012, a Philippine navy surveillance plane detected eight Chinese fishing vessels sailing near the shoal. In response, the Philippines deployed the BRP *Gregorio del Pilar*, a refurbished US Coast Guard cutter, to arrest the fishermen. China responded by sending in its own flotilla, and the situation escalated. American officials stepped in to mediate. By June, they had brokered what they thought was a deal for a mutual withdrawal from Scarborough Shoal. On June 15, the Philippines withdrew its ships; China's remained. The American response amounted to little more than a verbal protest. As Quezon put it, "We pulled out, the Chinese stayed, and no one could do a damn thing about it." There was a similar vacillating response in late 2013, when the Chinese started dredging sand and building artificial islands on disputed reefs and features in the Spratly Islands.

In fairness to the US government, the Scarborough Shoal imbroglio had put it in a difficult position. As Ely Ratner notes, Washington had been forced to mediate the dispute because of the poor lines of communication between Manila and Beijing, and the Chinese insistence on viewing the Philippines as a US proxy.[23] Once it became involved, the US had little interest in taking sides in a nationalistic squabble in the South China Sea. From Washington's perspective, the Philippines had often been a mercurial ally, its policies lurching with each change of administration. A senior official at Singapore's Foreign Ministry felt their pain: "Every time there is an election," the official said, "a new country is born in the Philippines." The vagueness of the MDT was thus an asset: it gave Washington a cushion against Manila's unpredictability.

All the same, to a growing number of Filipino defense officials and analysts, including many who were otherwise supportive of strong ties with the US, the perceived American inaction in the South China Sea contrasted unfavorably with the treatment given to other US allies. In April 2014, on a state visit to Tokyo, Obama confirmed that the US would come to Japan's aid in the event of a conflict with China over the disputed Senkaku/Diaoyu Islands, describing the American commitment to Japanese security as "absolute." A few days later, in Manila, he refused to extend a similar guarantee to the Philippines, describing its tensions with China as "disputes on a few rocks."[24] After fighting alongside US troops from Korea to Vietnam to Iraq, many Filipinos felt their nation was being treated, as Heydarian put it, like "a second-class treaty ally."

Duterte's foreign policy team concurred. They believed that confronting China had brought the Philippines the worst of both worlds: it had done little to loosen China's hold over Scarborough Shoal and its island-fortresses in the Spratlys, and it had soured relations with Beijing, effectively locking the Philippines out of participation in the Belt and Road Initiative (BRI), which was announced at the height of bilateral tensions in 2013. "What Duterte is doing is in some ways a correction of Aquino taking an outright confrontational stand against China," said Aileen Baviera, of the University of the Philippines' Asian Center. "He opted to be pragmatic: the only way to deal with China is to talk to China directly."

For all its apparent madness, Duterte's foreign policy represented a pragmatic adjustment to the changing security landscape in Southeast Asia. It reflected both the awkward realities of the Philippines' position—it is the only Southeast Asian nation that is both a US treaty ally *and* a claimant in the South China Sea—and the growing concern about the Trump administration's hostile posturing toward China. If the US had little interest in being sucked into a war over "a few rocks" in the South China Sea, the Duterte administration was equally uncomfortable about becoming the frontline of a shooting war between Washington and Beijing. In March 2019, when US Secretary of State Mike Pompeo visited Manila and offered the Philippines the security guarantee it had never received from the Obama administration—that any armed attack on Philippine forces in the South China Sea would trigger an American response under the MDT—Defense Secretary Delfin Lorenzana responded, "It is not the lack of reassurance that worries me. It is being involved in a war that we do not seek and do not want."[25]

Duterte's foreign policy recalibration didn't just involve China. Lost in the media coverage of his "pivot to Beijing" was the warmth of his relationship with Tokyo. As ever the silent achiever in Southeast Asia, Japan remained by far the largest source of foreign direct investment in the Philippines, while inciting few of the anxieties that attached to its East Asian rival. More importantly, it was also the one major power to have enjoyed equally balmy relations with both the Aquino and Duterte administrations.

Japan's relationship with the former dated back to World War II, when Aquino's grandfather had been a leading collaborator during the Japanese occupation. The Aquinos had since retained close ties to the Japanese nationalist right wing, particularly to Shintaro Ishihara, the conservative former governor of Tokyo who co-authored the 1989 nationalist manifesto, *The Japan That Can Say No*. (Ishihara's book would inspire the publication of a similarly titled Chinese tract in 1996.) At the same time, Japanese officials knew Duterte well from his time as mayor of Davao City. The Japanese had been present in Davao since the interwar period, when Japanese firms had controlled large plantations of *abaca* (Manila hemp), and downtown Davao was lined with Japanese businesses. As a result, Japan managed to negotiate a seamless transition from Aquino to Duterte. In January 2017, Prime Minister Shinzo Abe became the first national leader to visit the Philippines after Duterte's election. Visiting Davao City, the Filipino leader welcomed Abe at his home with a breakfast of sweet rice cakes and mung bean soup.[26] Duterte described Japan as a true friend of his country and a "preeminent and peerless" investor and development partner.[27]

In seeking workable relations with the nuclear-armed giant on his nation's doorstep, there was little Duterte's foreign policy team could look to for a precedent. A powerful maritime China was something altogether new in Philippine history. While Chinese sailors and merchants had been visiting the Philippine islands since at least the Song dynasty (960–1279), the wide sea generally kept the continental empire far away. At various times, China claimed vassals among the scattered rulers of the Philippine archipelago. In 1405, during

Admiral Zheng He's titanic ocean voyages, the Yongle Emperor sought to extend China's supremacy over the islands by appointing a "governor" in Luzon.[28] Twelve years later, Paduka Pahala, the Muslim king of Sulu, in the far south of the islands, died while on a tributary mission to Yongle's court, and was interred in an opulent tomb outside Beijing—the only foreign monarch to rest on Chinese soil.

However, these early connections withered after the Ming dynasty's fateful turn inward in the mid-fifteenth century, and the arrival of the Spanish in the Philippine islands a century later. Shielded for nearly four centuries by Spanish and American power—"Three centuries in a Catholic convent and fifty years in Hollywood," as the popular saying goes—the Philippines had less contact with the Chinese state than perhaps any other nation in Southeast Asia. Even the People's Republic of China's (PRC's) support to the Philippines' communist insurgencies was less robust than to those in other parts of Southeast Asia.[29]

All this changed with China's assertion of its "nine-dash line" claim in 2009, and its mammoth land reclamation activities in the Spratly Islands. Suddenly the wide sea shrank to a narrow strait. Justice Antonio T. Carpio of the Supreme Court of the Philippines, one of the most active and articulate defenders of the nation's maritime claims, said that unlike the Vietnamese, a people profoundly conditioned by their proximity to China, Filipinos were still trying to digest what it means to share a "border" with the rising superpower. "China is very close to us suddenly," he said one afternoon in his wood-paneled chambers in central Manila, its walls covered with framed antique maps. "So, we have this new mindset. We have not yet fully understood that."

This sudden contiguity is most apparent in the Spratly Islands, where just 18 kilometers separate Thitu Island, the largest feature occupied by the Philippines, from Chinese-occupied Subi Reef, one of its seven reclaimed island bases in the Spratlys. A coral-fringed speck known to Filipinos as Pag-asa, the Tagalog word for "hope," Thitu is the second-largest natural island in the Spratlys, and one of nine Philippine-controlled features in the contested island group. The 37-hectare islet supports a small military garrison and a population of 120 civilians, who live an isolated frontline existence in the shadow of an imposing Chinese naval presence. Subi Reef is the dragon's claw: starting in 2014, China transformed this band of turquoise waters and submerged coral banks into a fortified city, with multi-story concrete structures, a spherical radar station, a 3,000-meter airstrip capable of handling the largest Chinese bombers, jet hangars, and shelters for mobile missile launchers. From Thitu, the Chinese base is visible on the horizon; at night, it lights up the southwestern sky.

Thitu Island and the rest of the Kalayaan Island Group, as the Philippines refers to its scattering of possessions in the Spratlys, are administered from a green three-story office building in Puerto Princesa, the capital of Palawan, the nearest major Philippine island. Here, some 527 kilometers from his constituents on Thitu, Mayor Roberto M. Del Mundo works at a wooden desk with a name plaque. The wall behind him displays the Kalayaan municipal seal, a ring of embossed gold featuring images of local marine life: a green turtle, a leopard coral trout, and a gray gull. Another wall is taken up by a large map of his oceanic domain, with miniature flags marking out the Philippine-occupied features.

A former soldier with a quiet voice and easy-going air, Del Mundo presides over the Philippines' largest municipality by area, but smallest by population. Kalayaan embraces 168,287 square kilometers, an area larger than the nation of Bangladesh, but has fewer than 300 residents, of whom only 100 or so are present on Thitu Island at any given time. Because of its isolation, few stay for more than a year at a stretch.

Since being elected as mayor of Kalayaan in 2016—he won in a landslide, with 142 votes—Del Mundo has taken up the burden of supporting this far-flung civilian presence amid the constant circling presence of the Chinese navy and coastguard. Some of the island's residents are former army-men like Del Mundo; most are poor families from rural Palawan, lured out to Thitu by the promise of state subsidies. But when we spoke, Del Mundo brimmed with admiration for their sacrifice. "More than anyone else in this country, they are the ones that are the most patriotic," he said.

The Philippines owes its presence in the Spratlys to one Tomás Cloma, an eccentric businessman, lawyer, and adventurer from the province of Bohol. After World War II, Cloma dreamt up plans of opening a seafood cannery in the uninhabited islands off the coast of Palawan, and mining their natural guano deposits. On May 11, 1956, he sailed out into the blue with his brother and 40 men, and laid claim to 33 maritime features in the Spratlys. He declared them an independent micro-nation called the "Free Territory of Freedomland" and gave his new possession a flag: red and blue, with a white albatross.

Cloma was a man of flamboyant pretensions: he styled himself "Admiral" Cloma and often went about in a spotless white naval uniform. But his Spratly ambitions were never realized. No foreign nation ever recognized Freedomland, and Cloma struggled to hold onto his claim. When oil exploration began off the coast of Palawan in 1970, the Marcos administration brought the quixotic enterprise to a swift halt. In October 1974, Cloma was arrested for "illegally wearing uniform and insignia" and forced to sign his "rights" to the islands over to the central government for a single peso. Marcos renamed Freedomland the Kalayaan Island Group—*kalayaan* means "freedom" in Tagalog—and in June 1978 issued Presidential Decree 1596, officially incorporating Kalayaan as a municipality of Palawan.[30] Cloma, who died in 1996, is today remembered as a patriot, his strange career commemorated by a bronze bust on Thitu Island, situated next to the municipality's flagpole and flower beds, gazing out to sea.

Today, the Philippines bases its claims to the Kalayaan Islands on the 1982 UN Convention on the Law of the Sea (UNCLOS). Some features lie within its EEZ, while others (including Thitu) sit on Palawan's extended continental shelf. Justice Carpio described China's sweeping historical claims to these features, and the South China Sea more generally, as "totally fictitious" and legally dubious. "If historic rights still remained," he said, "we would be fighting because of what Genghis Khan did." In July 2016, the Permanent Court of Arbitration registered its agreement in the case brought by the Philippines, ruling that China's looping maritime claim was invalid under UNCLOS, and that Beijing had violated the Philippines' sovereign rights within its EEZ.

Yet asserting legal right over naval might is a constant struggle for the municipality of Kalayaan. The settlement on Thitu Island consists of little more than a basic municipal hall, police station, health center, lighthouse, and a dilapidated military airfield built in the 1970s. Del Mundo's domain embraces great latitudes, yet his office lacks its own transport vessels, forcing him to rely on naval supply runs. Where China has built a fortress on Subi Reef, his office struggles to muster the supplies of rice, cooking oil, diesel, and other basic items necessary to sustain a civilian presence on Thitu. In 2016, the municipality's budget was just 47 million pesos (around $900,000), and Del Mundo described resources as his main constraint. "Even a few coins in my pocket, I give them to my constituents," he said, adding, "My wife gets angry."

The Philippine presence on the rest of Kalayaan's islands, reefs, and atolls is even more threadbare. To establish a military toehold on Second Thomas

Shoal (Ayungin Shoal), the Philippine navy in 1999 deliberately grounded the *Sierra Madre*, a decrepit World War II-era transport ship. Today, the rusting hulk is manned by a small band of Filipino marines, who maintain a lonely watch over miles of vacant ocean.

This shortfall of resources reflects the broader challenges the Philippines faces in fully securing its permeable island geography. Despite consisting of more than 7,100 islands and some 35,000 kilometers of coastline, the state, like Indonesia, has mostly disregarded its ocean expanses. Protected after independence by the parasol of American power, and fighting to put down a raft of stubbornly persistent communist and Muslim separatist insurgencies, the Philippine armed forces have overwhelmingly focused on land operations over naval deployments. Corruption and mismanagement have also undermined modernization and defense reforms. Two recent rounds of defense modernization notwithstanding, the Philippine navy's fleet represents a minuscule deterrent to China's aggressive coastguard, let alone the rapidly expanding People's Liberation Army Navy.

In 2017, the Philippines committed 1.6 billion pesos (around $32 million) to the reinforcement of its frontline settlement on Thitu Island. When I met him, Del Mundo handed me a copy of the Kalayaan Municipality's Master Development Plan, which envisioned the construction of a seaport, the concreting of the airfield, and the erection of new residential and administrative buildings, including tourism facilities. But progress so far has been slow. Even more pressing than resources, one municipal staffer said on condition of anonymity, was the lack of "moral support" from Manila. Under President Aquino, when the Philippines stood David-like against the PRC Goliath, the Kalayaan authorities were empowered to publicize the frequent maritime skirmishes with China. The previous mayor, Eugenio Bito-onon Jr., was widely quoted in the international press, and often escorted journalists out to Thitu Island and other isolated ocean outposts. Duterte's pivot to China had left the Kalayaan municipal authorities in an awkward position, the official said, begging for resources from the central government to protect Philippine territory from Chinese incursions, while that same government was begging for resources from Beijing.

Under Duterte, the Philippines' position on the South China Sea has been erratic. The president has veered from tough-talking to sweet-talking, each of his "dramatic reversals" reversed dramatically in its turn. During his campaign for president, Duterte boasted that he would ride a jet-ski to the Spratlys and plant the Philippine flag there, but after taking office he struck a more conciliatory tone. In April 2017, he announced, and then canceled, a flag-planting trip to Thitu Island, citing "our friendship with China."[31] In March 2018, when China was found to have illegally surveyed parts of Benham Rise in the South China Sea, he said he would be willing to "go to war" to defend it from China; a month later, he declared, "I simply love Xi Jinping. He understands my problem and is willing to help, so I would say, 'Thank you, China.' "[32]

Duterte's vacillations paralleled his administration's broad retreat from multilateral diplomacy aimed at resolving the maritime disputes. Under Aquino, the Philippines had made energetic efforts to rally the ASEAN around the South China Sea issue, forcing China to intervene, via its Cambodian client, to purge critical language from an ASEAN joint communiqué in July 2012. When the bloc's rotating chairmanship passed to the Philippines in 2017, Duterte took a spongier line. The South China Sea issue was "better left untouched," he told a meeting of business leaders during the ASEAN Summit in November 2017, adding, "Nobody can afford to go to war."[33] Instead, member states agreed to start negotiating an ASEAN–China Code of Conduct (COC) to manage tensions in the South China Sea. Without any timeline for completion, however, many observers viewed the COC as China's way of buying diplomatic time. Absent in the announcement was any mention of the 2016 arbitral ruling in the Philippines' favor.

Redempto D. Anda, a journalist based in Puerto Princesa, said that since Duterte took office, information on incidents in the West Philippine Sea, as Manila officially terms its portion of the South China Sea, had been placed under tighter control. Media visits to the Kalayaan Islands were much less frequent; the government had become "very careful in terms of messaging." In February 2019, when the local *Palawan News* published an article, based on information from Mayor Del Mundo's office, alleging that dozens of Chinese vessels had blocked Filipino boats from accessing fishing grounds near Thitu Island, provincial officials denied it. So, too, did Vice Admiral Rene V. Medina, the head of the Philippine armed forces' Western Command, when I interviewed him at his headquarters in Puerto Princesa the following month. "The truth of the matter is, there's really no shoving off of the Filipino fishermen," he said. When I asked Del Mundo about the *Palawan News* report, he declined to comment.

A couple of weeks later, however, the Philippine government issued a press release acknowledging the presence of more than 200 Chinese boats in the area around Thitu, and lodged a diplomatic protest with the Chinese government. Once again, Duterte talked tough, warning China to "lay off" the island, saying he would send soldiers on a "suicide mission" to defend it.[34] A few weeks after that, he was back in Beijing for the second Belt and Road Forum, returning with a new stack of infrastructure funding commitments. Duterte's zigzagging stemmed partly from his mercurial leadership style. But the tensions were also baked into his China policy, which sought to preserve sovereignty over the Philippines' island possessions, while cultivating China for badly needed infrastructure funding.

Duterte's détente with China may also have scuttled plans for the expansion of the small naval installation at Oyster Bay, on the undeveloped west coast of Palawan. Under Aquino, Philippine officials had announced plans to convert the neglected naval station, the home port for the navy's three refurbished US cutters, into a larger base for its naval frigates, and eventually for American warships. "It will be a mini-Subic," Commodore Joseph Rostum O. Peña, commander of the Philippines' western navy, said in 2013.[35] The following year, the Philippines proposed opening Oyster Bay, a small cove within the larger Ulugan Bay, to the US Navy under EDCA. Around that time, it started building an access road through old-growth mangrove forests to the base, previously only accessible by water.

On a radiant morning in March 2019, I drove across the narrow waist of Palawan toward Ulugan Bay and the blue-green meridian of the South China Sea. At the fishing hamlet of Macarascas, a clutch of brightly painted wooden houses and schools spread out along the highway, the new access road snaked off toward Oyster Bay. The tarmac was black and freshly laid, with a double yellow line running down the center. Where it crested the shoulders of the hills, it revealed a breathtaking vista of Ulugan Bay: a flat jade expanse heaped with distant hills and a sky running a gradient from hazy blue to cloud.

Carving a naval base into this idyllic coast makes strategic (if not aesthetic or environmental) sense: it would give the Philippine navy much improved access to the Spratly Islands, which lie just 160 kilometers to the west, around half the distance from Subic Bay. But again, a lack of resources seems to have met an apparent lack of political will. In early 2016, when the Philippines approved five bases for a rotational US presence under EDCA, Oyster Bay was not among them. The access road to the base was completed a few months later, after Duterte's administration took office, but little seems to have happened since. Vice Admiral Medina told me that plans had been delayed "due to funding constraints," but were now moving forward. He declined to go into details, except to say that there were "ongoing developments" at the base. Anda, the local journalist, was more blunt. "It's been shelved," he said.

The road to Oyster Bay terminated in a hacked clearing with a deserted bamboo guard post marking the entrance to the naval station and the great blue beyond. Signs were posted, reading "THIS IS A NAVAL RESERVATION—KEEP OUT." Crickets hissed in the grass. Like the tiny municipality of Kalayaan, the new Subic Bay slumbered in the sun, awaiting another change in the political winds.

In November 2018, President Xi Jinping made a landmark trip to Manila, the first by a Chinese leader in 13 years. He and Duterte signed 29 economic agreements, covering everything from industrial development and infrastructure projects to joint oil and gas exploration in the South China Sea. They also announced Chinese plans to build an industrial park at the former US Clark Air Base: a telling symbol of the Philippines' shifting international alignments. Xi hailed the visit as a "milestone" and likened Sino-Philippine relations to "a rainbow after the rain."[36] Yet behind the champagne toasts and buoyant rhetoric, increasing numbers of Filipinos were beginning to ask what benefits Duterte's détente with China had actually delivered.

Resistance was particularly strong within the Philippine defense and security establishment. Whatever its reservations about the lack of clarity in the US alliance, they still saw Washington as their nation's surest strategic insurance policy in an age of rising Chinese power—to say nothing of the deep personal and cultural bonds linking the US and the Philippines. After Duterte took office, defense officials and military commanders had successfully dissuaded him from enacting his more outlandish threats to the American alliance, and quietly expanded joint exercises with the US military. Meanwhile, from outside the administration, Duterte's opponents, including former Aquino-era officials, accused him of setting aside the legal victory of the 2016 arbitral ruling for little apparent gain. On the second anniversary of the ruling, former Foreign Secretary Albert del Rosario had expressed his dismay at the Philippines becoming a "willing victim" and an "abettor" of China.[37]

The criticisms carried extra weight given that few of the billions in promised Chinese infrastructure funding had yet eventuated. In 2017, according to
the Philippines Statistics Authority, China contributed just 2.2 percent of
approved foreign direct investment, compared to 30.3 percent for Japan, 10.3
percent for Taiwan, and 8.3 percent for the US.[38] By the time of Xi's visit, just
one $62 million loan for a dam had been approved, according to one esti-
mate.[39] A year later, still not a single China-backed infrastructure project had
broken ground under Duterte, even as the Japanese continued to support and
finance major infrastructure developments.[40] Those few projects that had
moved forward were subject to harsh criticism on the financing arrange-
ments and the general lack of transparency that surrounded them. Justice
Carpio was particularly critical of the terms that attached to Chinese loans.
"We will be like Sri Lanka," he said, "having to cede our Hambantota Port."

The slow progress stemmed from problems on both sides. The Chinese
weren't the first outsiders to have problems operating within the chaotic
and polycentric Philippine system. To give Xi and Duterte something to
announce, projects were approved without sufficient due diligence, feasibility
analysis, or public consultation, and then ran headlong into the objections
of local officials and affected residents. The Chinese government was also
burdened by the memory of past experience. During the last "rainbow age" of
relations under the Arroyo administration, a series of planned Chinese infrastructure schemes, including a large railway project in Luzon, had collapsed
amid charges of graft by Filipino officials. Contrary to the charge that China
was pushing the Philippines into a "debt-trap," Chinese state banks were
erring on the side of caution in disbursing loans.

At the same time, China wasn't doing its cause any favors. Filipino officials
claimed the Chinese funding came with onerous conditions, including the
compulsory employment of Chinese workers and managers; Beijing also
seemed unwilling to co-finance projects with other lenders such as Japan and
the Asian Development Bank.[41] Then there was China's behavior offshore.
Even as Beijing wooed Duterte, the Chinese Coast Guard kept up its harass-
ment of Filipino fishermen around Thitu Island and elsewhere in the Spratlys.
In June 2019, the Philippine government filed a diplomatic protest after a
Chinese fishing vessel allegedly rammed and sank a Filipino boat near Reed
Bank, leaving 22 Filipino fishermen floating helplessly at sea before they were
rescued by a Vietnamese boat.

Here was another textbook case of Edward Luttwak's "great-state autism." Heydarian said that Beijing had been gifted a political opening by Duterte, but had failed to allow him to accrue the political capital necessary to shape public opinion in China's favor. "They're looking for some sort of a Hun Sen," he said of the Chinese. "They're not going to get a Hun Sen in the Philippines. . . . It's not like you get the president's phone number, and then you've got the country; that's not how it operates." In truth, China and the Philippines were almost perfectly mismatched: one had a strong state and weak civil society, the other a weak state and strong civil society. Neither found it easy to understand—let alone work constructively with—the other.

Filipino public opinion mirrored elite concerns about China's expanding influence in the Philippines. In the run-up to mid-term elections in May 2019, polls showed that Duterte was still wildly popular on every issue except one. Post-election surveys conducted by Social Weather Stations found that 87 percent of respondents believed the government should assert its legal right to disputed islands in the South China Sea; 93 percent said it was important for the Philippines to regain control of Chinese-occupied features.[42] During Xi's visit, thousands of Filipino Facebook users welcomed him by changing their profile pictures to Winnie the Pooh, a character banned in China for his supposed likeness to the Chinese leader. The hashtag #chinaout-ofph trended on Twitter.[43] A few months earlier, Filipino wags had unfurled banners in Manila reading, "Welcome to the Philippines, province of the People's Republic of China."

Another contributor to popular anti-China sentiment was the sudden increase in the number of mainland Chinese expatriates coming to live and work in the Philippines. Duterte's election had seen an easing of visa regulations for Chinese nationals, including an executive order facilitating the entry of foreign nationals via the port of Subic Bay, resulting in the cruise ship boom mentioned at the beginning of this book. From 2015 to 2018, the Philippines Department of Labor and Employment issued more than 85,000 alien working permits to PRC citizens. In addition, industry insiders estimated that between 100,000 and 250,000 Chinese nationals were working illegally on expired tourist visas.[44] Duterte opted not to take a hard line on these illegal migrants, worried about tit-for-tat retribution against Filipino workers in mainland China.

The new PRC arrivals quickly found themselves ensnared in the sorts of line-cutting, culture-clash controversies that have taken place in other

Southeast Asian countries. In February 2019, a viral pile-on ensued when a CCTV camera caught a Chinese student hurling a cup of *taho*, a soy-based breakfast snack, in the face of a train station guard in Manila. Mainland Chinese also drew negative attention for their involvement in Chinese online gambling operations, known locally as POGOs, or Philippine Online Gaming Operations. Like Cambodia, the Philippines provided a suitably fertile environment in which these semi-legal operations could take root. By mid-2019, POGOs had grown so extensive that they had overtaken call centers as the top users of office space in Manila.[45] Some security officials were even beginning to voice concerns that Chinese-run online gambling enterprises might be used as cover for intelligence activities, citing the unnerving proximity of some operations to key Philippine Army installations.[46]

More worryingly, the public's unhappiness about Chinese maritime actions and mainland Chinese workers was starting to color perceptions of the country's small Filipino-Chinese community. Shortly after Xi's state visit, the broadcaster and writer Solita Collas-Monsod wrote an article in *The Inquirer*, one of the Philippines' largest daily newspapers, questioning the loyalty of the local ethnic Chinese. "A Chinese Filipino will never state unequivocally that he/she is a Filipino first, and a Chinese second," she wrote.[47] A kindred view was expressed by the Filipino writer F. Sionil José, who declared, "The silence of our Filipino Chinese on this crucial issue is deafening." Accusing the Chinese of building their wealth "through exploitation of the land and the people," José praised Vietnam's history of fierce anti-Chinese resistance, and called for the Philippines "to see to it that the economic power of these ethnic Chinese, whose loyalty to the Philippines is in doubt, should be emasculated."[48]

These were minority views, and they quickly drew a wave of heated rebuttals from ethnic Chinese Filipinos. One of them was Carmelea Ang See, the managing director of the Kaisa Heritage Foundation, which researches the history of the ethnic Chinese communities in the Philippines. When we met for an interview in Quezon City, she said that the tensions in the South China Sea had surfaced a minority strain of sentiment against Filipinos with one-syllable surnames: usually a sign of Chinese ancestry. "The Chinese community gets caught in the middle," she said, "because at some subconscious level, many still see us as a foreign entity."

As elsewhere in Southeast Asia, the ethnic Chinese community in the Philippines, which numbers around 1.2 million, or just over 1 percent of the population, is far from homogeneous in its views of China. According to Ang See, many local Chinese see the new arrivals from the PRC as "totally foreign," and even refer to them by the derogatory term "TDK," short for *tai diok ka*, meaning "big country" in Hokkien. In the 1990s, to emphasize the community's local—and fundamentally Filipino—loyalties, Kaisa coined the term Tsinoy, a portmanteau of "Tsinong Pinoy," or Chinese Filipino, to differentiate locally born and raised Chinese from more recent immigrants.

Compared to nations like Indonesia and Malaysia, the Chinese community in the Philippines is well assimilated—perhaps more so than in any other Southeast Asian country outside Thailand and Cambodia. That is not to say that ethnic Chinese have always been welcome. Under the Spanish, the Chinese were subject to deportations and savage pogroms. Later, the US government applied the Chinese Exclusion Act of 1882 to the Philippines and refused entry to all but merchants and their sons: as a result, more than six of every ten Filipino Chinese can today trace their ancestry to a single locale: the county-level city of Jinjiang in Fujian province.[49] As in most other Southeast Asian nations, the community also faced restrictions during the Cold War, when contact with the mainland almost ceased.

However, certain unique factors smoothed the acceptance of the Chinese in the Philippines. Since the rise of Filipino nationalism in the late nineteenth century preceded, rather than followed, the appearance of nationalism in China, it did not acquire the same anti-Chinese resonance as in countries like Indonesia. Many pioneering Filipino nationalists came from Chinese-*mestizo* stock, not least the polymath national hero José Rizal, whose roots are marked today by a monument in Jinjiang county. When the Philippines formally recognized the PRC in 1975, the government granted Chinese Filipinos a legal path to Philippine citizenship. Since then, Tsinoys have become an authentic part of the Philippines' polyglot national community. Filipino-Chinese businesspeople consistently rank among the wealthiest in the country, as illustrated by the ornate tombs and mausoleums that line "millionaire's row" in Manila's fascinating Chinese Cemetery. But while ethnic Chinese have sometimes provoked envy, modern Philippine history has been blessedly free of the anti-Chinese violence that has stained other Southeast Asian countries.

Ang See said that she expected the Philippines' innate tolerance to prevail over the more racialized visions of nationalism asserted by a small minority of Filipinos. As she put it, "Southeast Asian Chinese are citizens of their countries first, Southeast Asians second, Chinese third." As elsewhere, however, a rising China has created new strains and dilemmas for the ethnic Chinese community in the Philippines. As long as tensions with Beijing persist, whispered questions of loyalty will never be far behind.

In May 2019, mid-term Senate elections delivered sweeping victories for the allies of President Duterte. His former police chief Bato dela Rosa, who oversaw the initial stages of the drug war, won election to the Senate; so did Imee Marcos, the daughter of Ferdinand and Imelda, who had gained Duterte's raised-fist endorsement. With the 2022 presidential elections now on the horizon, public opposition to Duterte's China policy seemed unlikely to translate into serious political problems for the Filipino leader, whose approval ratings on just about every other issue remained high. Jay Batongbacal of the University of the Philippines said that when people were asked in isolation, they had strong opinions about China's aggressive behavior in the South China Sea. When considered next to everything else, however, the issue often faded into the background. "While foreign policy may be a low point [for Duterte]," he said, "it's not enough to affect public perceptions about the administration as a whole."

In February 2020, Duterte dealt the US alliance a further blow when he announced the cancelation of the Visiting Forces Agreement (VFA), the 1999 accord governing the status of US troops stationed in the Philippines. The decision was sparked by the revocation of a US visa for his ally, Senator Dela Rosa. This was part of a broader suite of sanctions passed by US Congress earlier in the year, which imposed travel bans and other restrictions on senior Philippine officials involved in the war on drugs.

The scuttling of the VFA, which would enter into effect 180 days after Duterte's announcement unless otherwise agreed, was the most drastic step Duterte had taken to undermine the special relationship with the US. It threatened to complicate the rotational stationing of US troops on Philippine soil and jeopardized hundreds of annual joint military exercises. Supporters of the US alliance could take some consolation in the fact that Duterte was limited to a single presidential term. "Just like Trump," Justice Carpio said, "you just have to bear with him until he leaves office." But rumors swirled that Duterte was grooming his daughter Sara to succeed him as president, just as she had succeeded him as mayor of Davao City.[50] The founding of a putative

Duterte dynasty held out the prospect of a more sustained period of friendliness toward China, and further complications in the US alliance.

Regardless of what happened, the Philippines was unlikely to drift fully into China's orbit. The very things that granted Beijing its opening—the nation's weak institutions and idiosyncratic, personalized political culture—would limit its ability to maintain influence over the long term. The same political structures that gave Duterte the power to wrench foreign policy in the direction of China would give his successors the power to reverse course. Duterte's real revolution was altogether more subtle. While the inertia of the US alliance would sooner or later exert its pull, the gun-slinging mayor from Davao had broken a long-standing taboo. "Our relationship with the US is no longer sacrosanct," said Heydarian. "For 80 years, the idea was, the Philippines is in the US camp no matter what. That idea is no longer taken for granted." Under Duterte, the Philippines had left its American safe-harbor and was edging out into open ocean. Things would never be quite the same.

AFTERWORD

In December 2019, as I was putting the finishing touches to this book, an unknown strain of coronavirus emerged in the central Chinese city of Wuhan and quickly began its lethal migration across the globe. Within weeks, COVID-19, the disease caused by the novel coronavirus, had infected nearly 100,000 people and killed several thousand in China. In January and February, it paralyzed production and brought economic activity to a near-halt as tens of millions in central China were put under an unprecedented quarantine. The damage to China's economy was severe. Although the government swiftly brought the virus under control, its economic recovery was hamstrung by the collapse of global demand as the coronavirus hit Europe and North America. In April, Chinese officials announced that the nation's economy had shrunk 6.8 percent in the first three months of 2020 compared with the previous year, ending a streak of unbridled growth that survived the Tiananmen Square crackdown and the global financial crisis of 2008.[1]

By throwing its economy into turmoil, the virus threatened to derail China's strategic ambitions in Southeast Asia. From Boten in Laos to Bandung in Indonesia, work stalled on Belt and Road Initiative (BRI) infrastructure projects as Chinese laborers and engineers were barred from returning to their jobs across the region. Many major BRI projects were also premised on the continuing availability of massive amounts of cheap credit from Chinese state banks. The threat of a protracted global economic contraction, and an accompanying domestic credit crunch, therefore cast doubts on China's ability to meet billions of dollars in BRI commitments.

In this sense, the coronavirus pandemic served as a reminder of the many challenges, both internal and external, facing President Xi Jinping's rule. These ranged from environmental despoliation and an aging population to the violent unrest in Hong Kong and the growing international condemnation of China's mass internment of Uighur Muslims in Xinjiang. The coronavirus shutdown arrested an economy already growing at its slowest pace in 30 years, and some speculated that the crisis might speed a diversification of global supply chains away from China, furthering a process that had already begun with the onset of trade tensions with the US in mid-2018. Added to this was the threat of a global backlash over China's failures in the early stages of the COVID-19 outbreak, when it covered up early reports of the virus, and then delayed in locking down the epicenter of the contagion in Wuhan, allowing the disease to spread. All of these challenges were a reminder that the indefinite linear growth of Chinese wealth and power could no longer be taken for granted.

The effect of the pandemic on Southeast Asia, too, was profound. By March, as the coronavirus was scything across Europe and the US, the resulting economic downturn seemed likely to dwarf, by several orders of magnitude, the region's last major economic disturbance. The Asian financial crisis of 1997 had had far-reaching political aftereffects, catalyzing the fall of Suharto in Indonesia and prompting the rise of Thaksin Shinawatra in Thailand, the latter of which continued to resonate through Thai politics. Given the febrile state of politics in Thailand, Malaysia, Indonesia, the Philippines, and Burma, it was hard to imagine such a steep economic decline leaving the political landscape of Southeast Asia entirely unchanged.

The early stages of the contagion had also exposed the extent of Southeast Asia's reliance on Chinese trade, investment, and tourism. From Bali to Angkor Wat, temples, beaches, and food markets stood deserted as Chinese tour groups stayed away. Construction sites in Phnom Penh fell silent, and truckloads of Burmese watermelons rotted at the Chinese border. In Penang and Hanoi, factories idled in the face of disrupted China-centric supply chains and cratering Chinese demand. Even before it was declared a global pandemic, the coronavirus had showcased the region's vulnerability to any sudden Chinese downturn.

But when the pandemic finally petered out, Southeast Asia's relationship with China was unlikely to have been altered in any fundamental way. China's size and proximity ensured that it would remain a central player in the region, even if slowing growth forced it into retrenchment elsewhere. There was a good likelihood that the contagion would prompt some Southeast Asian nations to reduce their reliance on China-centered supply chains. If it was prepared, the region also stood to benefit from the expected relocation of production bases away from China. Nonetheless, past precedent suggested that China would play an important role in cushioning the region from the long-term economic and political fallout. Southeast Asian nations would find themselves in the same conflicted position as before, in which apprehension about China's power was balanced by a strong stake in its continued stability and growth.

At the same time, Beijing's many challenges in Southeast Asia were also likely to persist, if not deepen. For all its attempts at "soft power," including its campaign of global medical outreach during the COVID-19 crisis, China's communist leadership faced an uphill battle in convincing the region of its peaceful intentions and selling its vision of co-prosperity. From fears of Chinese debt and maritime bullying to the negative externalities of large-scale Chinese infrastructure projects, China's actions continued to undermine its promises. Conjoined to these worries was a simmering disquiet about new flows of Chinese immigration and the CCP's relationship with the region's Overseas Chinese, issues that pressed on an exposed nerve of sovereignty.

This points to the Chinese government's broader difficulties in transcending its solipsistic approach toward the region. Even as it regains its former power and wealth, China's behavior remains wrapped in the mythology of its victimization by imperial powers, past and present. As long as the Chinese leadership holds fast to this idea, it will mostly fail to understand why its power and behavior have prompted such abiding concerns. China's relationship with Southeast Asia is thus based on an increasingly tense contradiction, between the CCP's self-image as an aggrieved victim of Western designs and the reality of its own burgeoning imperial potential. Even as it champions the principle of national sovereignty, China is seen to threaten it.

As individual Southeast Asian nations struggle with this quandary, China's power also poses serious challenges for ASEAN as a whole. During the Cold War, ASEAN succeeded in allowing the small states of Southeast Asia to retain some measure of autonomy in the midst of great power competition. In the half-century since, it has maintained the peace between its members and given them a mechanism for preserving a minimum of cohesion and order. But the very thing that enables ASEAN to reconcile clashing sovereignties— its flexible, consensus-based form of decision-making—now threatens to paralyze it. As Amitav Acharya observes, the bloc's induction of Vietnam,

Cambodia, Laos, and Burma in the 1990s had a paradoxical effect: while making Southeast Asia look more like a single "coherent" region, it added to the bloc's political diversity, making it trickier to reach consensus on key issues.[2] This diversity is something that the Chinese leadership has been able to exploit to its own advantage.

The predicament facing ASEAN and its member states has been complicated by the mounting tensions between China and the US—a trend accelerated greatly by the onset of the coronavirus pandemic. While the Southeast Asian nations welcome a strong American presence as a counterbalance against China, many have misgivings about the erratic nature of US engagement under President Donald Trump, whose administration has veered between benign neglect and lashings of strident rhetoric.

In November 2019, when Southeast Asian leaders gathered in Bangkok for the 35th ASEAN Summit and its associated meetings, the US was notable for its absence. In place of President Trump, Vice President Mike Pence, and Secretary of State Mike Pompeo, the US sent a low-level delegation headed by recently appointed National Security Advisor Robert O'Brien. This was unusual: between 2011 and 2016, President Obama had missed just one US–ASEAN meeting and East Asia Summit (EAS). Trump's attention span was clearly less amenable to ASEAN-grade summitry. In 2018, he had skipped two Southeast Asia-focused meetings. The year before, he attended the US–ASEAN Summit in Manila, but then jetted off before the EAS immediately afterward.

The episode seemed to suggest that, for all of Washington's newfound focus on China as a systemic rival, Southeast Asia remained a blind spot on its radar. The US Indo-Pacific Strategy Report, released in 2019, declared the Indo-Pacific "the single most consequential region for America's future."[3] Yet in practice, the quintessential "Indo-Pacific" region seemed to figure only tangentially in the Free and Open Indo-Pacific (FOIP) strategy. One illustration was the fact that, throughout the Trump administration, key US diplomatic positions in Southeast Asia sat vacant. As of publication, this included the ambassadorial posts to Singapore and ASEAN, which had been unoccupied since the start of Trump's term. Meanwhile, Washington had no ambassador in Cambodia for nearly a year to September 2019. The same post in Thailand was vacant for even longer, while the administration's nominee for the Indonesian post, vacated in mid-2019, had yet to be confirmed.

To be fair, the Trump administration wasn't entirely ignoring Southeast Asia. It sent senior defense officials on frequent tours through the region, extended its security guarantee to the Philippines to encompass its portions of the South China Sea, and ramped up Freedom of Navigation Operations designed to push back against Chinese actions in contested waters. In July 2018, Pompeo also announced new funds for technological and infrastructure initiatives in the Indo-Pacific, even though the resources pledged were a small fraction of what China was offering under the BRI.[4] On the last day of 2018, Trump signed into law the Asia Reassurance Initiative Act (ARIA), which authorized $1.5 billion in annual spending for a range of US programs in East and Southeast Asia. The aim of the ARIA was to "develop a long-term strategic vision and a comprehensive, multifaceted, and principled United States policy for the Indo-Pacific region, and for other purposes."[5]

So far, these various US initiatives have done little to dispel the perception of American disengagement. In early 2020, Singapore's ISEAS–Yusof Ishak Institute published its annual survey of more than 1,300 Southeast Asian academics, government officials, and opinion-makers. Around 77 percent of them agreed that American engagement with Southeast Asia had either decreased or decreased substantially under the Trump administration; nearly half expressed little or no confidence in Washington's reliability as a strategic partner and provider of regional security.[6] The survey results betrayed a perception that the administration, focused narrowly on its contest with China, was overlooking the lands between. As always, the Middle Kingdom remained "the 'sun' around which America's interests in Asia revolved."[7]

The erratic nature of American engagement has been compounded by the increasingly zero-sum language with which some US officials were framing American competition with China. While Trump administration officials assured the region that the FOIP strategy "exclude[d] no nation" and that America did "not ask any country to choose between the United States and China," its promises were belied by its tendency to depict Sino-American rivalry in ideological, even civilizational, terms. Southeast Asia's leaders shared many American concerns about Chinese behavior, but positing a zero-sum struggle "between free and repressive visions of world order" (as the 2017 US National Security Strategy put it), or describing the CCP as "the central threat of our times" (as Pompeo did in early 2020) implied an invidious choice, something that the region has always been determined to avoid.[8]

Moreover, by presenting a simplistic picture of China's activities and intentions in Southeast Asia and elsewhere, the new US consensus risks generating a self-fulfilling prophecy—one that could ultimately play into Beijing's hands.

While it is true that China seeks revisions to an international order in which it has always been an uneasy participant, its approach has been a good deal more selective and strategic. As Howard French argues, "China takes a quite eclectic approach to the international order. It supports—and draws support from—institutions built in another era mostly through Western leadership, while creating new institutions and mechanisms ... when it senses a need and, especially, a vacuum."[9] Beijing wants a greater say in international governance, but it has no rational interest in tearing down the order that has undergirded its own economic renaissance.

Nor is China trying to export its authoritarian political system to the world. For all its loose talk about offering "lessons" to developing countries, it is not working to undermine liberal democratic systems as such, nor to evangelize its highly singular form of Confucian-Leninism. Beijing certainly offers succor to non-democratic governments and undermines liberal values in a broader sense, but as Jessica Chen Weiss of Cornell University has written, these efforts represent "less a grand strategic effort to undermine democracy and spread autocracy than the Chinese leadership's desire to secure its position at home and abroad."[10]

For all the illiberal and destabilizing impacts of China's growing influence in Southeast Asia, its behavior is roughly consistent with that of past great powers. Specifically, the Chinese government is using its economic and military wherewithal to expand its influence and shape political outcomes in a region that it views as essential to its national interest—an approach that more closely resembles the American engagement with Southeast Asia during the Cold War than it does the revolutionary evangelism of Mao. If governments in Southeast Asia happen to be corrupt, illiberal, or non-democratic, that says less about China than about the particular conditions—political, economic, and social—of the countries in question. The region's authoritarianism might be a worrying phenomenon, but it is an overwhelmingly Southeast Asian one.

Instead, the Chinese government presents itself as a conservative defender of national sovereignty and self-determination: two ideas with deep resonance in postcolonial Southeast Asia. Unlike the US and many Western powers, China seldom lectures ASEAN governments on how to run their societies, and asserts the right of every nation to choose its own political path. The result is that whenever Western governments pressure or sanction Southeast Asian governments over questions of political freedoms and human rights—from Duterte's "drug war" to the ethnic cleansing of Burma's Rohingya population—China reaps a reflexive strategic advantage. Under Beijing's shadow, Western values and Western interests increasingly pull in different directions.

In this sense, China's efforts represent one part of the broader reassertion of the Westphalian norm of state sovereignty that is taking place as global power shifts to the East—a phenomenon that the scholars David Fidler, Sung Won Kim, and Sumit Ganguly have described as "Eastphalia rising."[11] In practice, Beijing is wont to abridge this principle in accordance with its perceived national interests, and its economic bullying and influence operations very often amount to political interference by another name. But this, too, is unsurprising, hypocrisy being another frequent indulgence of great powers.

While the US government has a long list of pressing and legitimate concerns about Chinese behavior—from intellectual property theft to Beijing's mass internment of Uighur Muslims to its handling of the early stages of the coronavirus pandemic—the sharp turn in American policy toward China stems as much from American anxieties and self-perceptions as it does from Chinese actions. In *The Beautiful Country and the Middle Kingdom*, his sweeping history of US–China relations, John Pomfret describes how American views toward China have alternated between attempts to "convert" it—first to Protestantism, later to liberal democracy—and periods of hostility when China resisted American tutelage.[12] Viewing US–China competition as a new ideological showdown thus looms as a textbook example of "great-state autism" and mirror-imaging: one that projects an American missionary exceptionalism onto its Asian rival, transmuting a singular China into the inverted phantom of America's own virtuous self-image.

Dwelling in China's neighborhood, the Southeast Asian nations cannot afford to indulge in such binary thinking. As Singapore's Prime Minister Lee Hsien Loong told the *Washington Post* in September 2019, the American tendency to frame US–China rivalry in ideological terms—as "a conflict between two systems, almost two civilizations"—was "very worrying" for the world and the region. By ratcheting up isolated disputes into an all-encompassing struggle, he warned, the US could create a situation in which ASEAN and its member states might be forced to make difficult choices.[13]

Evan Laksmana, of Jakarta's Centre for Strategic and International Studies, concurred: "DC is just such a toxic place now when you talk about China," he said when we spoke in August 2019. "Everything becomes black and white."

This explains the generally agnostic view of Southeast Asian governments toward the Trump administration's FOIP strategy. In principle, the region is not opposed to the Indo-Pacific as a strategic concept, something that has been discussed in Southeast Asian capitals for years. Rightly or wrongly, however, many in the region view FOIP as being motivated primarily by an American desire bid to curb and contain China, and worry that it could dislodge ASEAN's centrality and polarize the region.

These concerns were articulated officially with the release in July 2019 of ASEAN's "Outlook on the Indo-Pacific," the bloc's first official position on the American strategy. Chock full of assertions of ASEAN centrality and the importance of its various diplomatic mechanisms, the outlook expressed worries about "the deepening of mistrust, miscalculation, and patterns of behavior based on a zero-sum game."[14] Its underlying premise was that Southeast Asia—a region connected to both the Indian and Pacific oceans—should lie at the core of any "Indo-Pacific" vision. The more buried subtext was that Southeast Asia is too economically intertwined with China to enlist in a US-led coalition aimed at curbing its rise.

For all their misgivings about China, Southeast Asian governments have continued to engage in the BRI and other Chinese-led initiatives, judging the benefits of participation to outweigh the risks. Of the 36 heads of state or government who attended the second Belt and Road Forum in Beijing in April 2019, nine came from ASEAN countries—a quarter of the total.[15] At the same time, Southeast Asian governments are becoming more sophisticated in how they negotiate the terms of Chinese projects. After suspending or reassessing overpriced Chinese infrastructure deals agreed by their predecessors, new governments in Malaysia and Burma renegotiated key strategic projects, including the East Coast Rail Line in Malaysia and the Kyaukphyu deep-water port on the coast of Burma. This demonstrated the agency of Southeast Asian governments in their relations with China: far from being the passive subjects of Chinese engagement, some were now playing important roles in shaping it.

The Southeast Asian position was expressed starkly by its response to the Trump administration's global campaign against the Chinese telecommunications giant Huawei. Claiming (probably correctly) that Huawei posed a security risk given its opaque ties to the Chinese state, Washington pressed foreign governments to exclude it from any involvement in their 5G telecommunications networks. Almost no Southeast Asian country complied with its demands. Spurning their treaty ally, Thailand and the Philippines let local firms sign agreements to utilize or trial Huawei's advanced and relatively inexpensive 5G technology; so, too, did Cambodia, Malaysia, Indonesia, and Singapore. The only nation to reject Huawei out of hand was Vietnam, which needed no American urging.

More telling were the justifications offered. In Malaysia, then-Prime Minister Mahathir said that if China posed an intelligence risk, the same was true of the US and other large powers. "I am quite sure for a long time the CIA have been reporting on everything that is done in Malaysia and China. We did not carry out a boycott of America because of that," Mahathir told an audience in Tokyo in May 2019.[16] This was echoed by George Yeo, Singapore's former foreign minister, who said that the US was worried "not only because Huawei represents a possible vulnerability, but because using Huawei also makes it harder for American intelligence to gain access into other people's systems."[17]

The Huawei affair demonstrated that the US government would not get far by expecting Southeast Asian countries to curtail their economic relationships with China. As the Center for a New American Security noted in a report on US–China relations in December 2019, "US policy will have to reflect the reality that countries in the region all view China to differing degrees as both an economic opportunity and geographic reality. As a result, attempts to construct an explicitly anti-China alliance will fail."[18] The same was true of the Trump administration's attempt to blame China for the coronavirus pandemic, by referring to the contagion as the "Chinese virus" and promising retaliation against China once the crisis was over. While Southeast Asian leaders will certainly want answers about the Chinese government's egregious failings during the early stages of the outbreak, there is little chance that they will support such a self-righteous and retributive approach.

If forced to choose between the US and China, some Southeast Asian nations—perhaps most—might find it hard to resist defaulting to proximity. In the ISEAS–Yusof Ishak Institute's 2020 survey, respondents were asked which side ASEAN should choose if hypothetically forced to align with either America or China. The US won out by a few percentage points on the whole, largely due to the overwhelming pro-American preference of respondents in Vietnam (85.5 percent) and the Philippines (82.5 percent). Aside from that, respondents in seven of the ten ASEAN member states—Cambodia, Indonesia, Laos, Brunei, Malaysia, Burma, and Thailand—expressed an overall preference for China.[19] As Chan Heng Chee, Singapore's former ambassador to Washington, warned, "Don't press countries in the region to choose. You may not like what you will hear."

There is no doubt that the US must respond more effectively to China's disruptive international behavior, and that measured actions would enjoy broad support in Southeast Asian capitals. However, an Indo-Pacific strategy based solely on organizing regional hostility toward China is unlikely to win the region's support. Instead, the US and its Quad partners will have to convince Southeast Asian leaders that the Indo-Pacific strategy is compatible with the principle of ASEAN centrality. It should also incorporate more ASEAN perspectives into FOIP in order to make the strategy "complementary and mutually beneficial."[20] An effective American approach will be one that broadens the choices of Southeast Asian nations rather than narrowing them: one that addresses the region's development challenges and increases its ability both to avoid an unhealthy overdependence on China, and to stand up to Beijing when necessary.

In some manner this will need to reflect the fact that China's primary challenge to the status quo in the Indo-Pacific is not military or ideological, but economic. Trump's withdrawal from the Trans-Pacific Partnership in 2017 left China free to push ahead with a number of alluring multilateral trade and investment initiatives, including the Regional Comprehensive Economic Partnership (RCEP), which could become one of the world's largest free-trade pacts. RCEP includes China and ASEAN, in addition to Australia, Japan, New Zealand, and South Korea, but does not include the US. In November 2019, leaders from the 15 Asian countries agreed to move forward with RCEP, hoping to conclude it sometime in 2020.[21] Without developing compelling alternatives for the region to stick with the US instead of China, the FOIP strategy will fail to gain lasting purchase in Southeast Asia.

Beyond Trump, there is a need for an American policy that takes a more nuanced approach to Southeast Asia: one that achieves a more realistic balance between values and interests, and creates a stable form of competition that avoids overheated zero-sum rhetoric. When the time comes, Washington can expect to draw on a considerable reservoir of goodwill in Southeast Asia. The region's publics remain broadly well disposed toward the US, which succeeds in many of the places where China fails: in drawing partners close through the force of cultural appeal and the attraction of the American creed. US businesses enjoy an enviable reputation across the region, and Southeast Asian governments remain more comfortable dealing with the US than China, even as they chafe at its liberal admonitions.

Here, too, geography forces itself into the equation. America's distance across the wide longitudes of the Pacific Ocean functions in an inverse way to China's proximity, blunting the fear of US power. Distance also serves as a reminder that there is nothing natural or inevitable about a strong US presence in Southeast Asia. The American commitment to the region is one that will have to be constantly renewed, through the quadrennial churn of presidential elections, and the uncertain commitment of the American public, worn down by never-ending conflicts in distant lands. As the historian Wang Gungwu put it when we spoke in Singapore, the Americans "have to justify being here." The Chinese, on the other hand, "are just here," he said. "It's their backyard."

At the dawn of the 2020s, Southeast Asia trembles on the cusp of a new era of superpower competition. The period of strategic tension is likely to be prolonged and uncertain, with no clear denouement. In the coming tug-of-war, ASEAN will come under increasing strain. It is hard to see the bloc recapturing the unity of purpose that marked its founding in 1967. The widening of ASEAN's membership since the end of the Cold War has made it trickier to find common ground, or to reconcile national with regional interests. It is a challenge that the potential induction of East Timor as ASEAN's eleventh member will further magnify.

While ASEAN will continue with its rota of summits, asserting its regional integrity and centrality, national interests will exert their centrifugal pull. On the burnished leagues of the South China Sea, Vietnam, the Philippines, and Malaysia will find some unity of purpose in confronting the power of the Chinese navy and coastguard, but most ASEAN members will balk at sacrificing their relationships with China for the sake of wider regional interests. Their attention drawn inward by the challenges of economic development and nation-building, Southeast Asian governments will prioritize pressing domestic concerns over the goal of regional integration. China will continue to engage in ASEAN processes, including in negotiations for a Code of Conduct on the South China Sea, but the most consequential negotiations will take place bilaterally, as Beijing prefers.

For as long as it sustains itself, China's rising power foretells a gradual widening of the existing division between the mainland and maritime halves of Southeast Asia—or more precisely, between those with strong connections to the oceans and those of a more continental orientation. In time, perhaps, China's re-emergence could begin to expose the limitations of "Southeast Asia" as a concept. As a region was "made," so, too, could it begin to be unmade. Yet ASEAN will almost certainly endure: in spite of its deficiencies, it remains the region's best and only vehicle for maintaining a modicum of agency in a new era of great power competition.

ASEAN's efforts will be aided by the continued presence and engagement of other outside powers with overlapping concerns about China's sudden return to wealth and power. Sooner or later, the US will awake from its Trumpian fever-dream, reverting perhaps to the storied tradition of realism that has so often lurked beneath the cloak of liberal evangelism. Japan will remain steadfast and engaged across the region, offering Southeast Asian governments a high-quality alternative to China's BRI infrastructure pitch. In many respects, it remains the region's preferred partner of choice. As confidence in the US has ebbed under President Trump, trust in Japan has risen.[22]

In addition to these nations, South Korea, Russia, Australia, and Taiwan will all remain closely engaged in the region. The European Union will continue to be an important economic player, in addition to a post-Brexit United Kingdom, determined to reinvigorate its relationships in Asia. On the western rim of Southeast Asia, India will continue to awaken to its huge demographic potential. The determination of these various nations to resist China's growing economic and military power provides a potential basis for "a regionally organized balance of power."[23]

Together or alone, the strategic meridian of the Southeast Asian nations will be one of balance. Far from being passive subjects of Chinese and American attentions—countries to be "won" and "lost" by dueling superpowers—the region's governments will do what they can to maintain their freedom of maneuver in a tenser, more constrained world. "To promiscuously and simultaneously balance, hedge, and bandwagon is embedded in our foreign policy DNA," writes Singapore's Bilahari Kausikan. "Not only do we not see any contradiction in doing so, this is an instinctive response honed by centuries of hard experience."[24] For the most ardent recipients of Chinese largesse—particularly the small satellites Cambodia and Laos—the challenge will be to find a more nuanced approach to China: one that allows them to benefit from its economic growth without submitting to conditions that will erode their sovereignty over the long term.

In the years to come, Southeast Asia's incoherence could work to its advantage. According to Kausikan, the region's fragmented nature has long made it resistant to any superpower gaining sole control. Historically, Southeast Asia has "slipped through the fingers of any power that has tried to grasp it as a whole," he said. "It's like trying to grab hold of Jell-O." Southeast Asia's future will not be one of linear and inexorable Chinese advance, but rather one in which past dynamics and contradictions reproduce themselves over time at varying pitches of tension. The coming century in Southeast Asia looms as one of flux and strain: less a new Cold War than a frosty, Eastphalian peace.

NOTES

INTRODUCTION

1. Gerald R. Anderson, *Subic Bay: From Magellan to Pinatubo* (4th edn) (Seattle: Amazon Digital Services, 2016), 251.
2. "Cruise ship tourism marks strong start in Subic," *Subic Bay News*, January 13–19, 2019.
3. Unless otherwise stated, all dollar amounts are given in US dollars.
4. Jason Gutierrez, "Philippines should take over shipyard to keep it from Chinese, officials say," *New York Times*, January 17, 2019; Seth Robson, "Chinese firms could gain footholds at both Subic and Clark in the Philippines," *Stars and Stripes*, May 7, 2019.
5. Nectar Gan and Zhou Xin, "Can Xi get things moving?" *South China Morning Post*, October 22, 2018.
6. Graham Allison, *Destined for War: Can America and China Escape Thucydides's Trap?* (Boston, MA: Houghton Mifflin Harcourt, 2017), 10.
7. See Sebastian Strangio, *Cambodia: From Pol Pot to Hun Sen and Beyond* (New Haven and London: Yale University Press, 2020).
8. *The State of Southeast Asia: 2020 Survey Report* (Singapore: ISEAS–Yusof Ishak Institute, 2020), 35.
9. Pál Nyíri and Danielle Tan, eds, *Chinese Encounters in Southeast Asia: How People, Money, and Ideas from China are Changing a Region* (Seattle, WA: University of Washington Press, 2017), 14.

1 PIVOT OF THE INDO-PACIFIC

1. Edward Wong, "China's global message: We are tough but not threatening," *New York Times*, October 2, 2019.
2. "Xi Jinping: 'Time for China to take centre stage'," *BBC News*, October 18, 2017.
3. For a good overview, see Orville Schell and John Delury, *Wealth and Power: China's Long March to the Twenty-first Century* (New York: Random House, 2013).
4. Mao spoke these words not at Tiananmen Square on October 1, 1949, but ten days earlier, in a speech to the Chinese People's Political Consultative Conference. Mao Zedong, *Selected Works of Mao Tse-Tung*, vol. 5 (Beijing: Foreign Languages Press, 1977), 17.
5. Evan A. Feigenbaum, "Reluctant stakeholder: Why China's highly strategic brand of revisionism is more challenging than Washington thinks," *MacroPolo*, April 27, 2018.
6. Linda Jakobson, "Reflections from China on Xi Jinping's 'Asia for Asians'," *Asian Politics & Policy* 8, No. 1 (2016).
7. Cited from Toshi Yoshihara and James R. Holmes, *Red Star over the Pacific: China's Rise and the Challenge to U.S. Maritime Strategy* (Annapolis: Naval Institute Press, 2010), 50.

8. See U.S. Energy Information Administration, "More than 30% of global maritime crude oil trade moves through the South China Sea," August 27, 2015, available at: www.eia.gov/todayinenergy/detail.php?id=36952

9. Ian Storey, "China's 'Malacca dilemma'," *China Brief*, April 12, 2006.

10. "China Dec crude imports at 2nd highest, gas imports at record," *Reuters*, January 14, 2019.

11. Frederick W. Mote, cited from Lynn Pan, *Sons of the Yellow Emperor: A History of the Chinese Diaspora* (Boston, MA: Little, Brown, 1990), 9.

12. Herold J. Wiens, *China's March Toward the Tropics* (Hamden, CT: The Shoe String Press, 1954).

13. Pan, *Sons of the Yellow Emperor*, 9.

14. Emperor Shizong, 1537. Cited from Geoff Wade, *The Ming Shi-lu as a Source for Southeast Asian History* (Asia Research Center, National University of Singapore, 2005), 28.

15. Martin Stuart-Fox, *A Short History of China and Southeast Asia: Tribute, Trade, and Influence* (St Leonards, NSW: Allen & Unwin, 2003), 33–34.

16. Cited from Howard W. French, *Everything Under the Heavens: How the Past Helps Shape China's Push for Global Power* (New York: Alfred A. Knopf, 2017), 178.

17. Gideon Rachman, *Easternization: Asia's Rise and America's Decline from Obama to Trump and Beyond* (New York: Other Press, 2017).

18. Wiens, *China's March Toward the Tropics*, 349.

19. For an early example, see Malcolm Howard, *Travels in South-Eastern Asia* (Boston, MA: Gould, Kendall, & Lincoln, 1839). For an authoritative survey of the term's origin, see Donald K. Emmerson, " 'Southeast Asia': What's in a name?" *Journal of Southeast Asian Studies* 15, No. 1 (March 1984).

20. According to Google's Ngram viewer, the term "Southeast Asia" makes a sudden appearance in 1941, two years before the formation of the South East Asia Command. It then rises steadily to an initial peak in 1967, the year of ASEAN's founding—and not coincidentally, also one of the peak years of American military involvement in Vietnam.

21. Benedict Anderson, *A Life Beyond Boundaries: A Memoir* (London: Verso, 2018), 51.

22. Emmerson, " 'Southeast Asia'," 21.

23. Cited from Amitav Acharya, *The Making of Southeast Asia: International Relations of a Region* (Ithaca, NY: Cornell University Press, 2012), 11.

24. David Shambaugh, "China engages Asia: Reshaping the regional order," *International Security* 29, No. 3 (Winter 2004/2005): 68.

25. Joshua Kurlantzick, *Charm Offensive: How China's Soft Power is Transforming the World* (New Haven, CT: Yale University Press, 2007).

26. Ian Storey, *Southeast Asia and the Rise of China: The Search for Security* (London: Routledge, 2011), 57, 65.

27. Benjamin Zawacki, *Thailand: Shifting Ground between the US and a Rising China* (London: Zed Books, 2017), 257.

28. Liu Hong, "Southeast Asian studies in Greater China," *Kyoto Review of Southeast Asia*, No. 3 (March 2003).

29. Jonathan Stromseth, "The testing ground: China's rising influence in Southeast Asia and regional responses" (Washington, DC: The Brookings Institution, November 2019), 2.

30. Kurlantzick, *Charm Offensive*, 65–66.

31. The first Confucius Institute was established in Seoul in 2004; today, there are 37 across the 10 nations of ASEAN. See: http://english.hanban.org/node_10971.htm

32. Valarie Tan, "Why more Southeast Asian students are choosing China for higher education," *Channel News Asia*, March 18, 2018.

33. Marvin Ott and Yilun Hao, "Chinese strategic assessments of Southeast Asia" (Washington, DC: Wilson Center, March 2018), 5.

34. "China needs to 'purchase' friendships, scholar says," *Nikkei Asian Review*, March 2, 2015.

35. Joseph Chinyong Liow, *Ambivalent Engagement: The United States and Regional Security in Southeast Asia after the Cold War* (Washington: Brookings Institution Press, 2017).

36. Yukon Huang, *Cracking the China Conundrum: Why Conventional Economic Wisdom Is Wrong* (Oxford: Oxford University Press, 2017), 3.
37. John Pomfret, *The Beautiful Country and the Middle Kingdom: America and China, 1776 to the Present* (New York: Henry Holt, 2016), 599.
38. A map featuring this claim was first published by the Republic of China in 1948, and subsequently inherited by the PRC. The line originally featured eleven dashes, before the removal of two in the Gulf of Tonkin in 1953, possibly as a gift to the Vietnamese communists. A tenth dash was added in 2013, embracing Taiwan to the east. China's 2009 submission of the line to the UN Commission on the Limits of the Continental Shelf was the first time the line had ever been employed in an official international context. For background to the claim, see Bill Hayton, *The South China Sea: The Struggle for Power in Asia* (London: Yale University Press, 2014), 50–59.
39. Christopher Walker and Jessica Ludwig, "The meaning of sharp power," *Foreign Affairs*, November 16, 2017.
40. "Xi Jinping: Let the sense of community of common destiny take deep root in neighbouring countries," Ministry of the Foreign Affairs of the PRC, October 25, 2013. Available at: www.fmprc.gov.cn/mfa_eng/wjb_663304/wjbz_663308/activities_663312/t1093870.shtml
41. Cited from Jay Taylor, *China and Southeast Asia: Peking's Relations with Revolutionary Movements* (New York: Praeger, 1976), 338.
42. Storey, *Southeast Asia and the Rise of China*, 60, 70; "ASEAN rises to be China's 2nd biggest trading partner," *Xinhua*, January 14, 2020.
43. Toru Takahashi, "Is China following Japan into the haven of Southeast Asian nations?" *Nikkei Asian Review*, January 18, 2020.
44. ASEAN and UNCTAD, *ASEAN Investment Report 2019* (Jakarta: ASEAN Secretariat, 2019), 22.
45. ADB, *Meeting Asia's Infrastructure Needs* (Manila: Asian Development Bank, 2017), vii.
46. Edward N. Luttwak, *The Rise of China vs. the Logic of Strategy* (Cambridge, MA: Belknap Press, 2012), 12–14.
47. John Pomfret, "U.S. takes a tougher tone with China," *Washington Post*, July 30, 2010.
48. Official estimates for the number of people of Chinese origin in Southeast Asian countries are approximate. Estimates vary from around 75 percent of the population in Singapore, 24–30 percent in Malaysia, 3–18 percent in Burma, 14 percent in Thailand, and 1–3 percent in Indonesia to under 2 percent in the Philippines, Cambodia, Vietnam, and Laos. See Benedict Anderson, "Riddles of yellow and red," *New Left Review*, January–February 2016, 11, n.17.
49. Michael Vatikiotis, *Blood and Silk: Power and Conflict in Modern Southeast Asia* (London: Weidenfeld & Nicolson, 2017), 270.
50. Wang Gungwu, "A short history of the Nanyang Chinese," in *Community and Nation: China, Southeast Asia and Australia*, ed. Wang Gungwu (St Leonards: Allen & Unwin, 1992), 26.
51. Alfred McCoy, *The Politics of Heroin: CIA Complicity in the Global Drug Trade* (Chicago: Lawrence Hill Books, 2003), 90.
52. Anthony Reid, *Imperial Alchemy: Nationalism and Political Identity in Southeast Asia* (Cambridge: Cambridge University Press, 2010), 64.
53. Julia Lovell, *Maoism: A Global History* (London: Bodley Head, 2019), 93.
54. Kenneth P. Landon, *The Chinese in Thailand* (New York: Institute of Pacific Relations, 1941), 35.
55. Benedict Anderson, "From miracle to crash," *London Review of Books*, April 16, 1998.
56. *Overseas Chinese Business Networks in Asia* (Canberra: East Asia Analytical Unit, Department of Foreign Affairs and Trade, 1995), 1.
57. Pan, *Sons of the Yellow Emperor*, 22.
58. Vatikiotis, *Blood and Silk*, 275.
59. Leo Suryadinata, *The Rise of China and the Chinese Overseas: A Study of Beijing's Changing Policy in Southeast Asia and Beyond* (Singapore: Institute of Southeast Asian Studies, 2017), 19–20.

60. Amy Qin, "Worries grow in Singapore over China's calls to help 'Motherland,'" *New York Times*, August 5, 2018.
61. Chris Buckley, "China gives Communist Party more control over policy and media," *New York Times*, March 21, 2018.
62. "Xi's secret economic weapon: Overseas Chinese," *Nikkei Asian Review*, April 3, 2017.
63. Suryadinata, *The Rise of China and the Chinese Overseas*, 9.
64. Ibid., 6, 20.
65. "Remarks by President Obama to the Australian Parliament," The White House, Office of the Press Secretary, November 17, 2011. Available at: obamawhitehouse.archives.gov/the-press-office/2011/11/17/remarks-president-obama-australian-parliament
66. "Summary of the 2018 National Defense Strategy" (Washington: US Department of Defense, January 2018), 2.
67. "Trump administration diplomacy: The untold story," speech by Secretary of State Mike Pompeo, Heritage Foundation President's Club Meeting, October 22, 2019. Available at: www.state.gov/trump-administration-diplomacy-the-untold-story/
68. The phrase "debt-trap diplomacy" was coined by the Indian analyst Brahma Chellaney in the early phase of the Trump administration. See Brahma Chellaney, "China's debt-trap diplomacy," *Project Syndicate*, January 23, 2017.
69. One could cite many sources. For paradigmatic examples, see Benjamin Reilly, "Southeast Asia: In the shadow of China," *Journal of Democracy* 24, No. 1 (January 2013); Josh Rogin, "China's foreign influence operations are causing alarm in Washington," *Washington Post*, December 10, 2017. For idealized invocations of the "international rules-based order," see Andrew J. Bacevich, "The 'global order' myth," *The American Conservative*, June 15, 2017; Patrick Porter, "A world imagined: Nostalgia and liberal order" (Washington, DC: The Cato Institute, June 5, 2018).
70. *National Security Strategy of the United States of America* (Washington, DC: The White House, December 2017), 45.
71. Joel Gehrke, "State Department preparing for clash of civilizations with China," *New York Times*, April 30, 2019.
72. Andrew J. Bacevich, *The Age of Illusions: How America Squandered Its Cold War Victory* (New York: Metropolitan Books, 2020), 5.
73. Elizabeth C. Economy, "China's new revolution," *Foreign Affairs*, April 16, 2018.
74. Cited from Jessica Chen Weiss, "A world safe for autocracy?" *Foreign Affairs*, July/August 2019.
75. Vatikiotis, *Blood and Silk*, 72.
76. *China and the World in the New Era* (Beijing: State Council Information Office, September 2019). Available at: www.xinhuanet.com/english/2019-09/27/c_138427541.htm
77. Yos Santasombat, ed., *Impact of China's Rise on the Mekong Region* (New York: Palgrave Macmillan, 2015), ix.
78. Ian Johnson, *The Souls of China: The Return of Religion after Mao* (New York: Pantheon, 2017), 79.
79. Cited from Acharya, *Making of Southeast Asia*, 139–140.
80. Lam Peng Er, ed., *Japan's Relations with Southeast Asia: The Fukuda Doctrine and Beyond* (London: Routledge, 2013), 1.
81. Takahashi, "Is China following Japan into the haven of Southeast Asian nations?"
82. Author interview with Richard Javad Heydarian, March 11, 2019.

2 MARCHING TOWARD THE TROPICS

1. John Keay, "The Mekong Exploration Commission, 1866–68: Anglo-French rivalry in Southeast Asia," *Asian Affairs* 36, No. 3 (November 2005): 290.
2. Milton Osborne, *The Mekong: Turbulent Past, Uncertain Future* (New York: Grove Press, 2000), 77.

3. Cited from ibid., 136.
4. Milton Osborne, *River Road to China: The Mekong River Expedition, 1866–1873* (New York: Liveright, 1975), 57.
5. Ibid., 170. A few weeks later his body was exhumed, and he was laid permanently to rest beneath the tricolor in Saigon's now-demolished Massiges Cemetery.
6. John Keay, *Mad about the Mekong: Exploration and Empire in South-East Asia* (London: HarperCollins, 2005), 280.
7. *Indo-China* (London: Naval Intelligence Division, Geographical Handbook Series, B.R. 510, December 1943), 438. Cited from Osborne, *The Mekong*, 152.
8. Edmund Leach, "The frontiers of 'Burma,'" *Comparative Studies in Society and History* 3, No. 1 (October 1960): 60.
9. James C. Scott, *The Art of Not Being Governed: An Anarchist History of Upland Southeast Asia* (New Haven, CT: Yale University Press, 2009), ix, 14–16. Although the term "Zomia" is indelibly associated with Scott, it was coined by the historian Willem van Schendel in 2002. See Willem van Schendel, "Geographies of knowing, geographies of ignorance: Southeast Asia from the fringes," *Environment and Planning D: Society and Space* 20, No. 6 (2002).
10. Historically, much of this trade was carried out by Yunnanese Muslims, initially converted following the Mongol conquests of the mid-thirteenth century. See Bin Yang, *Between Winds and Clouds: The Making of Yunnan* (New York: Columbia University Press, 2008), 23–71. For the role of the Yunnanese Muslims in the Southern Silk Road trade, see Ann Maxwell Hill, *Merchants and Migrants: Ethnicity and Trade among Yunnanese Chinese in Southeast Asia* (New Haven, CT: Yale University Southeast Asia Studies, 1998); Andrew Forbes and David Henley, *The Haw: Traders of the Golden Triangle* (Chiang Mai: Cognoscenti Books, 2011).
11. John W. Garver, "Development of China's overland transportation links with Central, South-west and South Asia," *China Quarterly*, 185, No. 1 (March 2006): 2.
12. Thant Myint-U, *Where China Meets India: Burma and the New Crossroads of Asia* (New York: Farrar, Straus & Giroux, 2011), 107.
13. William Clifton Dodd, *The Tai Race: Elder Brother of the Chinese* (Cedar Rapids, IA: Torch Press, 1923), 183–184.
14. Chen Bisheng, cited from Wiens, *China's March Toward the Tropics*, 338–339.
15. Dao Shixun, the last *tusi* ruler of Jinghong, died in Kunming in 2017, at the age of 89. For the evolution of the *tusi* system under the Qing, see C. Patterson Giersch, *Asian Borderlands: The Transformation of Qing China's Yunnan Frontier* (Cambridge, MA: Harvard University Press, 2006), 40–42.
16. Stuart-Fox, *A Short History*, 57.
17. Many of the transplants hailed from Hunan province, a regional "flavor" that persists to this day. Mette Halskov Hansen, *Frontier People: Han Settlers in Minority Areas of China* (London: Hurst & Co., 2004), 33.
18. Paul Handley, "River of promise," *Far Eastern Economic Review*, September 16, 1993.
19. Tim Summers, *Yunnan: A Chinese Bridgehead to Asia* (Oxford: Chandos, 2013), 76. In official translations, the term "bridgehead" (*qiaotoubao*) was soon amended to "gateway," presumably because of its less threatening connotations in English.
20. Owen Lattimore, "Yunnan, pivot of Southeast Asia," *Foreign Affairs*, April 1943.
21. This phrase was coined by Thai Prime Minister Chatichai Choonhavan in 1988. See Steven Erlanger, "Thailand seeks to shape a 'golden peninsula,'" *New York Times*, April 30, 1989.
22. "Xi Jinping urges Yunnan to open up further under BRI in Southeast Asia," *CGTN*, January 22, 2020.
23. Zheng Lan, *Travels through Xishuangbanna: China's Subtropical Home of Many Nationalities* (Beijing: Foreign Languages Press, 1981).
24. Zhuang Guotu and Wang Wangbo, "Migration and trade: The role of overseas Chinese in economic relations between China and Southeast Asia," *International Journal of China Studies* 1, No. 1 (January 2010): 190.

25. Chen Bisheng, *Dianbian sanyi (Miscellaneous Recollections of the Yunnan Frontier)* (Chongqing: Shangwu yinshuguan, 1941), 110–112. Cited from Wiens, *China's March Toward the Tropics*, 348.
26. C.P. Fitzgerald, *The Southern Expansion of the Chinese People* (New York: Praeger, 1972), xxi.
27. This section draws from two detailed investigations of the October 2011 murders: Andrew R.C. Marshall, "In Mekong, Chinese murders and bloody diplomacy," *Reuters*, January 26, 2012; Jeff Howe, "Murder on the Mekong," *The Atavist* No. 30 (2013).
28. McCoy, *The Politics of Heroin*, xxiii, 432.
29. Howe, "Murder on the Mekong."
30. Jane Perlez, "Chinese plan to kill drug lord with drone highlights military advances," *New York Times*, February 20, 2013.
31. "Dok Ngiew Kham Group pays US$6.3m in taxes," *Vientiane Times*, February 4, 2015. Dok Ngiew Kham is the Lao name of Kings Romans.
32. Pinkaew Laungaramsri, "Commodifying sovereignty: Special Economic Zones and the neoliberalization of the Lao frontier," in *Impact of China's Rise on the Mekong Region*, ed. Yos Santasombat (New York: Palgrave Macmillan, 2015), 125.
33. Marshall, "In Mekong, Chinese murders and bloody diplomacy."
34. "Beijing finds 122 people HIV-positive since 1985," *Reuters*, April 18, 1996. On the opening of drug smuggling routes to China, see Ko-Lin Chin, *The Golden Triangle: Inside Southeast Asia's Drug Trade* (Ithaca, NY: Cornell University Press, 2009), 111.
35. Andrew Jacobs, "Divided Chinese see a live TV program about executions as crass, or cathartic," *New York Times*, March 1, 2013.
36. Marshall, "In Mekong, Chinese murders and bloody diplomacy."
37. EIA, *Sin City: Illegal Wildlife Trade in Laos' Golden Triangle Special Economic Zone* (London: Environmental Investigation Agency, March 2015).
38. "Treasury sanctions the Zhao Wei transnational criminal organization," press release from the US Department of the Treasury, January 30, 2018. Available at: https://home.treasury.gov/news/press-releases/sm0272
39. Howe, "Murder on the Mekong."
40. Between 1909 and 1913, Pershing also spearheaded the defeat of the Islamic Moro rebellion in the Philippines, another formative episode in America's imperial expansion. Quoted in Jane Perlez and Bree Feng, "Beijing flaunts cross-border clout in search for drug lord," *New York Times*, April 4, 2013.
41. Tan Hui Yee, "Drought-hit Thailand taps Mekong water," *Straits Times*, February 20, 2016.
42. "Vietnam's southern delta faces worst drought in history," *Associated Press*, March 17, 2016.
43. *Mekong River in the Economy*, WWF–Greater Mekong Report, 2016, 20.
44. International Rivers, "Lancang River dams: Threatening the flow of the lower Mekong," August 2013.
45. "Requiem for a river," *The Economist*, February 11, 2016.
46. Brian Eyler, *The Last Days of the Mighty Mekong* (London: Zed Books, 2019), 288.
47. "Huge land loss predicted for Vietnam's Mekong Delta," *Voice of America*, February 18, 2019.
48. Hannah Beech, "Damming the Lower Mekong, devastating the ways and means of life," *New York Times*, February 15, 2020.
49. Alan Basist and Claude Williams, *Monitoring the Quantity of Water Flowing Through the Mekong Basin Through Natural (Unimpeded) Conditions* (Bangkok: Sustainable Infrastructure Partnership, April 2020).
50. Between 2006 and 2011, Chinese firms funded 46 percent of all new hydropower stations in Laos, Cambodia, and Burma. See Oliver Hensengerth, "Water governance in the Mekong basin," in *Chinese Encounters in Southeast Asia: How People, Money, and Ideas from China Are Changing a Region*, eds Pál Nyíri and Danielle Tan (Seattle, WA: University of Washington Press, 2017), 181.

51. "Lancang–Mekong Cooperation leaders' meeting hails achievements, maps out blueprint for future development," *Xinhua*, January 11, 2018; "China calls for joint efforts to ensure effective Lancang–Mekong cooperation," *Xinhua*, July 25, 2017.
52. Kurlantzick, *Charm Offensive*, 49.
53. Tom Miller, *China's Asian Dream: Empire Building Along the New Silk Road* (London: Zed Books, 2017), 43.
54. Bronson Percival, *The Dragon Looks South: China and Southeast Asia in the New Century* (Westport, CT: Praeger Security International, 2007), 37.
55. The earliest use of this phrase I could find in English was from "Slowly, the elephant stands up," *Newsweek*, November 26, 1962.

3 VIETNAM: DIFFERENT SHADES OF RED

1. Edward O'Dowd, *Chinese Military Strategy in the Third Indochina War: The Last Maoist War* (London: Routledge, 2007), 140.
2. Beijing and Hanoi released wildly contradictory casualty figures, ranging from 20,000 to 62,500 soldiers on the Chinese side, to 35,000 to 50,000 on the Vietnamese. See ibid., 45.
3. Xu Meihong and Larry Engelmann, "Chinese ordeal," *Vietnam*, October 1993. Cited from O'Dowd, *Chinese Military Strategy*, 142.
4. Cited from Henry J. Kenny, "Vietnamese perceptions of the 1979 war with China," in *Chinese Warfighting: The PLA Experience since 1949*, ed. Mark A. Ryan, David M. Finkelstein, and Michael A. McDevitt (Armonk, NY: M.E. Sharpe, 2003), 217.
5. Carlyle Thayer, "The tyranny of geography: Vietnamese strategies to constrain China in the South China Sea," *Contemporary Southeast Asia* 33, No. 3 (December 2011), 348–369.
6. Keith Weller Taylor, *The Birth of Vietnam* (Berkeley, CA: University of California Press, 1983), 298.
7. Christopher Goscha, *Vietnam: A New History* (New York: Basic Books, 2016), 32. For references to the Khmers as "barbarians," see Alexander Barton Woodside, *Vietnam and the Chinese Model: A Comparative Study of Nguyen and Ch'ing Civil Government in the First Half of the Nineteenth Century* (Cambridge, MA: Harvard University Press, 1971), 236.
8. This is a striking example of how power shifts in China often had far-reaching consequences in Southeast Asia. "In a minor way," Alexander Woodside notes, "the rise of the Manchus in China had contributed to the downfall of the Cambodians in the Mekong delta." Woodside, *Vietnam and the Chinese Model*, 248. Nayan Chanda notes the historic irony in the fact "that while a group of Chinese helped the Vietnamese to occupy Ha Tien, two hundred years later with Peking's military aid Cambodians would attempt to recover that territory." Nayan Chanda, *Brother Enemy: The War after the War* (New York: Macmillan, 1986), 437.
9. Taylor, *The Birth of Vietnam*, 297.
10. See Martin Stuart-Fox, "Southeast Asia and China: The role of history and culture in shaping future relations," *Contemporary Southeast Asia* 26, No. 1 (April 2004): 130–131.
11. Brantly Womack, *China and Vietnam: The Politics of Asymmetry* (New York: Cambridge University Press, 2006), 9.
12. "Chinese media threatens Vietnam with a 'lesson it deserves' over oil rig row," *Agence France-Presse*, May 6, 2014.
13. "Up to 21 dead, doctor says, as anti-China riots spread in Vietnam," *Reuters*, May 15, 2014.
14. Hayton, *The South China Sea*, 83.
15. Ibid., 174.
16. Robert Templer, *Shadows and Wind: A View of Modern Vietnam* (New York: Penguin, 1999), 295.
17. Frederick Logevall, *Embers of War: The Fall of an Empire and the Making of America's Vietnam* (New York: Random House, 2012), 11, 229.
18. Ibid., 133.

19. Benedict Anderson, *Imagined Communities: Reflections on the Origin and Spread of Nationalism* (London: Verso, 1983), 1.
20. "Constitution of the Socialist Republic of Vietnam," *Review of Socialist Law* 7, No. 3 (1981): 353. This passage was later dropped.
21. Quoted in Kenny, "Vietnamese perceptions of the 1979 war with China," 236.
22. Hayton, *The South China Sea*, 174.
23. Ibid., 177.
24. Mercedes Hutton, "Vietnam wants Chinese tourists, but only those willing to spend," *South China Morning Post*, July 18, 2018.
25. Khanh Vu, "Vietnam 2019 trade surplus $11.12 billion, beating $9.94 billion forecast: Customs," *Reuters*, January 13, 2020.
26. Le Hong Hiep, *Living Next to the Giant: The Political Economy of Vietnam's Relations with China Under Doi Moi* (Singapore: Institute of Southeast Asian Studies, 2017), 109.
27. By September 2011, there were 78,440 foreign workers in Vietnam, including Chinese nationals, of whom 31,330 were illegal. See ibid., 98.
28. "In Vietnam, China and bauxite don't mix," diplomatic cable from US Embassy Hanoi (09HANOI413_a), April 29, 2009.
29. Robert D. Kaplan, *Asia's Cauldron: The South China Sea and the End of a Stable Pacific* (New York: Random House, 2015), 53.
30. "Joint Statement by President Barack Obama of the United States of America and President Truong Tan Sang of the Socialist Republic of Vietnam," statement from the White House Office of the Press Secretary, July 25, 2013. Available at: https://obamawhitehouse.archives. gov/the-press-office/2013/07/25/joint-statement-president-barack-obama-united-states-america-and-preside
31. Womack, *The Politics of Asymmetry*, 9.
32. Nicola Mocci, "Vietnam 2017–2018: Strengthening the legitimacy of the VCP," *Asia Maior* 29 (2018): 228.
33. "Chinese, Vietnamese Communist parties have 'shared destiny': Beijing," *Reuters*, September 19, 2017.
34. Carlyle A. Thayer, "Not too hot, not too cold: A Vietnamese perspective on China–US relations," in *China–US Relations in Global Perspective*, ed. Bo Zhiyue (Wellington: Victoria University Press, 2016), 215–238.

4 CAMBODIA AND LAOS: PHOBOS AND DEIMOS

1. Andrew Mertha, *Brothers in Arms: Chinese Aid to the Khmer Rouge, 1975–1979* (Ithaca, NY: Cornell University Press, 2014).
2. Bertil Lintner, "The day of reckoning in Cambodia?" *Far Eastern Economic Review*, March 2009.
3. Storey, *Southeast Asia and the Rise of China*, 182.
4. "Visit to Cambodia by China's leader," *Agence France-Presse*, November 13, 2000; Saing Soenthrith, "Not all were happy to see the president," *Cambodia Daily*, November 14, 2000.
5. "Jiang makes 4-point proposal to boost China–Cambodian ties," *People's Daily*, November 14, 2000.
6. Ron Gluckman, "Concrete jungle," *Forbes Asia*, February 11, 2008.
7. "Why Cambodia has cosied up to China," *The Economist*, January 21, 2017.
8. For a detailed account of Cambodia's maneuvering behind the scenes at the 2012 ASEAN meeting, see Hayton, *The South China Sea*, 195–197.
9. Manuel Mogato, Michael Martina, and Ben Blanchard, "ASEAN deadlocked on South China Sea, Cambodia blocks statement," *Reuters*, July 25, 2016.
10. Prak Chan Thul, "Chinese President Xi Jinping visits loyal friend Cambodia," *Reuters*, October 13, 2016.

11. Available at: www.fmprc.gov.cn/mfa_eng/xwfw_665399/s2510_665401/t1489891.shtml
12. Tom Allard and Prak Chan Thul, "Cambodia's Hun Sen has an important election backer: China," *Reuters*, July 28, 2018.
13. "Chinese Ambassador: China-Cambodia long-lasting ties is like a good wine, glamorous," *Fresh News*, July 2, 2018.
14. Chanda, *Brother Enemy*, 109.
15. Cheunboran Chanborey, "Small state's hard strategic choices: Cambodia between ASEAN and China," in *The Belt and Road Initiative and Its Implications for Cambodia's Development*, ed. Neak Chandarith, Nguon Pheakkdey, and Sam Ath Sambath Sreysour (Phnom Penh: Royal University of Phnom Penh, 2019), 22–24.
16. Kuch Naren, "Rainsy says CNRP backs China, not Vietnam, in sea dispute," *Cambodia Daily*, January 11–12, 2014.
17. Anna Fifield, "This Cambodian city is turning into a Chinese enclave, and not everyone is happy," *Washington Post*, March 29, 2018.
18. Sheith Khidir, "China crime plaguing Cambodia?" *ASEAN Post*, October 9, 2019.
19. Tiziano Terzani, *A Fortune-teller Told Me: Earthbound Travels in the Far East* (New York: Three Rivers Press, 1997), 238–239.
20. See, for instance, Virginia Thompson, *French Indo-China* (London: George Allen & Unwin, 1937), 166; William E. Willmott, *The Chinese in Cambodia* (Vancouver: University of British Columbia, 1967), 35–36.
21. Zhou Daguan, *A Record of Cambodia: The Land and Its People*, trans. Peter Harris (Chiang Mai: Silkworm Books, 2007), 81.
22. "Cambodia's top ten tycoons," diplomatic cable from US embassy Phnom Penh (07PHNOMPENH1034), August 9, 2007.
23. Mech Dara and Alessandro Marazzi Sassoon, "Preah Sihanouk Governor bemoans Chinese influx," *Phnom Penh Post*, January 29, 2018; Sheridan Prasso, "Chinese influx stirs resentment in once-sleepy Cambodian resort," *Bloomberg*, June 21, 2018.
24. Devin Thorne and Ben Spevack, *Harbored Ambitions: How China's Port Investments Are Strategically Reshaping the Indo-Pacific* (Washington, DC: C4ADS, 2017), 54–64.
25. Hannah Beech, "A jungle airstrip stirs suspicions about China's plans for Cambodia," *New York Times*, December 22, 2019.
26. Jeremy Page, Gordon Lubold, and Rob Taylor, "Deal for naval outpost in Cambodia furthers China's quest for military network," *Wall Street Journal*, July 21, 2019.
27. Sam Rainsy, "China's Cambodian invasion," *Project Syndicate*, August 2, 2019.
28. Center for Global Development (CGD), "Examining the debt implications of the Belt and Road Initiative from a policy perspective," Policy Paper 121 (Washington, DC: CGD, March 2018), 12.
29. "If you have jobs, don't listen to propaganda: PM Hun Sen tells workers," *Fresh News*, February 20, 2019; "Cambodia's PM Hun Sen unveils 'strategy' to offset loss of EU trade scheme," *Radio Free Asia*, March 29, 2019.
30. Henry Kamm, "Look, cars! Rare species sighted in Laos," *New York Times*, September 10, 1995.
31. Tony Judt, *When the Facts Change: Essays 1995–2010* (New York: Penguin, 2015), 285.
32. "Latest plan aims to build high-speed rail network," *Global Times*, July 20, 2016.
33. Peter Janssen, "Land-locked Laos on track for controversial China rail link," *Nikkei Asian Review*, June 24, 2017.
34. Grant Evans, *A Short History of Laos: The Land In Between* (Crows Nest, NSW: Allen & Unwin, 2002), 71.
35. O.W. Wolters, *History, Culture, and Region in Southeast Asian Perspectives* (Singapore: Institute of Southeast Asian Studies, 1982), 17.
36. Victor Lieberman, *Strange Parallels: Southeast Asia in Global Context, c. 800–1830*, vol. 1: *Integration on the Mainland* (Cambridge: Cambridge University Press, 2003), 33.
37. See: www.the-monitor.org/en-gb/reports/2019/lao-pdr/view-all.aspx
38. Quoted in Bien Chiang and Jean Chih-yin Cheng, "Changing landscape and changing ethnoscape in Lao PDR," in *Impact of China's Rise on the Mekong Region*, ed. Yos Santasombat

(New York: Palgrave Macmillan, 2015), 89. Lan Xang was known to imperial China as *nanzhang* (南掌) or *lancang* (澜沧), the latter of which lives on as the modern Chinese word for the Mekong River.

39. "China becomes largest investor in Laos," *Xinhua*, January 30, 2014.
40. Eyler, *Last Days*, 155.
41. Danielle Tan, *Chinese Engagement in Laos: Past, Present, and Uncertain Future* (Singapore: Institute of Southeast Asian Studies, 2015), 10.
42. Victor Purcell, *The Chinese in Southeast Asia* (Oxford: Oxford University Press, 1965), 170.
43. Joel M. Halpern, *The Role of the Chinese in Lao Society* (Santa Monica, CA: Rand Corporation, 1961), 6.
44. Oden Meeker, *The Little World of Laos* (New York: Scribner, 1959), 195.
45. Florence Rossetti, "The Chinese in Laos," *Chinese Perspectives*, No. 13 (1997).
46. For instance, see Hansen, *Frontier People*, 189–192, 206–122.
47. Darren Schuettler, "China land deal rankles Laos capital," *Reuters*, April 7, 2008.
48. Center for Global Development, "Examining the debt implications of the BRI," 15–16.
49. Eyler, *Last Days*, 153.
50. "U.S. gives Laos extra $90 million to help clear unexploded ordnance," *Reuters*, September 6, 2016.
51. Molly McKitterick, "Obama to be first US president to visit Laos," *Voice of America*, November 5, 2015.
52. John McBeth, "Laos dances to survive between China and Vietnam," *Asia Times*, January 9, 2018.

5 THAILAND: BAMBOO IN THE WIND

1. Video available at https://www.youtube.com/watch?v=G5QTPUskwLY
2. "Chinese visitors to Thailand hit 10 million for 1st time," *Xinhua*, December 20, 2018.
3. Elizabeth Becker, *Overbooked: The Exploding Business of Travel and Tourism* (New York: Simon & Schuster, 2013), 293.
4. Oliver Smith, "The unstoppable rise of the Chinese traveller," *The Telegraph*, April 11, 2018.
5. These statistics are taken from Sadanand Dhume and Susan V. Lawrence, "Buying fast into Southeast Asia," *Far Eastern Economic Review*, March 28, 2002; Danson Cheong, "Documentary launched to sell Asean as tourist destination to Chinese," *Straits Times*, April 20, 2018.
6. Both statistics are taken from Zawacki, *Thailand*, 281.
7. King Bhumibol (Rama IX) died on October 13, 2016, and was succeeded by his son, Crown Prince Vajiralongkorn.
8. Scot Marciel, Testimony Before the House Committee on Foreign Affairs Subcommittee on Asia and the Pacific, Washington, DC, June 24, 2016. Available at: http://bangkok.usembassy.gov/062414_scot_marciel_testimony.html
9. Pongphisoot Busbarat, "Thai–US relations in the post-Cold War era: Untying the special relationship," *Asian Security* 13, No. 3 (2017): 269.
10. Pavin Chachavalpongpun, "Thai society maven uses neutral post to justify coup," *Asia Sentinel*, June 3, 2014.
11. Patrick Jory, "China is a big winner from Thailand's coup," *East Asia Forum*, June 18, 2014.
12. "Thai coup shows weaknesses of Western democracy," *Global Times*, May 25, 2014.
13. John Blaxland and Gregory Raymond, *Tipping the Balance in Southeast Asia? Thailand, the United States, and China* (Canberra: ANU Strategic and Defense Studies Center, 2017), 11.
14. Cited from Arne Kislenko, "Bending with the wind: The continuity and flexibility of Thai foreign policy," *International Journal* 57 (Autumn 2002): 543.
15. Chris Baker and Pasuk Phongpaichit, "Thailand is not lost," *New York Review of Books*, May 24, 2018.

16. Storey, *Southeast Asia and the Rise of China*, 134.
17. Percival, *The Dragon Looks South*, 48.
18. Ibid., 47.
19. Zawacki, *Thailand*, 299.
20. For a list of Confucius Institutes by country, see: http://english.hanban.org/node_10971. htm
21. Zawacki, *Thailand*, 192.
22. Ibid., 114–115, 202.
23. Diplomatic cable from US Embassy Bangkok, 06BANGKOK4254, July 18, 2006.
24. Thomas Parks and Benjamin Zawacki, *The Future of U.S.–Thai Relations: Views of Thai and American Leaders on the Bilateral Relationship and ways Forward* (Bangkok: The Asia Foundation, August 2018), 8–9, 16–17.
25. Zawacki, *Thailand*, 4. Emphasis in original.
26. Lieberman, *Strange Parallels*, vol. 1, 48.
27. Landon, *The Chinese in Thailand*, 1.
28. Chris Baker and Pasuk Phongpaichit, *A History of Thailand* (Cambridge: Cambridge University Press, 2014), 34.
29. Modern Thai also contains a large number of Chinese borrowings, including its number system, which date back to early Tai–Chinese contacts in the first millennium CE. See: www.sealang.net/thai/chinese/middle.htm
30. Anderson, "Riddles of yellow and red," 12; Baker and Phongpaichit, *A History of Thailand*, 34.
31. Anderson, "Riddles of yellow and red."
32. The pamphlet is reproduced in Landon, *The Chinese in Thailand*, 32–47.
33. Vatikiotis, *Blood and Silk*, 286.
34. Pavin Chachavalpongpun, *Reinventing Thailand: Thaksin and his Foreign Policy* (Singapore: Institute of Southeast Asian Studies, 2010), 17.
35. Vatikiotis, *Blood and Silk*, 285.
36. Anderson, "Riddles of yellow and red," 19.
37. Zawacki, *Thailand*, 114.
38. Ibid., 80.
39. Michael Vatikiotis, "Sino chic," *Far Eastern Economic Review*, January 11, 1996.
40. Kislenko, "Bending with the wind," 537.
41. Chas W. Freeman, Jr., "Reimagining China and Asia," speech delivered at the Watson Institute for International and Public Affairs, Brown University, March 23, 2017. Available at: https:// watson.brown.edu/files/watson/imce/people/fellows/freeman/ReimaginingChinaandAsia .pdf
42. Gregory Raymond, "Competing logics: Between Thai sovereignty and the China model in 2018," *Southeast Asian Affairs* 2019 (2019): 349.
43. John Bowring, *The Kingdom and People of Siam* (London: John W. Parker & Son, 1857), 5–6.
44. Zawacki, *Thailand*, 313.
45. Dominic Faulder, *Anand Panyarachun and the Making of Modern Thailand* (Bangkok: Editions Didier Millet, 2018), 86, 267.
46. Shawn Crispin, "China can't always get what it wants in Thailand," *Asia Times*, September 12, 2018.
47. Pechnipa Dominique Lam, "Will Thailand's Chinese high-speed railway be worth it?" *The Diplomat*, March 6, 2019.
48. Baker and Phongpaichit, *A History of Thailand*, 204.
49. Blaxland and Raymond, *Tipping the Balance*, 14–15.
50. Ibid., 12.
51. Raymond, "Competing logics," 341.
52. Thaksin Shinawatra, "The election in Thailand was rigged," *New York Times*, March 25, 2019.

6 BURMA: AMONG THE CACTUS

1. David I. Steinberg, *Burma/Myanmar: What Everyone Needs to Know* (Oxford: Oxford University Press, 2010), 79.
2. Keith B. Richburg, "Burma's military junta poses dilemma for foreign countries," *Washington Post*, March 11, 1989.
3. Thant Myint-U, "Asia's new Great Game," *Foreign Policy*, September 12, 2011.
4. Gary J. Bass, "China's unsavory friends," *Washington Post*, April 23, 2006.
5. Steinberg, *Burma/Myanmar*, 77.
6. Bertil Lintner, "China embrace too strong for Naypyidaw," *Asia Times*, November 29, 2011.
7. Thant Myint-U, *The Hidden History of Burma: Race, Capitalism, and the Crisis of Democracy in the 21st Century* (New York: W.W. Norton, 2020), 176.
8. Lucy Ash, "Burma learns how to protest—against Chinese investors," BBC, January 24, 2013.
9. Myint-U, *Where China Meets India*, 29.
10. Pan Qi, "Opening to the southwest: An expert opinion," *Beijing Review*, September 2, 1985.
11. The monument is described in Bertil Lintner, "As West recoils, China surges south in Myanmar," *Asia Times*, September 24, 2018.
12. Archibald R. Colquhoun, *China in Transformation* (London: Harper & Brothers, 1898), 117.
13. In order of defection, these four groups were the Myanmar National Democratic Alliance Army (Kokang), the United Wa State Army, the National Democratic Alliance Army (Mong La), and the New Democratic Army—Kachin.
14. The word is a possible derivation from "Turk." See Goh Geok Yian, "The question of 'China' in Burmese chronicles," *Journal of Southeast Asian Studies* 41, No. 1 (February 2010).
15. A detailed account of the fall of the Ming and their flight into Burma can be found in Lynn A. Struve, *The Southern Ming, 1644–62* (New Haven, CT: Yale University Press, 1984).
16. Maung Htin Aung, *A History of Burma* (New York: Columbia University Press, 1967), 181.
17. John S. Thomson, "Burmese neutralism," *Political Science Quarterly* 72, No. 2 (1957): 266.
18. The term, which has a strong connotation of two siblings born from the same womb, was used uniquely to describe Sino-Burmese relations. See David I. Steinberg and Hongwei Fan, eds, *Modern China–Myanmar Relations: Dilemmas of Mutual Dependence* (Copenhagen: Nordic Institute of Asian Studies, 2012), 7.
19. J. Mohan Malik, "Myanmar's role in China's Maritime Silk Road Initiative," *Journal of Contemporary China* 27, No. 111 (2018): 363.
20. Thomas Fuller, "Lo Hsing Han, Myanmar drug kingpin, dies at 80," *New York Times*, July 8, 2013.
21. "Obituary: Lo Hsing Han," *The Economist*, July 27, 2013.
22. Nicholas Farrelly and Stephanie Olinga-Shannon, "Establishing contemporary Chinese life in Myanmar," Trends in Southeast Asia 15 (Singapore: Institute of Southeast Asian Studies, 2015), 8.
23. Colquhoun, *China in Transformation*, 117.
24. Farrelly and Olinga-Shannon, "Establishing contemporary Chinese life in Myanmar," 3.
25. Bertil Lintner, "Burma and its neighbours," in *Indian and Chinese Foreign Policies in Comparative Perspectives*, ed. S. Mansingh (New Delhi: Radiant Publishers, 1998), 143.
26. Miller, *China's Asian Dream*, 140.
27. "Chinese influx transforming Myanmar's quintessential city," *Associated Press*, May 1, 2018.
28. Enze Han, "Under the shadow of China–US competition: Myanmar and Thailand's alignment choices," *Chinese Journal of International Politics* 11, No. 1 (2018): 101–102.
29. Jane Perlez and Bree Feng, "China tries to improve image in a changing Myanmar," *New York Times*, May 18, 2013.
30. Myint-U, *Hidden History of Burma*, 20.

31. Edmund Leach, "The political future of Burma," in *Futuribles: Studies in Conjecture*, vol. 1, ed. Bertrand de Jouvenel (Geneva: Droz Geneva, 1963), 125, 141.
32. Martin Smith, "Arakan (Rakhine State): A land in conflict on Myanmar's western frontier," Research paper (Amsterdam: Transnational Institute, December 2019), 8.
33. Myint-U, *Hidden History of Burma*, 35–36.
34. "'No one was left': Death and violence against the Rohingya in Rakhine State, Myanmar" (Geneva: Médecins Sans Frontières, March 2018), 5.
35. Doug Bock Clark, "Myanmar's internet disrupted society—and fueled extremists," *Wired*, September 28, 2017.
36. Tom Miles, "U.N. investigators cite Facebook role in Myanmar crisis," *Reuters*, March 13, 2018.
37. Michael Safi, "Aung San Suu Kyi says 'terrorists' are misinforming world about Myanmar violence," *The Guardian*, September 6, 2017.
38. "Amnesty International withdraws human rights award from Aung San Suu Kyi," press release from Amnesty International, November 12, 2018.
39. Barbara Victor, *The Lady: Aung San Suu Kyi, Nobel Laureate and Burma's Prisoner* (Boston, MA: Faber & Faber, 1998), 223.
40. Mary P. Callahan, *Making Enemies: War and State Building in Burma* (Ithaca, NY: Cornell University Press, 2003), 19–20.
41. Nan Lwin, "Myanmar military chief thanks Beijing for support on Rakhine crisis," *The Irrawaddy*, April 10, 2019.
42. Bertil Lintner, "Full steam ahead for China–Myanmar high-speed railway," *Asia Times*, February 21, 2019.
43. Larry Jagan, "Giants vie for influence in Myanmar," *Bangkok Post*, November 4, 2019.
44. Diplomatic cable from US Embassy Rangoon, 05RANGOON220_a, February 18, 2005.
45. "China's Myanmar strategy: Elections, ethnic politics and economics," Briefing 112 (Brussels: International Crisis Group, September 2010), 11.
46. Bertil Lintner, "China uses carrot and stick in Myanmar," *Asia Times*, February 28, 2017.
47. Myint-U, *Hidden History of Burma*, 177.
48. For Chinese military support to the UWSA, see Bertil Lintner, *The Costliest Pearl: China's Struggle for India's Ocean* (London: C. Hurst & Co., 2019), 48–50.
49. Yun Sun, "China and Myanmar's peace process," Special Report (Washington, DC: United States Institute of Peace, March 2017), 13–14.
50. Sui-Lee Wee, "Myanmar official accuses China of meddling in rebel peace talks," *Reuters*, October 9, 2015.
51. USIP, *China's Role in Myanmar's Internal Conflicts* (Washington, DC: United States Institute of Peace, September 2018), 25.
52. Sun, "China and Myanmar's peace process," 6.
53. Laura Zhou, "Locals still take dim view of dam," *South China Morning Post*, January 20, 2019.
54. Nan Lwin, "Behind the threats and warnings of Chinese ambassador's Kachin visit," *The Irrawaddy*, January 9, 2019.
55. Kanupriya Kapoor and Aye Min Thant, "Myanmar scales back Chinese-backed port project due to debt fears: Official," *Reuters*, August 2, 2018.
56. Malik, "Myanmar's role in China's Maritime Silk Road Initiative," 375.
57. Ying Yao and Youyi Zhang, "Public perception of Chinese investment in Myanmar and its political consequences," Policy Brief (London: International Growth Center, 2018).
58. Myint-U, *Hidden History of Burma*, 257.

7 SINGAPORE: THE GREAT LEAP OUTWARD

1. Terzani, *A Fortune-teller Told Me*, 140.
2. Tomé Pires, *The Suma Oriental of Tomé Pires*, trans. Armando Cortesão (London: The Hakluyt Society, 1944), vol. I, 228; vol. II, 287.

3. Howard, *Travels in South-Eastern Asia*, 96; Isabella L. Bird, *The Golden Chersonese and the Way Thither* (London: John Murray, 1883), 125.

4. Anthony Reid, *Southeast Asia in the Age of Commerce*, vol. 1: *The Lands below the Winds* (New Haven, CT: Yale University Press, 1988), 51.

5. Available at: https://web.archive.org/web/20070610100537/http://1421exposed.com/html/library_of_congress.html

6. Joseph Needham, Wang Ling, and Lu Gwei-Djen, *Science and Civilisation in China*, vol. 4: *Physics and Physical Technology*, Part III: "Civil engineering and nautics" (Cambridge: Cambridge University Press, 1971), 484. For the size of the Ming fleets, see Philip Ball, *The Water Kingdom: A Secret History of China* (London: Bodley Head, 2016), 144.

7. Wensheng Wang, *White Lotus Rebels and South China Pirates: Crisis and Reform in the Qing Empire* (Cambridge, MA: Harvard University Press, 2014), 100.

8. Wang Gungwu, *The Nanhai Trade: Early Chinese Trade in the South China Sea* (Singapore: Eastern Universities Press, 2003), xvii.

9. Howard J. Dooley, "The Great Leap Outward: China's maritime renaissance," *Journal of East Asian Affairs* 26, No. 1 (Spring/Summer 2012).

10. Nick Childs and Tom Waldwyn, "China's naval shipbuilding: Delivering on its ambition in a big way," International Institute for Strategic Studies blog, May 1, 2018.

11. David Lague and Benjamin Kang Lim, "How China is replacing America as Asia's military titan," *Reuters*, April 23, 2019.

12. Zhu Tingchang, "On the geostrategic status of Taiwan," *Forum of World Economics and Politics* 3 (2001): 67. Cited from Toshi Yoshihara, "China's vision of its seascape: The first island chain and Chinese seapower," *Asian Politics & Society* 4, No. 3 (2012): 303.

13. Cited from Pomfret, *The Beautiful Kingdom and the Middle Kingdom*, 544.

14. Merle Goldman and Leo Ou-Fan Lee, eds, *An Intellectual History of Modern China* (Cambridge: Cambridge University Press, 2002), 514. See also Han Minzhu and Hua Sheng, eds, *Cries for Democracy: Writings and Speeches from the 1989 Chinese Democracy Movement* (Princeton, NJ: Princeton University Press, 1990), 20–22.

15. Wang Gungwu, *The Chinese Overseas: From Earthbound China to the Quest for Autonomy* (Cambridge, MA: Harvard University Press, 2000), 111.

16. "A chained dragon," *The Economist*, July 6, 2019.

17. Deborah Bräutigam, "Misdiagnosing the Chinese infrastructure push," *The American Interest*, April 4, 2019. For the world's top container ports, see: www.worldshipping.org/about-the-industry/global-trade/top-50-world-container-ports

18. "A chained dragon."

19. *China's Military Strategy (2015)* (Beijing: State Council Information Office of the People's Republic of China, 2015), 16.

20. "Xi: Strong navy indispensable for promoting peace," *Xinhua*, April 24, 2019.

21. Kong Yuanzhi, cited from Geoff Wade, "The Zheng He voyages: A reassessment," Working Paper Series 31 (Asia Research Institute: National University of Singapore, 2004), 2.

22. Reid, *Southeast Asia in the Age of Commerce*, 53.

23. French, *Everything Under the Heavens*, 97.

24. "Remarks by H.E. Li Keqiang Premier of the State Council of the People's Republic of China at the 18th China–ASEAN Summit," Ministry of Foreign Affairs, PRC, November 21, 2015.

25. "Speech by Chinese President Xi Jinping to Indonesian Parliament," October 2, 2013. Available at: www.asean-china-center.org/english/2013-10/03/c_133062675.htm

26. Wade, "The Zheng He voyages: A reassessment," 18.

27. Philip Bowring, *Empire of the Winds: The Global Role of Asia's Great Archipelago* (London: I.B. Tauris, 2019), 4.

28. Fitzgerald, *The Southern Expansion of the Chinese People*, xvi.

29. Sophia Raffles, *Memoir of the Life and Public Services of Sir Thomas Stamford Raffles* (London: John Murray, 1830), 525.

30. World Bank statistics available at: https://tradingeconomics.com/

31. Reid, *Imperial Alchemy*, 59.
32. Howard, *Travels in South-Eastern Asia*, 89.
33. Lee Kuan Yew, *From Third World to First: The Singapore Story, 1965-2000* (New York: HarperCollins, 2000).
34. Cited from Stephen Hamnett and Belinda Yuen, eds, *Planning Singapore: The Experimental City* (London: Routledge, 2019), 2.
35. "Excerpts from an interview with Lee Kuan Yew," *New York Times*, August 29, 2007.
36. Rachman, *Easternization*, 107.
37. Ezra F. Vogel, *Deng Xiaoping and the Transformation of China* (Cambridge, MA: The Belknap Press, 2011), 290.
38. Cited from Nicholas D. Kristof and Sheryl WuDunn, *China Wakes: The Struggle for the Soul of a Rising Power* (New York: Vintage, 1995), 433.
39. George Yeo, "Deng Xiaoping visited S'pore in 1978: Here's the impact it left on Sino–S'pore relations 40 years on," *Mothership*, November 13, 2018.
40. Pomfret, *The Beautiful Kingdom and the Middle Kingdom*, 499.
41. Nectar Gan and Laura Zhou, "Lee Kuan Yew among foreigners honoured for helping China to open up," *South China Morning Post*, December 18, 2018.
42. Esther Teo, "China's President Xi Jinping praises Mr Lee Kuan Yew's 'outstanding contributions' to Asia," *Straits Times*, March 28, 2015.
43. Singapore Government Press Statement, May 5, 1988. Available at: www.nas.gov.sg/archivesonline/data/pdfdoc/831-1988-05-07.pdf
44. Faulder, *Anand Panyarachun and the Making of Modern Thailand*, 267.
45. Pomfret, "U.S. takes a tougher tone with China."
46. "Singapore urges respect for court ruling on South China Sea," *Today Online*, July 12, 2016.
47. Viola Zhou, "Blow-by-blow account of the China-Singapore spat over Global Times' South China Sea report," *South China Morning Post*, September 28, 2016.
48. "Singapore to name orchid hybrid after Obamas," *Channel News Asia*, August 3, 2016.
49. "China should make Singapore pay over South China Sea dispute, says PLA adviser," *Straits Times*, October 1, 2016.
50. Kishore Mahbubani, "Qatar: Big lessons from a small country," *Straits Times*, July 1, 2017; Bhavan Jaipragas, "As a small state, should Singapore hide when 'elephants' fight?" *South China Morning Post*, July 2, 2017.
51. See Bilahari Kausikan Facebook post, July 1, 2017, at: www.facebook.com/bilahari.kausikan/posts/1948237095433710
52. Ja Ian Chong, "Diverging paths? Singapore–China relations and the East Asian maritime domain," Maritime Awareness Project analysis, April 26, 2017, 2.
53. Qin, "Worries grow in Singapore."
54. Charissa Yong, "S'poreans should be aware of China's influence ops: Bilahari," *Straits Times*, June 28, 2018.
55. Hong Xiaoyong, "China does not manipulate other countries, says envoy," *Straits Times*, July 12, 2018.
56. Available at: https://www.pmo.gov.sg/Newsroom/pm-lee-hsien-loong-official-opening-singapore-chinese-cultural-centre
57. For the 1990 figure, see Antonio L. Rappa and Lionel Wee, *Language Policy and Modernity in Southeast Asia: Malaysia, the Philippines, Singapore, and Thailand* (New York: Springer, 2006), 85. For 2015, see Pearl Lee, "English most common home language in Singapore, bilingualism also up: Government survey," *Straits Times*, March 10, 2016.
58. Available at: www.reddit.com/r/singapore/comments/94vyiz/worries_grow_in_singapore_over_chinas_calls_to/
59. Andrew Jacobs, "In Singapore, vitriol against Chinese newcomers," *New York Times*, July 26, 2012.
60. IISS Shangri-La Dialogue, 2019, Keynote Address by Lee Hsien Loong, Prime Minister of Singapore, available at: www.iiss.org/events/shangri-la-dialogue/shangri-la-dialogue-2019

8 MALAYSIA: LORD OF THE RINGGITS

1. Jeevan Vasagar, "Chinese-backed Forest City rises above the sea," *Financial Times*, February 10, 2017.
2. Soo Wern Jun, "Mahathir launches bitter attack on Forest City project," *Free Malaysia Today*, December 30, 2017.
3. C.K. Tan, "Malaysia and China: The new 'lips and teeth' duo," *Nikkei Asian Review*, October 31, 2017.
4. Tom Wright and Bradley Hope, *Billion Dollar Whale: The Man Who Fooled Wall Street, Hollywood, and the World* (New York: Hachette, 2018), 14.
5. "Najib: I have never taken funds for personal gain," *The Star Online*, July 3, 2015.
6. Wright and Hope, *Billion Dollar Whale*, 234.
7. "Malaysia's 1MDB sells power assets to China firm for $2.3 billion," *Reuters*, November 23, 2015; "Malaysia's 1MDB to sell property project stake for $1.7 billion," *Reuters*, December 31, 2015.
8. Jeevan Vasagar, Caroline Binham, and Simeon Kerr, "China to help 1MDB settle multibillion-dollar legal dispute," *Financial Times*, December 7, 2016.
9. Tom Wright and Bradley Hope, "China offered to bail out troubled Malaysian fund in return for deals," *Wall Street Journal*, January 7, 2019.
10. Bhavan Jaipragas, "Has China offered to bail out Malaysia's 1MDB? At what cost?" *South China Morning Post*, December 7, 2016.
11. Umapagan Ampikaipakan, "What is wrong with Malaysia?" *New York Times*, May 7, 2018.
12. "Thousands rally in Malaysia to oust premier Najib," *Reuters*, October 14, 2017.
13. H.T. Ong, "A doctor's duty is to heal the unhealthy: The story of Tun Dr Mahathir Mohamad," *Annals of the Academy of Medicine, Singapore* 34, No. 6 (July 2005): 46C.
14. Chin Peng, *Alias Chin Peng: My Side of History* (Singapore: Media Masters, 2003), 410. For Chinese support to the CPM, see John W. Garver, *China's Quest: The History of the Foreign Relations of the People's Republic of China* (New York: Oxford University Press, 2016), 213–214; Lovell, *Maoism*, 102–106.
15. Bird, *Golden Chersonese*, 279.
16. Ibid., 282.
17. Jim Baker, *Crossroads: A Popular History of Malaysia and Singapore* (Singapore: Marshall Cavendish Editions, 2008), 171.
18. V.S. Naipaul, *Among the Believers: An Islamic Journey* (New York: Vintage, 1982), 227.
19. Rajendra Kumar Jain, *China and Malaysia, 1949–1983* (New Delhi: Radiant Publishers, 1984), xl.
20. "Race war in Malaysia," *TIME*, May 23, 1969.
21. This is the figure cited in John Slimming, *Malaysia: Death of Democracy* (London: John Murray, 1969), 47.
22. Cited from Storey, *Southeast Asia and the Rise of China*, 213.
23. Cited from ibid., 212.
24. Cheng-Chwee Kuik, "Making sense of Malaysia's China policy: Asymmetry, proximity, and elite's domestic authority," *Chinese Journal of International Politics* 6 (2013): 456.
25. Syahirah Syed Jaafar, "Malaysia–China trade sets new record in 2019," *The Edge Financial Daily*, January 21, 2020.
26. C.K. Tan, "For Malaysia, relations with China are good—maybe too good," *Nikkei Asian Review*, November 9, 2017.
27. Hayton, *The South China Sea*, 170.
28. Joseph Chinyong Liow, "Malaysia's post-Cold War China policy: A reassessment," in *The Rise of China: Responses from Southeast Asia and Japan*, ed. Jun Tsunekawa (Tokyo: National Institute for Defense Studies, 2009), 63.
29. Trefor Moss, "Indonesia blows up 23 foreign fishing boats to send a message," *Wall Street Journal*, April 5, 2016.

30. List of chiefs of the Malaysian navy, available at: www.navy.mil.my/index.php/en/component/k2/itemlist/category/76-former-cn
31. Kaplan, *Asia's Cauldron*, 88.
32. "Opinion of China: Malaysia," available at: www.pewresearch.org/global/database/indicator/24/country/my
33. "Envoy says China 'will not sit idly by' if its interests are infringed upon," *Straits Times*, September 26, 2015.
34. Trinna Leong and Andrew R.C. Marshall, "As Malaysia's PM struggles in graft scandal, his party plays the race card," *Reuters*, September 23, 2018.
35. Suryadinata, *The Rise of China and the Chinese Overseas*, 121.
36. Dennis Ignatius, "Ambassador Huang's behaviour is unacceptable," *Malaysiakini*, September 28, 2015.
37. Anderson, "From miracle to crash."
38. Adam Schwarz, *A Nation in Waiting: Indonesia's Search for Stability* (Boulder, CO: Westview Press, 2000), 116.
39. Vatikiotis, *Blood and Silk*, 188.
40. "Empires without umpires," *The Economist*, April 5, 2001.
41. From Robert Kuok's *Forbes* profile, available at: www.forbes.com/profile/robert-kuok/#7bc25af15eb5
42. Ngeow Chow-Bing and Tan Chee-Beng, "Cultural ties and states' interests: Malaysian Chinese and China's rise," in *China's Rise and the Chinese Overseas*, ed. Bernard P. Wong and Tan Chee-Beng (London: Routledge, 2018), 100.
43. Tash Aw, "A cultural revolution in Malaysia," *New York Times*, January 7, 2016.
44. Chow-Bing and Chee-Beng, "Malaysian Chinese and China's rise," 105.
45. "18% and growing, non-Chinese are turning to SJKCs," *Sinchew Daily*, July 10, 2017.
46. Chow-Bing and Chee-Beng, "Malaysian Chinese and China's rise," 105.
47. "Falling Malaysian Chinese population worrying: Analysts," *Straits Times*, January 24, 2017. The 2019 figure is from the Malaysian Department of Statistics, available at: www.dosm.gov.my/v1/index.php
48. Tash Aw, "What just happened in Malaysia?" *New York Times*, May 10, 2018.
49. Wright and Hope, *Billion Dollar Whale*, 328.
50. "Mahathir warns against new 'colonialism' during visit to China," *Bloomberg News*, August 20, 2018.
51. Josh Rogin, "In Malaysia, a victory for democracy—and an opportunity for the U.S.," *Washington Post*, June 7, 2018.
52. Kinling Lo, "Mahathir 'fully backs' drive but says routes must be open," *South China Morning Post*, April 26, 2019.
53. "Chinese Malaysian loyalty under spotlight as China flexes muscle," *Malay Mail*, March 7, 2018.
54. Nile Bowie, "Race and religion roiling Malaysian reform," *Asia Times*, March 27, 2019.
55. Shannon Teoh, "Thousands in KL for street protest against UN rights convention," *Straits Times*, December 8, 2018.
56. Anthony Burgess, *The Long Day Wanes: A Malayan Trilogy* (New York: W.W. Norton, 1977), 365.

9 INDONESIA: A LONG SPOON

1. Pan, *Sons of the Yellow Emperor*, 37.
2. Elisabeth Pisani, *Indonesia Etc.: Exploring the Improbable Nation* (New York: W.W. Norton, 2014), 288.
3. Cited from Susan Abeyasekere, *Jakarta: A History* (Singapore: Oxford University Press, 1987), 24.

4. The Dutch referred to this slaughter as *Chinezenmoord*—literally, "murder of the Chinese." See Pan, *Sons of the Yellow Emperor*, 36.

5. Rizal Sukma, *Indonesia and China: The Politics of a Troubled Relationship* (London: Routledge, 1999), 24–25.

6. Geoffrey B. Robinson, *The Killing Season: A History of the Indonesian Massacres, 1965–66* (Princeton, NJ: Princeton University Press, 2018), ix.

7. Robinson, *The Killing Season*, 3.

8. Harold Crouch, *The Army and Politics in Indonesia* (Jakarta: Equinox, 2007), 334.

9. For a detailed examination of this question, see Robert Cribb and Charles A. Coppel, "A genocide that never was: Explaining the myth of anti-Chinese massacres in Indonesia, 1965–1966," *Journal of Genocide Research* 11, No. 4 (December 2009): 447–465; Robinson, *The Killing Season*, 121–122, 144.

10. Resty Woro Yuniar, "Why are ethnic Chinese still being denied land in Indonesia?" *South China Morning Post*, March 10, 2018.

11. Jemma Purdey, *Anti-Chinese Violence in Indonesia, 1996–1999* (Singapore: Singapore University Press, 2006), 22; Pisani, *Indonesia Etc.*, 291.

12. Richard Borsuk and Nancy Chng, *Liem Sioe Liong's Salim Group: The Business Pillar of Suharto's Indonesia* (Singapore: Institute of Southeast Asian Studies, 2014), 1.

13. Amy Chua, *World on Fire: How Exporting Free Market Democracy Breeds Ethnic Hatred and Global Instability* (New York: Anchor Books, 2004), 44.

14. Borsuk and Chng, *Liem Sioe Liong's Salim Group*, xi.

15. Anderson, "From miracle to crash."

16. Reid, *Imperial Alchemy*, 75.

17. Charlotte Setijadi, "Ethnic Chinese in contemporary Indonesia: Changing identity politics and the paradox of sinification," *ISEAS Perspective* 12 (2016), 1.

18. Pankaj Mishra, "After Suharto," *London Review of Books*, October 10, 2013.

19. Storey, *Southeast Asia and the Rise of China*, 200.

20. Cited from Rizal Sukma, "Indonesia–China relations: The politics of reengagement," in *Living with China: Regional States and China through Crises and Turning Points*, ed. Shiping Tang, Li Mingjiang, and Amitav Acharya (New York: Palgrave Macmillan, 2009), 95.

21. Muhammad Zulfikar Rakhmat and Dikanaya Tarahita, "Indonesia could be Beijing's best Belt and Road friend," *South China Morning Post*, May 15, 2019.

22. Michael Leifer, "Indonesia's encounters with China and the dilemmas of engagement," in *Engaging China: The Management of an Emerging Power*, ed. Alastair Iain Johnston and Robert S. Ross (London: Routledge, 1999), 101.

23. Stuart-Fox, *A Short History*, 162.

24. Leifer, "Indonesia's encounters with China," 91.

25. Jeffrey Hutton, "Indonesia takes tough stance in fighting illegal fishing," *New York Times*, December 18, 2014.

26. The Foreign Ministry's comments are available at: www.fmprc.gov.cn/mfa_eng/xwfw_665399/s2510_665401/t1373402.shtml

27. "Indonesian leader visits Natuna Islands amid growing tensions," *ABC News*, June 23, 2016.

28. "FULL TEXT: Jokowi's inauguration speech," *Rappler.com*, October 20, 2014.

29. Pisani, *Indonesia Etc.*, 9.

30. Lex Rieffel and Jaleswari Pramodhawardani, *Out of Business and on Budget: The Challenge of Military Financing in Indonesia* (Washington, DC: Brookings Institution Press, 2007), 16–17.

31. Aaron L. Connelly, *Indonesia in the South China Sea: Going It Alone?* (Sydney: Lowy Institute for International Policy, 2016), 18.

32. Ibid., 8.

33. "Jokowi optimistic about China's Belt and Road Initiative," *Jakarta Globe*, May 16, 2017.

34. "Indonesia, China sign $23.3b in contracts," *Jakarta Post*, April 14, 2018.

35. Connelly, *Indonesia in the South China Sea*, 9.

36. Michael Leifer, *Indonesia's Foreign Policy* (London: Allen & Unwin, 1983), 29; Donald K. Emmerson, "Is Indonesia rising? It depends," in *Indonesia Rising: The Repositioning of Asia's Third Giant*, ed. Anthony Reid (Singapore: Institute of Southeast Asian Studies, 2012), 65.
37. Evan Laksmana, "Pragmatic equidistance: How Indonesia manages its great power relations," in *China, The United States, and the Future of Southeast Asia*, ed. David B.H. Denoon (New York: New York University Press, 2017), 113–135.
38. Ibid., 129.
39. Reid, *Imperial Alchemy*, 65.
40. "Indonesia to set up agency to combat fake news," *Agence France-Presse*, January 6, 2017.
41. Charlotte Setijadi, "Chinese Indonesians in the eyes of the Pribumi public," *ISEAS Perspective* 73 (2017).
42. Aubrey Belford, "Indonesia's gotta catch all the communists," *Foreign Policy*, August 12, 2016.
43. Robert W. Hefner, *Civil Islam: Muslims and Democratization in Indonesia* (Princeton, NJ: Princeton University Press, 2000), 202–204; Purdey, *Anti-Chinese Violence in Indonesia*, 106.
44. Edward Aspinall, "Oligarchic populism: Prabowo Subianto's challenge to Indonesian democracy," *Indonesia* 99 (2015).
45. Amy Chew, " 'Let's copy Malaysia': Fake news stokes fears for Chinese Indonesians," *South China Morning Post*, April 7, 2019.
46. Karlis Salna, "Indonesia's presidential challenger wants a better China trade deal," *Bloomberg*, January 17, 2019.
47. Amy Chew and Andre Barahamin, "Anti-China hoaxes stir fears over mob attacks," *South China Morning Post*, May 22, 2019.
48. Charlotte Setijadi, "Ethnic Chinese in contemporary Indonesia: Changing identity politics and the paradox of Sinification," *ISEAS Perspective* 12 (2016).
49. Ibid., 7.
50. Elizabeth Rosenthal, "Beijing students and women, defying ban, protest anti-Chinese violence in Indonesia," *New York Times*, August 18, 1998.
51. "ASEAN outlook on the Indo-Pacific," June 23, 2019, available at: www.asean2019.go.th/en/news/asean-outlook-on-the-indo-pacific/
52. Connelly, *Indonesia in the South China Sea*, 6.
53. Emmerson, "Is Indonesia rising?" 69.
54. That year, military spending totaled just 0.7 percent of its GDP. Data from the Stockholm International Peace Research Institute (SIPRI), available at: https://data.worldbank.org/indicator/ms.mil.xpnd.gd.zs
55. Evan Laksmana, "An Indo-Pacific construct with 'Indonesian characteristics'," *The Strategist*, February 6, 2018.
56. Emmerson, "Is Indonesia rising?" 73–74. Emphasis in original.

10 THE PHILIPPINES: SLOUCHING TOWARD BEIJING

1. Jonathan Miller, *Duterte Harry: Fire and Fury in the Philippines* (Melbourne: Scribe, 2018), 20.
2. Floyd Whaley, "Rodrigo Duterte's talk of killing criminals raises fears in Philippines," *New York Times*, May 18, 2016.
3. Miller, *Duterte Harry*, 4.
4. Joshua Berlinger, "Duterte tells rights investigators 'don't f*** with me' in speech," CNN, March 2, 2018.
5. Richard Javad Heydarian, *The Rise of Duterte: A Populist Revolt Against Elite Democracy* (Singapore: Palgrave Macmillan, 2018), 6–7.
6. "Satisfaction with the admin in its campaign against illegal drugs: Philippines, Sep 2016 to Jun 2019," Social Weather Stations, available at: www.sws.org.ph/swsmain/artcldisppage/?artcsyscode=ART-20190922154614

7. Heydarian, *The Rise of Duterte*, 10.
8. James Fallows, "A damaged culture," *The Atlantic*, November 1987.
9. The suffix "-co," common to the family names of some of the Philippines' more powerful political dynasties, derives from the Hokkien suffix of politeness for males. See Benedict Anderson, "Old corruption," *London Review of Books*, February 5, 1987.
10. Bob Drogin, "The King of Cronies eyes power in the Philippines," *Los Angeles Times*, January 1, 1991.
11. Federico D. Pascual Jr., "178 dynasties rule 72 of 80 provinces," *Philippine Star*, March 24, 2013.
12. William Mellor, "Democracy fails to deliver in Manila's 'Promised Land'," *Nikkei Asian Review*, March 13, 2019.
13. "Philippines is Asia's rising tiger – World Bank," *Philippine Star*, February 6, 2013; Ansuya Harjani, "Who is Asia's new darling of investors?" *CNBC*, October 8, 2012.
14. Cielito F. Habito, "Economic growth for all," *The Inquirer*, June 25, 2012.
15. Gerry Lirio, "Is Philippines ready for a state burial for Marcos?" *ABS-CBN.com*, March 14, 2016. Cited from Heydarian, *The Rise of Duterte*, 32.
16. Ben Blanchard, "Duterte aligns Philippines with China, says U.S. has lost," *Reuters*, October 20, 2016.
17. Stanley Karnow, *In Our Image: America's Empire in the Philippines* (New York: Random House, 1989), xi.
18. Global Indicators Database, "Opinion of the United States," data available at: www.pewresearch.org/global/database/indicator/1/
19. Indeed, the early 1970s saw the emergence of a small but vocal movement pressing for the Philippines' admission as the 51st state of the Union. See Rawlein G. Soberano, "The Philippine statehood movement: A resurrected illusion, 1970–1972," *South East Asian Studies* 13, No. 4 (March 1976).
20. Trefor Moss, "Behind Duterte's break with the U.S., a lifetime of resentment," *Wall Street Journal*, October 21, 2016.
21. Heydarian, *The Rise of Duterte*, 48.
22. John Lloyd, "How do you solve a problem like Duterte?" *Reuters*, September 9, 2019.
23. Ely Ratner, "Learning the lessons of Scarborough Reef," *The National Interest*, November 21, 2013.
24. Justin McCurry and Tania Branigan, "Obama says US will defend Japan in island dispute with China," *The Guardian*, April 24, 2014. "Remarks by President Obama and President Benigno Aquino III of the Philippines in Joint Press Conference," April 28, 2014, available at: https://obamawhitehouse.archives.gov/the-press-office/2014/04/28/remarks-president -obama-and-president-benigno-aquino-iii-philippines-joi
25. Jim Gomez, "Philippines worried it may get involved in war at sea for US," *Associated Press*, March 5, 2019.
26. Raul Dancel, "PM Abe visits President Duterte's modest Davao home for breakfast, bedroom tour," *Straits Times*, January 13, 2017.
27. Martin Petty and Linda Sieg, "Philippines' Duterte hits out at U.S., then heads to Japan," *Reuters*, October 25, 2016.
28. Karnow, *In Our Image*, 39.
29. Storey, *Southeast Asia and the Rise of China*, 253.
30. The preceding draws from Hayton, *The South China Sea*, 64–70; Marwyn S. Samuels, *Contest for the South China Sea* (New York: Methuen, 1982), 82–85.
31. "Philippines' Duterte cancels visit to disputed South China Sea island," *Reuters*, April 13, 2017.
32. Pia Ranada, "Duterte says he would 'go to war' to defend Benham Rise," *Rappler.com*, March 1, 2018; Hannah Beech and Jason Gutierrez, "Xi visits Philippines to celebrate 'rainbow after the rain' with Duterte," *New York Times*, November 19, 2018.
33. Chad De Guzman and Cecille Lardizabal, "Duterte: South China Sea issue 'better left untouched'," *CNN Philippines*, November 12, 2017.

34. Karen Lema, "Philippines' Duterte tells China to 'lay off' island in disputed waters," *Reuters*, April 4, 2019.

35. Andrew R.C. Marshall and Manuel Mogato, "As Obama plans Asia tour, postcard Philippines isle symbolizes U.S. pivot," *Reuters*, October 2, 2013.

36. "Full text of Xi's signed article on Philippine newspapers," *Xinhua*, November 19, 2018.

37. Paterno Esmaquel II, "Del Rosario: PH 'a willing victim' 2 years after Hague ruling," *Rappler*, July 12, 2018.

38. Luke Lischin, "US foreign policy is failing in the Philippines," *East Asia Forum*, March 23, 2018.

39. Beech and Gutierrez, "Xi visits Philippines."

40. Richard Javad Heydarian, "Duterte still waiting for China's ballyhooed bonanza," *Asia Times*, September 30, 2019.

41. Ibid.

42. Data is available at www.sws.org.ph/swsmain/artcldisppage/?artcsyscode=ART-2019071 2122047; www.sws.org.ph/swsmain/artcldisppage/?artcsyscode=ART-20190710213339

43. "Why Winnie the Pooh is popping up on your social media feeds," *Rappler*, November 19, 2018.

44. Aika Rey, "Duterte does not favor deporting illegal Chinese workers," *Rappler*, February 23, 2019.

45. Claire Jiao, "Online casinos to overtake call centers in Manila," *Bloomberg*, July 10, 2019.

46. Richard Javad Heydarian, "Philippine spy scare turns on Chinese-run casinos," *Asia Times*, August 28, 2019.

47. Solita Collas-Monsod, "Why Filipinos distrust China," *The Inquirer*, November 24, 2018.

48. F. Sionil José, "Can we still trust America?" *Philippine Star*, January 19, 2019.

49. Nick Aspinwall, " 'We are Filipinos, and we hate China': China's influence in the Philippines, and backlash against Tsinoys," *SupChina*, June 6, 2019.

50. "Rody eyes daughter Sara as successor," *Philippine Star*, September 23, 2017.

AFTERWORD

1. Keith Bradsher, "China's economy shrinks, ending a nearly half-century of growth," *New York Times*, April 16, 2020.

2. Acharya, *Making of Southeast Asia*, 41.

3. *Indo-Pacific Strategy Report: Preparedness, Partnerships, and Promoting a Networked Region* (Washington, DC: US Department of Defense, June 2019), 1.

4. Shi Jiangtao and Owen Churchill, "U.S. launches its answer to China's Belt and Road plan," *South China Morning Post*, July 30, 2018.

5. Ankit Panda, "Trump signs Asia Reassurance Initiative Act into law," *The Diplomat*, January 3, 2019.

6. *The State of Southeast Asia: 2020 Survey Report*, 39–40.

7. Pomfret, *The Beautiful Kingdom and the Middle Kingdom*, 625.

8. *National Security Strategy of the United States of America* (Washington, DC: The White House, December 2017), 45. "Secretary Michael R. Pompeo and British Foreign Secretary Dominic Raab discussion on the future of the special relationship," January 30, 2020. Available at: www.state.gov/secretary-michael-r-pompeo-and-british-foreign-secretary-dominic-raab-discussion-on-the-future-of-the-special-relationship/

9. Howard W. French, "What America's China debate gets right and wrong—and what it's missing," *World Politics Review*, July 31, 2019.

10. Chen Weiss, "A world safe for autocracy?"

11. David P. Fidler, Sung Won Kim, and Sumit Ganguly, "Eastphalia rising? Asian influence and the fate of human security," *World Policy Journal* 26, No. 2 (Summer 2009).

12. Pomfret, *The Beautiful Kingdom and the Middle Kingdom*, 55, 632.

13. Ishaan Tharoor, "The U.S. can't treat China the 'same way' it treated the Soviet Union, warns Asian leader," *Washington Post*, September 27, 2019.
14. "ASEAN outlook on the Indo-Pacific," 23 June 2019, available at: www.asean2019.go.th/en/news/asean-outlook-on-the-indo-pacific/
15. Stromseth, "The testing ground," 5.
16. Tashny Sukumaran, "Mahathir stands up for Huawei," *South China Morning Post*, May 30, 2019.
17. Josephine Ma, "Ban on Huawei technology 'will not stop spying'," *South China Morning Post*, March 30, 2019.
18. Ely Ratner et al., *Rising to the China Challenge: Renewing American Competitiveness in the Indo-Pacific* (Washington, DC: Center for a New American Security, 2020), 4.
19. *The State of Southeast Asia: 2020 Survey Report*, 29.
20. Parks and Zawacki, "Future of U.S.–Thai relations," 24, 34.
21. India also initially intended to join RCEP, but declined over concerns that the agreement would hurt the country's domestic producers.
22. *The State of Southeast Asia: 2020 Survey Report*, 39–40.
23. Chas W. Freeman, Jr., "The United States and a Resurgent Asia," speech prepared for delivery to the Watson Institute for International and Public Affairs, Brown University, April 14, 2020. Available at: https://chasfreeman.net/the-united-states-and-a-resurgent-asia/
24. Bilahari Kausikan, *Dealing with an Ambiguous World* (Singapore: World Scientific Publishing, 2017), 79.

FURTHER READING

Any attempt to provide a comprehensive list of suggested readings on China's history of relations with the kingdoms, sultanates, and nations of Southeast Asia would extend far beyond the scope of this present book. The following list includes books directly relevant to China's relations with Southeast Asia, as well as a selection of more general works on the nations and peoples of the region.

GENERAL WORKS

Acharya, Amitav. *The Making of Southeast Asia: International Relations of a Region*. Ithaca, NY and London: Cornell University Press, 2012.

Allison, Graham. *Destined for War: Can America and China Escape Thucydides's Trap?* Boston, MA: Houghton Mifflin Harcourt, 2017.

Andaya, Barbara Watson, and Leonard Y. Andaya. *A History of Early Modern Southeast Asia, 1400–1830*. Cambridge: Cambridge University Press, 2015.

Anderson, Benedict. *Imagined Communities: Reflections on the Origin and Spread of Nationalism*. London: Verso, 1983.

Anderson, Benedict. *A Life Beyond Boundaries: A Memoir*. London: Verso, 2018.

Bräutigam, Deborah. *The Dragon's Gift: The Real Story of China in Africa*. New York: Oxford University Press, 2011.

French, Howard W. *Everything under the Heavens: How the Past Helps Shape China's Push for Global Power*. New York: Alfred A. Knopf, 2017.

Garver, John W. *China's Quest: The History of the Foreign Relations of the People's Republic of China*. New York: Oxford University Press, 2016.

Hayton, Bill. *The South China Sea: The Struggle for Power in Asia*. London: Yale University Press, 2014.

Heydarian, Richard Javad. *Asia's New Battlefield: The USA, China and the Struggle for the Western Pacific*. London: Zed Books, 2015.

Huang, Yukon. *Cracking the China Conundrum: Why Conventional Economic Wisdom Is Wrong*. Oxford: Oxford University Press, 2017.

Kaplan, Robert D. *Asia's Cauldron: The South China Sea and the End of a Stable Pacific*. New York: Random House, 2015.

Kausikan, Bilahari. *Dealing with an Ambiguous World*. Singapore: World Scientific Publishing, 2017.

Khan, Sulmaan Wasif. *Haunted by Chaos: China's Grand Strategy from Mao Zedong to Xi Jinping*. Cambridge, MA: Harvard University Press, 2018.

Kurlantzick, Joshua. *Charm Offensive: How China's Soft Power Is Transforming the World*. New Haven and London: Yale University Press, 2007.

Lieberman, Victor. *Strange Parallels: Southeast Asia in Global Context, c. 800–1830*, vol. 1: *Integration on the Mainland*. Cambridge: Cambridge University Press, 2003.

Lintner, Bertil. *The Costliest Pearl: China's Struggle for India's Ocean*. London: C. Hurst & Co., 2019.

Lovell, Julia. *Maoism: A Global History*. London: Bodley Head, 2019.

Luttwak, Edward N. *The Rise of China vs. the Logic of Strategy*. Cambridge, MA: Belknap Press, 2012.

Mahbubani, Kishore, and Jeffery Sng. *The ASEAN Miracle: A Catalyst for Peace*. Singapore: National University of Singapore Press, 2017.

Nyíri, Pál, and Danielle Tan, eds. *Chinese Encounters in Southeast Asia: How People, Money, and Ideas from China Are Changing a Region*. Seattle, WA: University of Washington Press, 2017.

Osborne, Milton. *Southeast Asia: An Introductory History*. Sydney: Allen & Unwin, 2013.

Percival, Bronson. *The Dragon Looks South: China and Southeast Asia in the New Century*. Westport, CT and London: Praeger Security International, 2007.

Pomfret, John. *The Beautiful Country and the Middle Kingdom: America and China, 1776 to the Present*. New York: Henry Holt, 2016.

Reid, Anthony. *Southeast Asia in the Age of Commerce*, vol. 1: *The Lands Below the Winds*. New Haven, CT and London: Yale University Press, 1988.

Reid, Anthony. *Imperial Alchemy: Nationalism and Political Identity in Southeast Asia*. Cambridge, MA: Cambridge University Press, 2010.

Santasombat, Yos, ed. *The Sociology of Chinese Capitalism in Southeast Asia: Challenges and Prospects*. Singapore: Palgrave Macmillan, 2019.

Schell, Orville, and John Delury. *Wealth and Power: China's Long March to the Twenty-first Century*. New York: Random House, 2013.

Storey, Ian. *Southeast Asia and the Rise of China: The Search for Security*. London and New York: Routledge, 2011.

Stuart-Fox, Martin. *A Short History of China and Southeast Asia: Tribute, Trade, and Influence*. St Leonards, NSW: Allen & Unwin, 2003.

Swaine, Michael D. *America's Challenge: Engaging a Rising China in the Twenty-first Century*. Washington, DC: Carnegie Endowment for International Peace, 2011.

Tagliacozzo, Eric, and Wen-Chin Chang, eds. *Chinese Circulations: Capital, Commodities, and Networks in Southeast Asia*. Durham, NC: Duke University Press, 2011.

Vatikiotis, Michael. *Blood and Silk: Power and Conflict in Modern Southeast Asia*. London: Weidenfeld & Nicolson, 2017.

Vogel, Ezra F. *Deng Xiaoping and the Transformation of China*. Cambridge, MA: The Belknap Press, 2011.

Wang, Zheng. *Never Forget National Humiliation: Historical Memory in Chinese Politics and Foreign Relations*. New York: Columbia University Press, 2012.

MAINLAND SOUTHEAST ASIA

Atwill, David G. *The Chinese Sultanate: Islam, Ethnicity, and the Panthay Rebellion in Southwest China, 1856–1873*. Stanford, CA: Stanford University Press, 2005.

Chin, Ko-Lin. *The Golden Triangle: Inside Southeast Asia's Drug Trade*. Ithaca, NY and London: Cornell University Press, 2009.

Evans, Grant, Christopher Hutton, and Kuah Khun Eng, eds. *Where China Meets Southeast Asia: Social and Cultural Change in the Border Regions*. Singapore: Institute for Southeast Asian Studies, 2000.

Eyler, Brian. *The Last Days of the Mighty Mekong*. London: Zed Books, 2019.

Fitzgerald, C.P. *The Southern Expansion of the Chinese People*. New York: Praeger, 1972.

Gibson, Richard Michael, and Wen H. Chen. *The Secret Army: Chiang Kai-Shek and the Drug Lords of the Golden Triangle*. Singapore: John Wiley and Sons, 2011.

Giersch, C. Patterson. *Asian Borderlands: The Transformation of Qing China's Yunnan Frontier*. Cambridge, MA: Harvard University Press, 2006.

Keay, John. *Mad about the Mekong: Exploration and Empire in South-East Asia*. London: HarperCollins, 2005.

FURTHER READING

Lintner, Bertil, and Michael Black. *Merchants of Madness: The Methamphetamine Explosion in the Golden Triangle*. Chiang Mai: Silkworm Books, 2009.

McCoy, Alfred. *The Politics of Heroin: CIA Complicity in the Global Drug Trade*. Chicago: Lawrence Hill Books, 2003.

Myint-U, Thant. *Where China Meets India: Burma and the New Crossroads of Asia*. New York: Farrar, Straus & Giroux, 2011.

Osborne, Milton. *River Road to China: The Mekong River Expedition, 1866–1873*. New York: Liveright, 1975.

Osborne, Milton. *The Mekong: Turbulent Past, Uncertain Future*. New York: Grove Press, 2000.

Santasombat, Yos, ed. *Impact of China's Rise on the Mekong Region*. New York: Palgrave Macmillan, 2015.

Scott, James C. *The Art of Not Being Governed: An Anarchist History of Upland Southeast Asia*. New Haven, CT: Yale University Press, 2009.

Summers, Tim. *Yunnan: A Chinese Bridgehead to Asia*. Oxford: Chandos, 2013.

Swe, Thein, and Paul Chambers. *Cashing in across the Golden Triangle: Thailand's Northern Border Trade with China, Laos, and Myanmar*. Chiang Mai: Mekong Press, 2011.

Walker, Andrew. *The Legend of the Golden Boat: Regulation, Trade and Traders in the Borderlands of Laos, Thailand, China and Burma*. Honolulu: University of Hawai'i Press, 1999.

Wiens, Herold J. *China's March toward the Tropics*. Hamden, CT: Shoe String Press, 1954.

Wolters, O.W. *History, Culture, and Region in Southeast Asian Perspectives*. Singapore: Institute of Southeast Asian Studies, 1982.

Yang, Bin. *Between Winds and Clouds: The Making of Yunnan*. New York: Columbia University Press, 2008.

VIETNAM

Chanda, Nayan. *Brother Enemy: The War after the War*. New York: Macmillan, 1986.

Duiker, William J. *Ho Chi Minh: A Life*. New York: Hyperion, 2000.

Goscha, Christopher. *Vietnam: A New History*. New York: Basic Books, 2016.

Hai, Do Thanh. *Vietnam and the South China Sea: Politics, Security and Legality*. London: Routledge, 2017.

Hayton, Bill. *Vietnam: Rising Dragon*. London: Yale University Press, 2010.

Hiep, Le Hong. *Living Next to the Giant: The Political Economy of Vietnam's Relations with China under Doi Moi*. Singapore: Institute of Southeast Asian Studies, 2017.

Logevall, Frederick. *Embers of War: The Fall of an Empire and the Making of America's Vietnam*. New York: Random House, 2012.

O'Dowd, Edward. *Chinese Military Strategy in the Third Indochina War: The Last Maoist War*. London: Routledge, 2007.

Shaplen, Robert. *Bitter Victory*. New York: Harper & Row, 1986.

Taylor, Keith Weller. *The Birth of Vietnam*. Berkeley: University of California Press, 1983.

Templer, Robert. *Shadows and Wind: A View of Modern Vietnam*. New York: Penguin, 1999.

Womack, Brantly. *China and Vietnam: The Politics of Asymmetry*. New York: Cambridge University Press, 2006.

Woodside, Alexander Barton. *Vietnam and the Chinese Model: A Comparative Study of Nguyen and Ch'ing Civil Government in the First Half of the Nineteenth Century*. Cambridge, MA: Harvard University Press, 1971.

CAMBODIA AND LAOS

Becker, Elizabeth. *When the War Was Over: Cambodia and the Khmer Rouge Revolution*. New York: PublicAffairs, 1998.

FURTHER READING

Brown, MacAlister, and Joseph J. Zasloff. *Apprentice Revolutionaries: The Communist Movement in Laos, 1930–1985*. Stanford, CA: Hoover Institution Press, 1986.

Chandler, David P. *The Tragedy of Cambodian History: Politics, War, and Revolution since 1945*. Chiang Mai: Silkworm Books, 1994.

Chandler, David P. *A History of Cambodia*. 4th ed. Boulder: Westview Press, 2008.

Daguan, Zhou. *A Record of Cambodia: The Land and Its People*. Translated by Peter Harris. Chiang Mai: Silkworm Books, 2007.

Evans, Grant. *The Politics of Ritual and Remembrance: Laos since 1975*. Honolulu: University of Hawai'i Press, 1998.

Evans, Grant. *A Short History of Laos: The Land in Between*. Crows Nest, NSW: Allen & Unwin, 2002.

Ivarsson, Søren. *Creating Laos: The Making of a Lao Space between Indochina and Siam, 1860–1945*. Copenhagen: NIAS Press, 2008.

Kiernan, Ben. *The Pol Pot Regime: Race, Power, and Genocide in Cambodia under the Khmer Rouge, 1975–79*. New Haven, CT and London: Yale University Press, 1996.

Mertha, Andrew. *Brothers in Arms: Chinese Aid to the Khmer Rouge, 1975–1979*. Ithaca, NY: Cornell University Press 2014.

Osborne, Milton. *Sihanouk: Prince of Light, Prince of Darkness*. Chiang Mai: Silkworm Books, 1994.

Richardson, Sophie. *China, Cambodia, and the Five Principles of Peaceful Coexistence*. New York: Columbia University Press, 2009.

Short, Philip. *Pol Pot: Anatomy of a Nightmare*. New York: Henry Holt and Co., 2004.

Strangio, Sebastian. *Hun Sen's Cambodia*. London: Yale University Press, 2014.

Stuart-Fox, Martin. *A History of Laos*. Cambridge: Cambridge University Press, 1997.

Unger, Leonard, and Joseph J. Zasloff. *Laos: Beyond the Revolution*. New York: St. Martin's Press, 1991.

Willmott, William E. *The Chinese in Cambodia*. Vancouver: University of British Columbia, 1967.

THAILAND

Baker, Chris, and Pasuk Phongpaichit. *A History of Thailand*. Cambridge: Cambridge University Press, 2014.

Chachavalpongpun, Pavin. *Reinventing Thailand: Thaksin and His Foreign Policy*. Singapore: Institute of Southeast Asian Studies, 2010.

Handley, Paul M. *The King Never Smiles: A Biography of Thailand's Bhumibol Adulyadej*. London: Yale University Press, 2006.

Landon, Kenneth P. *The Chinese in Thailand*. New York: Institute of Pacific Relations, 1941.

MacGregor Marshall, Andrew. *Kingdom in Crisis: Thailand's Struggle for Democracy in the Twenty-first Century*. London: Zed Books, 2014.

Raymond, Gregory. *Thai Military Power: A Culture of Strategic Accommodation*. Copenhagen: NIAS Press, 2018.

Skinner, G. William. *Chinese Society in Thailand: An Analytical History*. Ithaca, NY: Cornell University Press, 1957.

Sng, Jeffery, and Phimpraphai Phisanbut. *A History of the Thai-Chinese*. Bangkok: Editions Didier Millet, 2015.

Winichakul, Thongchai. *Siam Mapped: A History of the Geo-body of a Nation*. Honolulu: University of Hawai'i Press, 1994.

Wongsurawat, Wasana. *The Crown and the Capitalists: The Ethnic Chinese and the Founding of the Thai Nation*. Seattle: University of Washington, 2019.

Wyatt, David K. *Thailand: A Short History*. London: Yale University Press, 2003.

Zawacki, Benjamin. *Thailand: Shifting Ground between the US and a Rising China*. London: Zed Books, 2017.

FURTHER READING

BURMA

Callahan, Mary P. *Making Enemies: War and State Building in Burma*. Ithaca, NY: Cornell University Press, 2003.

Charney, Michael W. *A History of Modern Burma*. Cambridge: Cambridge University Press, 2009.

Egreteau, Renaud. *Caretaking Democratization: The Military and Political Change in Myanmar*. Oxford: Oxford University Press, 2016.

Htin Aung, Maung. *A History of Burma*. New York: Columbia University Press, 1967.

Lintner, Bertil. *Outrage: Burma's Struggle for Democracy*. Hong Kong: Review Publishing Company, 1989.

Lintner, Bertil. *The Rise and Fall of the Communist Party of Burma*. Ithaca, NY: Cornell University Southeast Asia Programme, 1990.

Lintner, Bertil. *Burma in Revolt: Opium and Insurgency since 1948*. Chiang Mai: Silkworm Books, 1999.

Myint-U, Thant. *The River of Lost Footsteps: A Personal History of Burma*. New York: Faber & Faber, 2008.

Myint-U, Thant. *The Hidden History of Burma: Race, Capitalism, and the Crisis of Democracy in the 21st Century*. New York: W.W. Norton, 2020.

Popham, Peter. *The Lady and the Peacock: The Life of Aung San Suu Kyi*. London: Rider Books, 2011.

Smith, Martin. *Burma: Insurgency and the Politics of Ethnicity*. London: Zed Books, 1991.

Steinberg, David I. *Burma/Myanmar: What Everyone Needs to Know*. Oxford: Oxford University Press, 2010.

Steinberg, David I., and Hongwei Fan, eds. *Modern China–Myanmar Relations: Dilemmas of Mutual Dependence*. Copenhagen: NIAS Press, 2012.

Wade, Francis. *Myanmar's Enemy Within: Buddhist Violence and the Making of a Muslim 'Other'*. London: Zed Books, 2017.

MARITIME SOUTHEAST ASIA

Bowring, Philip. *Empire of the Winds: The Global Role of Asia's Great Archipelago*. London: I.B. Tauris, 2019.

Gungwu, Wang. *The Nanhai Trade: Early Chinese Trade in the South China Sea*. Singapore: Eastern Universities Press, 2003.

Laichen, Sun, and Geoff Wade, eds. *Southeast Asia in the Fifteenth Century: The China Factor*. Singapore: NUS Press, 2010.

Levathes, Louise. *When China Ruled the Seas: The Treasure Fleet of the Dragon Throne 1405–1433*. New York: Simon & Schuster, 1994.

Pires, Tomé. *The Suma Oriental of Tomé Pires*. Translated by Armando Cortesão. London: The Hakluyt Society, 1944.

Wang, Wensheng. *White Lotus Rebels and South China Pirates: Crisis and Reform in the Qing Empire*. Cambridge, MA: Harvard University Press, 2014.

Winchester, Simon. *Pacific*. New York: Harper Perennial, 2015.

Yoshihara, Toshi, and James R. Holmes. *Red Star over the Pacific: China's Rise and the Challenge to U.S. Maritime Strategy*. Annapolis, MD: Naval Institute Press, 2010.

SINGAPORE

Acharya, Amitav. *Singapore's Foreign Policy: The Search for Regional Order*. Singapore: World Scientific, 2007.

FURTHER READING

Allison, Graham, and Robert D. Blackwill. *Lee Kuan Yew: The Grand Master's Insights on China, the United States, and the World.* Cambridge, MA: MIT Press, 2013.

Baker, Jim. *Crossroads: A Popular History of Malaysia and Singapore.* Singapore: Marshall Cavendish Editions, 2008.

Barr, Michael D. *The Ruling Elite of Singapore: Networks of Power and Influence.* London and New York: I.B. Tauris, 2014.

Barr, Michael D. *Singapore: A Modern History.* London: I.B. Tauris, 2019.

George, Cherian. *Air-conditioned Nation: Essays about Singapore.* New York: Landmark Books, 2000.

Leifer, Michael. *Singapore's Foreign Policy: Coping with Vulnerability.* London: Routledge, 2000.

Yew, Lee Kuan. *From Third World to First: The Singapore Story: 1965–2000.* New York: HarperCollins, 2000.

MALAYSIA

Andaya, Barbara Watson, and Leonard Y. Andaya. *A History of Malaysia.* London: Macmillan, 1982.

Baker, Jim. *Crossroads: A Popular History of Malaysia and Singapore.* Singapore: Marshall Cavendish Editions, 2008.

Hooker, Virginia Matheson. *A Short History of Malaysia: Linking East and West.* Crows Nest, NSW: Allen & Unwin, 2003.

Jain, Rajendra Kumar. *China and Malaysia, 1949–1983.* New Delhi: Radiant Publishers, 1984.

Liow, Joseph Chinyong. *Piety and Politics: Islamism in Contemporary Malaysia.* New York: Oxford University Press, 2009.

Milner, Anthony. *The Malays.* Malden, MA: Wiley-Blackwell, 2008.

Mohamad, Mahathir. *The Malay Dilemma.* Singapore: Marshall Cavendish Editions, 2009.

Peng, Chin. *Alias Chin Peng: My Side of History.* Singapore: Media Masters, 2003.

Slimming, John. *Malaysia: Death of Democracy.* London: John Murray, 1969.

Wain, Barry. *Malaysian Maverick: Mahathir Mohamad in Turbulent Times.* London: Palgrave Macmillan, 2012.

Wright, Tom, and Bradley Hope. *Billion Dollar Whale: The Man Who Fooled Wall Street, Hollywood, and the World.* New York: Hachette, 2018.

INDONESIA

Elson, R.E. *Suharto: A Political Biography.* Cambridge: Cambridge University Press, 2001.

Leifer, Michael. *Indonesia's Foreign Policy.* London: Allen & Unwin, 1983.

McDonald, Hamish. *Demokrasi: Indonesia in the 21st Century.* New York: Palgrave Macmillan, 2015.

Mozingo, David. *Chinese Policy toward Indonesia, 1949–1967.* Jakarta: Equinox, 2007.

Pisani, Elisabeth. *Indonesia Etc.: Exploring the Improbable Nation.* New York: W.W. Norton, 2014.

Purdey, Jemma. *Anti-Chinese Violence in Indonesia, 1996–1999.* Singapore: Singapore University Press, 2006.

Robinson, Geoffrey B. *The Killing Season: A History of the Indonesian Massacres, 1965–66.* Princeton, NJ: Princeton University Press, 2018.

Roosa, John. *Pretext for Mass Murder: The September 30th Movement and Suharto's Coup d'État in Indonesia.* Madison: University of Wisconsin Press, 2006.

Schwarz, Adam. *A Nation in Waiting: Indonesia's Search for Stability.* Boulder, CO: Westview Press, 2000.

Sukma, Rizal. *Indonesia and China: The Politics of a Troubled Relationship.* London and New York: Routledge, 1999.

FURTHER READING

Vickers, Adrian. *A History of Modern Indonesia*. Cambridge: Cambridge University Press, 2005.

THE PHILIPPINES

Constantino, Renato. *A History of the Philippines: From the Spanish Colonization to the Second World War*. New York: Monthly Review Press, 1975.

Curato, Nicole, ed. *The Duterte Reader: Critical Essays on Rodrigo Duterte's Early Presidency*. Ithaca, NY: Cornell University Press, 2017.

Heydarian, Richard Javad. *The Rise of Duterte: A Populist Revolt against Elite Democracy*. Singapore: Palgrave Macmillan, 2018.

Karnow, Stanley. *In Our Image: America's Empire in the Philippines*. New York: Random House, 1989.

Miller, Jonathan. *Duterte Harry: Fire and Fury in the Philippines*. Melbourne: Scribe, 2018.

Nadeau, Kathleen. *The History of the Philippines*. Westport, CT: Greenwood Press, 2008.

THE ETHNIC CHINESE OF SOUTHEAST ASIA

Chirot, Daniel, and Anthony Reid, eds. *Essential Outsiders: Chinese and Jews in the Modern Transformation of Southeast Asia and Central Europe*. Seattle: University of Washington Press, 1997.

Choy, Lee Khoon. *Golden Dragon and Purple Phoenix: The Chinese and Their Multi-ethnic Descendants in Southeast Asia*. Singapore: World Scientific Publishing, 2013.

Cushman, Jennifer W., and Gungwu Wang, eds. *Changing Identities of the Southeast Asian Chinese since World War II*. Hong Kong: Hong Kong University Press, 1988.

Fitzgerald, Stephen. *China and the Overseas Chinese: A Study of Peking's Changing Policy 1949–1970*. Cambridge: Cambridge University Press, 1972.

Gungwu, Wang. *The Chinese Overseas: From Earthbound China to the Quest for Autonomy*. Cambridge, MA and London: Harvard University Press, 2000.

Gungwu, Wang, ed. *Community and Nation: China, Southeast Asia and Australia*. St Leonards: Allen & Unwin, 1992.

Pan, Lynn. *Sons of the Yellow Emperor: A History of the Chinese Diaspora*. Boston, MA: Little, Brown, 1990.

Purcell, Victor. *The Chinese in Southeast Asia*. Oxford: Oxford University Press, 1965.

Reid, Anthony, ed. *Sojourners and Settlers: Histories of Southeast Asia and the Chinese*. Honolulu: University of Hawai'i Press, 2001.

Suryadinata, Leo. *The Rise of China and the Chinese Overseas: A Study of Beijing's Changing Policy in Southeast Asia and Beyond*. Singapore: Institute of Southeast Asian Studies, 2017.

Wong, Bernard P., and Tan Chee-Beng, eds. *China's Rise and the Chinese Overseas*. London: Routledge, 2018.

Yong, C.F. *Tan Kah-Kee: The Making of an Overseas Chinese Legend*. Singapore: World Scientific, 2014.

ACKNOWLEDGMENTS

Given its wide geographic and temporal span, the research for this book extended far beyond my usual field of operations, sprouting tangential detours into precolonial Southeast Asian history, sociology, and international relations theory. As such, I benefited greatly from discussions with a large number of academics, scholars, and journalists, not all of whom are named in the text.

In Singapore, I learned a lot from conversations with Bilahari Kausikan, late of the Ministry of Foreign Affairs, P.J. Thum of Oxford University, journalist Kirsten Han, then-editor-in-chief of *New Naratif*, and Syed Farid Alatas of the National University of Singapore (NUS). Wang Gungwu of the East Asia Institute at NUS provided me with invaluable context for China's present re-emergence and the nation's fraught and ever-shifting relationship with Southeast Asia's ethnic Chinese.

In Vietnam, Dr. Truong Minh Huy Vu of Ho Chi Minh City's University of Social Sciences and Humanities, Do Thanh Hai of the Diplomatic Academy of Vietnam in Hanoi, and Vu Thanh Ca, the former president of the Viet Nam Institute for Sea and Island Research, offered important details on the maritime disputes in the South China Sea. In Kuala Lumpur, I enjoyed fruitful discussions with Edmund Terence Gomez of the University of Malaya, and Shahriman Lockman of the Institute of Strategic and International Studies. Rita Sim of the Centre for Strategic Engagement furnished me with a working knowledge of the changing status of Malaysia's ethnic Chinese community in a time of rising Malay Islamic identity.

In Phnom Penh, Pou Sothirak and Ou Virak kindly donated their time and insights, as, in Bangkok, did Jeffery Sng, Panitan Wattanayagorn of Chulalongkorn University, and Chulacheeb Chinwanno of Thammasat University. In Manila, I enjoyed speaking with Richard Javad Heydarian,

ACKNOWLEDGMENTS

Manolo Quezon III, Herman Joseph Kraft of the University of the Philippines Diliman, and the late Aileen Baviera at the university's Asian Center. Floyd Whaley tipped me off about the Chinese cruise ships at Subic Bay, which provided the book's opening montage.

Among the many other colleagues, scholars, and comrades who aided me in ways both large and small were Carmelea Ang See, Elizabeth Becker, David Boyle, Paul Chambers, Miguel Chanco, Liam Cochrane, Rica Concepcion, Adam Dedman, Penny Edwards, Brian Eyler, Jared Ferrie, C. Patterson Giersch, Orlando de Guzman, Kirsten Han, Boo Cheng Hau, Daniel Henderson, Murray Hiebert, Trasvin Jittidecharak, Kaiser Kuo, Josh Kurlantzick, Dien Luong, Calvin McLeod, Bennett Murray, Erika Pineros, Catherine Putz, Hishamuddin Rais, Ian Storey, Jim Stent, Michael Sullivan, Michael Tatarski, Max Walden, and Benjamin Zawacki. Special thanks to Zunar for the cartoon.

A number of institutions helped support the research of this book. The International Reporting Project in Washington, DC, sadly now defunct, provided financial support for my reporting of the Indonesia section of this book. Thupten Norbu at the Carolina Asia Center at the University of North Carolina at Chapel Hill offered me an institutional home during my two years in the US, and facilitated access to the university's large research collection. Dr. Chayan Vaddhanaphuti and all the staff at the Regional Center of Social Science and Sustainable Development (RCSD) at Chiang Mai University, offered welcoming and invaluable support during my final stretch of research and writing in Thailand.

During my field reporting, I leant heavily on the connections and knowhow of the following talented fixers and translators: Anh Chi in Hanoi; Alan Liu in Vientiane; Seng Nu Pan in Myitkyina; Mech Dara and Pheng Sokhenin in Phnom Penh; Febriana Firdaus in Jakarta; Bambang Muryanto in Yogyakarta; and Sakao Roberts in Sop Ruak/Chiang Saen. Your support was hugely beneficial.

It is hard to imagine this book having come together without the time invested by William Blakeley, Robert Carmichael, David Chandler, Minh Bui Jones, Mary Kozlovski, Milton Osborne, Abby Seiff, and Jim Stent, who braved an early draft of the manuscript and offered invaluable feedback on matters both stylistic and substantive. Miguel Chanco, Chas Freeman, Don Jameson, Tom Kean, George McLeod, Martin Rathie, Lex Rieffel, Gwen Robinson, and Carlyle A. Thayer did the same with individual chapters and sections of the text. I shudder to think of the errors and infelicities that would have slipped through the net without your careful scrutiny. I also owe a thanks to the anonymous reviewers who provided critical comments on both the initial proposal and the final manuscript.

Much thanks also goes to Heather McCallum, my editor at Yale University Press in London, who supported the project from its hazy inception in 2016 and kept the faith that it would all come good. Marika Lysandrou and Rachael Lonsdale were similarly invaluable in ushering the project to completion amid the disruptions of a global pandemic.

Last, but definitely not least, I owe a special debt of love and gratitude to my wife Hayley, who endured my long labors on this book either side of a daunting international move, and our son Felix, who joined us mid-way through the process and grew up as the book did. Thank you both for being there with me every step of the way.

INDEX

INDEX

INDEX